Mediterranean Sea

Strait of
Gibraltar

Madeira

Atlas Mountains

Haut Atlas

Grand Erg Occidental

Grand Erg Oriental

Gulf of
Sirte

Suez
Canal

Canary Islands

'Erg Iguïdi

Erg Chech

Ahaggar

Tibesti

Libyan Desert

Nile

Eastern Desert

Red Sea

Lake
Nasser

Nubian
Desert

S a h a r a

Cape Verde
Islands

El Mrayye

Massif
de l'Air

Ennedi

Senegal

Pointe des
Almadies

S a h e l

Niger

Lake
Chad

Murra
Hills

Darfur

White Nile

Blue Nile

Lake
Tana

Gulf of Aden

Raas
Xaafuun

Danakil
Desert

Chari

Sudd

Ethiopian
Highlands

Horn of
Africa

White Volta

Jos
Plateau

Shebshi
Mountains

Benue

Shebeli

Black Volta

Bandama

Lake
Volta

Niger

Adamawa
Highlands

Gulf of
Guinea

Isla de
Bioco

Príncipe
São Tomé

Uele

Lake Turkana
(Lake Rudolf)

Ngongerabeli
Plain

Ogooué

Sangha

Ubangi

Congo

Lake
Albert

Seychelles

Inner
Isands

ATLANTIC OCEAN

Congo
Basin

Lake
Victoria

Kasai

Lake
Tanganyika

Serengeti
Plain

Kilimanjaro
19,341 ft (5895m)

Pemba
Zanzibar

Mafia

Amirante
Isands

Lualaba

Wamba

Mitumba Range

Great Rift Valley

Great Rift Valley

Comoros

Farquhar
Group

Ngazidja
Mayotte

SCALE

Kilometres
0   500   1000

Miles
0   500   1000

Planalto
do Bie

Cubango

Zambezi

Lake
Nyasa

Mozambique Channel

Madagascar

INDIAN OCEAN

Mauritius

Réunion

Okavango
Delta

Victoria
Falls

Lake
Kariba

Zambezi

Limpopo

Namib Desert

Kalahari
Desert

Orange River

Great
Karoo

Drakensberg

Cape of
Good Hope

AFRICA

AFRICA

THE DEFINITIVE VISUAL HISTORY
OF A CONTINENT

DK London

Senior Editors	Simon Beecroft, Laura Sandford
Senior Art Editors	Jane Ewart, Lisa Lanzarini
Editors	Ankita Awasthi Tröger, Bridget Giles, Ian Fitzgerald, Scarlett O'Hara, James Smart, Anna Streiffert Limerick, Marcus Weeks
CGI Author and Researcher	Justine Willis
CGI Coordinator	Phil Gamble
CGI Artworks	Peter Bull Art Studio
Senior Cartographic Editor	Simon Mumford
Managing Editor	Carine Tracanelli
Managing Art Editor	Anna Hall
Senior Production Editor	Andy Hilliard
Production Controller	Jack Matts
Picture Researcher	Sarah Hopper
Jacket Design Development Manager	Sophia M.T.T.
Publishing Director	Jonathan Metcalf
Associate Publishing Director	Liz Wheeler
Art Director	Karen Self

DK Delhi

Art Editor	Debjyoti Mukherjee
Deputy Managing Art Editor	Vaibhav Rastogi
Senior Jacket Designer	Suhita Dharamjit
Senior Jackets Coordinator	Priyanka Sharma Saddi
Senior DTP Designer	Harish Aggarwal
DTP Designers	Bimlesh Tiwary, Anita Yadav
Hi-res Coordinator	Jagtar Singh
Pre-production Manager	Balwant Singh
Production Manager	Pankaj Sharma
Design Head	Malavika Talukder

First published in Great Britain in 2024 by
Dorling Kindersley Limited
DK, One Embassy Gardens, 8 Viaduct Gardens,
London, SW11 7BW

The authorised representative in the EEA is Dorling Kindersley Verlag
GmbH. Arnulfstr. 124, 80636 Munich, Germany

A CIP catalogue record for this book
is available from the British Library.
ISBN: 978-0-2415-0916-6

Printed in the UAE

www.dk.com

MIX
Paper | Supporting
responsible forestry
FSC™ C018179

This book was made with Forest
Stewardship Council™ certified
paper – one small step in DK's
commitment to a sustainable future.
Learn more at
www.dk.com/uk/information/sustainability

Use of historical language
Names of organizations and words used on historical images included in this book
retain the language and terminology of their time. Some of this language is now
outdated, and is deemed insensitive, inappropriate, and offensive. It is a reflection
of its time, and does not reflect the opinions of the publisher or of our contributors.

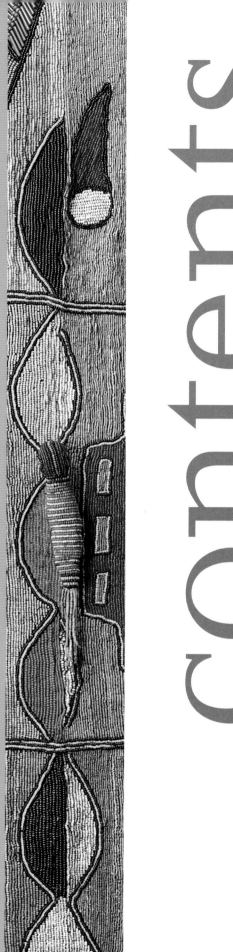

contents

1 African prehistory
5 MYA – 3500 BCE

2 Early civilizations
3000 BCE – 600 CE

3 African empires
600 – 1900 CE

4 European encounters
1440–1914

5 The age of independence
1914–1994

6 Contemporary Africa
1994–

contributors

FOREWORD AND CONSULTANTS

David Olusoga (foreword)
David Olusoga is a British–Nigerian historian, broadcaster, presenter, and BAFTA-winning film-maker. His books include the award-winning *Black and British: A Forgotten History*. In 2022, he received the British Academy President's Medal.

Dr Nemata Blyden
Dr Nemata Blyden is Professor of 19th Century African American History at the Carter G. Woodson Institute, University of Virginia. She teaches and publishes widely on African, African American, and African diaspora history.

Dr Marie Rodet
Dr Marie Rodet is a Reader in the History of Africa at SOAS (School of Oriental and African Studies), University of London. Her expertise is on the modern history of French-speaking West Africa.

Steven Snape
Steven Snape is Honorary Professor of Egyptian Archaeology at the University of Liverpool. His research interests focus on the sacred landscape of dynastic Egypt. He is the author of *Ancient Egypt: The Definitive Visual Guide* (DK, 2021).

AUTHORS

Dr Morenikeji Asaaju
Dr Morenikeji Asaaju is Cadbury Postdoctoral Fellow in African Studies at the Department of African Studies and Anthropology, University of Birmingham, UK. Her thematic interests are in gender, marriage, family, and the slave trade.

Dr Abidemi Babalola
Dr Abidemi Babatunde Babalola received his PhD from Rice University, Texas. He is an Andrew Mellon Fellow at the British Museum and a Marie Curie Postdoctoral Fellow at the Cyprus Institute, and has published widely.

Prof Jane Bryce
Prof Jane Bryce is a scholar of African literature and cinema. She is widely published in a range of academic journals and essay collections, and is the author of *Zamani: a Haunted Memoir of Tanzania* (Cinnamon Press, 2023).

Obert Mlambo
Obert Bernard Mlambo is Associate Professor of Classical Studies and History at the University of Zimbabwe. He is the author of *Land Expropriation in Ancient Rome and Contemporary Zimbabwe* (Bloomsbury, 2022).

Patience Motsatsi
Patience Motsatsi is a lecturer at the University of South Africa, specializing in Education and Academic Excellence, Organizational Studies, Colonization and Decolonization, Media Studies, and Culture and Identity.

Dr Butholezwe Mtombeni
Dr Butholezwe Mtombeni holds a PhD in History from the University of South Africa, where he is a lecturer in African History. His research interests include the Zulu people, gender, religion, slavery, and social and agrarian history.

Dr Girma Negash
Dr Girma Negash is Associate Professor of History and current Head of the Department of History at Addis Ababa University, Ethiopia. His book, *The Education of Children Entangled in Khat Trade in Ethiopia*, was published in 2017.

Prof Raphael Chijioke Njoku
Prof Raphael Chijioke Njoku teaches History and Global Studies at Idaho State University. He has published 12 books and 50 academic articles, including *West African Masking Traditions and Diaspora Masquerade Carnivals* (2020).

Philip Parker
Philip Parker studied International Relations at Johns Hopkins School of Advanced International Studies. He is a specialist in medieval and military history and the author of DK's *Eyewitness Companions: World History* (2010).

Luke Pepera
Luke Pepera is a writer, broadcaster, and historian of African history and cultures. He is the author of *Motherland: 500,000 Years of African History, Cultures, and Identity* (Weidenfeld & Nicolson, 2025).

Dr Marilee Wood
Dr Marilee Wood, an Honorary Research Associate in the School of Geology, Archaeology, and Environmental Studies at the University of the Witwatersrand, specializes in glass beads traded into Africa in the Islamic period.

▷ **Beaded tunic (detail)**
This highly decorative, beaded tunic would have been worn by a Yoruba king, or *oba*, on important occasions.

▷ **Following page**
Ewe *kente* cloth from Eastern Ghana or Togo

Foreword

Africa is the continent upon which humans first emerged and, therefore, where the history of us all began. Yet Africa's astonishing past – even today – remains poorly understood. This book is a huge, sweeping introduction to the history of the African continent and its many diverse peoples.

That diversity is astounding; greater in Africa than in any other continent. There are around 3,000 ethnic groups living on the continent today who, between them, speak around 2,000 languages. Behind that incredible diversity lies a long history of movement, migration, and adaptation; a history within which numerous African states and empires have risen and fallen over the centuries.

The scope of this book is thus inevitably vast. It begins in Africa's prehistory and introduces the reader to those very first humans who walked the immense spaces of Africa when it was the "cradle of humankind". It goes on to show how those early African peoples became the creators of the world's very first civilizations and cultures. The book then explores the age of Africa's great empires, before introducing the reader to colonial European empires in Africa, and the independence struggles of the late 20th century that toppled them. Finally, it takes us to modern Africa, with its massive and youthful populations, vibrant music, cinema, and art, and its growing megacities, like Lagos – the city of my birth.

This book also confronts the most painful chapters in Africa's history. It explores how Africa became a source of enslaved people – first to the Arab world from the 7th century onwards. From the 16th century, Africa was ravaged by the Atlantic slave trade, which sparked wars and disastrously disrupted African societies as at least 12 million Africans were trafficked to European colonies in the Americas. Later, this book examines how towards the

end of the 19th century almost the whole of the continent was colonized and exploited by European imperial powers – despite constant resistance from African peoples.

Another theme addressed by this book is how Africa has been imagined and misrepresented by non-African peoples – in maps, through legends, and within the racial and cultural theories that were used to "justify" slavery and imperialism.

The real Africa, which was concealed behind those myths, is a continent of cultural sophistication whose people have their own sense of history. It is also a continent whose landscapes are almost as diverse as its people. Through stunning photography, this book offers a glimpse of Africa's ancient deserts, sweeping grasslands, and verdant rainforests. The history of Africa has always mattered to me. My work as a historian has repeatedly led me back to African history, as I have sought to understand how Africans were seen by the

outside world and how they interacted with the various peoples, from different continents, with whom they have had contact for centuries. For far too long, Africa's place in global history has been underappreciated. This book is an effort to bring to the reader the remarkable story of the continent upon which human history first began.

David Olusoga
British–Nigerian historian and broadcaster

Introduction

Africa is a land of great diversity. Hot deserts sit alongside high mountain ranges formed over billions of years by immense geological forces. Lush rainforests border extensive grasslands. The continent's topography exists on an epic scale, with awe-inspiringly spectacular coastlines and some of the world's longest rivers, largest lakes, most stupendous waterfalls, and widest, deepest valleys.

The pages that follow explore how those landscapes were formed, then focus on the historical events that make Africa truly unique. Some 2 million years ago, the first humans emerged on the continent, either in East Africa or possibly further south. As they evolved, our early ancestors learned to hunt, to master their environment, to form communities, to manufacture tools, and to create culture. They moved around their continent and, eventually, beyond it. As they did so, the first civilizations were born. One of these, of course, was Egypt. But the Nile Valley in which it developed was also home to other early African civilizations such as Kush, Kerma, Napata, Meroë, and Aksum, all of which feature here, alongside lesser-known but important cultures like that of the Nok of West Africa.

In classical antiquity, North Africa was home to the mighty Carthaginian Empire and was one of the key sites involved in Rome's rise to power. By this time, a distinction had emerged between the "Mediterranean" North Africa and the regions of Africa south of the Sahara, which remains to this day. This idea was reinforced by the arrival in Africa of Christianity, which would go on to spread across the west and south, and the later advance of Islam in the north. After this era, great African empires formed: Wagadou in present-day Ghana, for example, and the Mali and Songhai empires. Their stories, and those of many other kingdoms and peoples, are told here through their artefacts, archaeology, architecture, and art, and through the biographies of their leaders and the customs and practices of Indigenous groups such as the Asante, Bedouin, Maasai, Tuareg, Yoruba, and Zulu.

The medieval period saw Africa develop deeper contacts with Europe, the Middle East, and Asia. Trade became an important aspect of these contacts, with states importing cloth, glass, ceramics, and spices, and exporting gold, ivory, leather goods, timber, and many other items. The period saw an escalation in the enforced trafficking of people from

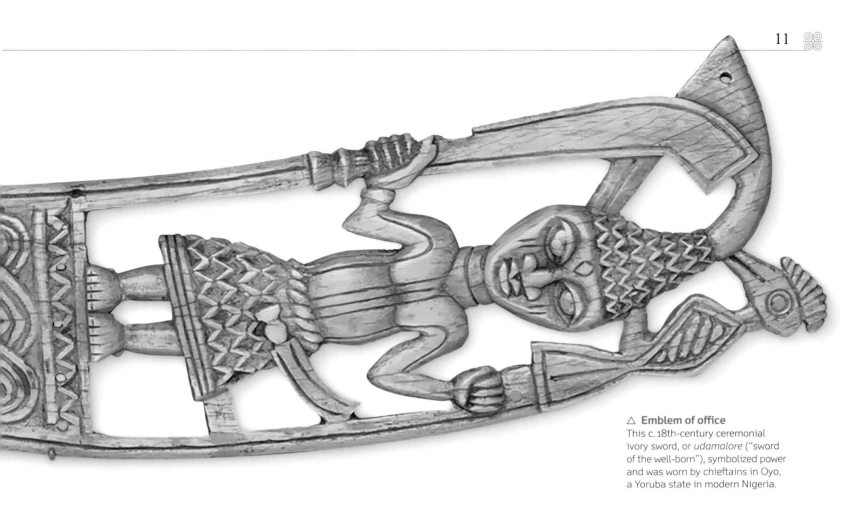

△ **Emblem of office**
This c.18th-century ceremonial ivory sword, or *udamalore* ("sword of the well-born"), symbolized power and was worn by chieftains in Oyo, a Yoruba state in modern Nigeria.

Africa, which had begun in the 7th century with the slave trade between Africa's northern and eastern states and the Arab world. The arrival of European explorers in West Africa in the 15th century led to many more millions of Africans being transported to the Americas in the Atlantic slave trade.

Imperialism and beyond

An examination of the complex relationship between Africa and Europe forms an important part of this book. The Portuguese arrived first, exploring the West African coast, followed by the British, Dutch, French, and others. By the end of the 15th century, Europeans had established military and commercial outposts on African soil. From these beachheads, as many as 15 million enslaved people would be forced to work on plantations in the Americas.

The "Africa" the Europeans encountered was not the "primitive" or "dark" continent that they later portrayed it to be, but a place of sophisticated cultures. Many of the continent's great empires continued to thrive – some in part due to their entanglement in the slave trade. Old kingdoms such as that of Kongo in Central Africa endured alongside newer powers like the West African kingdom of Dahomey. Islamic Sultanates, notably that of Zanzibar, along the East African coast enjoyed a golden age.

From the early 19th century onwards, Europe increasingly involved itself in Africa's affairs. Explorers and Christian missionaries paved the way for the era of formal colonization that followed. African people resisted fiercely and sometimes successfully, but from around 1880 to the 1960s the majority of the continent was under European control – a short but highly significant period in Africa's long history. It was the aftermath of World War II, Cold War politics, and liberation movements within Africa that finally ended imperialism.

Independence was not a magic cure for all the issues that affected Africa in the wake of colonization, such as poverty, political instability, corruption, over-powerful militaries, and a lack of economic development. But through self-rule, African nations are regaining control of their own destiny. Today, people around the continent are increasingly contextualizing the past, celebrating it, and using history to understand the present – and building a future based on confidence in who Africans are and what Africa can be.

1

African prehistory

5 MYA–3500 BCE

African prehistory

Africa is a continent of diverse climates and landscapes. It is also the home of humankind, the origin point from which the first anthropoids (primates that resembled humans) emerged from ape-like creatures, evolved over millions of years into *Homo sapiens* – modern humans – and spread across the rest of the world.

Early origins

Africa spans around 8,000 km (5,000 miles) from the north to its southern tip, and 7,400 km (4,600 miles) east to west. Geologically, the continent was formed about 180 million years ago by the break-up of the "super-continent" Pangaea, which split into Africa, South America, Arabia, Madagascar, India, Australia, and Antarctica. Most of Africa sits on a single tectonic plate (the African Plate) that extends into the middle of the Atlantic Ocean. The eastern edge of the plate is bordered by the Arabian Plate, situated in the northeast, and the Somalian Plate, which extends from the Horn of Africa to the Southern Cape. The fault lines where these plates join are responsible for geological formations such as the Ethiopian Highlands and the Great Rift Valley.

The landscape of Africa has changed over millions of years, shaped by tectonic movement and the effects of successive ice ages and interglacial warmer periods. The continent today is characterized by a hot, dry north that encompasses the Sahara; a central band of tropical forests and savannas, or grasslands, either side of the Equator; and the more temperate south, with its plateaus and mountains, such as the Drakensberg range.

The first human-like creatures emerged around 5 million years ago, descended from the order of primates that includes apes and monkeys. Why this happened in Africa and nowhere else is a mystery, as is where in Africa it originally happened. Two million years ago, *Homo erectus* ("upright man") appeared in Africa, and the human story took a great step forward. This species evolved into *Homo sapiens* ("wise man") 1.7 million years later. Numbers of both species moved out of Africa, spawning subspecies and other species (such as the Neanderthals) that all, with the exception of *Homo sapiens*, eventually died out.

The birth of culture

As well as being the birthplace of humanity, Africa is also where culture and society were born. The first humans did not exist as solitary creatures that only came together to mate. From the beginning, our ancestors lived and worked together. Initially, and for many hundreds of thousands of years, humans were hunter-gatherers, traversing the landscape with the changing seasons in search of food, water, and shelter. By necessity, those early hunters began to fashion tools and weapons from stones and worked out how to make and control fire. Cooking with fire allowed humans to improve their diet, which helped make their bodies more efficient and their brains bigger. Humans began to express themselves through art and body adornment, such as jewellery. In time, in Africa and beyond, humans learned how to gain some control over their environment. Settled agriculture arose, towns and cities were built, civilizations emerged, and the next phase of human development began.

◁ **The Makapansgat pebble, found in South Africa**

c. 5–4 million BCE Evolution of *Australopithecus afarensis*, the earliest human ancestor

c. 3 million BCE Makapansgat pebble is thought to be the oldest known object that hominids recognized as having a symbolic face

c. 180 million BCE Break-up of the Pangaea supercontinent; Africa and other separate landmasses form

c. 3–2 million BCE Evolution of *Homo habilis* ("handy man"), the first of the *Homo* species and the first tool-maker

c. 2 million BCE Emergence of *Homo erectus*, the first species with human-like proportions

Africa 7,000 years ago
The main map (below) shows Africa's vegetation 7,000 years ago, before the Sahara was a desert. It also locates significant prehistoric sites. The inset map (right) shows Africa's vegetation today.

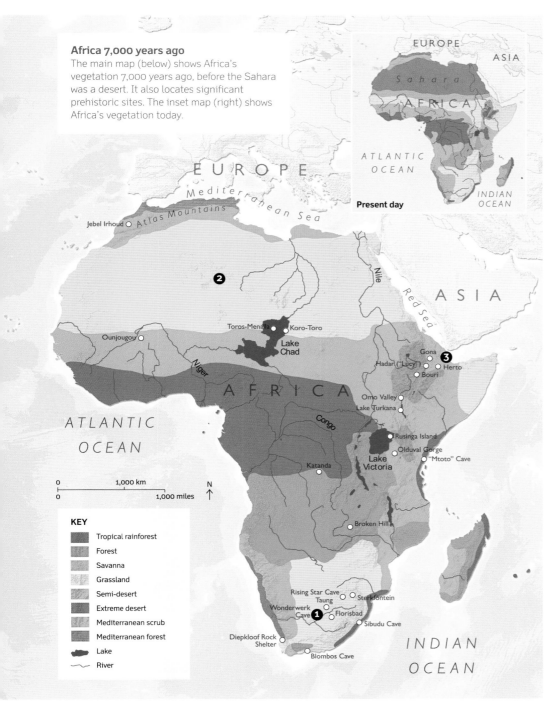

EUROPE

Mediterranean Sea

Atlas Mountains

Jebel Irhoud

EUROPE

ASIA

Sahara

AFRICA

ATLANTIC OCEAN

INDIAN OCEAN

Present day

❷

Toros-Menalla

Koro-Toro

Lake Chad

Ounjougou

Niger

AFRICA

Congo

Nile

Red Sea

ASIA

Hadar ("Lucy")

Gona

❸ Herto

Bouri

Omo Valley

Lake Turkana

Rusinga Island

Olduvai Gorge

"Mtoto" Cave

Katanda

Lake Victoria

ATLANTIC OCEAN

0 — 1,000 km
0 — 1,000 miles

N ↑

Broken Hill

KEY

▮	Tropical rainforest
▮	Forest
▮	Savanna
▮	Grassland
▮	Semi-desert
▮	Extreme desert
▮	Mediterranean scrub
▮	Mediterranean forest
▮	Lake
～	River

Rising Star Cave
Taung

Sterkfontein

Wonderwerk Cave ❶

Florisbad

Sibudu Cave

Diepkloof Rock Shelter

Blombos Cave

INDIAN OCEAN

❶ South Africa's Wonderwerk Cave

❷ Tassili n'Ajjer, Algeria, a site of ancient cave art

❸ Laas Geel Caves, Somalia

c. 430000 BCE First appearance of Neanderthal species in Europe and Asia

c. 150000 BCE The first languages begin to develop

c. 40000 BCE *Homo sapiens* becomes the sole surviving human species

c. 3500 BCE Earliest migrations of Bantu-speakers across Africa

c. 1.75 million BCE The first "out of Africa" migrations by small groups of *Homo erectus*

c. 300000 BCE First appearance of *Homo sapiens*

c. 73000 BCE The first rock art appears, in South Africa

c. 9000 BCE Domestication of livestock begins

△ **Coastal desert**
Considered to be the world's oldest desert, the Namib stretches for almost 2,000 km (1,200 miles) along the Atlantic coast of Southern Africa.

Africa's environment

The continent's rich and varied topography

Africa's varied climatic zones – deserts, mountains, islands, rainforests, and temperate coastal plains – and its plant and animal life have shaped the history of this vast continent for millennia.

Africa covers more than 30 million sq km (12 million sq miles), contains the world's longest river and largest hot desert, and is second only to Asia in size. Its tallest peaks are Kilimanjaro in Tanzania at 5,895 m (19,341 ft) and Mount Kenya at 5,199 m (17,057 ft). East Africa is also home to the Great Rift Valley, a vast sequence of trenches and valleys that includes Lake Assal in Djibouti, 155 m (509 ft) below sea level. Africa's great mountain ranges include the Atlas Mountains of North Africa, East Africa's Ethiopian Highlands, and the Drakensberg Mountains in South Africa.

These high areas are the source of some of Africa's mighty rivers, including the Congo, Niger, Zambezi, and Orange. The Nile is the world's longest river, running 6,650 km (4,132 miles) from Lake Victoria –

the world's largest tropical lake – to Egypt's Nile Delta. Africa's river systems have enabled civilizations to flourish, with the Niger supporting the empires of Ghana, Mali, Songhai, and Kanem-Bornu, while Egypt's population hugs the Nile.

Climate and civilization

The equator cuts Africa in two, bringing heavy rainfall and warm temperatures to a central belt of rainforests. This region is rich with plant life, including majestic mahogany trees and spectacular orchids, and animal life, including chimpanzees and elephants.

North and south of this lush rainforest stretch different climatic zones, with conditions generally becoming drier further from the equator. To the

"I am an African. I owe my being to the hills and the valleys… the ever-changing seasons."

THABO MBEKI, FORMER PRESIDENT OF SOUTH AFRICA, 1996

northeast, towards the Horn of Africa (Eritrea, Ethiopia, and Somalia) lies a temperate rainforest that the ancient Greeks saw as an earthly paradise, with plentiful rainfall and rich soil. As the land rises into the Ethiopian Highlands, the climate becomes drier and hotter, and human settlement relatively sparse.

To the west of here, woodlands and vast grasslands fringe the central rainforests and provide a home for megafauna such as giraffes, hippos, and lions. Further north, the Sahel runs across north-central Africa from Mali to Sudan. Its minimal rainfall and coarse soil mean vegetation is mostly thin and shrubby, although in medieval times the region was more verdant and supported a considerable population.

Deserts, forests, and bush

The world's largest hot desert, the Sahara, along with the Egyptian, Libyan, and Nubian deserts, lies to the north of the central savannas. These desert landscapes contain rock-strewn plains, dunes, sand seas, and oases where camels and human travellers have quenched their thirst for thousands of years. The Atlas Mountains separate the Sahara from the fertile and more populous plains that border the Mediterranean.

South of the equator, from central Gabon to Tanzania and down to Botswana in Southern Africa, the central belt of rainforest transitions to grassland and forests, and parts of Botswana's Okavango Delta, Zambia, Zimbabwe, and Tanzania are sparsely

△ **Forest habitat**
The largest living primates, mountain gorillas, make their home in the rainforests of the Congo Basin. These forests, the largest in Africa, cover 1.6 million sq km (1 million sq miles).

populated but abundant with wildlife. In the Indian Ocean, Madagascar is one of the world's largest islands, with unique flora and fauna.

Southern Africa is generally dry, with grass or bush, and the Kalahari and Namib deserts stretching to the southwest. There are small mountain ranges such as the Karas, as well as large national parks, while the tip of South Africa has a Mediterranean-like climate. In Southern Africa, human settlement is most dense close to major rivers and seas, with drier regions supporting thinner or nomadic populations.

▽ **Lake Nakuru**
Flamingos gather at Kenya's Lake Nakuru, one of the Rift Valley lakes, 1,754 m (5,755 ft) above sea level.

Namib Desert

A gemsbok stands in the Namib, a desert that stretches for almost 2,000 km (1,200 miles) along the coasts of Angola, Namibia, and South Africa. The Namib is believed to be the world's oldest desert, existing in an arid state for at least 55 million years. Beyond a few coastal cities, the region is virtually uninhabited by humans. But there is life. Vegetation includes grasses, lichens, and even some trees. Beetles, geckos, and snakes are found across the region, birds throng the coast, and antelope, elephants, and lions can be found in the north. Gemsbok, a variety of oryx, are particularly well suited to hot conditions thanks to adaptations including a vein-packed nose that cools their blood.

The shifting Sahara

Changing climate of the world's largest hot desert

The Sahara occupies around 9 million sq km (3.5 million sq miles), or one-third of Africa's total landmass. Today, the Sahara is a place of endless sands, rocks, and mountains. But over 5,000 years ago, the region was a lush, verdant land.

Evidence of the past

Early travellers have left eyewitness accounts of the Sahara, including Muslim scholar Ibn Battuta's famous book *The Rihla (The Travels)* in the 14th century. But to reconstruct the ancient ecology of the Sahara, scientists use archaeological remains and paleoclimate (historical climate) evidence, such as pollen found in sediment. Earlier than about 5,000 years ago, these sources indicate, the Sahara had regular rainy monsoon seasons that created networks of rivers, rivulets, and lakes. At this time, the region supported diverse flora, including grasslands and forests, and fauna, including river animals such as fish and crocodiles. These wetter conditions also encouraged the establishment of vibrant settlements and transhumance (the movement of livestock around different regions). Rock carvings and paintings in Tassili, southern Algeria, dating from more than 6,000 years ago, show people and animals, including elephants, giraffes, hippos, and rhinos, that flourished in the vast, lush savanna before desiccation set in.

Examination of ocean sediments along West African coasts, including dust, pollen, and other materials deposited by the wind, suggests that about 8,000 years

△ **Lake Chad**
A freshwater lake with a surface area that varies by season as well as year by year, Lake Chad is the remaining portion of a larger ancient sea sometimes called Mega Chad. It covers territories in four countries: Nigeria, Cameroon, Niger, and Chad.

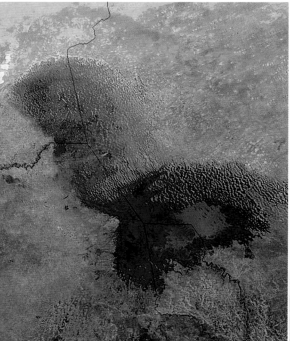

△ **Shrinking waters**
Satellite images taken over several decades provide startling visible evidence of the shrinking of the once "Great" Lake Chad. It now spans less than a tenth of the area it covered in the 1960s. Many initiatives, such as planting trees to avoid soil erosion, are being taken by local communities to protect their lake environment.

△ **The Sahel**
The Sahel is a region of grasslands, forests, savannas, and shrublands between the Sahara to the north and the Sudanian savanna to the south. Deforestation and drought have caused much of it to turn to desert – a trend that is likely to continue.

"We found much water... in pools left by the rains."

IBN BATTUTA, *THE RIHLA* (*THE TRAVELS*), 1354

ago the middle of the Sahara experienced a period of dryness. This period lasted about 1,000 years, forcing a wave of migration to the north and south and marking a cultural shift among the ancient inhabitants. Those who returned after the dry period survived on a more diverse diet, moving from hunting and gathering to cattle herding and dairy production.

Desert on the move

The current more intense period of dryness set in some 5,000 years ago, forcing further migrations from the Sahara as groups of people moved to the better-watered grasslands and forests of West Africa and northeastwards into Egypt's fertile Nile Delta. These movements helped to foster a cultural interaction on which ancient Egypt's 3,000-year-old civilization was built. For around 2,000 years, the Sahara's climate has been relatively stable. However, scientists at the University of California Los Angeles (UCLA) have shown that the desert is now expanding steadily southwards by 1.5 km (0.9 miles) a year. Lake Chad in West-Central Africa, which provides food and water to over 50 million people, has shrunk by 95 per cent since 1960, threatening the lives of many in the region. Trends indicate that this drift will continue until at least 2050. However, some models of future climate change suggest that the West African monsoon could strengthen again naturally, which would trigger an increase in green vegetation: a new chapter in the story of the Sahara.

△ **Desert settlement, Morocco**
Communities in desert settlements in the the High Atlas Mountains, Morocco, are highly vulnerable to the effects of climate change. Many barely scrape a living as labourers and agriculturalists, and face the constant threat of drought.

△ **Ships of the desert**
Dromedary camels were first introduced to the Sahara around 200 CE as part of trade caravans from the Arabian Peninsula. Their tremendous endurance, strength, and ability to withstand the effects of intense heat and food and water deprivation make them ideally suited to the harsh desert environment.

△ **The hamada**
The majority of the Sahara is a type of desert known as hamada, meaning "rock" in Arabic. These landscapes consist of high, hard, rocky plateaus, generally lacking in vegetation, where most of the sand has been removed through wind erosion.

Cradle of humanity

From *Ardipithecus* to *Australopithecus*

△ **Facial reconstruction**
Researchers recreated the face of a 4–3.3-million-year-old hominid, known as "Lucy", using sophisticated forensic techniques.

A wealth of fossil finds across the continent of Africa provides evidence for the earliest humans, who evolved from the family of hominids, or "great apes" (chimpanzees, orangutans, and gorillas), about 5–4 million years ago (MYA).

The confirmation of humanity's African origins began in the 1920s. Ever since, experts have been reconstructing humankind's family tree, tracing its branches back over millions of years to show how evolution progressed not in a straight line, one species after another, but contingently.

In 1924, the Australian anthropologist Raymond Dart discovered a child's skull at Taung, in South Africa. "Taungboy", as Dart described the 2.8-million-year-old fossil, was the first specimen found of the upright-walking bipedal early human, or hominin, *Australopithecus afarensis* ("the southern ape from afar").

At this time, the scientific community believed that humans originated in Europe or Asia, not Africa, and many dismissed Dart's assertion that *Australopithecus afarensis* represented a "missing link" between apes and humans. In time, however, scientists recognized his claim, helped in part when the palaeontologist (a scientist who studies fossils) Robert Broom discovered adult *australopithecine* remains in South Africa in 1936.

Following Dart's and Broom's discoveries, similar, older finds in Tanzania, Ethiopia, and Kenya left little doubt as to humankind's place of origin. In 1978, the British paleoanthropologist Mary Leakey found sets of

"The **driving force of evolution** is **environment**."

YOHANNES HAILE-SELASSIE, 2019

◁ **Place of origin**
Olduvai Gorge in Tanzania is one of the world's most important sources of hominin fossil remains and early stone tool artefacts.

3.5-million-year-old footprints made by upright-walking hominins at Laetoli, south of Tanzania's Olduvai Gorge. This complemented her earlier discovery at Olduvai Gorge in 1959 of what is now known as *Australopithecus boisei*, which lived 3–2 MYA and had a larger cranium than *Australopithecus afarensis*. This species was later linked with *Paranthropus robostus*, a hominin found in Southern Africa.

Unlike *Australopithecus boisei*, *Paranthropus robostus*, which lived 2–1.2 MYA, was able to make tools. *Homo habilis*, an advanced species of *Paranthropus robostus*, is credited with creating sharpened stone tools that allowed it to hunt game effectively and harvest wild roots and crops for food.

The past reveals the present

A landmark find came in 1974, when French geoscientist Maurice Taieb's team in Hadar, Ethiopia, excavated "Lucy", an ape-like creature 1.1 m (3 ft 8 in) tall and weighing 29 kg (65 lb). "Lucy" was a small-brained bipedal hominid, classed as *Australopithecus afarensis*, who lived 4–3.3 million years ago. Her ability to stand upright and walk placed her species in a prominent position in the human evolution tree.

In 1998–99, a team led by paleoanthropologists Louise and Meave Leakey made another important discovery in Lake Turkana, Kenya. *Kenyanthropus platyops* lived 3.5 MYA and its flat facial features and small teeth have led some to believe that this species is a direct ancestor of modern humans. Then, in Ethiopia in 2009, came the earliest find yet — the 4.4-million-

year-old *Ardipithecus ramidus*. An older fossil, the 7-million-year-old *Sahelanthropus tchadensis* from Chad, is not yet fully accepted as a true human ancestor due to doubt as to whether the species could walk on two legs.

How humankind developed in Africa, and why some species thrived while others died out, depended on a number of factors. The tool-making capabilities of some species played a role, as did Africa's ecology, with its climate, landscape, flora, and fauna determining which species prospered. With each new fossil discovery, our understanding of human evolution expands.

△ **"Lucy" skull**
Scientists have reconstructed the skull of "Lucy" from fragments of bone. Her third molars ("wisdom teeth") are erupted and slightly worn, indicating that "Lucy" was fully adult.

◁ **Find from Ethiopia**
Yohannes Haile-Selassie, a paleoanthropologist from Ethiopia, helped to discover the skull of an *Australopithecus anamensis*, an ancestor of *Australopithecus afarensis*. The two species coexisted for around 100,000 years.

Figures were painted using
ground-up minerals mixed with
water, saliva, blood, fat, or urine

Elaborate
decorations on
limbs and torso

△ **Rock paintings of Tassili n'Ajjer**
This rock art, from Tassili n'Ajjer, Algeria, dates to c. 6000 BCE.
Of all ancient human species, only *Homo sapiens* seems to
have created figurative art, a skill demonstrating its ability to
understand and represent the world.

The rise of sapiens

Tracing the birth of humankind

From the Latin for "wise man", *Homo sapiens* is the species to which all modern humans belong. It first appeared in Africa and developed a complex culture and technology that allowed it to adapt to a wide range of different environments.

Homo sapiens, the first recognizable humans, evolved in Africa. Scientists view Southern Africa or Ethiopia as the likeliest sites, although the earliest remains discovered so far were found in Jebel Irhoud in Morocca, and date from around 300,000 years ago.

Like all of humankind's ancestors, *Homo sapiens* derived from primates, the zoological order whose groups also include monkeys and apes. Indeed, humans (*Homo*) are actually part of the ape "superfamily" Hominoidea. The *Homo* genus of the Hominoidea family tree branched off around 3 million years ago (see pp. 22–23) and evolved through a number of species, including *Homo habilis*, *Homo erectus*, and *Homo heidelbergensis*. *Homo sapiens* is the most recent *Homo* species and has outlived all the others, which have gone extinct.

The defining characteristic of *sapiens* against all earlier species is that it had a bigger brain, housed in a high-vaulted, thinly walled skull. Why this bigger brain developed is the subject of scientific debate, but some environmental and cultural factors are generally agreed. *Sapiens* came about at a time when Earth's climate was relatively dry and cold. Food and water were scarce, meaning that our ancestors had to invent strategies for finding and keeping sustenance when they could. In this respect, *sapiens* profited from earlier *Homo* species' development of the first stone tools and their harnessing of fire as a means of keeping warm and cooking food.

Origins of the species

With their bigger brains and the evolutionary experience of hundreds of thousands of years of tool-making by earlier species, *sapiens* made and used cutting and hunting implements that were better and more effective than ever before. Being able to gather, store, and cook food – particularly meat – more efficiently allowed *sapiens* to evolve into a strong, healthy, long-lived, practical, organized, and intelligent species. All of these characteristics in combination ensured that *sapiens* would flourish where other species, which possessed only some of these characteristics, would die out.

In addition, the earliest *sapiens* discovered that those groups able to accumulate knowledge, share it, and pass it on to others were more likely to thrive. Devising ways of working together (or against each other) allowed groups of *sapiens* better chances of survival, especially in harsh, unforgiving environments as they moved around, and ultimately out of, Africa. Cooperation by necessity means communication, and this led to the emergence of language and, in time, art, religion, culture, social organization, and the first civilizations – and *sapiens* becoming who we are today.

SEARCHING FOR **AFRICA'S EARTH MOTHER**

In recent decades, scientific studies have sought to discover the origin site of humankind by looking at mitochondrial DNA, which is found within cells and inherited only by females. Comparing mitochondrial DNA in the oldest *Homo sapiens* fossils with that of Indigenous populations of parts of Africa, the aim is to discover people with the strongest or longest unbroken genetic links. A study among the Khoisan people (below) of northern Botswana placed the Makgadikgadi basin region as a strong candidate, but the quest to find the definitive "Mitochondrial Eve" continues.

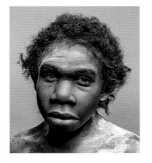

△ **Turkana Boy**
This model is based on a *Homo ergaster* skeleton from c. 1.6 million years BCE, discovered in 1984 in Kenya and known as "Turkana Boy". From a species predating *Homo sapiens*, he appears remarkably "modern".

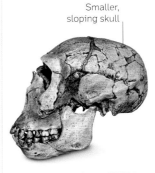

Smaller, sloping skull

HOMO ERGASTER SKULL

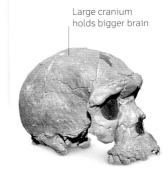

Large cranium holds bigger brain

HOMO SAPIENS SKULL

▷ **Brain development**
A comparison of the "Turkana Boy" skull (above right) with a *sapiens* skull (right), found in Ethiopia and dating to 200,000 years ago, shows the remarkable increase in cranium size.

Stone tools

Inventing the earliest implements

Africa's Stone Age began 3.3 million years ago and ended around 2000 BCE. In modern times, archaeologists have uncovered a wide variety of tools and artefacts used by humankind's ancient ancestors, including sharp flakes, arrowheads, hammerstones, handaxes, and other utensils.

Flaked on both sides

Flaked on one side only

▷ **Stone Age selection**
These tools are from a find of 300,000-year-old artefacts at Jebel Irhoud, Morocco. "Limace", "Unifacial", and "Levallois" describe different "flaking" styles.

LIMACE   **UNIFACIAL**   **LEVALLOIS**

Edges flaked off by hammer

Expertly rendered serrated edge

Patch of iron-rich pink in otherwise blue-grey jasper

Green jasper

Skilfully created symmetrical shape

Slender carved shaft

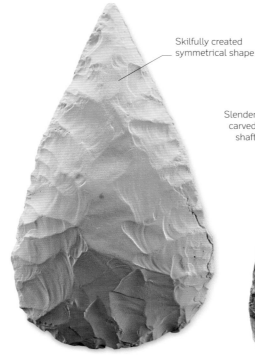

Inward-curving wings

△ **Regional rarity**
Discovered in Mali, this scraper was made 280,000–500,000 years ago. It is 7 cm (2.75 in) in length and is of a style and material unique to West Africa.

△ **On the hunt**
Sharp items like this 195,000-year-old projectile point from Omo Kibish in Ethiopia were attached to sticks to use as spears for hunting animals.

△ **Neolithic arrowhead**
Found in the western Sahara, this slender arrowhead measures 4.5 cm (1.77 in) long and dates from about 10000 BCE–2000 BCE.

△ **Saw-toothed tool**
Designed with double faces, this elongated cutting implement dates from the Neolithic era. Discovered in Mali, it measures 16.4 cm (6.45 in) in length.

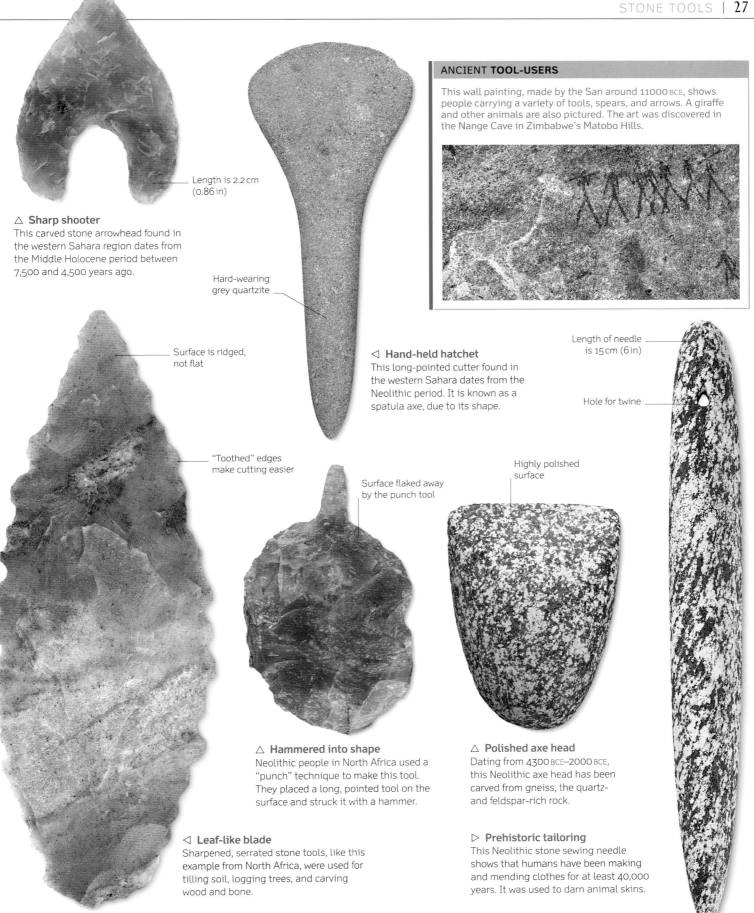

△ Sharp shooter
This carved stone arrowhead found in the western Sahara region dates from the Middle Holocene period between 7,500 and 4,500 years ago.

Length is 2.2 cm (0.86 in)

Hard-wearing grey quartzite

Surface is ridged, not flat

"Toothed" edges make cutting easier

ANCIENT TOOL-USERS
This wall painting, made by the San around 11000 BCE, shows people carrying a variety of tools, spears, and arrows. A giraffe and other animals are also pictured. The art was discovered in the Nange Cave in Zimbabwe's Matobo Hills.

◁ Hand-held hatchet
This long-pointed cutter found in the western Sahara dates from the Neolithic period. It is known as a spatula axe, due to its shape.

Length of needle is 15 cm (6 in)

Hole for twine

Surface flaked away by the punch tool

Highly polished surface

△ Hammered into shape
Neolithic people in North Africa used a "punch" technique to make this tool. They placed a long, pointed tool on the surface and struck it with a hammer.

△ Polished axe head
Dating from 4300 BCE–2000 BCE, this Neolithic axe head has been carved from gneiss, the quartz- and feldspar-rich rock.

◁ Leaf-like blade
Sharpened, serrated stone tools, like this example from North Africa, were used for tilling soil, logging trees, and carving wood and bone.

▷ Prehistoric tailoring
This Neolithic stone sewing needle shows that humans have been making and mending clothes for at least 40,000 years. It was used to darn animal skins.

Out of Africa

The first human migrations

Groups of early humans moved from their homelands and out of Africa in phases, with the first, *Homo erectus*, dispersing about 2 million years ago, followed by *Homo sapiens* around 60,000 years ago.

Homo sapiens (modern humans) was not the first species to leave Africa. Fossil records show that small numbers of an earlier human ancestor, *Homo erectus* ("upright man"), made their way through the Middle East and on to Europe and parts of southeast Asia and China around 2 million years ago, surviving for hundreds of thousands of years.

The Ubeidiya archaeological complex in northern Israel, for example, contains the remains of *Homo erectus* dating from 1.5 million to 700,000 years ago, alongside a variety of "Acheulean" tools – oval and pear-shaped handaxes that were first developed in Africa around 1.76 million years ago. It is believed that Acheulean tool-making (of which the oldest examples have been found in Ethiopia) emerged from Oldowan technology, a very early form of tool manufacture from around 2.9 million years ago associated with the Olduvai Gorge in Tanzania. These finds offer additional confirmation of a lineage of early human – and technological – evolution spreading outwards from the African continent.

◁ **Pointing the way**
These finger bones date from c. 85000 BCE and were found in the Arabian Peninsula – one of the routes by which *Homo sapiens* left Africa.

Beyond Israel, it is thought that *Homo erectus* arrived in China 700,000 years ago. The remains known as "Peking man" found in northern China in 1921 are recognized as *Homo erectus pekinensis*, a subspecies of *Homo erectus*. Further subspecies made it to Indonesia between one million and 500,000 years ago (*Homo erectus erectus*, or "Java man") and to Europe around 500,000 years ago (*Homo heidelbergensis*, or "Heidelberg man").

Evolutionary steps

Although *Homo erectus* was dispersed widely across the world, it failed to thrive in great numbers. Around 300,000 years ago, it was joined outside Africa by the first migratory *Homo sapiens*. As with *Homo erectus*, Israel appears to have been an early stopping-off point for the new species. Archaeological digs at the Mislaya Caves on the slopes of Mount Carmel, in northern Israel, have uncovered a 200,000-year-old *Homo sapiens* jawbone and teeth, together with advanced flint tools and sophisticated handaxes.

This may have been part of an advance wave of *Homo sapiens* migrations that were ultimately failures. It was not until around 60,000 years ago that the species began to leave Africa in larger numbers and successfully flourish in new locations. Reconstructions of the era's climate indicate that conditions in Africa (particularly the east of the continent) were dry, with sea levels much lower than today, and this made it easier for populations to move north and east, towards the Middle East, Europe, and Asia across land bridges between continents that have since disappeared beneath the rising waters of the oceans. The arid, drought-like conditions in their African homelands may also have made *Homo sapiens*' exodus

▽ **On the move**
Waves of human-like *Homo* species moved around and out of Africa from 2 million years ago. The Americas were the last landmasses early humans reached.

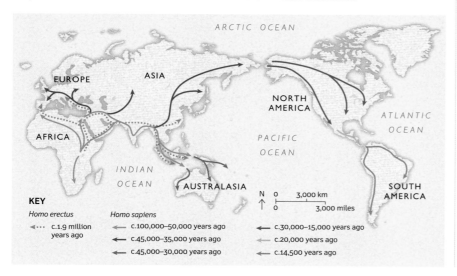

KEY

Homo erectus
◁···· c.1.9 million years ago

Homo sapiens
← c.100,000–50,000 years ago
← c.45,000–35,000 years ago
← c.45,000–30,000 years ago
← c.30,000–15,000 years ago
← c.20,000 years ago
← c.14,500 years ago

◁ **Leaving a mark**
Dating to c. 20000–6000 BCE, these fossilized *Homo sapiens* footprints lie at the base of Ol Doinyo Lengai, an active volcano in Tanzania. The depth and angle of the prints indicate they were made by people jogging.

Layer of volcanic ash and mud in which prints are preserved

Indentation of footprint, one of 400 left by up to 20 individuals

necessary, forcing them out in search of water, nutrient-rich plants, and a varied diet. In 2020, footprints from hundreds of elephants, cattle, and horses were discovered in a dried lake in Saudi Arabia, along with the footprints of three humans – the oldest evidence of *Homo sapiens* in Arabia – demonstrating the close ties between the movements of early humans and the animals they hunted. Finally, there is simply the possibility that *Homo sapiens* migrated spontaneously, as populations in Africa became more dense.

As *Homo sapiens* settled in new areas, they coexisted and to some extent interbred with other species, such as *Homo erectus* and *Homo neanderthalensis* (Neanderthals). Eventually, *Homo sapiens* began to supplant all other species, and, by between 40,000 and 15,000 years ago, all *Homo* species except *sapiens* had died out.

SOUTH-TO-EAST **EXODUS**

Scientists and anthropologists continue to speculate on the movements of our ancestors within and out of Africa. One scenario suggests an early migration from Southern Africa into East Africa in around 70000–60000 BCE when a naturally climate-induced wet corridor opened up. *Homo sapiens* from the south of Africa showed the earliest and clearest examples of complex tool-making and self-expression, including rock art depicting humans and animals. Transferring these new skills and abilities to existing populations in the east could have provided the means for further migratory exploration beyond the continent.

SAN ROCK ART, SOUTH AFRICA

Origins of human culture

The conscious creation of things

As human evolution progressed, from *Homo erectus* to *Homo sapiens*, the first stirrings of culture developed. Tool-making, the use of fire, social organization, and communication through art and language emerged.

As the era of *Homo erectus* came to an end and that of *Homo sapiens* began, the development of culture accelerated, diversified, and became more sophisticated. This is not "culture" in its modern sense – though it certainly paved the way for it and contains elements of it – but more a shift in the way that humans acted, how they thought, and how they expressed those thoughts. The period runs roughly from 300000 BCE, when *Homo sapiens* (modern humans) first emerged, to around 40000 BCE, when it was on the way to becoming the sole surviving human species.

Causes, effects, and cultural shifts

A significant factor that allowed culture to develop was early humans' mastery of fire. This happened around 2 million years ago, in the era of *Homo erectus*. At sites such as Wonderwerk Cave in South Africa and Koobi Fora in northern Kenya, scientists have found evidence of controlled fire use, including remnants of burned bone and plants, and what appear to be hearths. Using fire to cook meat and fish had an evolutionary outcome. Cooked food took less of the body's energy to digest than raw food – and the energy saved was channelled towards evolving a smaller, more efficient digestive tract and a larger, more powerful brain. Evolution progresses slowly, so it would be hundreds of thousands of years before these changes came to fruition, in the shape of *Homo sapiens* and its contemporaries such as Neanderthals, found in Europe and Western Asia.

A bigger brain allowed early humans to see the world differently, and begin to attribute meaning and significance to the things they experienced. It also

△ **On point**
This 90,000-year-old harpoon head was found at an archaeological site on the Semliki River in the Democratic Republic of the Congo. The harpoon is carved from bone.

◁ **Art supplies**
This sea snail shell, used for mixing paint, was found in South Africa's Blombos Cave. At c.100,000 years old, it is among the oldest art objects ever discovered.

gave them the ability to remake the world in ways that better suited their needs and wants. Tools are a good example of this process at work. The earliest tools, found in places such as Kenya and Ethiopia, were made around 3.3 million years ago and were simple rock hammerstones and sharp flakes and shards of stone. By the time of *Homo sapiens*, tools had evolved into far more complex and practical items, designed for specific purposes and relatively easy to use (see pp. 26–27). Discovered at many sites, particularly in North and East Africa, and dating to around 300,000 years ago, these tools included blades, awls (piercing tools), points, scrapers, and burins (chisels). By at least 90,000 years ago, barbed points made of

Motif of lines

△ **Early engravings**
At 60,000 years old, the engravings on these ostrich shell water containers are early examples of graphic art. These fragments were discovered at the Diepkloof Rock Shelter, South Africa.

bone – like those discovered at sites on the Semliki River in the Democratic Republic of the Congo – were used to spear fish. Other composite tools, including axes, arrows, and bows, were made of materials such as stone, animal hide, and wood. Many of these designs are still in use today.

What these sophisticated tools showed was that humans were now able to think in abstract and symbolic terms. Not uncoincidentally, at around the same time humans were producing new and better tools, they also began to make art. One of the first ways humans left their mark was through rock art and cave paintings, the oldest of which – patterns made with an ochre crayon on a piece of rock – dates from around 73,000 years ago and was found in South Africa. Mark-making began to be used to represent the world and express or invoke beliefs and expectations, complementing the other form of communication humans acquired at around this time: language.

Birth of the decorative arts

Initially, humans would probably have decorated practical objects in some way – carving axe handles or inscribing patterns onto bowls, for example. Eventually, this morphed into the making of decorative items purely for their own sake, or for possibly ceremonial or symbolic purposes.

From around 130000 BCE, humans began to bury their dead, as evidenced by sites in Europe and Asia. The earliest intentional burial site found in Africa is

at Panga ya Saidi, a cave site on the Kenyan coast that dates back 78,000 years – where a three-year-old child whose head appears to have been laid on a support, like a pillow, is buried.

Artefacts and ornaments have been found at burial and other sites. In 2014–18, a team of archaeologists in Morocco found 33 shell beads dating from around 150000–130000 BCE that were designed to have been strung on some form of cord and worn as decorative items. Body piercing and tattooing seem also to have been practised: bones of a 12,000-year-old man found in Tanzania show teeth damage thought to have been caused by a piercing on the lower lip.

With most of the elements associated with the creation of culture in place by 40,000 years ago at the latest, the scene was set for the next phase of human development. This was the era of settled agriculture, the building of towns and cities, and the formation of the first civilizations.

△ **Patterned plaque**
This ochre plaque, dating to c. 70000 BCE, is engraved with possibly the first geometric pattern made by a human hand. It was found in Blombos Cave, South Africa.

▽ **Cave of wonders**
The 100,000-year-old sediments in South Africa's Blombos Cave contained some the earliest and richest cultural artefacts made by early humans yet discovered.

Rock art

Visual representation in the Neolithic era

Art forms such as drawings and paintings (known as pictographs), carvings and inscriptions (petroglyphs), rocks arranged in patterns (petroforms), and carved motifs (engravings) are modes of expression as old as humankind. Africa offers rich and varied examples of rock art created in all of these techniques.

Creating a visual record

Archaeologists have discovered millennia-old artworks over the entire continent, from Namibia and South Africa to Mali and Niger in West Africa, across the Sahara to the plains of Egypt and south to Uganda, Tanzania, and Kenya. The study and interpretation of these paintings, carvings, and rock formations offers a wealth of insights into a long-vanished past.

These artworks reveal that our earliest ancestors shared a common interest in documenting their existence. The similarity of works found across the whole expanse of Africa suggests that the impulse or need for expression was common to peoples as they began to form into groups and acquire the first trappings of domesticity and civilization.

Africa's Neolithic cave paintings, drawings, carvings, and sculptured forms are the earliest images of how peoples were organized, where they found shelter, how they moved and migrated across the land, how they gathered food, what and how they hunted, and much more. In the absence of written records and, in many cases, a lack of extensive archaeological remains, ancient art has also supplied the modern

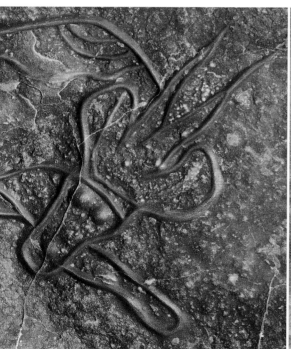

△ **Designs in the desert**
The engravings at southeast Algeria's Tin Taghirt site were made around 8000 BCE by nomadic pastoralists and include representations of cattle, buffalo, and crocodiles. This antelope appears to be sleeping with its head resting on a forelimb.

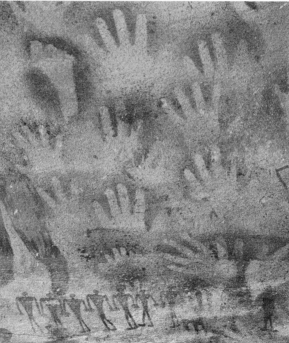

△ **Stencils and paintings**
Egypt's Wadi Sura ("Valley of Pictures") is famed for its Neolithic rock art, which is more than 7,000 years old. The "Cave of Beasts", as it is known to archaeologists, features thousands of painted animals, including elephants, ostriches, and giraffes, and, as here, depictions of human figures and stencils of small hands.

△ **Preserved by nature**
The "Great God of Sefar", in Tassili N'Ajjer, Algeria, was painted around 12,000 years ago and is over 3m (10ft) high. The Sahara's hot, dry climate has helped preserve much rock art, including the image of this mysterious, horned, faceless figure.

"Africa's **rock art**… is the **common heritage** of humanity."

KOFI ANNAN, FORMER UN SECRETARY-GENERAL, 2005

△ **Animal magic**
Seven quartzite slabs found from 1969–72 in a cave in Namibia depict human and animal figures and have been dated to around 28000 BCE. Archaeologists called the cave "Apollo 11" after the then-recent NASA Moon mission.

world with invaluable information on how humanity's ancestors thought about issues such as gender and sexuality, ethnicity, religious beliefs, and fertility, as well as how they entertained themselves with music and dance, wore decorative clothing and headdresses, made technological advances, and developed a material culture and lived their daily lives.

Methods and impulses

The earliest rock art discovered in Africa so far is in Namibia (see right). Early humans experimented with production techniques and invented methods for communicating their artistic impulses. They ground coloured rocks into fine powders – for example, ochre for yellow, orange, and brown, limestone for white, and hematite for red – and used charcoal for black and shells for more white. They mixed these with binding agents such as plant sap, animal fat, or saliva, and applied them to walls using their hands or with brushes made from feathers, animal hair, or the ends of chewed sticks. Sometimes, they drew with solid lumps of pigment or blew powdered pigment onto surfaces through a pipe.

Why Neolithic people created rock art is open to question. It is thought that the main reasons were to express religious beliefs, to appease or ask for help from spirits or providence, to celebrate a good hunt, or to simply make something beautiful or interesting.

△ **Expressive figures**
The hunter-gatherer San people created many images on rock surfaces in South Africa's Cederberg Mountain region, many as recently as 2,000 years ago. These dancing women are thought to be involved in a ritual or ceremony.

△ **Everyday life**
Among the 15,000 examples of rock art that have been identified so far in Algeria's Tassili N'Ajjer National Park are many scenes of daily and social life that display remarkable naturalistic realism. Such depictions include people hunting and herding animals, and, as here, what appears to be children taking part.

△ **Set in stone**
Dabous, in Niger's Ténéré Desert, hosts prehistory's most extensive collection of animal petroglyphs. The celebrated "Dabous Giraffes" are at least 6,000 years old and were probably carved and etched into the soft sandstone using flint tools.

△ **Cattle drive**
Livestock is rounded
up for inspection in this
Egyptian tomb painting
from c. 1350 BCE. Cattle
herding in Egypt began
around 6000 BCE.

The development of agriculture

Cultivation and settlement in Africa

From the late Neolithic period, farming became established across the African continent in different ways and at different rates. This had a profound effect on how African societies were organized.

Although humans originated in Africa (see pp. 22–23), agriculture did not. The first farmers emerged around 12,000 years ago in the area known as the "Fertile Crescent". This was the well-watered land between the Euphrates and Tigris rivers that included modern-day Lebanon, Syria, southern Turkey, Iraq, and western Iran. From here, the understanding of how to domesticate animals and cultivate plants and crops spread east to India and China, and southwest to the Nile Valley.

Agriculture and settlement

Egypt was the first place in Africa to acquire knowledge of agriculture – the management of crops, livestock, fish, and forestry for food and other purposes. It is no coincidence that the continent's first settled civilization also developed there. Hunter-gatherers tend to operate in small groups, always on

Animal-hide binding

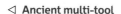
Wooden handle

◁ **Ancient multi-tool**
This model of an adze (a type of axe) used in
Egypt c. 1981 BCE has a copper blade. Adzes were
used for cutting, chopping, and planing wood.

the move, their time largely spent finding sources of food, preparing it, and seeking suitable places to shelter. Settled communities, by contrast, are larger and more diverse. Once they master the principles of agriculture, people in these communities have more time for other pursuits. Religions develop, social hierarchies are established, leaders emerge, and complex forms of social organization can then arise.

One outcome of settlement is that there is now time for the manufacture of tools to begin. The first farmers were able to plant crops and improve yields through the use of a variety of tools. At first, these were fairly crude stone items (see pp. 26–27), ridged, shaped, and sharpened to clear overgrown land, make furrows in soil, and cut down harvests.

This activity began to take place in small pockets of Egypt in the Lower Nile Valley around 6000 BCE, and by 3000 BCE – around the time of the First Dynasty in c. 3100–2890 BCE – agriculture was well established. By this time, agriculture in Africa had spread west and southwest into the modern-day countries of Libya, Morocco, and the southern, non-desert parts of Mauritania. Barley and wheat were cultivated, and cattle, sheep, and goats domesticated. Saharan rock paintings from the 5th millennium BCE begin to show cattle herding and milking as well as hunting scenes, and the cattle are often depicted in huge herds.

The crops grown

Plant and animal domestication took place later in regions south of the Sahara, some time in the 3rd millennium BCE. This probably occurred spontaneously in the area around modern-day Nigeria and Cameroon rather than being imported from Egypt. Millet was the first cereal crop cultivated south of the Sahara, followed by sorghum – a nutrient-rich cereal grain that remains one of the continent's most important crops. These grains were probably initially grown as food for animals; it is likely that Africa's first farmers domesticated livestock long before they began to grow crops for their own consumption.

In addition to millet and sorghum, in West Africa people began to grow rice between 2,000 and 3,000 years ago along the floodplains in a bend in the Niger River. A type of rice called *Oryza glaberrima* is native to the regions of Africa south of the Sahara and is one of the world's two cultivated rice species (the other being *Oryza sativa*, which is found in Asia). Africa is still a major producer of rice today, and the crop ranks fifth among the continent's cash exports after cassava (a potato-like root vegetable), sugar cane, and maize – which were all introduced by Portuguese colonizers after 1500 – as well as yams, an indigenous tuber similar to the sweet potato.

"The **best** of mankind is a **farmer**; the best food is **fruit**."

ETHIOPIAN PROVERB

Farming spreads south

While agriculture was developing in West Africa, it was also spreading further south from Egypt into what is today Sudan, and across into the Great Lakes region and to East Africa. In Ethiopia, however, farming probably developed independently of any outside influence, as it did in West Africa, as early as 5000 BCE. The crops grown in Ethiopia were indigenous rather than introduced from other regions. They included the cereal grains *tef* and *dagusa*, also known as finger millet; *enset*, a banana-like plant used to make flatbreads, pancakes, and porridge; and *nug*, a flowering herb grown for its oil and edible seeds.

The development of African agriculture proceeded more slowly south of the equator. Bantu-speaking people migrating out of West and Central Africa brought their knowledge of farming with them as they gradually travelled further south from c. 2500 BCE. Settled agriculture was not practised in any significant way in Southern Africa until around 250 CE – more than 6,000 years after the continent's earliest farmers had planted their first crops in Egypt around 7,000 km (4,350 miles) away.

▽ **Farmer at work**
This 4th-century CE carved relief once decorated the walls of the Ghirza Mausoleum in western Libya. It shows a farmer using a tool to harvest a wheat crop.

The Bantu migrations

The spread of farming and iron-making culture

Around 3,500 years ago, Bantu-language speakers began leaving their home near the border of modern-day Nigeria and Cameroon. They dispersed techniques of farming and iron-smelting to hunter-gathering groups across the continent.

△ **Migration routes**
This map gives an approximate indication of the migration paths that different Bantu-speaking groups are thought to have taken across Africa.

KEY
■ Bantu homeland, c.2000 BCE
■ Northwestern Bantu by c.500 CE
■ Eastern Bantu by c.500 CE
■ Western Bantu by c.500 CE
← Spread of Bantu

Evidence for the Bantu migrations is mainly linguistic, drawing on the strong language resemblances in vastly different areas. Scholars believe this movement may have been caused by climatically induced overpopulation: following a period of cold, dry, erratic weather about 10,000 years ago (known as the Younger Dryas), the Earth gradually became warmer, wetter, more stable, and richer in carbon dioxide (today's epoch, known as the Holocene).

Plant life became increasingly abundant and, instead of frequent foraging, the Bantu-speaking groups stayed in specific areas for longer, where they collected and stored as much of the local foods as possible. This increase in the availability of food meant that their societies could sustain a greater number of people. To feed the higher numbers, they began cultivating local produce, working the land harder, for longer, and developing a wider range of tools to increase efficiency and productivity.

◁ **Lydenburg pottery fragment**
This pottery fragment, c.500 CE, was retrieved from Lydenburg, South Africa, one of the areas populated by the Bantu-speakers.

Eventually, their populations grew so large they were unsustainable, and some Bantu-speaking groups migrated in search of other fertile lands. Other Bantu-speaking groups migrated to the edges of the Central African forest, which, from 2000 BCE, was traversable, inhabitable savanna – although the core of the forest remained dense and inhospitable.

Learning and spreading new skills

In 500 BCE, a new climatic shift took place: the climate, and the sea surface, became warmer, prompting more rainfall, which washed away the soil in the Central African forest. Trees were unable to grow and savanna replaced the dense vegetation at the heart of the forest. Some of the Bantu-speakers moved into it, occupying areas such as modern-day north Gabon; others migrated into what is now eastern Congo, before using nearby waterways to migrate east and south. By around 300 BCE, some of them had ventured as far as the Great Lakes of East Africa.

▷ **Ironworkers**
A watercolour, made around 1650 CE by Italian missionary Giovanni Antonio Cavazzi da Montecuccolo, shows ironworkers in the Bantu-speaking Kingdom of Kongo forging weapons and tools.

"**Iron… so pure** that I doubt in Europe they would achieve **such perfection.**"

CAVAZZI DA MONTECUCCOLO, FROM HIS HISTORY OF CONGO, MATAMBA, AND ANGOLA, 1687

There, they met farmers and skilled iron-tool users who spoke the languages of Central Sudan, and from them they acquired greater knowledge about farming.

Many diverse hunter-gathering groups populated the areas into which the Bantu-speakers had moved since 2000 BCE. The Bantu-speaking communities conquered or displaced these people, or adapted to their environments, exchanging knowledge and cultural practices. Hunter-gatherers adopted ironworking technology from the Bantu-speakers, who in turn borrowed words and customs from hunter-gatherers.

Multiple migrations
Between 300 and 200 BCE, some of the Bantu-speakers who had been influenced by the Central-Sudan-language-speakers migrated back west, along the south edge of the Central African forest, into north Angola. There, they encountered Bantu-speakers who, rather than settling in north Gabon or moving east following the climatic shift of 500 BCE, had migrated down Africa's west coast to south Congo. By 1 CE, many had settled in north Angola and adopted the ironworking, farming culture of the Central-Sudan Bantu-speakers.

Some of the north Angolan Bantu-speakers migrated south, moving deeper into Angola, gradually spreading themselves over much of southwest Africa; others went east, into the Democratic Republic of the Congo and Zambia, settling there by 500 CE. Meanwhile, between 100 and 200 CE, instead of migrating westwards, some of the Central-Sudan-speaking Bantu who had settled near the Great Lakes travelled south and east, finally settling in Kenya, Tanzania, and possibly Somalia. Between 300 and 400 CE, some of them had continued further south, moving first into Zambia and Malawi, before entering Zimbabwe and South Africa.

In this way, the Bantu-speaking people from West Africa gradually spread a sophisticated ironworking, farming culture across most of the continent of Africa.

△ **San archer**
This detail from a cave painting, c. 6000 BCE, in the Cederberg Mountain range in South Africa, shows a San artist's representation of an archer. Bantu-speakers helped to spread methods of farming and ironworking to peoples across Africa, including hunter-gatherer San-speaking groups.

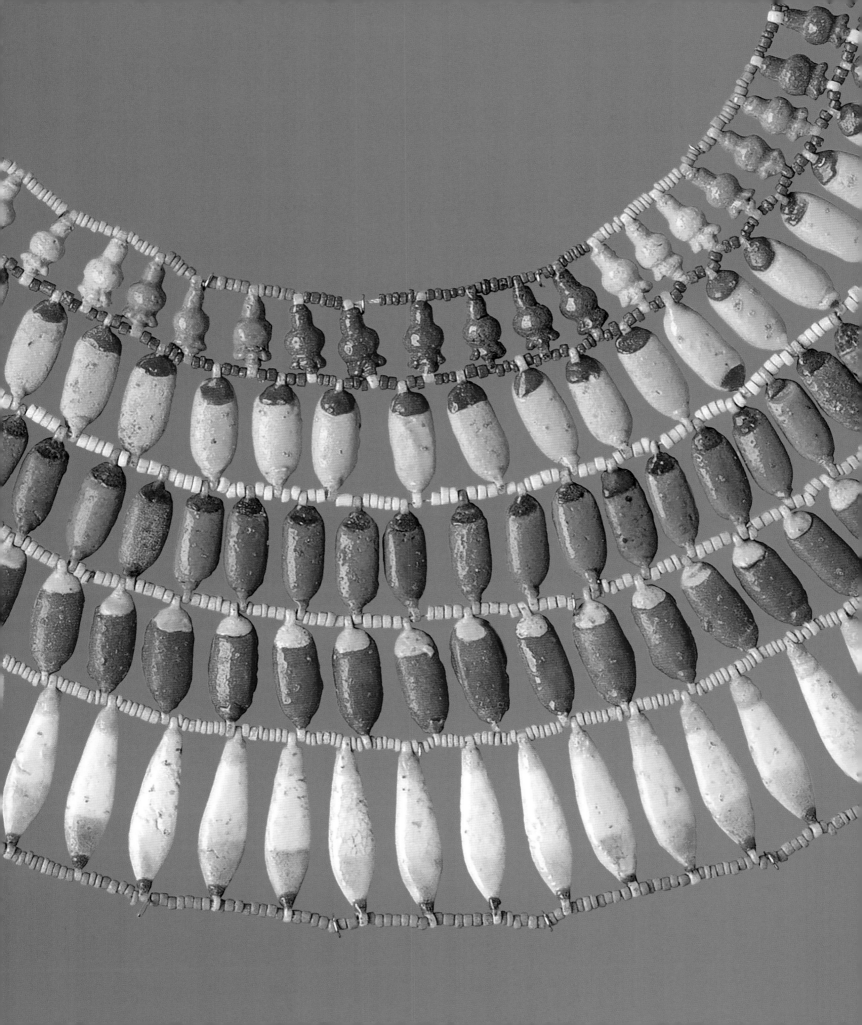

◁ **Precious collar**
Wealthy ancient Egyptians wore beaded necklaces known as *wesekh*, or broad collars. The faïence beads in this collar, made in 1353–1336 BCE, symbolize fruits and flowers.

2
Early civilizations

3000 BCE–600 CE

Introduction

During ancient times, a variety of peoples and civilizations thrived in Africa, particularly in the north. Some were known to non-African cultures, such as those of Assyria, Greece, and Rome; others rose and fell, unknown beyond their own – often considerable – spheres of influence in Africa.

Kingdoms of the Nile

The most notable ancient African civilization was Egypt, whose long and complex history embraces not just the Old, Middle, and New Kingdoms, but the state's incorporation into the Roman Empire and the later arrival of Coptic Christianity and Islam.

South of Egypt, in what is now Sudan, Kerma flourished from around 2500 BCE, followed by the Kingdom of Kush and the ancient Nubian city-state of Meroë. Further south, present-day Eritrea and Ethiopia were home to the little-known D'mt along with the extensive Aksum Kingdom.

Early colonizers and hidden histories

North Africa's coast was home to several cultures that helped to shape the history of the ancient world. Carthage, in modern Tunisia, was founded by traders from the East Mediterranean seaboard and, in the Punic Wars, battled with Rome to dominate the Mediterranean. To the west of Carthage lay Mauretania, while further east was Cyrenaica. Surrounding and at times subsuming them all was the vast, shifting territory of Numidia.

Beyond the Nile and the Mediterranean, however, were African civilizations unknown to the contemporary "Western" chroniclers on whom we have tended to rely today for much of our knowledge of the ancient world. Now, modern research methods and archaeology are helping to expand our knowledge of once little-known cultures such as the Nok, which existed up to 3,500 years ago in present-day Nigeria, and the Sao civilization, which flourished from as early as the sixth century BCE in what is now Chad.

A shared heritage

By looking at Africa's earliest civilizations, we recognize the diverse influences that shaped the continent's different cultures and the importance of recognizing those diverse influences within a shared "African" context. It is clear that while parts of Africa in ancient times developed with little or no contact with outside civilizations, large areas of the continent were impacted and indeed changed by their contacts with Rome, Greece, and Phoenicia, for example, and by the effects of Christianity or Islam on their cultures.

It may be argued, indeed, that the Carthaginians and some later rulers in Egypt (of Phoenician and Macedonian descent respectively) were of different ethnicities to Black Africans who lived south of the Sahara. But this does not necessarily mean that they are less African than those with a longer lineage on the continent or whose cultures had less contact with the wider world. What an examination of Africa's earliest civilizations reveals is the diversity of development experienced by its peoples who, at the same time, share a heritage on the continent that makes all of them Africans.

◁ **Anthropomorphic figure from Sao civilization**

C. 5000 BCE People begin to settle in Egypt

C. 3000 BCE Egypt is unified as a single state under King Narmer

C. 2500 BCE Kerma culture begins to flourish

C. 1500 BCE Earliest evidence of Nok culture in West Africa

1 The ancient ruins of Kerma

2 Nubian pyramids at Meroë

3 The Ezana Stone, Aksum

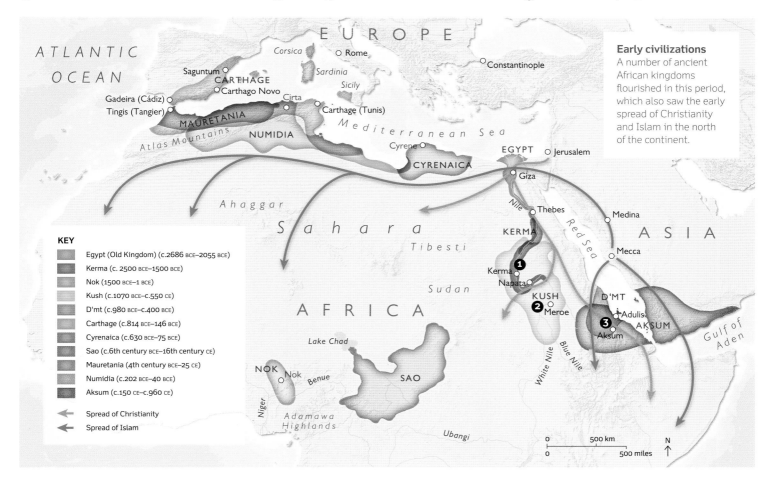

Early civilizations
A number of ancient African kingdoms flourished in this period, which also saw the early spread of Christianity and Islam in the north of the continent.

KEY

Egypt (Old Kingdom) (c.2686 BCE–2055 BCE)

Kerma (c. 2500 BCE–1500 BCE)

Nok (1500 BCE–1 BCE)

Kush (c.1070 BCE–c.550 CE)

D'mt (c.980 BCE–c.400 BCE)

Carthage (c.814 BCE–146 BCE)

Cyrenaica (c.630 BCE–75 BCE)

Sao (c.6th century BCE–16th century CE)

Mauretania (4th century BCE–25 CE)

Numidia (c.202 BCE–40 BCE)

Aksum (c.150 CE–c.960 CE)

→ Spread of Christianity

→ Spread of Islam

c. 1070 BCE Kingdom of Kush forms to the south of Egypt

980 BCE Origin of D'mt Kingdom in modern-day Eritrea and northern Ethiopia

c. 630 BCE Kingdom of Cyrenaica established by colonists from Greece

202 BCE Establishment of Amazigh (Berber) Kingdom of Numidia in northwest Africa

25 BCE Ancient Amazigh kingdoms of Mauretania annexed to Rome

c. 814 BCE Founding of Carthage by Phoenician settlers from Tyre (a city in modern-day Lebanon)

c. 500 BCE The Sao civilization develops to the south of Lake Chad

30 BCE Egypt becomes a part of the Roman Empire

c. 150 CE The Kingdom of Aksum is established

The Age of the Pharaohs

Ancient Egypt under absolute rule

The Old, Middle, and New Kingdoms of ancient Egypt flourished in the third and second millennia BCE, an era that saw the state's greatest political, artistic, and architectural accomplishments.

△ **Palette of King Narmer**
Found at Hierakonpolis, the first African city, this palette (c. 3200 BCE) is thought to depict the unification of Upper and Lower Egypt.

Egypt's first settled cultures developed around 10000 BCE. By 6000 BCE, climate change and overgrazing led to the creation of the Sahara, forcing people to concentrate into villages, towns, and cities along the Nile. This was predynastic Egypt, where, under cultures such as the Badari and Naqada, deities such as Osiris, Isis, and Set and some of the forms of local government and tax collection associated with the later Egyptian civilization were introduced. These developments culminated in the rule of Narmer, a chieftain-king from southern Egypt who, around 3200 BCE, headed north and conquered the Nile Delta, unifying the region into a single kingdom.

Societal organization

In time, Egypt's kings became known as pharaohs, a word meaning "great house", indicating the palace in which the king lived. Not just the head of state, the pharaoh was also Egypt's religious leader, the divine intermediary between the people and the gods. The pharaoh's authority included the power to make laws, collect taxes, and wage war. The pharaoh also owned all of the country's land and its people. Below the pharaoh, the state was administered by an upper class of priests, officials, and military officers. Then came a middle class of merchants and artisans, followed by a lower class of labourers and land-workers.

A golden age

The Age of the Pharaohs is divided into three eras: the Old, Middle, and New Kingdoms. The Old Kingdom lasted from c. 2686 to 2055 BCE, and followed the so-called "Early Dynastic Period" inaugurated by Narmer's son, Hor-Aha, which saw Memphis emerge as the capital of newly united Egypt. The most remarkable visual symbols of the Old Kingdom are the Great Pyramids of Giza and the Sphinx – a sculpture thought to represent the godlike power of the king. On a practical level, the organization of Egypt into a regulated state took place during the Old Kingdom.

There was a period of political instability at the end of the Old Kingdom. Order was restored – and the Middle Kingdom initiated – with the reign of Montuhotep II (c. 2055–2004 BCE). He reunited Egypt, initiated ambitious building programmes, and began to expand Egypt's borders to the south and west, after which the state enjoyed a golden age of peace and prosperity. However, by c. 1700 BCE regional unrest undermined the power of successive pharaohs; within 150 years the Middle Kingdom was over.

The New Kingdom

The first ruler of the New Kingdom was Ahmose I and his sister-wife Ahmose-Nefertari (1550–1525 BCE). Later New Kingdom pharaohs included Hatshepsut, Thutmose III, Amenhotep III, Tutankhamun, and

◁ **Stairway to heaven**
Built in the Old Kingdom in around 2670 BCE, the Djoser Pyramid, in Saqqara, close to Cairo, is the oldest monumental stone building in Egypt still standing.

Abydos in southern Egypt is one of the country's oldest and most sacred cities. It is home to many temples and pharaonic burial sites including those of kings in the Early Dynastic Period. One of the city's most extraordinary ancient buildings is the temple of the New Kingdom pharaoh, Seti I (reigned c. 1294–1279 BCE), whose wall carvings include the Abydos King List (right). It is inscribed with the names, in hieroglyphics, of 76 Egyptian pharaohs from the legendary king Menes to Seti I himself.

KING SETI I AND HIS SON RAMESSES II, SHOWN ON THE ABYDOS KING LIST

Ramesses II and III. The great temple complexes at Luxor and Karnak and the Valley of the Kings were all either built or reached their greatest extent in the New Kingdom. The Book of the Dead, Ancient Egypt's most famous text, was composed in this era.

Decline and fall

The New Kingdom's last pharaoh was Ramesses XI (1099–1069 BCE). His long reign – the longest since Ramesses III – was followed by political volatility, economic decline, and a smallpox epidemic that left the state vulnerable to a succession of foreign rulers that included Libyans, Nubians, Assyrians, and Persians. The Macedonian Greeks arrived in 332 BCE and installed the Ptolemaic dynasty, which was still in power 300 years later when the Romans defeated the last pharaoh, Cleopatra VII, and her lover Mark Antony at the Battle of Actium in 31 BCE. The three-millennia-long Age of the Pharaohs ended the following year, when Cleopatra died by suicide.

△ **Face from the past**
Weighing 11 kg (24 lb), the solid gold funerary mask of New Kingdom pharaoh Tutankhamun was among the treasures discovered in his tomb in the Valley of the Kings in 1922.

◁ **Representing power**
As queen, regent, then pharaoh, Hatshepsut was one of Egypt's few female rulers. At her own request, she was depicted in sculpture as a man, as here.

"**Respect the nobles**, support **your people**, fortify your **borders**."

ADVICE FROM *THE TEACHING FOR KING MERYKARA*, WRITTEN DURING THE MIDDLE KINGDOM

The *Uraeus* is a symbol of kingship in the form of a cobra snake

"A savage lion... advancing **bravely** and returning only when he has **triumphed**."

POEM ON RAMESSES II'S "VICTORY" AT KADESH, INSCRIBED ON KARNAK TEMPLE

Khepresh, or war crown

Heqa sceptre, denoting power and dominion

Pleated robe with hieroglyphic inscriptions

Ramesses II
This magnificent, life-size statue, which dates from the first half of his reign, depicts the king as a young man, wearing the robes and emblems of office.

Ramesses II

Egypt's greatest and most powerful king

Ramesses II (r. 1279–1213 BCE) was one of Egypt's most influential leaders, famous for his military campaigns in the Middle East and his impressive building programmes, including the spectacular rock-cut temples at Abu Simbel.

Few of Egypt's kings were as revered as Ramesses II, also known as Ramesses the Great. He was the third ruler of the 19th Dynasty (1293–1185 BCE), one of the three New Kingdom dynasties in Egypt between 1550 and 1069 BCE. In boyhood, Ramesses joined his father, Seti I, on military exploits, and became king in 1279 BCE, aged 24. Ramesses ruled for 66 years, making him one of the few pharaohs to take part in two of the Heb Sed festivals that were held every 30 years to rejuvenate the pharaoh.

The rise of the warrior-king

Under Ramesses II, the New Kingdom rose to its greatest heights in military strength and stability. To establish a base for his military campaigns in Syria, Ramesses founded a new capital in the Nile River Delta in his name, Pr-Ramesses (House of Ramesses). His early successes included campaigns in Nubia to the south and an assertion of Egypt's foothold in Libya and Syria. In western Syria, the king attempted to dislodge the Hittite Empire at the famous battle of Kadesh in 1274 BCE. The outcome was inconclusive, but Egyptian propaganda depicted Ramesses as the courageous victor (see opposite). The two sides eventually signed a peace treaty in 1259 BCE.

Ramesses was an adept self-publicist, and his building programmes served as potent symbols of his wealth and power. His construction projects include the temple of Karnak at Thebes and, near the border with modern Sudan, the magnificent rock-cut temples at Abu Simbel, as well as cities, monuments, and colossal statues. Among his greatest architectural achievements was his mortuary temple in Thebes, the Ramesseum (see pp. 46–47). He also memorialized his principal wife, Nefertari, with a tomb in Thebes and a temple – next to his own – at Abu Simbel.

Ramesses's reign was one of the longest and most glorious in Egyptian imperial history. He strengthened the country's borders, increased its wealth, and widened its scope of trade. After Ramesses died in c. 1213 BCE, aged about 90 years, nine more pharaohs took his name in honour of their illustrious forebear.

△ **Queen Nefertari**
This detail from Nefertari's tomb in Thebes shows her bearing two ritual vessels.

▽ **King's temple**
The entrance to Abu Simbel is flanked by four rock-hewn statues of Ramesses II that are 20 m (66 ft) tall.

c. 1303 BCE Ramesses II is born to King Seti I and Queen Tuya

1279 BCE Ramesses II is crowned king

1274 BCE Battle of Kadesh

1255 BCE Abu Simbel is completed

c. 1289 BCE Appointed Prince Regent by Seti I at the age of 14

c. 1277 BCE Construction of Ramesses' mortuary temple, the Ramesseum, begins

1259 BCE Peace treaty with the Hittites is signed

1213 BCE Ramesses dies and is succeeded by his son Merneptah

▷ **Temple decor**
This relief of Ramesses II decorated the rear wall of the largest hypostyle hall leading to the sacred heart of the temple. The hall contained 48 columns with papyrus blossom capitals, representing the primeval marsh from which Egypt was believed to have emerged.

The gods bestow emblems of kingship on the pharaoh

Administrative office for recording incoming and outgoing provisions

Columns in the mummified guise of the god Osiris

Artisans' workshops for weaving and stone vase-cutting

Temple of Queens Tuya and Nefertari

Thirty bakehouses ensured the supply of food and offerings

School for scribes and artisans

A small palace accommodated the visiting pharaoh

The entrance pylon was faced with dressed limestone blocks

Waterways linked the complex to the Nile

▷ **King in Life Colonnade**
The first courtyard's northern side was bordered by 11 columns, each fronted by a statue of Ramesses II. They presented the king dressed as in life, but holding the crook and flail of the god Osiris, whose emblems were closely associated with regal power.

▽ **Mansion of Millions of Years**
In Ramesses II's day, the Ramesseum was referred to as his "Mansion of Millions of Years". Construction began in the second year of his reign (c. 1278 BCE) and lasted some 20 years. This reconstruction depicts the complex as it may have looked upon completion.

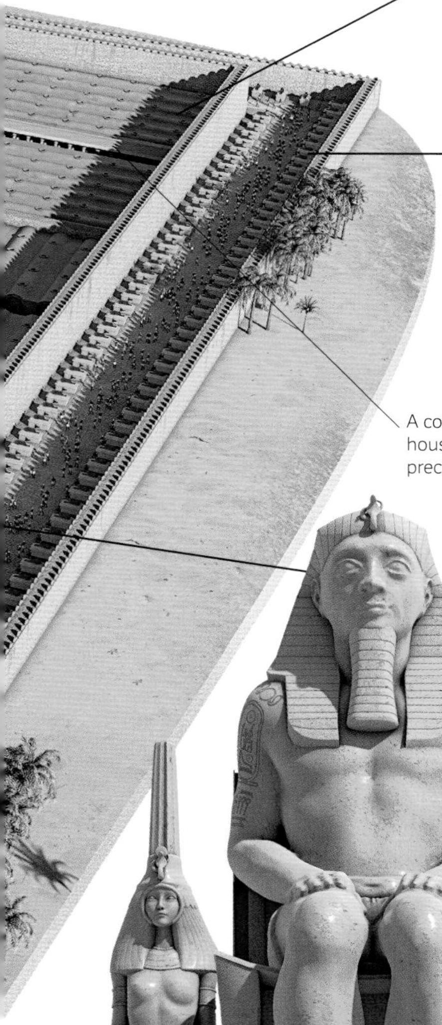

◁ **Royal stores**
This model of a Middle Kingdom granary shows scribes recording deliveries of grain. The Ramesseum had dozens of such storerooms, demonstrating the king's ability to provide for the gods and his people.

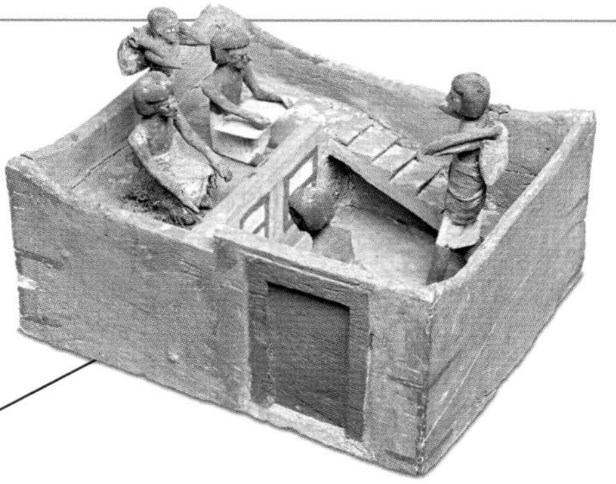

◁ **Processional avenues**
Surrounding the complex on three sides, the processional avenues are unique to the Ramesseum. This reconstruction shows how the northern avenue, lined by jackals, may have looked. Excavations indicate that sphinxes with the head of Ramesses II lined the other avenues.

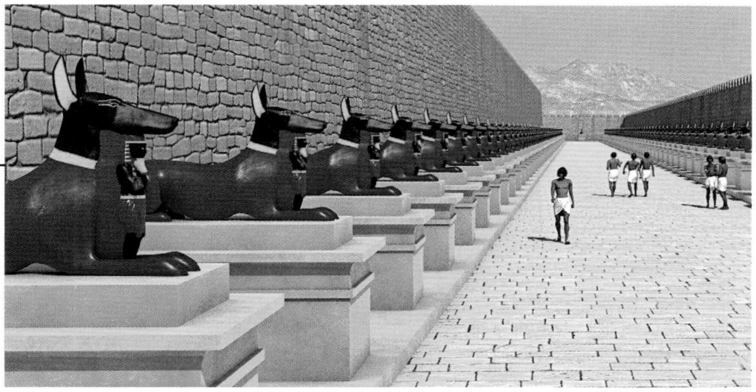

A columned treasury housed the most precious items

The Ramesseum

Thebes (present-day Luxor), Egypt

The Ramesseum was built for Ramesses II as his mortuary temple, dedicated both to the worship of his cult after his death, and to the god Amun. Designed to demonstrate Egypt's power and wealth, the complex introduced a new level of monumental architecture and was an inspiration for succeeding pharaohs, particularly Ramesses III. The walls tell a story of Ramesses II's greatness on earth and in heaven, with brightly painted reliefs depicting his military victories and kinship with the gods. Beyond the sacred temples at its core, the Ramesseum was a hub of economic activity, even during the pharaoh's lifetime. A vast arrangement of outbuildings included kitchens, artisans' workshops, a scribes' school, and dozens of storerooms.

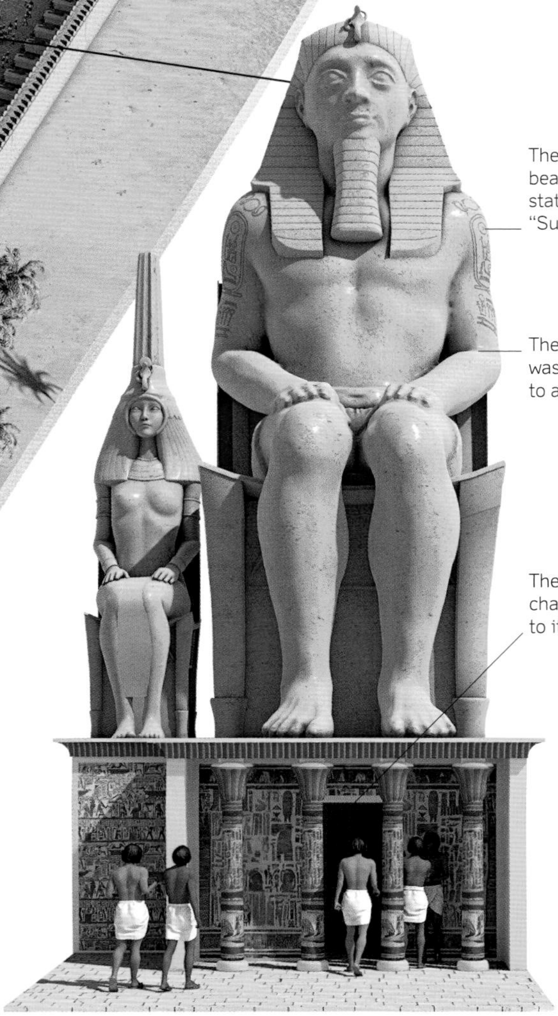

The shoulder bears the statue's name: "Sun of Princes"

The granite was polished to a sheen

The statue had a chapel dedicated to its own cult

◁ **The Sun of Princes**
A monumental colossus of Ramesses II dominated the first courtyard. Hewn from a single block of pink granite and shipped in one piece along the Nile from the quarries of Aswan, further south, it was nearly 18 m (59 ft) tall and weighed over 1,000 tonnes.

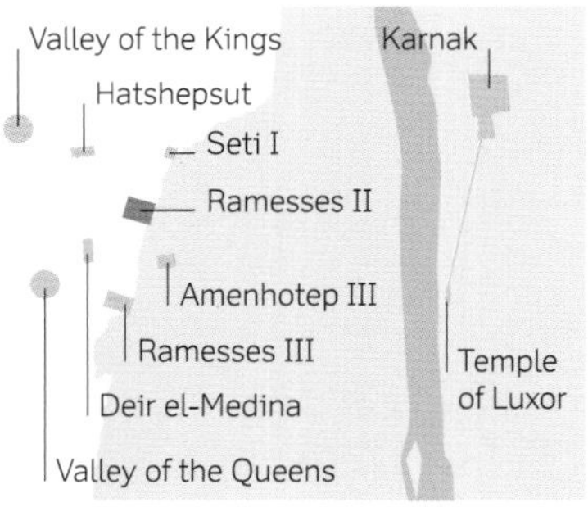
Valley of the Kings
Karnak
Hatshepsut
Seti I
Ramesses II
Amenhotep III
Ramesses III
Temple of Luxor
Deir el-Medina
Valley of the Queens

◁ **Thebes**
c. 1150 BCE
Ramesses II built his temple on the west bank of the Nile at Thebes, in close proximity to the great temples of Karnak and Luxor on the east bank. The Ramesseum was linked to the river by channels.

Egyptian artefacts
Treasures from across the ages

Ancient Egypt has bequeathed to the world a vast collection of beautiful decorative and practical items, jewellery, and artworks that show the full range of the culture's creativity and crafting excellence, while simultaneously offering fascinating glimpses of everyday life in this civilization.

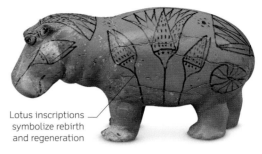

Lotus inscriptions symbolize rebirth and regeneration

△ **Animal statuette**
This hippopotamus figure, from c. 1900 BCE, is moulded from faience, a ceramic composed of ground quartz. The brilliant blue glaze represents the life-giving waters of the Nile.

Dancers providing entertainment

△ **Heavenly delights**
This fresco from palace official Nebamun's tomb dates from c. 1350 BCE. The scene shows the entertainments he will enjoy in the afterlife.

Arghul (double flute)

Hatshepsut's name in hieroglyphs

Engraved cartouche (pharaoh's name in hieroglyphs)

△ **Scarab amulet**
This thumbnail-sized, glazed steatite (soapstone) scarab beetle amulet from c. 1460 BCE was recovered from Queen Hatshepsut's funerary temple.

Tripartite wig is a symbol of elite status

Kilt typically worn by pharaohs

△ **Royal representations**
Once brightly painted, this life-sized sandstone statue from c. 2490 BCE is an idealized embodiment of Pharaoh Menkaura and one of his wives.

Finely carved hairstyle

△ **Happy couple**
This statue of Demedji, an official, and his wife Hennutsen dates from c. 2450 BCE. Non-royal statuary has a "rougher", less refined finish.

△ **Arm defenders**
This gold and lapis lazuli bracelet was owned by Pharaoh Shoshenq II (d. 885 BCE). The design incorporates the protective Eye of Horus.

▷ **Journey to the afterlife**
This *Book of the Dead* papyrus from c. 1275 BCE shows a heart weighed against a feather from the goddess Maat to assess if its owner can enter *Duat*, the underworld.

Ani, the scribe who commissioned the papyrus

Anubis, the jackal-headed god of funerary rites

Ammit, the beast-goddess that devours hearts that "fail" the feather test

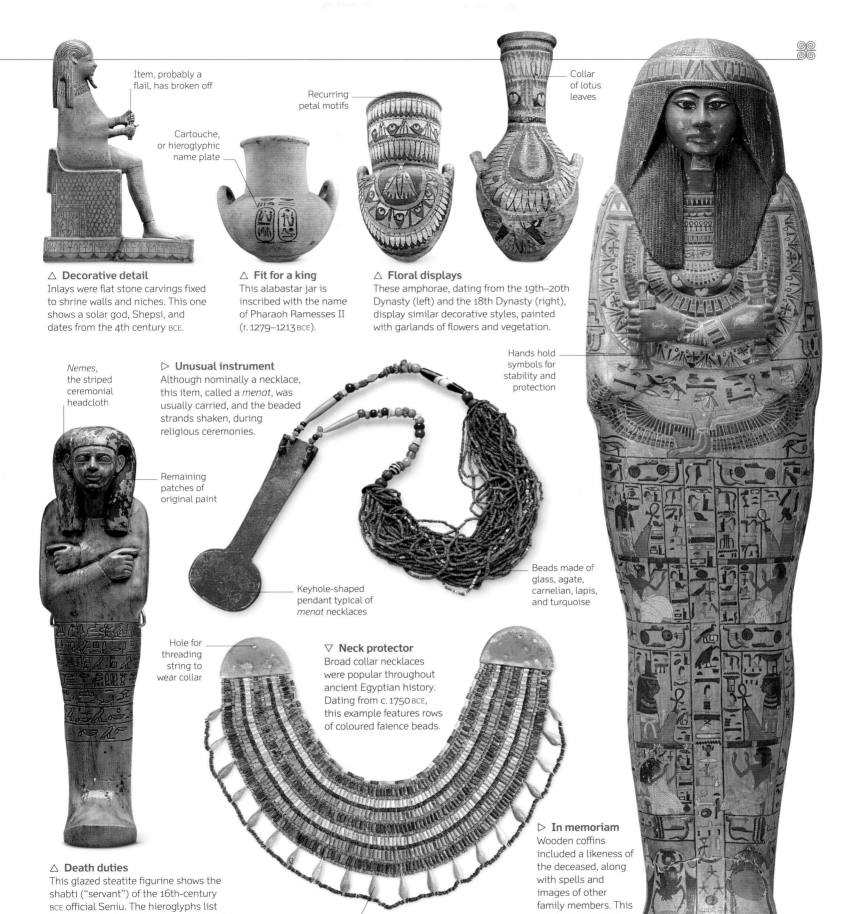

△ **Decorative detail**
Inlays were flat stone carvings fixed to shrine walls and niches. This one shows a solar god, Shepsi, and dates from the 4th century BCE.

Item, probably a flail, has broken off

Cartouche, or hieroglyphic name plate

△ **Fit for a king**
This alabastar jar is inscribed with the name of Pharaoh Ramesses II (r. 1279–1213 BCE).

Recurring petal motifs

△ **Floral displays**
These amphorae, dating from the 19th–20th Dynasty (left) and the 18th Dynasty (right), display similar decorative styles, painted with garlands of flowers and vegetation.

Collar of lotus leaves

Hands hold symbols for stability and protection

Nemes, the striped ceremonial headcloth

▷ **Unusual instrument**
Although nominally a necklace, this item, called a *menat*, was usually carried, and the beaded strands shaken, during religious ceremonies.

Remaining patches of original paint

Keyhole-shaped pendant typical of *menat* necklaces

Beads made of glass, agate, carnelian, lapis, and turquoise

Hole for threading string to wear collar

▽ **Neck protector**
Broad collar necklaces were popular throughout ancient Egyptian history. Dating from c. 1750 BCE, this example features rows of coloured faience beads.

△ **Death duties**
This glazed steatite figurine shows the shabti ("servant") of the 16th-century BCE official Seniu. The hieroglyphs list the servant's obligations towards his master in the afterlife.

Row of decorative drop beads

▷ **In memoriam**
Wooden coffins included a likeness of the deceased, along with spells and images of other family members. This one houses a man known as Khonsu.

Kerma and Kush

Early civilizations of the Sudan

The Nubian civilization of Kerma, in modern-day northern Sudan, prospered from 2500–1500 BCE and for a time rivalled Egypt as a regional power. Kerma was followed by the more Egyptophile Kingdom of Kush.

Named after its capital city, the Kerma civilization grew out of a Neolithic culture known as the A-group, which emerged around 3500–3000 BCE, at the same time as predynastic Egypt (see pp. 42–43). The A-group traded – and, it appears, competed – with its northern neighbour. By 2800 BCE, however, Egypt's First Dynasty had established its regional ascendancy, forcing the A-group Nubians southwards. Here, they evolved into a culture known as the C-group, which became the precursor to the Kerma state.

Rise and fall

By 2000 BCE, Kerma was well established in Upper Nubia, an area corresponding to central and southern Sudan – "Upper" refers to regions upstream on the Nile, therefore further south. Over the next three centuries, Kerma also conquered Lower Nubia (downstream on the Nile, or further north), bringing its territory up to the border with Egypt. Perhaps inevitably, the two civilizations clashed. Egypt, by now in its expansionist Middle Kingdom period, dominated at first. However, when Egypt's power declined after 1650 BCE, Kerma seized the opportunity to consolidate its control of Upper and Lower Nubia. The city of Kerma encompassed around 10,000 people and its rulers built palaces, tomb complexes, and *deffufas* – large temples. Between 1575 and 1550 BCE, Kerma allied

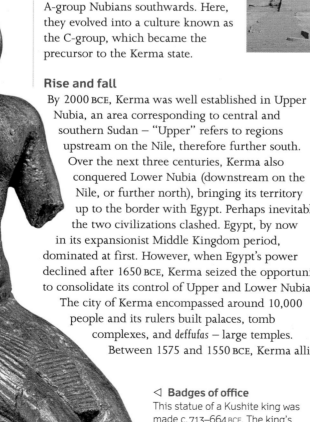

Crown, with double *uraei* (cobras) repesenting Nubia and Egypt

◁ **Badges of office**
This statue of a Kushite king was made c. 713–664 BCE. The king's name was engraved on his belt, but is now indecipherable.

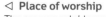

◁ **Place of worship**
The monumental temple known as the Western Deffufa dominates Kerma. The word *deffufa* derives from the Nubian term for a mudbrick building.

with Hyksos – Canaanites who occupied the Nile Delta – and threatened the survival of the remaining Egyptian state based at Thebes. Egypt's Middle Kingdom had collapsed and a spell of military and political turmoil, known as the Second Intermediate Period, ensued. This turmoil encouraged Kerma and Hyksos to strike at Egypt. However, the establishment of the New Kingdom after 1550 BCE restored order in Egypt. Within 50 years, a resurgent Egypt had conquered and colonized Kerma. Sporadic rebellion continued for a couple of hundred years, but over time Kerma became increasingly Egyptianized and tied to Egyptian imperial government, and was never to regain its position as an autonomous power.

The people of Kerma left no written records, and it is not known which language they spoke. The names of only a few of their kings survive. As well as the royal family, Kerma had elite classes of priests and merchants and sizable urban populations at its capital city and at the town of Sai Island in the Nile River. The economy was based on agriculture and trade, though there is also evidence of gold mining. Kerma was also endowed with cattle, dairy products, ebony, ivory, and incense – and produced fine bronzework and pottery, including blue glazing known as faïence.

A change of the guard

As Kerma's civilization began to wane, a new Nubian culture was on the rise: the Kingdom of Kush. Egyptian texts refer to "Kush" as a general name for Upper Nubia, but scholars also use the term to refer to

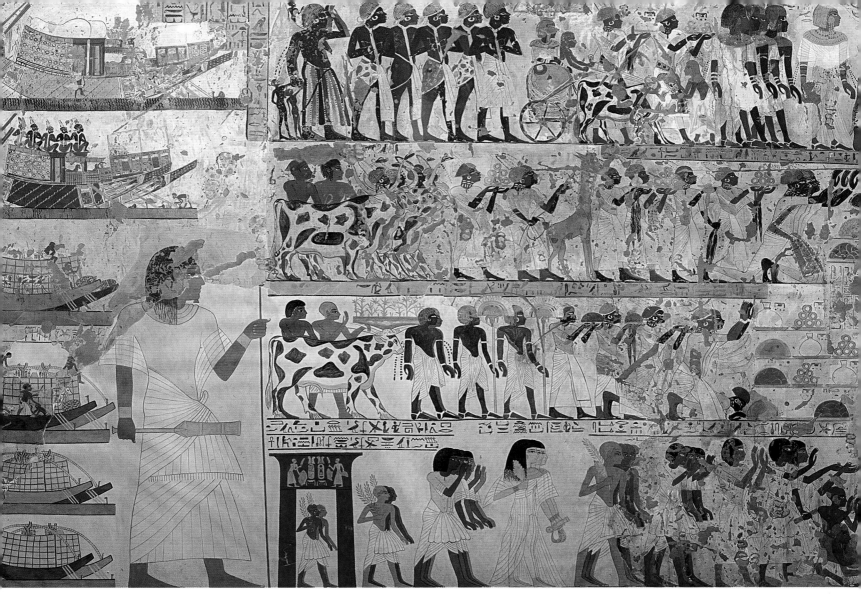

△ **Nubian delegation**
Nubian tribute-bearers appear in the top three rows of this painting, the original of which dates to 1353–1327 BCE and appeared in the tomb of Amenhotep, the viceroy of Kush.

the kingdom that emerged in Nubia after the Egyptian New Kingdom. Unlike Kerma, the Kushite rulers borrowed from Egyptian culture, especially in royal art and state religion. The chief state deity was Amen, a god associated with kingship, whose cult was celebrated at temples in Kush's capital city, Napata,

and at many other places. Kush also had the good fortune to emerge just as the great age of the pharaohs was drawing to a close, leaving it well placed to fill the power vacuum left by Egypt's decline.

Historians believe the Kushite rulers were in charge of the state religion and maintained the houses of the gods. But many specifics of the early Kushite civilization's social and economic organization remain unclear. More visible would be the later Kushite civilization that emerged in the 8th century BCE, based first in Napata and then Meroë (see pp. 54–55).

▽ **Royal ornament**
This gold ram's head amulet was once strung on a Kushite ruler's necklace. A ram's head was the symbol of the god Amen.

"We realized that **the tombs, palaces, and temples** stood out from Egyptian remains… **We were in another world.**"

ARCHAEOLOGIST CHARLES BONNET, ON UNCOVERING ANCIENT KERMA'S RUINS

Nubian temple
Dating from the 1st century BCE, the Lion Temple at Naga in modern-day Sudan is carved with figures in relief on all four of its sides. The southern side, shown here, depicts the gods Horus (with a falcon's head) and Apedemak (with a lion's head), and the Nubian (or Kushite) king Natakamani and his wife Queen Amanitore paying homage to the gods. Apedemak was the Nubian god of war, while Horus was an Egyptian deity, marking a fusion of cultures at this time.

Napata and Meroë

The later kingdoms of Kush

Beyond Egypt's southern border lay Nubia, a territory from which arose cultures whose civilizations would compete with, absorb, submit to, and — in the case of Meroë — ultimately outlast the pharaohs.

For two millennia after 3000 BCE, Egypt dominated Africa's Nile region (see pp. 42–43). But other African civilizations rivalled Egypt's power, in particular the kingdoms of Kerma and Kush (see pp. 50–51). By 1450 BCE, however, Kerma had disappeared and Egypt was experiencing a period of political instability and economic decline. Kush, the newest of these civilizations, filled the power vacuum and for the next 1,000 years held sway over the region south of Egypt known as Nubia.

Ram-headed god, Amen

◁ **Royal artefact**
This gold "shield ring" was found within the pyramid of Queen Amanishakheto, who was ruler of Kush from approximately 10 BCE–1 CE.

The capital of Kush was Napata, and around 750 BCE it was the base from which the Kushite king Kashta launched his conquest of Upper Egypt. His son and successor, Piye, annexed the rest of Egypt, and so-called "Nubian Pharaohs" ruled Egypt and Kush until an Assyrian invasion forced them out in the 660s BCE (see pp. 56–57). The Kushites regrouped in their stronghold of Napata, but within two generations a resurgent Egypt went on the attack. Egyptian attempts to reconquer the northern part of Kushite territory may have been a factor that encouraged King Aspelta to move his capital from Napata 240 km (150 miles) upriver to Meroë.

Meroë's history is traditionally divided into four Meroitic periods. The first, from 542–315 BCE, saw the city grow steadily and witnessed the construction of

the earliest of the royal pyramid tombs that would be erected over the next several hundred years and are today the civilization's most distinctive archaeological remains. The second and third Meroitic periods took the kingdom into the 1st century CE. More pyramids were built, along with grand palaces, temples, residences, and industrial buildings and warehouses, attesting to Meroë's importance as a major centre of iron production and as a trading crossroads between North Africa, Central Africa, and Asia.

In the fourth Meroitic period, from the 1st to the 4th centuries CE, the kingdom came to the attention of Rome. After taking Egypt, the emperor Augustus invaded Nubia in 23 BCE, but withdrew the following year having plundered Napata. Meroë remained more or less unmolested by Rome after this, surviving for another three centuries until its final destruction by the new Aksumite Empire (in present-day Ethiopia) in 350 CE.

Meroitic culture

As a long-lasting Nubian power, Meroë is today cited as an early example of a successful "Africanized" civilization, especially in contrast to the more Mediterranean- and Middle Eastern-facing Egypt. In truth, both states were highly culturally and ethnically diverse – although contemporary references by writers to the "Ethiopians" (a synonym for Black Africans) of Nubia perhaps indicates a greater preponderance of peoples from south of the Sahara there than in Egypt.

One unusual aspect of Meroitic society was the position of the *kandakes* – the queens, queen mothers, and female relatives of the king. They held great power in Meroë, especially when serving as regents to child monarchs. Shanakhdakheto, the first known *kandake*, is said to have ruled without a king, holding sole power from 170–150 BCE, while it was the warrior-queen Amanirenas who fought the Romans in Nubia following their attack on Napata in 23 BCE. Almost a century later, *Kandake* Amanikhatashan sent cavalry and archers to fight for Rome during the First Jewish-Roman War of 66–73 CE.

△ **Pyramids of power**
Almost 200 royal tomb pyramids were built at three sites in and around Meroë, ranging in height from 6–30 m (20–98 ft).

▷ **Stele of Nubian Queen**
A stone stele from the late 1st century BCE shows warrior *Kandake* Amanishakheto (right) being embraced by the protector goddess Amesemi.

Winged solar disc

"[Meroë has] the **biggest concentration** of **pyramids in the world.**"

MAHMOUD SULIMAN BASHIR, NATIONAL CORPORATION FOR ANTIQUITIES AND MUSEUMS, SUDAN

Victorious king
In this c. 7th-century BCE relief added to the 15th-century BCE temple complex at Karnak, in Upper Egypt, King Taharqa grasps the hair of multiple defeated enemies.

Taharqa

A Nubian king of Egypt

Hailing from Egypt's southern neighbour, Taharqa initiated the last great age of pyramid-building. As a warrior-pharaoh, his long-running fight with the mighty Assyrian Empire defined his reign.

Taharqa was born to Piye, Nubian ruler of the Kushite kingdom of Napata in modern-day Sudan. He was a cousin of the Kushite pharaoh of Egypt, Shebitku, and joined the imperial court at Thebes when he was just out of his teens. In 701 BCE, in his early twenties, Taharqa led an Egyptian-Kushite force against an Assyrian army that was laying siege to Jerusalem, the capital of Egypt's neighbour, Judah. According to the Bible's Book of Kings, "Tirhakah" (who scholars identify as Taharqa) and the Judeans won the ensuing Battle of Eltekeh; the Assyrian king, Sennacharib, by contrast claimed a victory for his side.

In 690 BCE, Taharqa became Egypt's ruler, probably after usurping his predecessor, Shabaka. As both monarch of the Kingdom of Kush and pharaoh of Egypt, Taharqa was the main regional

◁ **Royal statue**
Shown here as a bronze statue, Taharqa was pharaoh and *qore* (king) of the Kingdom of Kush. He was fourth of the five "Kushite Pharaohs" who made up Egypt's 25th Dynasty.

bulwark against the expansionist Assyrian emperor, Esarhaddon. In 674 BCE, Taharqa repulsed an Assyrian invasion force. Three years later, however, the Assyrians captured Egypt's capital, Memphis, forcing Taharqa into exile in the south. He retook Memphis in 669 BCE, but Esarhaddon's successor, Ashurbanipal, soon reasserted Assyrian hegemony. An Assyrian vassal, Necho I, replaced Taharqa, who never regained full control of Egypt. He died in Thebes in 664 BCE.

Building a legacy in Egypt and Nubia
Throughout his reign, Taharqa had maintained an ambitious building programme. In the 680s BCE, he ordered the construction of a temple to the sun and fertility god, Amun-Re, at Kawa in his native Nubia. He also rebuilt and restored several other temples to Amun-Re across his empire. Most strikingly, he restarted the practice of pyramid-building after 1,000 years, creating the first and largest of 20 or so pyramids at Nuri, in modern Sudan, erected between c. 670 BCE and c. 310 BCE.

△ **Kiosk of Taharqa**
This is the only remaining example of the ten 21-m- (69-ft-) columns that lined Karnak's Kiosk of Taharqa, a vast chamber built as part of the processional route of the god Amen out of the temple.

> "I was **brought from Nubia** amongst the **royal brothers** that **his Majesty** had brought."
>
> TAHARQA'S TEMPLE INSCRIPTION AT KAWA

725 BCE Birth of Taharqa

690 BCE Taharqa becomes pharaoh

670 BCE Work begins on Pyramid of Taharqa at Nuri

668 BCE Ashurbanipal becomes Assyrian king

705 BCE Taharqa is taken to Thebes

680 BCE Building of Amun-Re temple, Kawa

674–669 BCE Wars against Esarhaddon of Assyria

664 BCE Death of Taharqa

Writing systems

From ancient symbols to modern scripts

Some of the earliest marks or symbols made by early humans have been found in Africa. Examples include symbolic patterns engraved on 60,000-year-old ostrich eggshells, found at Diepkloof, South Africa (see p. 30), and symbols and patterns painted on cave walls at Wonderwerk, in northern South Africa. Rocks by the Kharga oasis in present-day Egypt bear traces of writing-like inscriptions, called "Proto Saharan" by some scientists, that date from at least 4000 BCE.

Ancient scripts

In around 3000 BCE, hieroglyphic writing developed in Egypt. Egyptian hieroglyphs were initially used as simple labels, but soon developed into a complex writing system using a mixture of both phonetic and pictorial signs. Ancient Egyptians also used an abbreviated, cursive form of the hieroglyphic script, known as Hieratic, which could be written at a greater speed. In the 1st century BCE, an even simpler script, called Demotic (from a Greek word meaning "popular script"), came into everyday, general use, such as for writing documents.

In around 800 BCE, an alphabetic script known as Meroitic arose in Nubia (modern-day Sudan). Meroitic takes two forms: a cursive script, derived from Demotic, and hieroglyphs, developed from Egyptian hieroglyphs. The cursive form could be written with a stylus and was used for general records on parchment or papyrus. The hieroglyphic form appears mainly as royal or religious inscriptions in stone.

△ **Egyptian hieroglyphs**
Hieroglyphs can be read from right to left, left to right, or top to bottom. The direction in which humans and animals face indicates the starting point of the text. In this right-facing wall-carved inscription, the text is intended to be read from right to left.

△ **Meroitic**
Shown here on a stone inscription from the 1st century BCE, Meroitic was used to write the language of the kingdom of Meroë in modern-day Sudan. The script is not fully deciphered, but scholars know how the letters sounded: there are vowels, and consonants are assumed to be followed by "a", unless another vowel is provided.

△ **Punic**
This Punic inscription on a funerary stele in Carthage, Tunisia, dates from 300–200 BCE. Punic was spoken in Carthage until about the 4th century CE and was derived from the earlier Phoenician alphabet, with influences from coastal Amazigh (Berber) languages.

From the 1st century CE in Ethiopia, the Ge'ez script, based on Arabic and consisting of 231 characters, was used; it is one of the oldest writing systems in continuous use in the world.

Since at least the 10th century CE, people throughout Africa have used an Arabic-derived script called Ajami to write phonetic renderings of about a dozen languages, including Swahili, Wolof, and Hausa. The rediscovery of Ajami texts, from love letters to business records, provides historians with valuable insights into everyday life in Africa.

Many parts of Africa developed ideographic scripts, which use symbols to represent ideas. In parts of Central and Southern Africa, Sona pictograms are mnemonic devices for remembering fables, riddles, and proverbs. The system was documented in drawings by European visitors in the 17th century, but may date back to antiquity. *Adinkra* symbols, developed by the Akan people in Ghana, represent concepts and aphorisms, and are printed on fabric for events such as weddings and funerals.

In recent times, scripts have been developed for specific languages. Created in the 1980s, Adlam transcribes the Fula language, spoken by 25 million people in West Africa, and can be typed on phones and computers. The Luo script, developed in 2009–2012, transcribes the Dholuo language spoken in East Africa. In North Africa, Tifinagh, used for writing Amazigh (Berber) languages, has been modernized as Neo-Tifinagh for use on computers and phones.

△ **Nsibidi headdress**
This wooden bird-beaked headdress is engraved with Nsibidi script using a heated tool or fine flame. Developed by secret societies in what is now Nigeria in around 2000 BCE, Nsibidi comprises nearly 1,000 symbols.

△ **Ge'ez**
This illuminated manuscript of the Christian Bible was created at a monastic centre in Ethiopia around the beginning of the 15th century CE. The text is in Ge'ez, a Semitic language still used in religious ceremonies in the region.

△ **Libyco-Berber**
A cave painting at Tadrart Acacus, Libya, dated to between 12000 BCE and 100 CE, shows Libyco-Berber script alongside pictograms of animals. The Libyco-Berber alphabet developed into Tifinagh, a script used to write the Amazigh languages spoken across North Africa today.

△ **Adinkra**
This early example of Ghanaian *adinkra* mourning cloth, dating from 1817, features 15 symbols, including *nsroma* (stars) and *dono ntoasuo* (double *dono*, or talking, drums). The patterns were printed using carved calabash (gourd) stamps and a vegetable-based dye.

"These works **define our history**. They **define who we are.**"

ALHAJI LAI MOHAMMED, MINISTER OF
INFORMATION AND CULTURE, NIGERIA, 2020

Nok terracotta figure

Celebrating the artistry of West Africa's oldest civilization

In 1943, a British archaeologist in Nigeria named Bernard Fagg noticed a terracotta head that had been used on a scarecrow in a local yam field. Recognizing the object was of great antiquity and of a style not seen before, Fagg began to search for and collect similar sculptures. By Fagg's estimate, the sculptures had been made around 500 BCE – much earlier than any civilization known to have existed in that region. Fagg named this largely forgotten West African culture the Nok, after the village where several of the finds had been located.

Sophisticated culture

Radiocarbon dating has since shown that the Nok flourished even earlier than Fagg thought, from 1500 BCE, disappearing around 1 CE. As yet, little is known about Nok life and culture. What has been established, however, is that the Nok were imaginative and technically advanced. Excavations at artefact sites have revealed iron-smelting furnaces – 13 at one dig close to the village of Taruga. Scientists have dated the furnaces to 280 BCE, which would make the Nok people the first to master iron smelting south of the Sahara. As many of the terracotta heads were found in and around smelting sites, some historians believe the sculptures were intended as objects of worship, used to bring good luck in the manufacture of iron tools, weapons, and decorative objects.

To date, close to 200 terracotta sculptures have been retrieved across the 80,000 sq km (30,000 sq miles) of Nok territory, centred on the town of Jos – suggesting that the Nok civilization was large and widespread. Surviving Nok terracotta pieces range in size from 10 cm (4 in) to 1.22 m (4 ft) tall (based on sculptural fragments). Craftworkers made the sculptures not by a casting process, but by carving individual pieces of clay – such as an arm, head, leg, or beads – and then joining them together to form a single composite work that was fired in a furnace. Some scholars have argued that the Nok's creativity may have influenced the sculptors of the 14th-century Yoruba Ilé-Ifè culture (see pp. 110–11), whose naturalistic, copper-alloy life-size heads are among humanity's greatest artistic achievements.

Distinctive styling

The object shown here is a particularly complex example of Nok terracotta work. Its date of manufacture is not known, but it contains details typical of Nok sculpture including the oversized, cylindrical heads with elongated features such as the distinctive oval-shaped eyes. This sculpture was one of three items purchased against Nigerian law by the French government in 1998 and, with post-factum consent from the Nigerian government, is currently displayed in the Musée du Quai Branly in Paris.

△ **Female figure**
Subjects are often shown seated, sometimes with their hands on their knees or in stylized poses. The purpose, if any, of Nok sculpture is still unknown.

Finely worked headwear

Perforations allowed heat to be equalized during the firing process

Figures carved separately and added to main structure

Sculpture is 54 cm (21 in) in height and appears to be the base of a larger piece

Triangular or oval-shaped eyes are an identifying characteristic of Nok sculptures

◁ **Nok sculpture**
This is a rare example of a Nok sculpture with multiple heads. After controversially acquiring the piece, France signed an agreement with Nigeria to lease it for 25 years.

The Kingdom of Aksum

East Africa's first Christian state

The Kingdom of Aksum ruled a large tract of East Africa for four centuries. A great trading hub, it was an entry and exit point into the continent for peoples, products, ideas, and faiths.

Centred around what is today the Tigray Region of northern Ethiopia, the Kingdom of Aksum was founded around 150 CE. At its height, it controlled parts of modern Eritrea, Djibouti, and Somalia, as well as territory across the Red Sea in Yemen. Little is known of Aksum's origins. Its earliest myths claim it was the home of the Queen of Sheba (ruler of the Kingdom of Saba or Sheba in southwestern Arabia) and the resting place of the Ark of the Covenant (a gold chest said to have held the tablets of the law in Judaism and Christianity). Though both assertions are implausible, they illustrate how this part of the continent was considered a cultural crossroads.

The capital, also called Aksum, was located on a high, fertile plateau 2,000 m (6,560 ft) above sea level. It sat at the intersection of the major trading routes south and west into Africa, north towards the Middle East and the Mediterranean, and east across the Indian Ocean to Asia from the Red Sea port of Adulis. Ivory and gold were the main products bought and sold here, along with frankincense, myrrh, obsidian, rhinoceros horn, emeralds, salt, livestock, textiles, iron, steel, weapons, olive oil, glassware, and much more. Enslaved people were also traded here.

One of the kingdom's most significant imports was Christianity. It arrived south of the Sahara in the 4th century CE, introduced as the state religion by Aksum's king, Ezana I (r. 320s–c. 360). This was possibly a diplomatic move by Ezana to align his kingdom's faith with that of its most important trading partner, the eastern Roman Empire in Constantinople. Around 270 CE, Aksum became the first African nation to mint its own coinage. It was manufactured according to standardized Roman imperial weights and matched the compositions of Roman coins. Aksumite coins have been found as far away as Israel and India.

Expansion and challenge

Aksum reached its peak between the 3rd and 7th centuries. The city of Aksum's population numbered up to 20,000, and art and architecture – including distinctive stone stelae – flourished there. Erected as grave markers, the stelae were carved to resemble multi-storeyed royal palaces or houses of the nobility. Ruins of one stele indicate it was 30 m (97 ft) tall.

As well as trade, Aksum acquired power and prosperity through conquest. The early Aksumite king Gedara expanded into southern Arabia at the beginning

△ **Carved stelae**
Aksum's commemorative stelae are tall structures with representative doors and windows carved into their facades. This, in the Northern Stelae Park in Aksum city, stands 24 m (79 ft) high.

Gold coin shows ears of wheat or barley

100 per cent pure silver

Bronze coins were the most common

▷ **Use of coins**
Aksum introduced Roman-style coinage in the 3rd century CE. This was at a time when other states south of the Sahara were using shells, beads, or bartered goods as currency.

of the 3rd century CE, and Ezana I conquered the Sudanese city-state of Meroë (see pp. 54–55) a century later. Around 520, Aksum's King Kaleb (also known as Saint Elesbaan) sent a large naval force to subdue the Himyarite kingdom in what is today southern Yemen. This was done partly at the request of the Byzantine emperor, Justin I, who wanted to punish the Himyarites for their persecution of Christians. This conquest saw Aksum's empire reach its greatest extent.

Within a decade, however, rebels in the Himyarite kingdom were challenging Aksum's authority. Aksum struggled to retain its Arabian holdings for the next 50 years, until, around 575, it was driven out of the peninsula by an army invading from the Sassanian Empire (modern-day Iran).

Aksum under threat
On the African mainland, nomadic herding peoples such as the Afar, the Saho, and the Beja migrated into Aksum territory. Their livestock overgrazed the land, and this degraded the soil, leading to crop failures and famine that destabilized the state. More significantly, the rapid spread of Islam across North and East Africa after its founding in 610 presented Christian Aksum

with an existential threat. By 648, the Rashidun Caliphate based in Medina had taken control of the Red Sea, cutting off Aksum's access to the Indian Ocean. The caliphate also assumed control of the overland trade routes that Aksum had benefited from for so long. Now isolated and surrounded, Aksum's inhabitants abandoned their capital, moving further inland to the Ethiopian highlands and founding a new capital whose name and location are lost to history.

The kingdom continued for several hundred years, but was much diminished. The exact date of its demise is not known, but at some point between 900 and 1200 its lands were taken by the Zagwe dynasty, who were based at Lalibela in northern Ethiopia (see pp. 122–23). The remains of the city of Aksum were designated a UNESCO World Heritage Site in 1980.

▷ **Man of God**
This 10th-century Byzantine painting shows King Kaleb (r. 514–42). Also known as Saint Elesbaan, he abdicated in old age and retired to a monastery.

△ **Popular story**
Known as "Sheba's Palace", these extensive remains at Dungur, close to Aksum city, actually date from the 7th century CE – 1,700 years after the biblical queen's era.

"And so went **in peace** to his land this **Christ-loving Kaleb** and all his army with him."

THE BOOK OF THE HIMYARITES

Carthage
The empire that rivalled Rome

Carthage in North Africa was a Phoenician settlement that went on to rule much of the Mediterranean. This wealthy trading empire became a target for Roman plans for dominance in a great rivalry that brought about its eventual downfall.

The Phoenicians, one of the great peoples of antiquity, emerged in modern-day Lebanon and Syria. They came to prominence as important sea traders in the mid-12th century BCE, and in around 814 BCE settlers from the Phoenician city of Tyre founded Carthage in what is now Tunisia, North Africa. The city-state became the richest in the ancient world with a multi-ethnic African culture, encompassing many Indigenous Amazigh (Berber) people.

Carthage has roots in myth. According to the Roman poet Virgil, the Phoenician founder of Carthage, Elissa, renamed Queen Dido by Virgil, met Aeneas, a hero of the Trojan war. They fell in love, but Aeneas left Dido and the queen cursed him, foreshadowing the enmity that was to arise between Carthage and the Romans, who claimed descent from Aeneas.

Trading empire

Carthage's site was a fine one: the port occupied a key position on maritime trade routes and had access to fertile land for agriculture. By the middle of the 6th century BCE, the city had grown powerful. In addition to Northern African territory, Carthage eventually encompassed much of Sicily, as well as Corsica, Sardinia, and parts of modern-day Spain.

Carthage traded heavily with the Iberian Peninsula, although its traders also crossed the Sahara, ferrying between Africa and Europe everything from wine and ivory to ostrich eggs, as well as trading silver and tin with other Phoenician cities in the Mediterranean. Tin, possibly sourced from the Canary Islands and Britain, was an important ancient article of trade, since it was used to make bronze.

As Carthage rose to power, the Phoenician heartland was fading. The city-states in modern-day Lebanon and Syria fell under the sway of the Assyrians, the Babylonians, the Persians, and finally Alexander the Great. Yet Phoenician culture continued to shape Carthage. The Carthaginians spoke a Semitic language, Punic, and their religion was of Phoenician origin, involving worship of the gods Baal Hammon, Eshmun, Bes, and Melqart, and the goddess Tanit.

△ **Miniature mask**
This 3rd-century BCE mask, made from glass paste, is believed to have been a funerary pendant.

◁ **Carthaginian god**
This limestone carving of Baal Hammon, the weather deity and chief god of Carthage, dates from the 2nd century CE. At this time, Carthage was under Roman control but worship of Phoenician deities continued.

> "Carthage… rich in **wealth** and **most harsh** in the **arts of war**."

VIRGIL, *THE AENEID*

By the 3rd century BCE, the city of Carthage had as many as 500,000 inhabitants, mostly of African heritage, and the empire had fought wars against Greeks and Libyans. Initially, relations with Rome were friendly, but as Rome grew in strength the two empires clashed over Sicily.

Wars with Rome

The First Punic War (264–241 BCE) ended with Sicily becoming a province of the victorious Romans. In the Second Punic War (218–201 BCE), Rome and Carthage fought over the Iberian Peninsula, and the great Carthaginian general Hannibal (see pp. 68–69) surprised the Romans by crossing the Alps and attacking Italy from the north. He won several battles before his final defeat in 202 BCE at Zama, Tunisia.

Carthage was now a weakened state, confined to North Africa. But the Romans still desired the kingdom's rich farmland, and the Roman statesman Marcus Porcius Cato demanded the destruction of Carthage, convinced that Rome could never be safe while it remained. He ended many senatorial addresses, irrespective of the subject of debate, with the famous words "Delenda est Carthago" ("Carthage must be destroyed"). In the Third Punic War (149–146 BCE), despite fierce resistance, Rome destroyed Carthage and killed many of its people.

It was the end of an empire, but not the end of the city. Carthage was rebuilt and became one of the wealthiest Roman cities. Punic (Carthaginian) and Amazigh culture persisted through such writers as Numidian-born Apuleius (c. 124–170).

▽ **Antonine Baths**
Built in the 2nd century CE, the now-ruined Antonine Baths of Roman Carthage were the largest Roman baths in Africa.

Kingdoms of the northwest

Carthage's ancient neighbours

Carthage and Egypt may be North Africa's most famous ancient states, but in the northwest, the Amazigh (Berber) kingdoms of Numidia and Mauretania flourished for hundreds of years.

North Africa supported several ancient civilizations. To the west of Carthage (see pp. 64–65) stood Mauretania and Numidia. These were the kingdoms of the Amazigh, who had lived in the Maghreb for thousands of years. Mauretania included parts of what is now Algeria and Morocco. Its first known ruler, Baga, reigned in the 3rd century BCE, but evidence of trade with Carthage goes back still further. The kingdom had close relations with Numidia to the east in modern Algeria. According to the Roman historian Sallust, the Numidians had nomadic ancestors, although they later adopted a more settled existence, built great monuments and tombs, and traded with what would become Spain.

Rival states

Numidia was divided into two states: the Massylii in the east and the Masaesyli in the west. Both were famous for their nimble, javelin-wielding horse riders. At the start of the Second Punic War, in 218 BCE, the Massylii were allied with Carthage and the Masaesyli with Rome. But in 206 BCE, the new king in the east, Masinissa, allied with Rome instead, since he believed it would prevail in the war. The western king, in opposition to him, joined Carthage. When the war ended in 201 BCE, the Romans gave all of Numidia to Masinissa.

Masinissa and his descendants ruled a large kingdom, which now extended beyond the Atlas Mountains in the south, but in 118 BCE civil war broke out between his grandson Adherbal and Jugurtha, the illegitimate son of Mastanabal, Masinissa's youngest son.

△ **Jugurtha**
This coin, minted in c. 50 BCE, decades after the Jugurthine War, depicts Jugurtha on the right kneeling in chains before the Roman dictator, Sulla.

△ **Juba I**
Juba I, depicted on a coin from around 50 BCE, sided with Pompey in the Roman civil war of 49–45 BCE.

△ **Juba II**
This Mauretanian coin shows Juba II, who was educated in Rome and ruled both Numidia and Mauretania as a client king.

◁ **Jugurthine War**
Numidian forces under Jugurtha (in the woodland at the top left) face the Roman legions of Quintus Caecilius Metellus during the Jugurthine War.

Jugurtha besieged the Numidian capital, Cirta (modern Constantine, in Algeria), and when Adherbal surrendered, killed him and all armed adult males that he found. Romans were among the dead, and Rome declared war. During the Jugurthine War (112–106 BCE), Jugurtha was captured and executed.

Numidia remained independent, but when civil war broke out between Julius Caesar and Roman general Pompey in 49 BCE, King Juba I took Pompey's side. In 46 BCE, the two armies met at Thapsus on the Tunisian coast, and Juba, foreseeing defeat, died by suicide. After the war, western Numidia came under Mauretanian rule and the eastern part became a Roman province, Africa Nova. In 40 BCE, western Numidia was annexed to Africa Nova.

Juba's son, Juba II, is said to have been one of the most educated Roman citizens of the time. He ruled Africa Nova (30–25 BCE) and then Mauretania (25 BCE–23 CE) as a client king — a monarch who ruled only with Rome's consent — and married Selene II, daughter of Queen Cleopatra VII of Egypt and Roman politician and general Mark Antony.

Rome finally annexed Mauretania in 44 CE, putting the whole northwest under direct control. The region supplied grain to the empire, and many cities grew significantly and gained Roman infrastructure — the Mauretanian city of Volubilis acquired a basilica and a temple. In 428 the Vandals, a Germanic peoples, invaded the region, and the Mauro-Roman Kingdom, an independent Amazigh state in what is now Algeria, challenged both the Vandals and the Byzantine conquerors. The Byzantines eventually occupied the kingdom from 578, until the forces of the Rashidun and Umayyad Caliphates ousted them in the 7th century. But the kingdoms of the northwest left their mark: Amazigh, or Tamazight, is now an official language of Morocco and Algeria.

Headband typical of Hellenistic rulers

Beardless jawline indicative of idealized youth

▷ **Bust of Juba II**
This bronze head of Juba II, dating to around 25 BCE, was found in Volubilis, then part of Mauretania, near the modern-day Moroccan city of Meknes.

"One of **the most gifted rulers** of his time."

GREEK HISTORIAN PLUTARCH ON JUBA II

◁ **Bust of Hannibal**
This Roman marble bust, dating from the 2nd century BCE and thought to be of Hannibal, was found at the ancient city of Capua in southern Italy.

Decorated helmet

"**What else** do you believe the Alps are, but **high mountains**?"

HANNIBAL TO HIS ARMY,
AS REPORTED BY ROMAN HISTORIAN LIVY

Paludamentum (military cape)

Hannibal

Africa's most famous general

Hannibal commanded the armies of Carthage against the Romans during the Second Punic War (218–201 BCE). He crossed the Alps and won a succession of crushing victories, bringing Rome to its knees, before being overcome at Zama.

In the third century BCE, the powerful North African empire of Carthage clashed with Rome in the Punic Wars (see pp. 64–65). Hannibal, born in 247 BCE, swore hostility to Rome from childhood and spent much of his life fighting Carthage's great rival.

In 221 BCE, Hannibal became commander of the Carthaginian army and began expanding Carthage's territory in the Iberian Peninsula. After his forces sacked the city of Saguntum in Spain in 219 BCE, the Romans declared war. Hannibal's response was to strike at Rome's heart, and in 218 BCE he chose to attack from the north by marching across the Alps.

During the crossing, Hannibal lost many men and several of the war elephants he rode on, but in Italy his skilful tactics and strong leadership helped him outwit his opponents time after time. The Romans adopted delaying tactics but faced him again at Cannae, southeast Italy, in 216 BCE, where Hannibal's troops surrounded and almost destroyed a larger Roman and Italian army. Hannibal subsequently established winter quarters at Capua in southern Italy, an area noted for its wealth and power. The Romans laid siege to Capua in 212 BCE. Hannibal attempted to draw the Romans away from the city by mounting his own siege of Rome itself – unsuccessfully, as Capua fell to the Romans shortly afterwards.

In 203 BCE, after 15 years in Italy, Hannibal was recalled to North Africa to face a Roman invasion of Carthage. The following year, at the Battle of Zama, the Roman general Scipio defeated the Carthaginians and stripped Carthage of its European territories.

Final act

Hannibal was not finished. As a statesman in Carthage, he attempted to eliminate corruption and restore the economy. He then used his battlefield experience to command troops for the Seleucid Empire of the Eastern Mediterranean and the Kingdom of Bithynia, in what is now Turkey. He is said to have died by suicide in c. 183 BCE, when, finally cornered by the Romans, he took poison concealed in a ring.

△ **Silver shekels**
These silver Carthaginian shekels, showing a man wearing a laurel wreath and an elephant and its rider, were produced in Spain in the 3rd century BCE.

◁ **Crossing the Alps**
The Italian Renaissance artist Jacopo Ripanda painted *Hannibal in Italy* in c. 1510. Hannibal's armies included war elephants and an Amazigh (Berber) cavalry.

221-219 BCE Defeats the Olcades and Carpetani in Spain and captures Saguntum

218 BCE Second Punic War begins and Hannibal crosses the Pyrenees, then the Alps, with his army

202 BCE Having returned to North Africa, Hannibal's army is defeated at Zama in what is now Tunisia

c. 183 BCE Dies in exile in modern-day Turkey

247 BCE Born in what is now Tunisia

216 BCE Hannibal's forces are victorious at the Battle of Cannae in Italy

207 BCE A Carthaginian army under Hannibal's brother Hasdrubal is defeated in northern Italy

201 BCE Rome and Carthage agree a peace treaty, ending the Second Punic War

Roman North Africa

Annexation and assimilation with the Mediterranean world

In 146 BCE, Rome defeated the great Mediterranean power Carthage in the third and final Punic War. So began the empire's advances into North Africa — an occupation that would continue for the next 600 years.

By the 1st century BCE, both Cyrenaica (modern Libya) and Egypt had been brought under Roman control, followed by the territories encompassing the North African coast and all cultivable lands north of the Sahara. The last kingdom taken by Rome was Mauretania, to the far west, annexed in 40 CE. This extended Rome's imperial frontier along a border more than 6,500 km (4,000 miles) long.

Collectively, the Romans called these territories (excluding Cyrenaica and Egypt) *Africa*, possibly derived from the name of an Amazigh (Berber) people, the *Aourigha* (pronounced "Afarika"). In time, Rome divided the region into four provinces: *Africa Proconsularis* (Tunisia and coastal Libya); *Numidia* (eastern Algeria); *Mauretania Caesariensis* (the remainder of Algeria); and *Mauretania Tingitana* (northern Morocco).

Lines of defensive forts, called Limes, along the provinces' borders were manned by troops including the Third Augustan Legion. Their role was to stave off external attacks, control internal dissent, and safeguard the region's rich resources of wheat, wine, corn, and olive oil. These goods were mostly exported overseas, to Italy, along with large quantities of ivory and cedarwood, used for ship construction and house building.

Rome expropriated the best agricultural land from Imazighen (Berbers) and Indigenous groups and consolidated it into estates. Land in the mountains, borderline desert areas, and other zones that were hard to farm were left to the Imazighen. Whatever crops they managed to produce were subject to Roman taxes and tithes.

△ **Artistic legacy**
This lion mosaic from the House of Liber Pater in Sabratha dates from the mid-4th century CE.

With Roman control came Romanization. The authorities encouraged the inward migration of settlers, including merchants, magistrates, other civic officials, and former Roman soldiers – enticed with rewards of free land for their years of military service. The Romans rebuilt existing settlements and cities such as Carthage (in modern Tunisia) and Leptis Magna (in modern Libya) according to Roman town-planning models, and established new, wholly Roman cities, such as Timgad (in modern Algeria) around 100 CE.

Divisions and decline

The Romans also achieved the Romanization of North Africa through assimilation. They progressively extended Roman citizenship throughout the 1st and 2nd centuries, allowing locally born men of ability to attain positions of power. The high point of this process came in 193, when Leptis Magna-born Septimius Severus became the first Roman emperor of African origin. In 212, Septimius's son and successor Caracalla extended Roman citizenship to free peoples across the empire, which increased opportunities for social advancement among the inhabitants of North Africa and other provinces. Despite these attempts at integration, Roman North Africa remained divided along class and ethnic lines. Roman and Romanized

NORTH AFRICA'S **GREATEST THEOLOGIAN**

St Augustine (*right*) was one of the most significant examples of the cultural exchange resulting from Rome's control of North Africa. A man of Amazigh heritage, Augustine (354–430 CE) rose to become not just the bishop of Hippo Regius in Numidia (modern Algeria), but one of the foremost theologians and philosophers of the early Roman Catholic church. His writings helped lay the foundation for much of medieval and modern Catholic thought, including the concept of original sin.

citizens controlled its towns and coastal cities, while peoples whose culture, language, and way of life remained distinctly Amazigh populated more rural and marginalized areas.

Rome was in decline by the 5th century, its control in Africa, as elsewhere in the empire, falling away. But all of the civilizations of North Africa – including Egypt and Cyrenaica – continued to be connected with those of the Mediterranean, with cities such as Alexandria and Carthage important centres of Christian scholarship and worship. The region's destiny would change again in the decades and centuries to come, but its contact with Rome left an imprint that is still visible today.

Pharos Lighthouse was one of the Seven Wonders of the World

Walls once stood 9 m (30 ft) high

Romans introduced camels to North Africa in c. 200 CE

◁ **Major city**
Alexandria was, after Rome itself, one of the largest and most populous cities of the empire. This engraving shows it in the 16th century.

The arrival of Islam

The Muslim empire expands into Africa

Following the establishment of Islam in the 7th century CE, an Islamic empire spread rapidly from Arabia into Africa, as Muslim conquests displaced the Christian rule of the Byzantine Empire.

Muhammad, the founder of Islam, was born in Mecca, Arabia, in around 570 CE. By the time of his death in 632, Islam had grown from having a handful of followers to being the predominant religion of the Arabian Peninsula, unifying the previously disparate Arabic peoples in a single, powerful Islamic nation.

Initially, the new religion's doctrine of a single deity met with hostility from adherents of polytheistic religions. Muhammad and his followers faced persecution and were forced to flee from Mecca. Many went with Muhammad to the city of Medina, but some sought refuge in Abyssinia (present-day Ethiopia and Eritrea) in 614, a migration known as the First Hijra. Despite requests to surrender them to the Meccans, King Najasi (r. 614–630) of the Christian Kingdom of Aksum gave them safe haven, and himself went on to convert to Islam.

Most of the Muslims sheltering in Abyssinia later returned to Medina, but some remained, and established the first mosques in Africa, notably at Zeila in present-day Somalia and Massawa in Eritrea. Under Islamic rule, Arabia prospered, and after Muhammad's death his successors, the Rashidun caliphs, expanded its influence into neighbouring regions to form an Islamic empire.

During the reign of the second caliph, Umar, Islamic forces conquered Egypt in 641, took much of Persia and the Levant, and, the following year, went on to occupy what is today Libya. This involved some cunning strategy: when Muslim soldiers attacked Tripoli, seven of them managed to enter secretly and by inciting riot gave the false impression that the Muslim forces had already entered the city en masse.

Eastward expansion

By the time the Rashidun Caliphate was succeeded by the Umayyad dynasty, the Islamic Empire extended as far as present-day Tunisia. Forces led by General Uqba Ibn Nafi then made further inroads into the Maghreb, the western part of North Africa, and in 670 established the city of Kairouan as a military base. This became the capital of the Islamic province of Ifriqiyya (a name sharing the same root

◁ **African protector**
This 14th-century manuscript illustration shows the King of Aksum refusing to surrender Muslim refugees to the Meccans.

> "**All those who listen to me** shall pass on **my words to others**."

MUHAMMAD, FINAL SERMON (c. 630 CE)

THE **BLUE QUR'AN**

Produced in Kairouan, Tunisia (or, possibly, Córdoba, Spain) and believed to date from the late 9th or early 10th century, the Blue Qur'an is one of the most celebrated early Qur'anic manuscripts. It takes its name from the unusual indigo-coloured parchment on which the text is written. Most striking is the gold calligraphy in Kufic script (the oldest calligraphic form of the various Arabic scripts).

as "Africa"), and the site of a magnificent mosque. The push westwards along the Mediterranean coast continued through the 670s, and by 681 Islamic forces had reached present-day Morocco. General Uqba failed to occupy Tangier, however, and it would be another century until Morocco became a Muslim state.

Campaigns and conquest

A key moment in the conquest of North Africa came in 695, when Muslim forces invaded Carthage, an important Byzantine stronghold. The Muslims were initially victorious, but the Byzantine army eventually repulsed them. Later, in 698, the Muslims retook Carthage, sacking the city to prevent it falling under Christian rule again.

Soon after, General Musa Ibn Nusair began a campaign against the Imazighen (Berbers) in the quest to extend the Umayyad Empire across the Maghreb. The Imazighen put up a fierce resistance, but their queen, Al-Kahina, was slain in the Battle of Tabarka, and the Muslims continued their conquests, reaching the Atlantic coast in 708. Almost all of North Africa was now under Muslim control, and, in place of the Christian social order, an Islamic society was set up, which persists to the present time.

◁ **The Great Mosque of Kairouan, Tunisia**
Distinctive horseshoe arches line the colonnade alongside the courtyard of the Mosque of Kairouan, which was established in 670 CE, but extensively rebuilt in the 9th century.

Christian states of the northeast

The establishment of Christianity in northern Africa

The Christian Church in northern and northeastern Africa can trace its roots back as far as 1st-century Ethiopia and Egypt, developing into a distinctively African Orthodox tradition.

△ **Aksumite gold coin**
King Ezana of Aksum's conversion to Christianity was marked by a change in design of the coinage from a pagan disc and crescent motif to the Christian cross.

▽ **Ethiopian convert**
This illustration from the Menologion of Basil II (c. 1000 CE) depicts the conversion and baptism of the Ethiopian eunuch by Philip the Evangelist.

According to the Acts of the Apostles, the first African convert to Christianity was described as an Ethiopian eunuch, who was returning home from Jerusalem when he met Philip the Evangelist, who baptized him. In Ethiopian tradition, this event marked the foundation of the Ethiopian Church, but it was almost 300 years until Christianity was formally adopted here in the 4th century CE.

In Egypt, the apostle St Mark established the Coptic Orthodox Church in Alexandria around 42 CE. This was initially linked to the Greek-speaking Orthodox Church, but by the 2nd century had developed distinctive characteristics, including worship in the local languages and the use of the *Agpeya*, a breviary or prayer book in the Coptic language. Also in the 2nd century, Christianity began to rise in the western half

▷ **Ethiopian cross**
This processional cross with typically elaborate, stylized design was created by the Tigrinya people of Tigray province in about 1500.

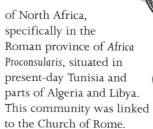

of North Africa, specifically in the Roman province of *Africa Proconsularis*, situated in present-day Tunisia and parts of Algeria and Libya. This community was linked to the Church of Rome.

Christian communities were also growing in northeastern Africa. The kingdom of Aksum, situated in modern-day Ethiopia, Eritrea, northern Djibouti, and eastern Sudan, was first to formally adopt the religion, after the conversion of King Ezana of Aksum around 330. This marked the establishment of the Ethiopian Orthodox Church, linked to the Coptic Orthodox Church of Alexandria.

Spread and schisms

From Aksum, Christianity began to spread into neighbouring Nubia to the north. In about 350, Aksum invaded the Meroitic kingdom, in modern-day Sudan, causing its decline and eventual collapse. It was replaced by three smaller kingdoms: Nobatia, Makuria, and Alodia. The Nobatian king and aristocracy officially converted to Orthodox Christianity in 543, and Alodia followed suit soon

"Philip and [the Ethiopian] went down into the water and Philip baptized him."

ACTS OF THE APOSTLES 8:37

Text in classical Ge'ez script

Page made of vellum (prepared animal skin)

▷ **Illuminated manuscript**
This tempera and ink painting is one of 20 from an illuminated manuscript of the Four Gospels that monks in the Amhara region of northern Ethiopia created in the 14th or 15th century. This scene depicts the appearance of the resurrected Christ.

after. Christian influence had also made its way into Makuria in the 6th century, and after it annexed the kingdom of Nobatia at the beginning of the 8th century, it too officially adopted the religion.

Although the Coptic Orthodox Churches were initially a part of the Greek Orthodox Church of Alexandria, differences of belief developed between them. This culminated in a schism in 451, separating the Oriental (Coptic) Orthodox Churches of Africa from the Eastern (Greek) Orthodox Church. The dispute centred around the nature of Christ: while the Eastern Orthodox Church took the mainstream Christian view (shared with the Roman Catholic Church) that Jesus has two distinct natures, divine and human, the Oriental Orthodox Churches held that Jesus' two natures are united as one. Indeed, the Ethiopian Orthodox Tewahedo Church contains in its name the Ge'ez (Classical Ethiopic) word for "united as one" – *tewahedo*.

Another schism came in the Maghreb, this time between the Roman Church of Carthage and a breakaway sect, Donatism, which flourished in the 4th and 5th centuries. Donatists presented a challenge to the Christian clergy by arguing that ministers must be faultless for their ministry to be effective. The Donatist church survived until the arrival of Islam in North Africa in the 7th century (see pp. 72–73).

3

African empires

600–1900 CE

African empires

Several African empires such as Napata, Meroë, and Aksum had emerged during antiquity, but numerous kingdoms across the continent entered their golden age during the medieval period and beyond. These empires were made rich by networks of international trade and they developed wealthy elites. Potent belief systems, including Islam and Christianity, became closely linked with state power. The kingdoms also developed and utilized writing systems, as part of a sophisticated bureaucracy, and nurtured distinctive, world-class artistic traditions.

Empires in the North and West

The first medieval empires to rise to prominence were North African. After the fall of Rome at the end of the 7th century, a succession of caliphates ruled great swathes of the region, spreading Islam as they went. The Fatimid Caliphate stretched as far east as the Arabian Peninsula, while the Almoravids conquered much of North Africa and Spain and reached south to Gao, in what is now Mali.

The Almovarids clashed with the Wagadou Empire (ancient Ghana), one of the great powers in the West African Sahel between the 9th and 16th centuries. The mighty Mali Empire that followed was founded in the early 13th century by the Mandingo (Malinke) warrior-prince Sundiata Keita and peaked during the reign of Mansa Musa a century later. In the 15th century, the Songhai dominated the region and its rich trade routes, which crossed the Sahara and reached into Central and East Africa.

To the west of these kingdoms, in what are now Senegal and the Gambia, the Jolof Empire prospered between the 14th and 16th centuries. To the south, in modern-day Ghana, Osei Tutu and his childhood companion Okomfo Anokye founded the Asante Empire in the early 18th century. In what is now Nigeria, the Oyo formed a Yoruba kingdom with a cavalry that was the scourge of surrounding states from the 17th to the 19th centuries. Among their conquests was the 18th-century Kingdom of Dahomey, in modern-day Benin, which was eventually overrun despite its use of European firearms.

East, Central, and Southern Africa

In the northeast of the continent, around modern-day Ethiopia, the Zagwe dynasty ruled from the 11th to the 13th century. Its most famous king, Lalibela, commissioned magnificent rock-hewn churches at a site that now bears his name. The Zagwe were overtaken by the Solomonids who formed the Ethiopian Empire, which was only briefly colonized by Europeans and survived until the 20th century.

Much of Central and Southern Africa was less densely populated, but the Christian Kingdom of Kongo, founded in the 14th century in what is now Angola, grew rich on commerce and endured for six centuries. East of there, between the 12th and 16th centuries, the super-state of Great Zimbabwe profited from Indian Ocean trade and built a capital whose massive stone walls still stand. In today's South Africa, in the 19th century, the warrior-king Shaka used groundbreaking tactics to strengthen the Zulu Kingdom, which redrew the map of Southern Africa before falling to European colonizers expanding their own empires.

◁ **Gold pendant crafted by the Asante people**

969 Tunisia's Fatimid Caliphate conquers Egypt, and soon makes Cairo its capital

c. 1200 The Yoruba empire of Ife, well known for its sculptures, emerges in what is now Benin

9th century CE The Wagadou (Ghana) Empire enters its peak, powered by trade in gold, ivory, and horses

c. 1120 The Amazigh (Berber) Almoravid Caliphate stretches from Mauritania to Spain

12th–13th centuries Great Zimbabwe becomes the heartland of a Shona kingdom

Major empires
This map shows African empires that existed from the medieval era onwards. Most sit by the coast, near major rivers, or on trading routes, which brought many benefts.

EUROPE

Black Sea

Córdoba
Seville
ALMOHAD CALIPHATE
Grenada
Marrakech
Atlas Mountains
AGHLABID EMIRATE
Mediterranean Sea
Kairouan
Cairo
FATIMID CALIPHATE
Red Sea
ASIA
Nile

Sahara

ALMORAVID CALIPHATE
WAGADOU EMPIRE
Koümbi Saleh
Timbuktu
Gao
MALI EMPIRE
Jenne
SONGHAI EMPIRE
Niger
KANEM–BORNU EMPIRE
Gonder
ETHIOPIAN EMPIRE
Addis Ababa
ZAGWE KINGDOM

MOSSI STATES
Oyo
IFE EMPIRE
Ife
Edo
ASANTE EMPIRE
OYO EMPIRE
KINGDOM OF BENIN
AFRICA
Congo

ATLANTIC OCEAN

KONGO KINGDOM
LUNDA KINGDOM
LUBA KINGDOM
Lake Victoria

SULTANATE OF ZANZIBAR
SULTANATE OF KILWA

LOZI KINGDOM
KINGDOM OF ZIMBABWE
Great Zimbabwe

ZULU KINGDOM

INDIAN OCEAN

0   1,000 km
0   1,000 miles
N

KEY
- Wagadou Empire (600–1000)
- Kanem-Bornu Empire (c.800–1893)
- Aghlabid Emirate (800–909)
- Zagwe Kingdom (c.900–c.1200)
- Fatimid Caliphate (909–1171)
- Sultanate of Kilwa (957–1513)
- Almoravid Caliphate (1050s–1147)
- Almohad Caliphate (1121–1269)
- Kingdom of Benin (1180–1897)
- Ife Empire (1200–1420)
- Kingdom of Zimbabwe (1220–1450)
- Mali Empire (1230–1660)
- Ethiopian Empire (1270–1974)

- Oyo Empire (c.1300–1896)
- Kongo Kingdom (c.1390–1862)
- Songhai Empire (1464–1591)
- Mossi States (1500–1895)
- Luba Kingdom (1585–1889)

- Lunda Kingdom (c. 1665–c. 1887)
- Lozi Kingdom (c.1700s–1890)
- Asante Empire (1701–1901)
- Zulu Kingdom (1816–1887)
- Sultanate of Zanzibar (1856–1964)

1 Great Zimbabwe's Hill Complex

2 The rock-cut Church of Saint George, Lalibela

3 The Larabanga Mosque in what is now Ghana

c.1270 The Solomonic dynasty defeats the Zagwe dynasty and founds the Ethiopian Empire

c.1350 The Jolof Empire, once a vassal of the Mali Empire, gains its independence

1580s The Luba Empire emerges in what is now the Democratic Republic of the Congo

1700s The Oyo Empire wages war on the Kingdom of Dahomey, eventually defeating its rivals

1901 After two centuries of rule, and four wars with the British, the Asante Empire finally falls

c.1312 Mansa Musa becomes ruler of the Mali Empire, gathering immense wealth

1460s Under Sunni Ali, the Songhai Empire adopts Islam and dominates much of West Africa

1623 The Kingdom of Kongo defeats a Portuguese army in what is now Angola

1816 Shaka becomes ruler of the Zulu nation and begins building a powerful army

Languages

From Arabic to Zulu

Around 2,000 different languages are used in Africa, some spoken by millions of people, others on the verge of extinction. In addition, non-verbal means of communication include beadwork and "talking" drums. Spoken languages are grouped into several major families, their geographical spread reflecting thousands of years of communication and settlement.

The largest family, Niger-Congo, includes Bantu languages such as Swahili, Zulu, and Shona, as well as the Mande and Dogon languages of West Africa. Thanks in part to the movements of Bantu-speaking peoples, it is the most widespread language group. Most Niger-Congo languages use tone to change word meaning and feature noun classification (in which nouns are grouped by theme).

Afro-Asiatic languages are spoken in North Africa and the Horn of Africa. They include Semitic (such as Arabic, spoken across much of North Africa), Chadic (including Hausa, spoken primarily in northern Nigeria and southern Niger), Cushitic (such as Oromo, spoken in Ethiopia and parts of Kenya), and Amazigh (Berber) languages, as well as Ancient Egyptian. Most Afro-Asiatic languages require syllables to start with consonants, and share a common set of pronouns.

Between these two large language groups, some peoples in the Sahel and Sahara speak the Saharan, Nilotic, and Sudanic languages. More than 100 languages fall into these families, which can be grouped together as Nilo-Saharan languages, and are characterized by their use of different tones to change

△ **Bantu-speakers**
Bantu-speaking peoples live across Central and Southern Africa – the musicians shown in this 19th-century Italian print are from modern-day Angola. Bantu-speakers use around 500 distinct but related languages in the Niger-Congo language family.

△ **San storyteller**
The San peoples are hunter-gatherers from Southern Africa with a rich storytelling tradition that is both a regular pastime and a way to preserve a threatened culture. The San, like the pastoralist Khoikhoi, speak a variety of languages that feature clicking sounds, which function as consonants.

△ **Tuareg**
The Tuareg (shown here in a 19th-century European depiction) are an Amazigh people who live in Niger, Mali, Algeria, Libya, and Burkina Faso. Tuareg languages are part of the Afro-Asiatic language family; the most widely spoken dialect is Tawellemet.

"If you know… the **language of your culture**… that is **empowerment**."

NGŨGĨ WA THIONG'O, KENYAN WRITER, 2017

meaning and by rules of vowel harmony (in which two sets of contrasting vowels never coexist in the same word). Many speakers live in Sudan or South Sudan, although Songhai languages (deriving from the empire of the same name) are spoken in West Africa.

In contrast to these thriving language groups, many of Africa's most ancient languages are endangered. Once widespread, the hunter-gatherer San and the pastoralist Khoikhoi have been forced to the margins of their homelands, which mainly lie in Southern Africa. One of the most notable features of the speech of the Khoikhoi and San is their use of clicking sounds, produced when air is released in a burst past the tongue, teeth, and palate. These clicks have been borrowed by Bantu languages such as Xhosa and Zulu,

but are not found on any other continent. Some languages, such as Khoikhoi (spoken in Namibia, Botswana, and South Africa) and Sandawe (Tanzania), are used by many thousands of people, but others have been driven to extinction.

Languages from outside Africa also have a significant presence, with English an official tongue in over 20 nations, especially in Southern and East Africa, and French widely used in West Africa. Creole languages such as Krio (Sierra Leone) and Kreyol (Liberia) are also spoken, while Madagascar's Malagasy is the westernmost Austronesian language in the world, having been introduced by traders from the Malay archipelago over 1,500 years ago.

△ **Message beads**
Aroko is a form of non-verbal communication used by the Yoruba of West Africa. Meaning is determined by different combinations or colours of leaves, cowrie shells, weapons, and beads.

△ **Nilotic speakers**
The Nilotic-speaking Samburu (pictured) are cattle and sheep herders, who mostly live in northern Kenya. Nilotic languages are part of the Nilo-Saharan linguistic family and are spoken by over 50 million people across East Africa.

△ **Talking drum**
Griots (poets and musicians) in West Africa have used talking drums as a storytelling tool for centuries. The instrument can be played to mimic the rhythm and tone of human speech, but was also used to spread messages between villages, conveying news over long distances more rapidly than a horse and rider.

△ **N|uu language**
South African government minister Nathi Mthethwa hands a N|uu dictionary to Ouma Katrina Esau, one of the remaining fluent speakers of this San dialect. Esau created a school to pass on the language, which has 45 clicks, 30 non-click consonants, and 39 vowels.

The development of East African trade

Trade and transformation in East Africa

East Africans have been trading with people in the Persian Gulf, along the Arabian Sea, and on the coast of the Indian Ocean for 2,000 years, taking advantage of the prevailing winds to journey to and from Asia.

△ **Chinese connection**
This tomb pillar from the East African settlement of Kunduchi (in modern-day Tanzania) is embedded with plaques from medieval China, evidence of links between the two regions.

From at least the 1st century BCE, Cushitic (ancient Somali) livestock herders were bartering goods with travelling Arab merchants. These contacts continued for the next 200 years, with the Cushites setting up trading ports on the coast along the Horn of Africa, including one known today as Hafun West, where archaeological finds include pottery fragments from the region occupied by modern-day Iraq.

The Bantu-speakers and sea trading
By the 1st and 2nd centuries CE, Bantu-speaking people (see pp. 36–37) from the Great Lakes region around modern-day Burundi, Rwanda, and the Democratic Republic of the Congo (DRC) had migrated eastwards, displacing or assimilating Indigenous groups as they progressed. On reaching East Africa's coast, they founded new settlements and took over those already constructed by the migratory Cushite pastoralists. Rhapta in modern Kenya, for example, had been established in the 1st century BCE by the Cushites and was known to the Romans but only became a major sea-trading centre under Bantu-speakers 200–300 years later.

Generally speaking, the prevailing winds in the region blew from west to east in the summer, making this the season for traders to sail to Asia or up and down East Africa's coastline. They would buy and sell goods such as the elephant ivory and animal skins that were popular in Arabia, India, and China. Merchants travelled in a vessel called a *mtepe*, a long, square-sailed cargo boat. The wooden planks of its hull were sewn together using coir, the hair-like husk of a coconut shell, which made the boats notoriously leaky. By winter, with the winds blowing east to west, Asian merchants arrived in East Africa with grain, glass beads, and pottery to trade for local produce.

All of this activity made East Africa's ports diverse and ever-changing places. Their inhabitants were not simply sailors and traders, but also acted as middlemen, facilitating deals between Arab, Indian, and Iranian merchants, and with local suppliers and vendors along the coast as well as much further inland.

Birth of a new culture
From the 8th to the 12th centuries, East Africa's trading links with the nations across the Arabian Sea and the Indian Ocean intensified. Iran and the

◁ **Port of call**
Ancient ruins at Gedi (in modern-day Kenya) include a palace with arched gateways, as well as houses, tombs, and a mosque. Gedi was a coastal trading centre during the medieval period.

Mountains with rivers
running down to the sea
appear inland from the
East African coast

The "Mountains
of the Moon", the
fabled source of
the River Nile

Mecca is at
the centre of
the map

جبل القمر وهو منبع النيل

The representations of
India, China, and South
Asia owe more to guesswork
than informed knowledge
on the map-maker's part

Straits of
Gibraltar

▷ **World turned upside-down**
This 1154 world map by Arab cartographer
Mohammed al-Idrisi is displayed as his
contemporaries would have seen it: with Africa
at the top and Europe below.

The Iberian
Peninsula of Spain
and Portugal

southern Arabian territory of present-day Yemen
became particularly important destinations for
African merchants. A range of goods, including
gold, ivory, and rock crystal, were traded for textiles,
glass beads, and ceramics as part of a rich cultural
exchange. In addition, enslaved people were trafficked
across the region (see pp. 148–49). With ports and
city-states such as Shanga and Pemba (islands off
Kenya and Tanzania, respectively) and Kilwa (in
Tanzania) growing in size, population, and reputation,
East Africa's wealthier citizens now lived in homes
built from a stone-like coral called *porites* rather than
the usual mud, wood, and leaves, and they imported
large quantities of Arabian pottery and Chinese
porcelain to display as a visible sign of their status.

Arrival of Islam

Islam also made an impact, with many East Africans
adopting the faith, observing whichever branch
of the religion – Sunni or Shia – was practised by
the Muslims they transacted with. The growing
cosmopolitanism of East Africa's trading centres
led to major social change. With large numbers
of Indian, Chinese, Iranian, and particularly
Arab people settling in East Africa, the population's
composition began to alter. As incomers began to
mix with and intermarry among the Islamized
Bantu-speaking people, a new culture and language
known as Swahili emerged. Today, Swahili is still the
name given to both the language and the people of
much of the East African coastal region.

△ **The usual view**
When Mohammed al-Idrisi's
map is shown in a more
recognizable orientation,
Africa, Europe, and Asia
are easier to visualize.

The rise and fall of Wagadou

An empire built on gold and trade

On the southern edge of the Sahel, the Wagadou (Ghana) Empire emerged in the 6th century CE as the first great trading state of West Africa, thriving for seven centuries until its eventual collapse in the 14th century.

Wagadou (Ghana), meaning "the land of gold", arose among the Soninke peoples of modern-day southeastern Mauritania and western Mali around 600 CE. The existence of a stone-built town at Dhar Tichitt in the southwestern Sahara, dating from about 1600 BCE, suggests that the empire developed from several existing local cultures.

The rulers – known as the *ghana* – of the new state enjoyed considerable wealth. This was partly due to the availability of copper and salt, which could be traded and on which tolls could be levied. The region's position on trans-Saharan trade routes carrying gold from sources at Ghiyaru,

Bure, and Bambuk on the Senegal and Upper Niger also brought wealth, and the *ghana* possessed a monopoly on the gold itself, of which most citizens were allowed to possess only the dust.

Much of what we know about Wagadou comes from early Arab travellers who passed through it (see box), beginning with the astronomer Ibrahim al-Fazari (d. 777). The first king was said to have been Dyabe Sissé, whose successors expanded to the east and west, seeking to dominate all routes through the Sahara. They built relations with the Sanhaja Amazigh (Berber) rulers of Aoudaghost north of Wagadou, and with the buffer states at Sili and Takrur in the west.

The capital city

Described as possessing an army of 200,000 men, including 40,000 archers, the Wagadou kings ruled from a capital at Koumbi Saleh, which was divided into two sections. The royal city – which Arab writers called *al-Ghaba* ("the grove") – housed the palace, which was surrounded by a stone wall and circular wooden huts for the majority of the population. It was also the site of the wooden-domed royal tombs and sacred copses where Wagadou priests carried out their rituals.

Islam had reached Wagadou by the 11th century, and the other district was the Muslim town, which had twelve mosques, special food shops, and resident Islamic legal scholars. Modern excavations suggest

△ Prime location
At its height in the 1050s, the Wagadou Empire dominated trade passing between the goldfields to its south and the Muslim states of North Africa.

KEY
- ▓ Wagadou Empire
- ▒ Sahara Desert
- — Trade route
- ○ Trading centre
- △ Goldfield

N ↑ 0 — 1,000 km
       0 — 1,000 miles

Corded patterning

Net-like decoration

◁ Wagadou crafts
Pottery vessels provided storage and a way to transport everyday items such as grain, and have been found at many Wagadou sites.

that the site may have held a population of 15,000. It occupied around 45 hectares (110 acres), and had two large cemeteries outside its walls.

The decline of Wagadou

Trade routes gradually moved further east due to desertification, which had extended the borders of the Sahara southwards. Border regions such as Takrur broke away and eventually the Wagadou Empire became far less significant. The last great king was probably the *ghana* Tunka Menin, who ascended the throne in 1063. Menin succeeded his maternal uncle to become king – Wagadou royal succession was matrilineal. In 1054, the Almoravids – a movement of Islamic renewal with its roots in the desert fringes of Mauretania (see pp. 100–101) – swept south and captured the important Amazigh trading town of Aoudaghost. In 1076, they sacked Koumbi Saleh – a devastating blow to Wagadou.

Although Wagadou recovered a little after the Almoravid Empire collapsed in the 1140s, it was unable to bring together the rival Soninke chieftaincies or compensate for the loss of revenue from the gold trade. The capital, Koumbi Saleh, could no longer support the large population it once held. Instead, Wagadou was obliged to pay tribute to the growing Mali Empire (see pp. 90–91), and by the mid-13th century Koumbi Saleh had disappeared.

△ **Trading post**
Ouadane, once an important stage on the gold-trading route north of Aoudaghost in the southwest Sahara until its decline in the 13th century, now lies in ruins.

"From every donkey **loaded with salt**... the king takes a duty of **one gold dinar**."

ABU UBAYD AL-AZIZ AL-BAKRI, 1068

Dogon settlement
On the Bandiagara Escarpment in Mali's central plateau, these adobe buildings are houses and granaries for the Dogon people. The Dogon arrived here around the 15th century when the area was occupied by the Tellem people, who had been here since the 11th century. Some Tellem were pushed out; others intermarried and became part of the Dogon community. There is evidence that the Dogon drew on Tellem customs in their own faith. The approximately 600,000 Dogon live as farmers, mainly near the top or bottom of the cliffs – where there is a water supply – and the area is also a popular place for tourists.

Riches of the trade routes

The exchange of goods, people, and ideas

The trade routes that crossed the Sahara, known as the trans-Saharan trade routes, carried gold, salt, and enslaved people, bringing huge wealth and influences that helped shape Africa's economic, cultural, and political development.

African merchants have traded across the continent and beyond since ancient times. From at least Egypt's Old Kingdom in the 3rd millennium BCE, the vast sand sea of the Sahara (see pp. 20–21), far from being a barrier, proved a highly effective conduit for trade. Here, merchants went in search of products available in Africa south of the Sahara, such as ivory and hides, in exchange for grain and manufactured goods. The immense hardships of desert travel during this period channelled the trade from oasis to oasis along certain routes, where towns began to spring up, eventually deriving great wealth from the provisions sold to travellers and the tolls imposed on them.

Caravans of gold

Further west, a network of routes developed, carrying gold, spices, kola nuts, and other forest products, as well as enslaved people, in exchange for jewellery, textiles, and salt, which was scarce in West Africa. From the northern terminus of the trade – towns such as Sijilmasa (in modern-day Morocco), Tripoli (in Libya), and Kairouan (in Tunisia) – caravans of merchants travelled south. From around the 3rd century CE, the merchants used camels to carry both goods and people. The ability of these animals to travel long distances without food and water made the journey less risky and arduous.

The trade greatly enriched African rulers south of the Sahara, giving rise from the 6th century to the formation of larger empires such as Ghana, whose kings controlled access to the Bambuk goldfields beyond the Senegal River. Further east, the Kanem-Bornu Empire (see pp. 108–109) flourished on the fringes of Lake Chad. In addition, trade brought

with it the exchange of ideas and beliefs, including the transmission of Islam (see pp. 72–73). The religion began to penetrate North Africa from the 8th century, although it did not become established among rulers and the bulk of the populace for several centuries yet.

The new-found wealth helped the growth of trading hubs like Gao, Djenné, and Timbuktu, which became centres of learning and of industries – such as textile production – as well as the focus of competition between rival powers. Later, they developed into substantial towns, with royal palaces and mosques, including the Djinguereber mosque at Timbuktu, built

△ **Gold dinar**
The Islamic Almoravid dynasty based in Morocco minted this mid-12th-century coin from gold traded across the Sahara.

Europe

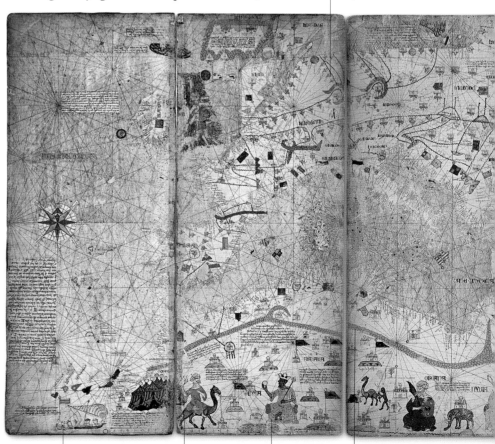

▷ **The Catalan Atlas**
Created in 1375 by a cartographer in Majorca, this map situates North Africa and the Sahara region at the bottom left. The Atlas demonstrates the significant European interest in the lucrative trade routes that had developed across Africa.

European sailors en route to Africa

Camel-riding desert trader

Mansa Musa of Mali

Gold band representing Atlas Mountains

in 1327. The discovery of new goldfields at Bure (modern-day Guinea) led trade routes to shift slightly to the east, bypassing Ghana, which had lost the key trading town of Aoudaghost by 1050. A new empire, Mali, founded by Sundiata Keita in the 1230s, would eclipse Ghana as the preeminent power in the region.

Mali profited so much from trans-Saharan trade that its ruler Mansa Musa (see pp. 92–93) went on a pilgrimage to Mecca in 1324–25, during which he spent and gave away such vast quantities of gold that it caused the overall value of gold to decrease for at least a decade afterwards. Mali was, in turn, eclipsed by the Songhai Empire (c. 1464–1591), which again relied for its wealth on the profits from trading gold and enslaved people northwards.

By this time, however, the ancient trading routes were already endangered. From the 1440s, the arrival of the Portuguese in Africa opened up alternative sea routes for trade, and the beginnings of the transatlantic slave trade destabilized new regions of coastal West Africa.

The decline of trade

In 1591, the Moroccan sultan Ahmad al-Mansur sacked Timbuktu, bringing the Songhai Empire to an end. Although trade across the desert continued, and even became easier with the advent of modern roads and railways in the 19th century, the demand for gold among Mediterranean states had also slackened. By 1600, the heyday of the trans-Saharan trade routes was over.

△ **Ivory salt cellar**
Created by West African craftspeople for a European market, the snakes on this exquisitely carved ivory salt cellar represent wealth.

"We came next to [the oasis of] **Tisarahla**… **where the caravans halt**."

IBN BATTUTA, *THE TRAVELS*, 1354

Caravan with camels, on the Silk Road, China

Sultan of Babylon (Cairo, Egypt) | Legendary Queen of Sheba | Trading ships on the Red Sea | Islands along the coast of China | Kingdom of Taprobane (Ceylon, now Sri Lanka)

△ **Impressive landmark**
The Great Mosque of Djenné, in modern-day central Mali, was built around the 13th century, though the current structure dates to 1907.

The Empire of Mali

The creation of Africa's most famous empire

Born from the defeat of a king said to have been a sorceror, the Mali Empire stretched across West Africa in the 13th and 14th centuries. Its wealth in gold made it famous from Europe to Mecca.

Between the 9th and 11th centuries, the Ghana Empire dominated the region around the Niger River (see pp. 84–85). Its empire encompassed Mande, the homeland of the Mandingo (also known as the Mandinka or Malinke), in what is now southern Mali and northeastern Guinea. But after a disastrous war in the 11th century with the Almoravids, an Islamic dynasty centred on modern Morocco, its grip weakened and several provinces began to break away.

◁ **Archer figure**
This terracotta archer, dating from the 13th–15th centuries, is depicted in ceremonial military attire and may represent warriors who were allies of the Malian emperor Sundiata Keita.

By the 12th century, Mande had conquered the nearby Kingdom of Do, as well as other towns around the Niger, to create the Kingdom of Mali.

Sumanguru and the Lion King

Mali was not the only nation to rise in Ghana's wake. Under its ruler Kemoko Kanté, the Kingdom of Sosso conquered much of the declining empire. When he died, his son Sumanguru continued to expand Sosso territory. An impressive but reportedly cruel leader, Sumanguru was believed to have mystical powers, and is remembered as the inventor of the *balafon*, a xylophone made from gourds. Sumanguru sacked Mande nine times, but each time the Mandingo regrouped and counterattacked. However, when the

Malian king Maghan died in around 1218, he left the crown to his less military-minded son, Dankaran Tuman, who sued for peace. Unable to maintain the support of his people, Dankaran fled Mande. His younger brother, Sundiata – or Mari-Diata (Lion King) – returned from travels across the Ghana Empire and led the Mandingo to war. He raised an army of troops and cavalry, and at the Battle of Krina in around 1235, he defeated Sumanguru's army.

The victorious Sundiata conquered the lands of the Sosso and created an oral constitution, named *Kurukan Fuga* after the plain on which it was agreed, that made him ruler of the Mali Empire. His generals conquered the gold fields of Bondu and Bambuk to the south and desert trading towns to the north, and by Sundiata's death his empire stretched west and east to the Senegal and Niger rivers respectively.

Prosperity and decline

The empire's central West African location and its control of goldmines, fertile land, and trade routes put it in a commanding position. Taxes on the trade in gold, salt, copper, ivory, and enslaved people made its kings wealthy. Yet Sundiata's descendants struggled to make a mark, and several decades of instability caused by succession rivalries followed his death in around 1255. The empire still prospered, thanks in part to powerful court officials, and Islam became increasingly influential.

In around 1307, Mansa Musa ascended to the throne, and the empire reached its peak. Musa (see pp. 92–93) almost doubled its possessions, conquering the cities of Gao and Timbuktu and enslaving thousands of captured people. But while he spent most of his reign in conflict with his non-Muslim neighbours, he encouraged closer links with the sultanates of North Africa.

By now, the multiethnic and multilingual Mali Empire supported a large army that included mail-clad cavalrymen and archers. Muslim scholars gathered in libraries and

> #### FOUNDER OF **THE MALI EMPIRE**
>
> Much of our knowledge of Mali's founder, Sundiata Keita, comes from the *Epic of Sundiata*, a poem that mixes history and myth and was originally recited by *griots* (storytellers). According to the poem, Sundiata was born to King Maghan and a formerly enslaved woman named Sogolon. The young prince was disabled from birth, but miraculously learned to walk. He left Mande and grew into a skilled warrior and statesman. Finally, his people, the Mandingo, called him back to lead them and he commanded a large army made up of calvary and infantry – as had been foretold by prophecy.
>
> **HORSEMAN FIGURINE, MALI, 13TH–14TH CENTURY**

universities in cities such as Timbuktu. For several decades after Musa's death in around 1337, Mali's golden age continued. But the empire's size made it hard to defend. Arguments over the succession weakened Mali, and rebellions gradually shrank its borders in the 14th and 15th centuries. Portuguese ships challenged for trade, the nomadic Tuareg raided settlements, and by the early 16th century, the Songhai (see pp. 104–105) had taken over much of the empire. Mali remained a regional power, but its legendary riches were long gone.

Bumps are thought to depict ornaments or sores from illness

▷ **Seated figure**
This 13th-century sculpture from Djenné, present-day Mali, may represent mourning, though its exact meaning is unknown.

Toes and and other expressive, intimate details bring the sculpture to life

Wealthy emperor
Mansa Musa is represented on the 1375 Catalan Atlas of the Jewish-Spanish cartographer Abraham Cresques. Musa's crown and orb are rendered in vivid gold, the source of his great wealth.

Mansa Musa

The greatest ruler of the Mali Empire

Mansa Musa oversaw the growth of the Mali Empire in the 14th century. His pilgrimage to Mecca was one of the most notable events of the medieval age.

Born into the Mali Empire's royal family, Musa became *mansa*, or emperor, around 1307. His predecessor headed a fleet of ships on an expedition that sought to discover whether any lands lay beyond the Atlantic Ocean – and was never seen again.

The Mali Empire reached its greatest extent during Musa's reign, encompassing large areas of present-day Guinea, Senegal, Mauretania, and the Gambia, as well as Mali itself. Mali's imperial might was backed by impressive resources, too. As well as gold and salt deposits, Musa's empire also benefited from the lucrative trade in ivory. Such were Mali's riches that Mansa Musa has often been described as the richest man that has ever lived.

Raising Mali's public profile

In 1324, Musa embarked on the *Hajj*, or pilgrimage, to Mecca that every devout Muslim is expected to attempt. His reasons for making the long and hazardous journey from West Africa to Arabia were complex. Piety played a role, as did guilt – a year earlier Musa had caused his mother's death by accident, and his court counsellors advised him to visit the tomb of the Prophet Muhammad in Medina, close to Mecca, as penance.

Going on the *Hajj* also gave Musa an opportunity to display his wealth and prestige to the outside world. He reportedly travelled to Mecca and Medina with 60,000 porters bearing gifts made of gold, 500 silk-clad servants, and 15,000 camels laden with sacks of gold, perfume, salt, and provisions. His retinue gifted and spent so much gold while staying in Cairo that they debased the precious metal's value there for more than 10 years afterwards.

Once in Mecca, Musa recruited a number of scholars to help modernize his empire. Chief among these was the Andalusian lawyer, poet, and architect Abu Ishaq al-Sahili, whose finest creation was the Djinguereber Mosque in Timbuktu. This, and other mosques, *madrasas* (centres of learning), and schools, turned Timbuktu from a busy trading hub into the home of one of the world's first universities.

△ **Timbuktu texts**
Under Mansa Musa, Timbuktu's libraries grew to hold countless texts on science, medicine, and, as shown here, mathematics and astronomy.

▽ **Seat of learning**
Built during Musa's reign, Sankoré Madrasa in Timbuktu was a great medieval seat of learning.

1235 Mali's empire founded by Sundiata Keita, Musa's great-uncle

1324/5 Mansa Musa's pilgrimage to Mecca and Medina

1325/6 University of Timbuktu established

1330 Timbuktu invaded by neighbouring Mossi kingdom, but later recaptured

c. 1307 Musa becomes *mansa* (emperor) of Mali

1325 Mali conquers Gao, capital of the rival Songhai people

1327 Djinguereber Mosque commissioned

c. 1337 Death of Mansa Musa

Djinguereber Mosque

Timbuktu, present-day Mali

The city of Timbuktu benefited from a strategic location on a trans-Saharan trade route between goldfields to the south and salt mines to the north. It began to prosper in the 14th century under Mansa Musa, who promoted Islam and established the first of the city's three great mosques: Djinguereber. In the 15th to 16th centuries, through its mosques and trade network, Timbuktu developed into a renowned centre of religious and intellectual learning, with a prestigious university attracting scholars from North Africa and beyond. In 1591, Morocco invaded, bringing the city's golden age to an abrupt end.

The roof was constructed using *golettes* (small sticks) overlaid with mudbricks.

Tuareg tents made from wood and straw matting

Extensions to the original prayer hall arcades feature arches

Wells provided the community with easy access to water

The main courtyard provided additional prayer and teaching space

Long drainpipes reduce erosion by rain

▷ **A Timbuktu library**
As a city of scholarship, Timbuktu became renowned for the production and trade of quality manuscripts on a wide variety of subjects. Tutors of the university built up prized collections in their personal libraries, and often drew on these to lead the study and copying of texts in their own homes.

◁ **Focus of prayer**
The prayer hall is cool and dim, with simple mudbrick arcades. A moulded frieze confers special significance on the *qibla* wall and *mihrab* (prayer niche) and may date to the 16th century.

△ **Secondary courtyard**
The courtyards of Timbuktu's mosques provided space for prayer, theological discussion, and study: much of the university teaching took place there, in individual tutor groups. The secondary courtyard at Djinguereber, reconstructed here, also allowed access to the main minaret.

Palmwood *torons* provide support, in-built scaffolding, and decoration

Current mosque   Original mosque

▷ **Evolution of Djinguereber Mosque**
Excavations suggest the original mosque, built around 1325 for Mansa Musa, had a simple rectangular plan (marked in red on this floorplan of the current building). It has since been remodelled and enlarged several times, most notably in 1570–83.

The conical minaret is situated above the *mihrab* in the prayer hall

The *qibla* wall indicates the direction of prayer

Camel trains from the Sahara desert brought in salt slabs weighing 25–30 kg (55–66 lb) apiece

Manuscripts were among the most valuable trade goods

ANNUAL **RESTORATION**

The distinctive earthen architecture of Timbuktu's mosques is durable, but requires regular maintenance to survive weathering by wind, sand, and rain. Restoring the mosques is an important tradition, carried out annually at the request of the relevant imam and directed by one of two families of master masons, who claim descent from the original builders of the 14th century. Using the decorative wooden posts (*torons*) in the minaret as scaffolding, local residents replaster the surface with fresh mudbrick. Every member of the community contributes in some way, be it labour, money, or materials.

REPLASTERING THE DJINGUEREBER MOSQUE

△ **Djinguereber district**
Djinguereber district lay on a north–south trade route at the southwest limit of old Timbuktu. This reconstruction depicts the area in the 1580s, at the peak of Timbuktu's prosperity and renown. Trade was thriving, and the Great Mosque had just been reconstructed on a grand scale.

"The **word of God** and the treasures of **wisdom** are only to be found **in Timbuktu**."

15TH-CENTURY MALIAN PROVERB

Timbuktu manuscript

Written records of West Africa

Timbuktu's position between the southern Sahara and the Niger River in West Africa made it a crucial medieval trading post. However, for all the gold that passed through this legendary city, its greatest legacy has arguably been cultural. Part of the Mali Empire in the 13th century, Timbuktu became known for its mosques, *madrasas*, and libraries.

In Timbuktu, students and scholars wrote, translated, and collected hundreds of thousands of texts. The city's written works, collectively known as the Timbuktu Manuscripts, represent a unique treasure, and span 900 years, with the oldest texts dating from around the 12th century. Many of the manuscripts are written in the Arabic and Spanish languages, but also in Ajami, an Arabic-derived script used to write other local languages, including Songhai, Fula, and Bambara, reflecting the variety of cultures that interacted with Timbuktu's heritage.

Classification and preservation

The collection includes some of the earliest known Islamic texts of philosophy and mathematics, while astronomy, medicine, botany, architecture, music, law, and history are also represented. Multiple copies of the Qu'ran are present, as well as religious treatises and guides to morality, while literary works include the *Epic of Sundiata* (see pp. 90–91), an account of the founding of the Mali Empire.

The Timbuktu Manuscripts are significant to many African countries and their diasporic communities. They are evidence of the vibrant civilization of West Africa, a testament to the resilience and strength of its people, and a reminder of the region's rich written, as well as oral, cultures.

Yet these texts, many of which date from the Mali and Songhai Empires in the 14th to 16th centuries, have often been under threat. After a Moroccan invasion in the late 16th century, Timbuktu declined, although new works continued to be written. Under French colonial control (1892–1960), Arabic education was neglected, and more manuscripts were damaged, lost, or entered private ownership.

In 2012, Tuareg militants occupied Timbuktu, destroying thousands of manuscripts that did not meet their interpretation of Islam. Librarians battled to save the texts, with a team led by Malian librarian Dr Abdel Kader Haïdara saving thousands of manuscripts and smuggling them via all-terrain vehicles, carts, and boats to Mali's modern-day capital, Bamako. While many documents have been lost, others have been stored or digitized by Malians, as well as by global giants such as Google, which has uploaded 40,000 for public use under the banner "Mali Magic". Mali's ancient gold may be gone, but its scholarship lives on.

Red Morocco leather used to encase pages

▽ **Decorated Qu'ran**
This 12th-century Qu'ran, one of the finest
of the Timbuktu Manuscripts, comes from
the collection of Dr Abdel Kader Haïdara.

Decorative panel
enhances the text

The Arabic script
used is typical for
12th-century Morocco

Note records that this Qu'ran was
owned by several Moroccan kings

The rise and fall of the Aghlabids and Fatimids

Two great powers in North Africa

Eastern North Africa, conquered by Muslim armies around 700 CE, gave rise to two immensely powerful dynasties – the Aghlabids, who ruled for a century, and the Fatimids, who ruled for more than 200 years.

Until the late 8th century, the Arab Islamic Abbasid dynasty controlled Egypt and North Africa. However, in parts of the empire, a series of local rulers began to govern more or less independently. In 800, Ibrahim ibn al-Aghlab, the commander of a small Abbasid garrison, quelled a rebellion by Arab soldiers and seized the important city of Kairouan. He was rewarded with the province of Tunisia and ruled the region for 12 years, founding the Aghlabid dynasty, paying lip service to the Abbasids but in reality operating independently.

△ **Fatimid goldwork**
This 11th-century pendant shows filigree and cloisonné enamel of birds. It is a rare surviving example of the fine work of Egyptian goldsmiths from the Fatimid era.

Aghlabid rule

Al-Aghlab moved the capital to al-Abbasiya, just outside Kairouan, and built a series of *ribats*, or fortified garrison posts. His successor Ziyadat Allah I (r. 817–38 CE) faced a serious challenge when the *jund*, the troops of Arab descent, rebelled in 824, an uprising that took three years to suppress. In part as an outlet for these disaffected *jund* troops, the Aghlabids invaded Sicily in 827, leading to a Muslim occupation of the island for 200 years.

Aghlabid rule was opulent, financed by a fixed tax that paid for a lavish lifestyle and a series of grand building projects. These included the Great Mosque at Sousse, and reconstruction of the Zitouna Mosque in Tunis and the Great Mosque at Kairouan, all completed in the reign of Abu Ibrahim Ahmed (r. 856–63). However, the Aghlabid emirate descended into tyrannical bloodshed, as Ibrahim II (875–902) massacred *jund* garrisons and put down an Amazigh (Berber) revolt. In 903, Ibrahim's grandson Ziyadat Allah III (r. 903–909) killed his own father, Abdullah II. Ziyadat Allah also went on to murder his brother.

The Fatimids take over

Order was restored by a new dynasty, the Fatimids, whose origins lay with a Shia missionary, Abu Abdullah al-Shii. He had converted the Kutama Amazigh of eastern Algeria, raised them in revolt against the Aghlabids, and by 909 had taken Kairouan. Abu Abdullah was executed by his superior, Ubaydullah al-Mahdi, who declared himself caliph and imposed Shia Islam on Tunisia. In 914, he launched an invasion into Egypt. The Egyptian forces repulsed the attack and Ubaydallah al-Mahdi instead concentrated on securing his power base, building a capital at Mahdia in 916, and invading Idrisid Morocco, an Arab Muslim dynasty (788–974) whose capital Fès he took in 921.

△ **Fatimid miniature**
This painting shows two traders weighing merchandise on a set of scales. Fatimid merchants profited from Egypt's strategic position between Africa and West Asia.

The Fatimids continued the Arab conquest of Sicily, but struggled to hold together their extensive empire. They lost control of northern Morocco to the Umayyad Caliphate of Córdoba between 931 and 973, and faced a serious revolt from 944 by Abu Yazid (known as "the old man on the donkey"), an Amazigh rebel of humble origins who became a spiritual leader and gained support for his opposition to the Fatimids.

Peak of Fatimid power

It took twelve years to put down Abu Yazid's uprising, after which the Fatimids regrouped, partially retaking Algeria in 958 and, under al-Mansur (r. 946–53), building a new capital at al-Mansuriyya south of Kairouan. In 969, Caliph al-Muizz (r. 953–75) ordered the invasion of Egypt. A weakened Ikshidid dynasty of Muslim Turks, which controlled Egypt and Syria at this time, offered little resistance. Al-Muizz's general Jawhar al-Katib had established a new capital at al-Qahira (Cairo) and in 973 the Fatimid court moved to Egypt, never to return.

Control of Tunisia was now handed to Zirid governors (Sanhaja Amazigh from modern-day Algeria), who rapidly installed an independent dynasty. The Fatimids also overran Syria and Palestine and secured peace in Egypt. As part of their campaign to promote Shia Islam, the Fatimids built *madrasas* and mosques in Cairo, including the splendid al-Azhar.

End of the Fatimids

Fatimid rule was briefly threatened in the mid-11th century by the migration of nomadic Arab peoples, the Banu Hilal and Banu Sulaym. After the Fatimids successfully diverted these groups westwards towards Tunisia, they instead wrought devastation on the Zirids.

Infighting, aggravated by famines, led to provinces in the east and far west breaking away, and in 1099, the capture of Jerusalem by the Christian crusaders dealt a devastating blow to Fatimid prestige. In 1073, the caliph al-Mustanşir sent an army officer, Badr al-Jamali, to restore order. Al-Jamali executed dissident commanders and his success established a military regime and reduced the power of the caliphs. In 1171, the Kurdish general Saladin took over the office of vizier and deposed the last Fatimid caliph, putting an end to the dynasty.

> "We will **defend you and protect you** against [enemies]. We will **not let you be harmed**…"

FATIMID COMMANDER JAWHAR'S PROMISE TO THE EGYPTIANS, CITED IN SCHOLAR IDRIS AL-DIN'S *UYUN AL-AKHBAR*, 1467

▽ **Clay plate**
This 12th-century plate from Egypt shows Fatimid art and uses a lustreware technique. Metallic oxide glaze applied before firing leaves a shimmering, yellow-gold surface.

Dancing girl depicted in a sensuous and naturalistic style

The Almoravid and Almohad dynasties

Conquerors of the Western Mediterranean

From the 10th century, several Muslim dynasties emerged across North Africa. While the Fatimid Caliphate, a dynasty of Arab origin, controlled the east and central region, in the west two short-lived but influential powers emerged.

△ **Empire builder**
Possible portrait of Almoravid commander Abu Bakr ibn Umar, from a 15th-century Spanish map. As well as founding Marrakech, ibn Umar spread Islam to the southern edges of the western Sahara.

The Almoravid dynasty – the name deriving from the Arabic *al-Murabitun*, meaning "men of the *ribat*", a fortified place of religious practices – was founded in the 11th century. From the 1040s, a Muslim theologian, Abdallah ibn Yasin, began preaching among the Sanhaja. These nomadic Amazigh (Berber) peoples had until then practised their own religion. Abdallah ibn Yasin's interpretation of Islam emphasized the importance of conquest as a means of spreading the word of the Prophet Muhammad. Among his many supporters was Yahya ibn Umar, leader of the most powerful Sanhaja group, the Lamtuna. Together, Ibn Yasin and Ibn Umar established the Almoravid dynasty.

The Almoravid dynasty
Yahya ibn Umar died in 1056 and Abdallah ibn Yasin in 1059. By this time, the Almoravids controlled the most important trans-Saharan trading cities in the region, Sijilmasa and Aoudaghost, and had conquered most of western North Africa. Yahya ibn Umar's brother, Abu Bakr ibn Umar, founded the city of Marrakech around 1070, making it the imperial

△ **Lighting the way**
This early 12th-century engraved Almoravid lamp shows the fine craftsmanship of which the warlike dynasty was capable. The handle may depict a lion or a wolf.

capital, and from here the Almoravid Empire began to grow. In 1086–87, the Almoravids took control of the *al-Andalus* region of southern Spain and Portugal, and by the early 1100s their empire had penetrated as far south as modern Senegal, covering an area 3,000 km long (1,900 miles) from north to south.

The Almoravids' successes were spectacular but short-lived. Barely a century after the dynasty was formed it collapsed when, in 1147, a new rival in the region – the Almohads – killed the last Almoravid king, Ishaq ibn Ali, and took the capital, Marrakech.

Almohad ascendancy and defeat
The Almohad Caliphate, as it came to be known, had grown out of an earlier rebellion against Almoravid rule by Masmuda Amazigh peoples in the Atlas Mountains. The rebels' leader was Muhammad ibn Tumart, who died around 1130, and whose adherence to Sufism, a mystical branch of Islam, contrasted with the more austere beliefs of the Almoravids.

Having toppled the Almoravids, the Almohads inherited their Western Mediterranean empire in North Africa and Iberia. They administered it by

◁ **Almoravid pavilion**
The exquisitely decorated Qubba al-Ba'adiyyin in Marrakech dates from the early 12th century and is one of the few surviving examples of Almoravid architecture in the city.

Design of lions and harpies
(human-headed birds)

> "When you strive after **much-desired glory**, cease not to aspire until you **reach the stars**."

IBN TUMART, QUOTING 10TH-CENTURY
POET AL-MUTANABBI

operating a huge fleet based at Rabat on the Atlantic coast. Such was the fleet's reputation that the great Muslim warrior Salah al-Din Yusuf ibn Ayyub (commonly known as Saladin) called for its help during the Third Crusade in 1183, and it held its own against major powers such as Pisa, Genoa, and Venice. However, the caliphate's fortunes begin to decline after a land defeat against southern Spain's Christian kingdoms at the Battle of Las Navas de Tolosa in 1212. After a series of revolts in the Almohads' North African heartland, the dynasty's end came when the Banu Marin, an Amazigh people from northern Morocco, captured the capital Marrakech in 1269.

△ **Almoravid shroud**
This fragment of an early 12th-century shroud was made during the Almoravid conquest of southern Spain. Its intricate design is woven with red, green, and light brown silk and gold thread.

All worshippers face the *qibla* wall

The pattern of arcades creates a sense of order

Mats provide a clean, individual space to pray

△ **Inside the prayer hall**
Row upon row of rhythmic horseshoe arches divide the vast prayer hall into 17 naves, capable of accommodating 25,000 worshippers. The central nave leads to a decorative *mihrab*, the focal point for prayer, at the midpoint of the *qibla* wall.

▷ **Inside the courtyard**
The courtyard – centred on an ablutions fountain – provided a calm space for the faithful then, as now, to cleanse and prepare themselves for prayer, in keeping with Muslim practice. It was laid out over a garden belonging to the destroyed Almoravid palace.

The central nave is widest, signifying its importance

The *mihrab* is at the midpoint of the *qibla* wall

The imam and rulers accessed the prayer hall through private chambers

A triangular area shows the difference in alignment

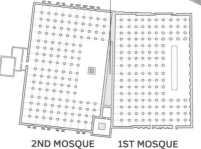

2ND MOSQUE   **1ST MOSQUE**

◁ **The two mosques**
As seen in this plan, both mosques shared one minaret and an almost identical layout, but their orientation differed. The second mosque may have been built to better align with the desired direction of prayer.

The *qibla* wall indicates the direction of prayer

The hall contains 112 columns

Three golden spheres top the minaret

The minaret is 77m (250ft) tall

A ramp allowed the *muezzin* to ride up the tower on horseback to give the call to prayer

The mosque is built from local pink brick and sandstone

Booksellers traded outside the mosque

Koutoubia Mosque

Marrakech, present-day Morocco

In 1147, the Almohad dynasty, an Amazigh (Berber) Muslim people from the Atlas Mountains, captured Marrakech from the Almoravid dynasty. In a show of supremacy, the Almohad ruler, Abd al Mu'min (r. 1130–63), destroyed the Almoravid palace and constructed a great mosque in its place. Within a decade, for reasons that remain unclear, Abd al Mu'min began building a second mosque next to the first. This second mosque, still in use today, became the most important in the Almohad dynasty. Its landmark minaret is quintessentially Almohad, and closely resembles two other great towers: the Giralda in Seville (Spain) and the (unfinished) Hassan Tower in Morocco's modern capital, Rabat. Historically, this district was the booksellers' quarter, hence the name "Koutoubia", from the Arabic for booksellers: *kutubiyyin*.

△ **Intricate stonework**
The ornamental elements on the minaret reappear frequently in Almohad architecture. Each face bears different patterns of horseshoe and polylobed arches – some blind, some open – intricately carved in symmetrical arrangements.

△ **Koutoubia mosques**
This reconstruction depicts the two mosques around 1200. They are believed to have coexisted for several decades before the first mosque was demolished, though it is not clear what function the first mosque served during that time.

MASTERFUL **MINBAR**

In 1137, the Almoravid ruler 'Ali ibn Yūsuf commissioned Andalusian artisans to create a *minbar* (pulpit) for his mosque in Marrakech. They delivered a masterpiece: an eight-stepped wooden structure exquisitely panelled with intricately carved and inlaid patterns and inscriptions using coloured woods and bone. Recognizing its quality, Abd al Mu'min saved it for the Koutoubia Mosque, where, according to historical accounts, it rolled magically into position when needed. Evidence suggests it may have used a counterbalance mechanism, perhaps triggered by the imam's footfall.

MEDIEVAL MINBAR

The Songhai Empire

The rise and fall of one of Africa's great states

After a slow rise to power, the Songhai Empire grew to control the Niger River in West Africa. It became rich on trans-Saharan trade and spread Islam across the region before internal strife weakened it fatally.

The Songhai people emerged in the northwest African kingdom of Gao (also known as al-Kawkaw) around the 9th century. This stretch of the western Sahel, known as the Sudan region, was home to fertile savanna and the Niger River, which offered abundant opportunities for fishing and trade.

Farming, fishing, and war

Songhai society had three divisions of trades: fishermen (*sorko*), hunters (*gabibi* or *gow*), and agriculturists (*do*), who specialized in arable farming and cattle rearing. Although the Songhai gained territory and grew more prosperous in the 10th century, their rise to greatness was gradual. Their heartland, in what is now Mali, was a long way from the gold-producing areas of Bambuk and Bure to the southwest, and they had many rivals.

From the 11th century, the Songhai had to protect their territory from the neighbouring Mandingo (Malinke), Sosso, and Soninke, and in the 14th century, Gao fell under the yoke of the Mali Empire (see pp. 90–91). As the Mali Empire started collapsing in the late 14th century, the Songhai won their independence, but it was only with the defeat of the nearby Mossi, Dogon, and Fulani

during the late 15th century and early 16th century that the kingdom became an empire. Trans-Saharan trade had been significant for centuries, but its extension into territories such as the Hausa Kingdoms, in what is now northern Nigeria, made Songhai a major hub of desert-caravan and river routes connecting North and West Africa.

Sunni the Great

Sunni Ali, who came to the throne in 1464, became the first emperor of the Songhai. Under his reign, the Songhai expanded their land through conquest until they controlled all the major trading ports along the Niger — extending their authority further than the Empire of Mali ever had. Now trade flowed between the salt mines of Taghaza in northern Mali and great commercial cities such as Djenné and Timbuktu.

HISTORIES OF **THE SONGHAI**

The 17th-century chronicles, *Tarikh al-Sudan* ("History of the Sudan") and the *Tarikh al-fattash* ("The Researcher's Chronicle"), are important primary sources for the history of the Songhai Empire. The books were written by Muslim scholars in Timbuktu.

PAGE FROM THE
TARIKH AL-SUDAN

◁ **Archer figure**
This figure of an archer was made on the Niger Delta between the 11th and 17th centuries. The Songhai Empire had a professional army of infantry and cavalry.

"**Ali was always victorious**… his armies were **never defeated**."

THE *TARIKH AL-SUDAN* ON SUNNI ALI

△ **City of scholars**
The fabled city of Timbuktu, shown in a 19th-century European drawing, became an important place of learning during the Mali Empire and remained so under the Songhai.

Fine North African horses were traded for gold, ivory, and the enslaved people who had been captured during the empire's wars of expansion.

In the oral tradition of the *griots* (narrators of those traditions), Sunni Ali is remembered as Sunni Ali Ber, meaning "Sunni the Great", a strong and wise ruler who commanded the powers of magic. But in the histories that Muslim scholars wrote in the 17th century (see box, left), he is depicted as a bloodthirsty tyrant, who was capable of great generosity but also committed numerous acts of cruelty and treated the scholars in Timbuktu with contempt.

The rise of Islam
As the Songhai Empire expanded, its belief system was shifting. Islam had spread from the Mahgreb along the trade routes, and was stronger in the west and in great river cities such as Djenné and Timbuktu, which were key centres of education. But it had not yet become the faith of the state, with pre-Islamic Songhai beliefs a strong force, especially among pastoralists and in the historic Songhai nucleus around Gao.

Sunni Ali followed both Islamic and Songhai beliefs, and sought to balance the two groups, but his son Sunni Dao, who succeeded to the throne in 1492, favoured the pre-Islamic Songhai belief that everything contains a spirit or soul. Only a year later he was deposed by one of his generals, Askia Muhammad I (see pp. 106–107). Askia made Islam the state religion, established Islamic schools and a university at Timbuktu, and encouraged conversion

throughout the empire. In the years that followed, Islam became the basis not just of the state religion, but also of royal authority, spreading its culture and practices to distant lands. Askia conquered the desert trading post of Agadez (in modern-day Niger), fought campaigns against the Hausa Kingdoms and extended the empire west towards the coast.

Power and decline
By now, the empire was at its peak, ruling a vast strip of inland West Africa that took in much of modern Mali, Niger, Mauritania, Nigeria, Senegal, Guinea, Gambia, Burkina Faso, and Côte d'Ivoire, as well as parts of southern Algeria. Timbuktu now rivalled the old Songhai heartland around Gao and the early-16th-century Andalusian traveller Leo Africanus wrote admiringly of its "corn, cattle, milk, and butter… in great abundance" and its "magnificent and well-furnished court".

In the decades that followed, Askia's children and grandchildren tussled for power, as the lack of an internal succession system saw instability weaken the Empire. The Songhai's crucial role in West Africa's gold and salt trade continued through the 16th century, but also made it attractive to other powers. Moroccan raids culminated in an invasion, and in 1591 the country's Saadi Sultanate, equipped with muskets and cannons, crushed the Songhai forces. The remaining Songhai elite fled to the Songhai and Dendi provinces, in southwestern Niger, but would never regain their great empire.

Lance confers high status on the bearer

Hunter's hat

Seated position denotes authority

▷ **Seated hunter**
A Bamana maker crafted this figure of an idealized male leader as early as the 16th century, when the Bamana people were part of the Songhai Empire. The Bamana later founded an empire of their own.

Askia Muhammad I

The Songhai's mightiest emperor

Under Askia Muhammad I's rule, Songhai became the largest empire West Africa had ever seen. Askia established a unique and efficient bureaucracy and made Islam the state religion, transforming West Africa.

△ **Malian manuscript**
This medieval manuscript, written in Arabic and Songhai, comes from Timbuktu. Askia Muhammad was a keen promoter of scientific and Muslim scholarship in the city.

Askia Muhammad was a prominent minister in the late 15th-century court of Sunni Ali, the first king of the Songhai. Ali had expanded his empire from the Songhai heartland in what is now Mali to control much of the area around the Niger River. On Ali's death in 1492, his son, Sunni Dao, succeeded him. But Askia Muhammad desired the throne and challenged the succession. In 1493, his forces defeated the king's armies and he founded the Askia dynasty.

A devout Muslim, Askia took the *Hajj* to Mecca in 1497, building a hostel for Songhai pilgrims and reportedly bringing 300,000 gold pieces with him — a third of which he gave away as alms. He continued to allow non-Muslims to practise their own religions, as they had done under the Sunnis, but he was keen to spread his Islamic faith. At home, he recruited Islamic scholars from Egypt and Morocco, set up centres of learning in cities including Gao, Djenné, and Walata, and enforced the veil for Muslim women.

War and justice
Askia built a large standing army of cavalry and archers, and used it to expand his borders west into what is now Senegal, northeast to the Saharan city of Agadez, in modern Niger, and southeast into the Hausa Kingdoms of Nigeria. The resulting empire was one of the largest Africa had ever seen.

Askia was also an astute administrator. He established an efficient bureaucracy, which was responsible for taxation and justice. He divided the kingdom into provinces with governors to oversee them and set up a council of ministers that included a commander of the fleet, a minister of forests and fisheries, and a master of the court.

This administration, unparalleled in West Africa at the time, allowed Askia to expand Songhai trade across the Sahara, with commerce reaching as far as Europe and Asia. But by the 1520s, Askia was ageing and had become blind. He spent his last years as a powerless witness to dynastic rivalries that weakened his empire. In 1528, one of his sons, Askia Musa, deposed him in a bloodless coup.

△ **The tomb of Askia**
This wood and mud structure, built during Askia's reign, is believed to contain his tomb. The 17-m- (55-ft-) high building includes a mosque that is still used for worship.

c. 1443 Born in the Songhai city of Gao

1493 Askia wins the Battle of Anfao and seizes the throne

c. 1500 Songhai armies capture territory in modern Niger and Burkina Faso

1537 Askia dies and is buried in a tomb that still stands today

1492 Songhai king Sunni Ali dies, and is succeeded by his son, Sunni Dao

1497 Askia takes the *Hajj* to Mecca, staying until 1498

c. 1510 The Songhai fight campaigns against the Fulani in Senegal

1591 The Songhai Empire, weakened by civil war, falls to Moroccan troops

Terracotta horseman

This sculpture from Mali dates to between the 12th and 16th centuries. Successive West African empires developed cavalry, including Wagadou (Ghana) and Mali. Under Askia, the Songhai cavalry reached its peak as a formidable force.

Ornate necklace was a symbol of wealth

Rich caparison (decorative protective covering)

Details painted with red ochre pigment

△ **Mounted warriors**
Heavily armoured cavalry formed the heart of the Bornu army, enabling it to dominate vast areas.

Kanem-Bornu

A major empire in northern Central Africa

Centred around the shores of Lake Chad, the Empire of Kanem-Bornu was one of Africa's longest-lasting states. It dominated the region from the 10th to the 19th century.

△ **Horse protection**
This brass horse harness is ornately worked, an indication of the importance of the cavalry to the Bornu.

The origins of the Kanem state are probably linked to the nomadic Zaghawa people who migrated south from Amazigh (Berber) communities in North Africa around the 7th century. They settled on the edges of the Sahara north of Lake Chad. Their ironworking skills and use of horses enabled them to dominate local communities and control the trading routes that led to the Mediterranean.

Arab travellers, such as al-Yaq'ubi in the 9th century and Ibn al-Nadim in the 10th, wrote that the Zaghawa created a state based on a sacred kingship, with a royal capital at Nijmi northeast of Lake Chad. Towards the end of the 11th century, a Muslim noble named Humai ibn Salamna drove out the ruling Zaghawa dynasty and founded the Sayfawa dynasty that would rule Kanem-Bornu for 770 years, making it one of the world's longest reigning royal houses.

A Muslim state
Although Islam had already reached Kanem, Humai was the first Muslim *mai* (king), and his successor Dunama (r. 1098–1151) performed the *Hajj* to

"Before the **age of our Sultan**, [non-Muslims] used to wander about in the **land of Bornu**... Idris [Alawma] **stopped all this**."

BOOK OF THE BORNU WARS, IBN FARTUWA, 1576

△ **Royal audience**
Visitors to the Bornu court in the 19th century have an audience with the *mai*, who is, as tradition demanded, seated inside a cage made from bamboo.

Mecca three times. Under *Mai* Dunama Dabbalemi (r. 1221–59), Kanem reached its peak, with its borders extended to the Fezzan, an arid region that lay to the north. However, his destruction of the *mune*, a sacred object said to protect the power of the king but which Dabbalemi associated with non-Islamic local religion, angered many of the people and weakened the monarchy. The 13th and 14th centuries were marked by struggles to maintain the Kanem Empire: four *mais* died in war with the Sao, a powerful people to the west, and an equal number fighting Bulala pastoralists from 1377 to 1387. There were also civil wars between the descendants of *Mai* Idris and *Mai* Dawud. By 1387, the court had abandoned Nijmi and fled west across Lake Chad, establishing a new capital at Ngazargamu (in modern-day northern Nigeria).

A new empire

The Sayfawa rulers established the Bornu Empire, although it remained unstable until the accession of *Mai* Ali Gaji (r. 1470–1503), who fortified Ngazargamu. His son Idris Katakarmabe (r. 1507–29) managed to drive the Bulala out of the old Kanem capital, Nijmi. Skirmishes with the Bulala over Kanem continued for a century, leading the Bornu *mais* to seek allies elsewhere, including with the Ottoman commander and *Pasha* of Tripoli, Turgut Reis, in the mid-16th century. Meanwhile, the empire's expansion to the south and west continued with the occupation in 1532 of the Amazigh Sultanate of Agadez in the Air mountains.

The Bornu Empire reached its peak in the reign of Idris Alawma (r. 1570–1619), who conquered the Hausa peoples of northern Nigeria, aided by a camel cavalry and Turkish musketeer recruits. Idris also reformed the administration and integrated local groups who had previously been semi-independent. Less able successors faced challenges from Agadez and the state of Kwararafa in Hausaland, as well as from Tuareg warriors. The last great *mai*, Hajj Ali, defeated attacks on Ngazargamu by both Agadez and Kwararafa in 1668. He was followed by *mais* who struggled with

famines and a declining grip on vital trade routes. A devastating defeat against Mandara rebels from northern Cameroon in 1781 shattered the Bornu army. Then, in 1808, Fulani Muslims, led by Usman dan Fodio (see pp. 194–95), attacked Bornu and proclaimed a jihad (holy war) against non-observant Muslims. *Mai* Dunama Lefiami called for the help of an Islamic scholar, Muhammad al-Kanemi, who saved Bornu by rallying resistance and repelling the Fulani, becoming effective ruler until his death in 1837.

The Sayfawa *mais* remained monarchs in name only until 1846, when al-Kanemi's son Umar deposed the last one and declared himself *shehu* (sheikh). The Bornu Empire struggled on for a few more decades until a Sudanese military leader named Rabih az-Zubayr conquered it in 1893. In 1900, French colonial forces killed Rabih and reestablished the *shehu*. Today, descendants of al-Kanemi still rule the Bornu state, which is located in northeastern Nigeria.

▽ **Fine craftwork**
This highly decorated women's cotton robe was created in Bornu state, Nigeria, and dates from the 19th century.

Brightly coloured silk embroidery

Rise of the Yoruba

An iconic African culture

The Yoruba claim descent from Oduduwa – their founder king. From their beginnings as a highly spiritual, artistic people, this West African ethnic group would create a powerful city-state and worldwide diaspora.

There are around 45–50 million Yoruba-speaking people in West Africa, the vast majority living in Nigeria. The first Yoruba settlement was Ilé-Ifè in the southwest of the country, whose earliest archaeological artefacts date from the 4th century BCE. In Yoruba mythology, the city was built by their founder and first king, Oduduwa. Among those who follow Indigenous beliefs, Ilé-Ifè is the Yoruba's most important religious site and the seat of their spiritual leader, the *Ooni*.

Ilé-Ifè was also a centre of art. During the city-state's "golden age" from 1000–1500, artisans produced some of Africa's finest stone, terracotta, and bronze sculpted heads depicting royal and political figures. In addition, Ilé-Ifè was the only African state south of the Sahara able to manufacture the coloured glass beads that were widely exchanged as currency and were used as decorative items on royal and religious regalia. The city-state's position as sole supplier of these valuable items made Ilé-Ifè wealthy.

Despite its affluence and technological expertise, Ilé-Ifè declined due to political divisions and emigration. By the 17th century, the wealth and power had moved away to other city-states such as Ilesha, and, especially, Oyo (see pp. 112–13). Founded around 1300, Oyo was the largest and the most powerful Yoruba city-state by the mid-18th century, its empire covering southern Nigeria, the Kingdom of Dahomey, and parts of Benin.

Power and trade

Yoruba culture centred around large towns and cities rather than dispersed villages. The centralized power structure, based around divine kingship, that had developed in Ilé-Ifè was used in many other city-states. Each Yoruba state was organized slightly differently, but most were ruled by a powerful – but not absolute – monarch, or *oba*, who was assisted by a prime minister, an administrative body, and an advisory council of elders and religious officials. Trade brought goods and revenue, with salt, leather, horses,

△ **Mythical monument**
This 5.5-m- (18-ft-) tall granite stele in Ilé-Ifè is known as "Oranmiyan's Staff". Oranmiyan was the son of Oduduwa and the founder of the Oyo dynasty.

▷ **Capturing a king's likeness**
This copper alloy mask is said to represent the Ilé-Ifè ruler Obalufon II, who reigned in the 14th century. It was probably used in religious rites.

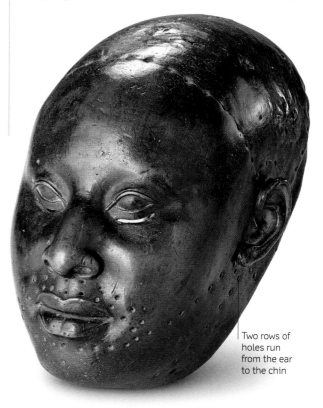

Two rows of holes run from the ear to the chin

> "All the [peoples] of the **Yoruba Nation** trace their **origin from Oduduwa** and the City of Ilé-Ifè."

S.O. JOHNSON, *THE HISTORY OF THE YORUBAS*, 1959

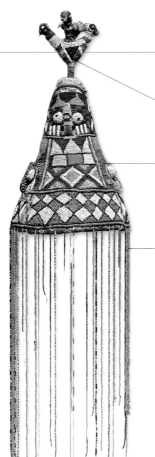

A bird connects the *Ooni* to Oduduwa

Cap is divided into three sections representing youth, adolescence, and old age

Beaded veil hides the *Ooni*'s face

◁ **Ceremonial crown**
The *Aare* – sacred beaded crowns – symbolize power and authority for the Yoruba. The *Ooni* of Ilé-Ifè still wears a headdress like this during festivals.

kola nuts, ivory, and textiles bought and sold among the Yoruba and their neighbours. Humans were also trafficked extensively, as captives in warfare and as part of the Atlantic slave trade (see pp. 162–63) that saw at least one million Yoruba transported to the Americas.

An enduring culture

The city-states began to decline in the late 18th century. Most could not resist the incursions into their territory by the Muslim Fulani people, whose Sokoto Caliphate became West Africa's dominant empire in the late 18th century (see pp. 194–95). In 1900, most of the Yoruba were absorbed into the British Empire's Southern Nigeria Protectorate.

Today, the Yoruba are Nigeria's second-largest ethnic group, with around 20 per cent of the population. Yoruba culture remains important in the diaspora, particularly Brazil, where the popular Candomblé religion blending Catholic, Yoruba, and other African ritualistic practices has several million followers.

▷ **Yoruba deity**
This 12th–15th century copper alloy head represents Olokun, the Yoruba deity of the sea, wealth, and glass bead-making – Ilé-Ifè's profitable and prestigious industry.

Decorative headdress with rosette

Striped facial markings, or "scarifications"

The Oyo Empire

Yoruba's most powerful state

The Yoruba state of Oyo was one of many powerful competing kingdoms in West Africa. From the 17th century until the beginning of the 19th, Oyo held sway, thanks to its innovative political structure and military strength.

According to Yoruba history, Oranmiyan (sometimes called Oranyan), the son of Oduduwa, founder of the Yoruba people (see pp. 110–11), established the city of Oyo-Ile around 1300 CE and his descendants expanded it into the Oyo Empire. Historical evidence shows that Yoruba farmers in southwest Nigeria set up an organized political entity around the 9th century and cemented Oyo-Ile's status as a metropolis between the 13th and the 15th centuries. By the late 15th century, as a result of its stable political system and a strong army, Oyo's influence was growing.

Dynamic statecraft

Like other Yoruba states and kingdoms, Oyo was ruled by an *oba*, or king. In Oyo, the king was known as the *alaafin* ("the owner of the palace"). As the head of state, the *alaafin* was owed both the loyalty of the people and the tribute of goods and army recruits from local chieftains and leaders of conquered territories. The *alaafin*'s power was not absolute, however. A privy council, the *Oyo Mesi*, consisted of seven of the state's most powerful noblemen and was headed by a prime minister, or *bashorun*. No *alaafin* could assume the throne without the *Oyo Mesi*'s approval, and any *alaafin* who ignored their advice – and whose behaviour

threatened the empire – could be banished, forced to abdicate, or compelled to die by suicide. There were *alaafins* in Oyo into the 21st century. The power-sharing government exercised authority through its army.

Some time around 1535, a devastating invasion by the Nupe people to the east forced Oyo's rulers to abandon Oyo-Ile and resettle at Igboho for about 80 years. They reorganized their state along militaristic lines. Its large, semi-standing army was supplied with arms and armour that included elephant- and ox-hide shields and formidable 2.7 m (9 ft) swords. Oyo was one of a few states to adopt the use of cavalry, which gave it a competitive advantage against infantry-only enemies. By the early 17th century, Oyo had retaken all of the territory lost to the Nupe, including the capital Oyo-Ile, to which a triple ring of walls and earthen barriers was added. The walls stood up to 7.5 m (24 ft 6 in) high, with an outer wall 21 km (13 miles) long.

Expansion and destablization

From the early 17th century, Oyo State began to build an empire. Oyo had subdued the Nupe and taken control of the territory occupied by the other Yoruba towns and city-states. It was also receiving tribute from the Kingdom of Benin (see pp. 128–29) in the southeast in return for not attacking it, and had conquered the Kingdom of Dahomey (see pp. 178–79) to the west. In 1764, Oyo led a coalition of armies that repelled an invasion by the powerful Asante Empire (see pp. 190–91). Oyo's territorial expansion gave it control of the southern end of the trade route from North Africa to what is now the Nigerian coast, allowing it to collect vast sums in taxes from merchants. These taxes were

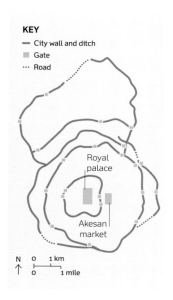

KEY
— City wall and ditch
▪ Gate
··· Road

Royal palace

Akesan market

N
0   1 km
0   1 mile

△ **City defences**
The multiple concentric walls at Oyo-Ile comprised ditches and embankments, and were constructed during the heyday of the Oyo Empire for protection against attacks.

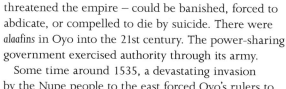

◁ **Oyo palace**
The thatched-roof palace of the *alaafin* of Oyo was a multi-room and multi-chamber building. The complex housed the royal family and palace administrators.

> "**Oyo** had reached the **zenith** of its territorial **expansion** by the middle of the **18th century**."

PROFESSORS ARIBIDESI USMAN AND TOYIN FALOLA, 2019

Edun ara (sacred stone) embedded in battle-axe

▷ **Thunder god**
This *ose Sango* (Shango's staff) represents the Shango deity – the god of thunder and fire, who was worshipped during the 18th century. His might is symbolized by a double-edged battle-axe.

Ayan (drummer)

Worshipper of Sango

△ **Royal portrait**
Wearing a veiled beaded crown and holding an *irukere* (fly whisk), Adeniran Adeyemi II, *alaafin* of Oyo State, poses with his son in 1950. His political sympathies led to exile in 1954.

paid in money – usually cowrie shells – or as tributes, with customs officials taking a portion of the traded goods, which included gold, ivory, leather, cloth, and salt. Enslaved people were also traded.

It was during the Oyo's expansionist period that the annual Bere festival was initiated. Taking place in January or February, it both celebrated the yearly harvest of valuable *bere* grass in Yorubaland and served as a means by which vassal states paid tribute to the *alaafin*. They did this by bringing bundles of *bere* grass to the capital to re-thatch the roof of the royal palace. Another important source of produce for Oyo was its colony of Ede-Ile (south of Oyo-Ile), whose reserves of clay were used for pottery and iron ore for smelting.

Oyo's power began to wane in the early 19th century, when its regions and vassal states began to chafe against central control. The destabilization this caused was followed in the 1830s by attacks from Muslim jihadists known as the Fulani – who would go on to establish the Sokoto Caliphate (see pp. 194–95). As Oyo's empire dissolved, a number of Oyo refugees established a new city-state to the south, at Ibadan. This became Oyo's new power base, from which it was able to reassert a small degree of its former influence. However, by the late 19th century, the European-controlled slave trade further weakened the Yoruba states. In 1900, Britain forced Yorubaland – including the Oyo territories – into its Southern Nigeria Protectorate. Oyo still exists today as a thriving city, with a majority Yoruba population, within Oyo State.

The Igbo states
A unique civilization of the Niger Delta

Igbo people lived in egalitarian village-based communities in the forests of southeastern Nigeria. This distinctive culture traded widely, developed exceptional craft making abilities, and was known for freeing enslaved people.

Around a fifth of Nigeria's population today is made up of Igbo people, with sizable groups in nearby Cameroon, Gabon, and Equatorial Guinea. But while the Igbo have a shared language, they have never formed a single nation.

Archaeological discoveries – particularly jewellery, ceramics, and finely worked bronze items – from the town of Igbo-Ukwu in the south of Nigeria suggest that a sophisticated Igbo society existed from at least the 9th century CE. Communities to the east and west of the Niger River formed groups made up of several villages, with many Igbo people living as subsistence farmers, cultivating crops of nutritious root vegetables such as cassava, yams, and taro. These communities spoke different dialects, and today the Igboid language has several dialects including Delta Igbo, Enuani Igbo, Ika Igbo, Ikwerre, and Ukwuani.

Igbo political organization was broadly democratic, and accounts from Portuguese traders – who first arrived in the region in the 15th century – describe groups governed by consultative assemblies of the common people, led by councils of elders. Discussions took place in the market square and the aim was to reach a consensus on local disputes. In these communities there was no "ruler", though elders were male and the position was generally passed on to other male relatives.

Igbo culture
Glass beads from the Middle East, palm-leaf textiles, and bronze artefacts – including cups, pendants, and swords – found in Igbo-Ukwu suggest technological sophistication and wide trade links. Symbols called *nsibidi*, drawn on gourds, drinking vessels, and houses, conveyed information about sexual relationships, land and property, or local crimes and journeys. The Igbo developed a calendar with four days in a week, seven weeks in a month, and thirteen months in a calendar year, with the thirteenth month having an extra day.

Unlike many West African peoples, the Igbo did not practise slavery for much of their history. They did operate a system of indentured servitude, but the differences in status between the free people

△ **Igbo terracotta statue**
This 19th- or 20th-century figurine shows a woman holding a child. Igbo culture featured expressive statues known as *ntekpe* (meaning "children of the shrine"), which are linked with healing and worship.

"Among **the Igbo**… **proverbs** are the **palm oil** with which **words are eaten**."

CHINUA ACHEBE, *THINGS FALL APART*, 1958

◁ **Igbo ceremonial dress**
Igbo people are seen here in a photograph from the early 20th century wearing ceremonial dress, including headdresses, feathered pieces, and tall metal leg bands.

and servants appear to have been limited. Olaudah Equiano, an Igbo man who was forced into slavery in the Americas in the 18th century, reports in his memoir of the experience (see box, right) that the servants did not do more work than the rest of the community, and had the same clothing and food, though they were not permitted to eat with people who were free-born.

Kingdoms and conquest

In the late medieval period, increasingly centralized states developed. The neighbouring empire of Benin, which reached its peak in the 16th century, ruled over some of the western Igbo people. However, the Igbo formed several kingdoms, especially in the eastern regions. According to oral tradition, the kingdom of Nri was established around the 9th century, and had political and religious dominion over about a third of Igbo territory by the 17th century. The state, ruled by priest-kings called *eze nri*, who managed trade, was known for setting enslaved people free. Its artists produced many exceptional bronzes that have survived to this day (see pp. 116–17).

By this time, other Igbo-dominated communities, including Onitsha and Arochukwu, had kings or priest-kings. The European demand for enslaved people to work in the Americas from the 16th century had led to conflict and territorial shifts, and the Aro people of Arochukwu fought a series of campaigns against the neighbouring Ibibio people in the southeastern region of modern-day Nigeria in the 17th and 18th centuries. Nri populations declined, while the Aro and other nearby Igbo and non-Igbo communities traded in increasing numbers of enslaved people.

Igbo people were also captured and enslaved by the Efik people, who had settled in the Cross River Delta, near the border with Cameroon. The area, which was

OLAUDAH EQUIANO

In 1789, an Igbo man published a memoir that helped end slavery. *The Interesting Narrative of the Life of Olaudah Equiano* describes Equiano's youth in Igboland in the 1740s and '50s, his capture, and his life as an enslaved person in Britain, North America, and the Caribbean. As the first popular "slave narrative", it made a significant contribution to the abolitionist cause. Equiano went on to buy his freedom, and returned to London, where he married. He died in 1797, but his memoir has been repeatedly reprinted and adapted.

known as Old Calabar, became a major port for enslaved people, and was governed by the Ekpe (Leopard) society, made up of wealthy Efik men.

British influence

In 1807, Britain, which had shipped large numbers of enslaved people to its colonies, prohibited slavery and put pressure on other nations to do the same. As the trade declined, British influence grew, and European merchants established trading posts in Igboland, where the plentiful palm trees were a ready supply of oil.

Many people converted to Christianity, but Igbo identity remained strong. After Nigeria gained its independence from Britain in 1960, the Igbo-dominated state of Biafra, in southeastern Nigeria, went on to declare its independence from Nigeria in 1967. Nigeria crushed and reabsorbed the state in 1970, and many Igbo have since felt marginalized by Nigeria's Hausa and Yoruba majorities. Igbo nationalists continue their struggle for recognition through celebrations of Igbo culture and calls for increased autonomy.

△ **Igbo woman**
This photograph of an Igbo woman wearing brass anklets was taken in 1922 by British anthropologist Northcote Thomas. Women played a key role in trading in the Igbo marketplace.

Surface is decorated with carved symbols

▷ **Brass anklet**
Dating from around 1930, this is an Igbo brass anklet or *ogba*. Anklets were a status symbol for young Igbo women. They were worn in pairs, with smaller anklets on the lower leg and larger ones towards the knee.

Nri bronzes

Fine decorative craftwork

The Nri culture, which developed among the Igbo of eastern Nigeria around the 9th century CE, created a series of exquisite bronzes. Excavated mainly from three sites at the town of Igbo Ukwe, these artefacts employed a sophisticated version of the lost wax technique (see pp. 132–33) using latex.

◁ **Bowl on stand**
Produced during the 9th or 10th century, this is a leaded bronze bowl resting on top of a bronze stand. It is decorated with small raised coils.

Fine exterior decoration

▷ **Fly whisk handle**
A small bronze figure riding an animal (probably a horse) sits atop a base, which was fitted to a fly whisk. The oversized human figure has scarification marks to indicate high status.

Scarification marks

Inward sloping rim with spiral pattern

Lip on which to rest the altar

Four rows of loops indicate hair or headdress

Decorative beading

△ **Altar stand**
Carved with snakes, frogs, female figures, and male figures with wavy hair and wearing two necklaces, this open cylinder measuring 27 cm (10.5 in) in height was an altar stand.

△ **Pendant**
This ornament in the shape of a human head is 8 cm (3 in) high, with a loop for attaching to a pendant. The oblique lines on the face indicate scarification.

△ **Roped pot**
Cast in two pieces and standing 32 cm (12.5 in) high, this water pot is slightly oval-shaped. It is decorated with raised lines and an elaborate rope-like design of two intertwining strands.

▷ **Ceremonial bowl**
All cast in one piece, with a single handle on one side, this bowl is 26 cm (10 in) in diameter. It is decorated with patterns of triangles and quatrefoils.

Underside of the bowl decorated with three bands of quatrefoil patterns

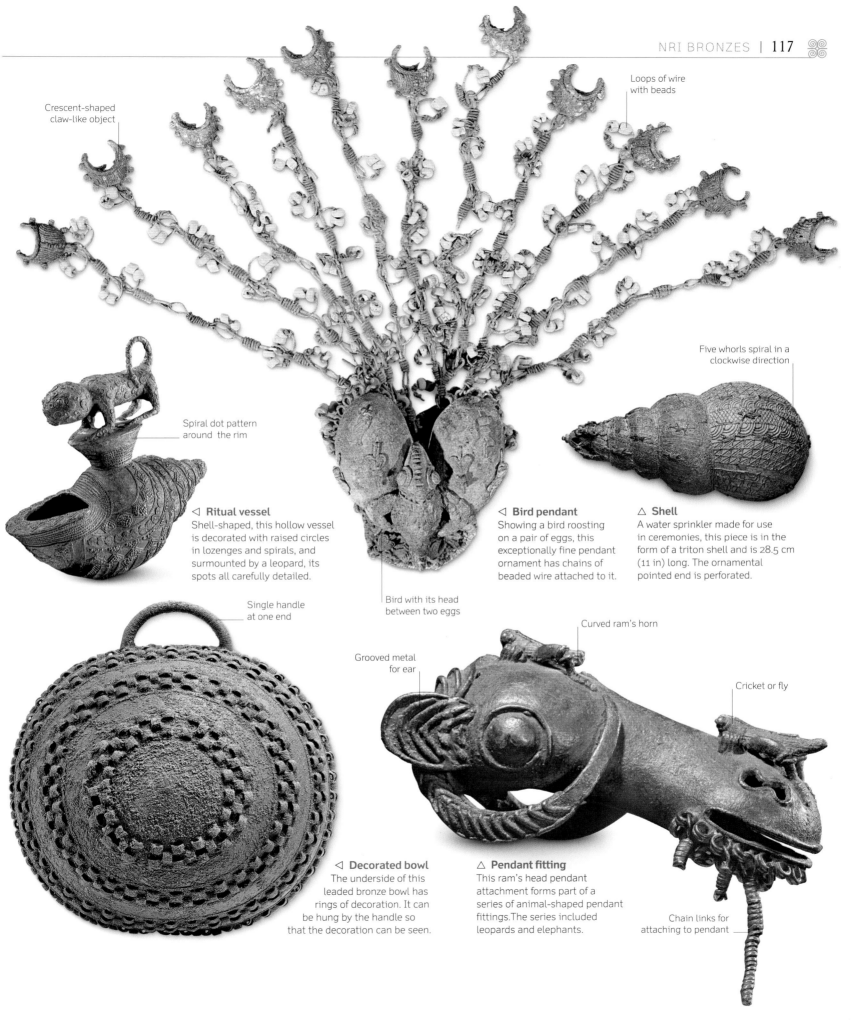

Crescent-shaped claw-like object

Loops of wire with beads

Spiral dot pattern around the rim

Five whorls spiral in a clockwise direction

◁ Ritual vessel
Shell-shaped, this hollow vessel is decorated with raised circles in lozenges and spirals, and surmounted by a leopard, its spots all carefully detailed.

◁ Bird pendant
Showing a bird roosting on a pair of eggs, this exceptionally fine pendant ornament has chains of beaded wire attached to it.

△ Shell
A water sprinkler made for use in ceremonies, this piece is in the form of a triton shell and is 28.5 cm (11 in) long. The ornamental pointed end is perforated.

Bird with its head between two eggs

Single handle at one end

Curved ram's horn

Grooved metal for ear

Cricket or fly

◁ Decorated bowl
The underside of this leaded bronze bowl has rings of decoration. It can be hung by the handle so that the decoration can be seen.

△ Pendant fitting
This ram's head pendant attachment forms part of a series of animal-shaped pendant fittings. The series included leopards and elephants.

Chain links for attaching to pendant

Medieval Ethiopia: the Zagwe and Solomonids

East Africa's Christian empires

The East African kingdom of Aksum was replaced by the Zagwe dynasty, which in turn succumbed to the Solomonids. This Orthodox Christian empire fended off several Islamic incursions and the dynasty reigned until 1974.

△ **King of kings**
In this colourful 15th-century Ethiopian icon, King Gebre Meskel Lalibela is shown on horseback and carrying a spear.

Much of modern-day Ethiopia and Eritrea is made up of the ancient kingdom of Aksum (see pp. 62–63), which arose in the 2nd century CE. Aksum's dominance ended between the 8th and 12th centuries, when the Zagwe people assumed control of the kingdom's territory.

The Zagwe heartland was northern Ethiopia's Lasta Mountains. On seizing power, the Zagwe moved the kingdom's capital from Aksum to Roha (sometimes called Adefa). How the Zagwe deposed the Aksumites is not clear, and the names of the dynasty's earliest rulers are lost to history. The most notable Zagwe king was Gebre Meskel Lalibela (r. 1181–1221). The Zagwe had carved 11 extraordinary Christian churches into the rocks at Roha (see pp. 122–23). Legend says that the churches were built in one night during Lalibela's reign, though historians agree that they were actually built over the course of the Zagwe dynasty. The capital city was renamed Lalibela in honour of the king and it became an important pilgrimage site.

The Zagwe Kingdom's economy was based on farming, but this was supplemented by trade in ivory, gold, and enslaved people with states around the Arabian Gulf. Much of this trading took place in the Red Sea port of Dahlak Island and later at Zeila in the Gulf of Aden.

According to most accounts of Zagwe's history, the dynasty's end came about as a result of regional unrest and palace intrigues, which weakened the last (or, in some sources, penultimate) Zagwe ruler, Yitbarek. He was defeated and killed at the Battle of Gaynt Qirqos in 1270 by a prince of the Amhara people of northwest Ethiopia named Yekuno Amlak. Yekuno established the Solomonic dynasty, which would reign for 700 years.

King Solomon's heirs
Yekuno Amlak claimed descent from Ethiopia's first emperor, Menelik I, the supposed son of King Solomon and the Queen of Sheba – this

> "The excellent and **hallowed**... glorified and blessed, **wearer of purity**..."

DESCRIPTION OF KING LALIBELA, *GADLA LALIBELA* (ACTS OF LALIBELA)

Symmetrical latticework design

◁ **Sign of faith**
This early 15th-century copper alloy cross was designed to be used in religious processions, and to ward off evil spirits.

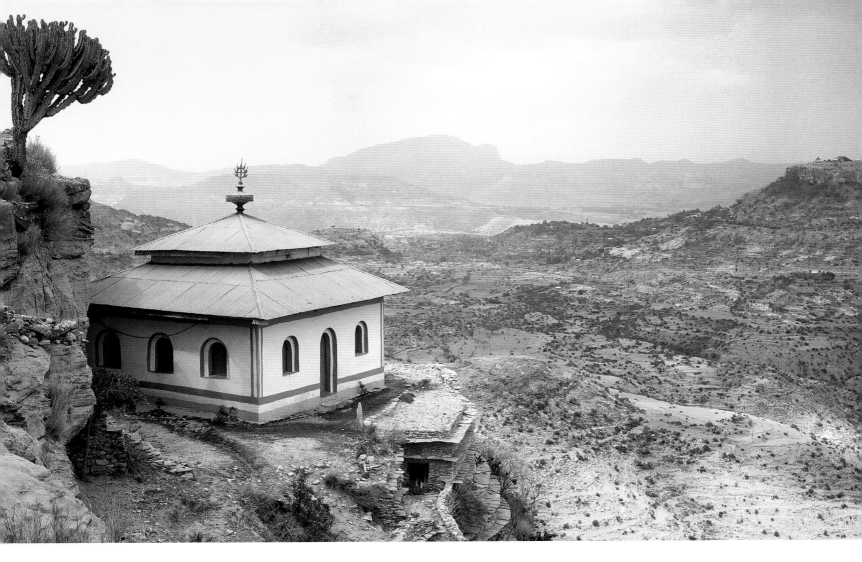

△ **Christian place of worship**
The Debre Damo Monastery on a mountain in northern Ethiopia is only accessible by rope. It dates from the 6th century, indicating how long the Christian faith has existed in the area.

is where the name "Solomonic" came from. The Solomonids' territory expanded and contracted over the centuries, but their stronghold always remained the highlands in northern Ethiopia. For this reason, and because of the Solomonids' strict adherence to the Ethiopian Orthodox Church, the state Yekuno Amlak established was also known as the Christian Highland Kingdom. To ensure the new state's stability, after each Solomonic king named his chosen heir all other possible claimants to the throne were imprisoned for life in a mountain fortress called Amba Geshen in northern Ethiopia.

Initially, the dynasty had no capital city. Instead, it set up what the 14th-century Arab historian Al-Umari called "tent capitals", moving the royal court from place to place. This was in part an effort to incorporate newly conquered territories in the north towards Beja and south towards Berara into the Solomonids' expansionist empire. The most successful Solomonic ruler was Amda Seyon I (r. 1314–44), who annexed regions to the north and south of the highland heartlands, as well as land along the Red Sea coast.

These last conquests were part of the Christian Solomonids' long-running conflicts with the emerging Islamic sultanates of East Africa (see pp. 146–47) such as Adal (incorporating areas of modern Somalia and Sudan) and Ifat (parts of modern-day Ethiopia, Djibouti, and Somaliland). Religious rivalries and trade disputes led to two centuries of intermittent warfare, which ended in 1543 when the Solomonids were able to fend off an attempted conquest by Ahmad ibn Ibrahim al-Ghazi of the Adal Sultanate. They were only able to do this, however, with help from the Portuguese. This was a sign that their empire was in decline and that Europeans were playing an ever more active role in African affairs.

By the mid-16th century, the Solomonids' best days had already passed, although later rulers such as Fasiledes would temporarily revive the empire's fortunes, building a permanent capital city at Gondar (see pp. 120–21) in 1636, for example. The dynasty continued to reign until 1974.

△ **Yekuno Amlak**
This wall portrait may show the Solomonic king, Yekuno Amlak. He is shown holding symbols of his kingship and his Orthodox Christian faith.

Cherubic angel is one of 123 that decorate the ceiling

Wooden beam supports

Murals show the evangelists Matthew, Mark, Luke, and John

St George, slaying the dragon

The Trinity: God the Father, Jesus the Son, and the Holy Spirit

△ **Illustrated shrine**
Gondar's Debre Birhan Selassie Church was built by Fasiledes' grandson, Emperor Eyasu II. It was damaged by lightning and rebuilt in the 1880s. Almost every surface in its interior is covered in murals depicting stories from the Bible.

The splendour of Gondar

A city fit for royalty

Founded by Emperor Fasiledes in the 17th century, Gondar was the capital of the Ethiopian Empire for two centuries. This wealthy and cosmopolitan city became known for its stone architecture, including a royal castle and many churches.

For centuries, Ethiopia's emperors moved their court around the country in great processions, exploiting the best agricultural land and forests for firewood. By 1636, Fasiledes (r. 1632–67) decided a permanent capital would better allow him to conduct the affairs of government and manage his growing empire.

The chosen place was Gondar, which sat on a high, fertile plain, close to the caravan routes running to and from modern-day Sudan and the Red Sea. At its height in the 17th and 18th centuries, Gondar had a population of 10,000 people, many of them traders, artisans, and court officials. Its greatest architectural treasure is the Fasil Ghebbi ("the Royal Enclosure"), a complex of palaces, fortresses, churches, a swimming pool, and other buildings. Much of the compound was built under Fasiledes, but significant portions were constructed by the Empress Mentewab in the mid-18th century. These include the castle that bears her name and a grand banqueting hall.

Gondar was the capital of a Christian empire, with nobles and wealthier residents occupying the Qagn Bet district. Those who practised other faiths tended to live in their own areas: Muslims occupied the Addis Alem quarter, while many of Ethiopia's large population of Jews occupied the Kayla Mayda neighbourhood.

Into the present

Gondar was replaced as Ethiopia's capital by the eastern city of Mekele in the 1880s, but remains an important religious centre and popular tourist destination. Today, Fasil Ghebbi is a UNESCO World Heritage Site, in recognition of the Royal Enclosure's variety of finely detailed Nubian, Indian, Arab, and Baroque buildings and artistic styles.

△ **Empire-builder**
No contemporary images of Fasiledes exist. This stamp, designed by 20th-century Ethiopian artist Afewerk Tekle, depicts him beside the capital city he created.

◁ **Palatial surroundings**
Fasiledes' Castle is the most intact building in the Fasil Ghebbi ("Royal Enclosure"). It stands 32 m (105 ft) tall, with a crennelated parapet and four towers topped by egg-shaped domes.

Bete Giyorgis, Lalibela

The church of Bete Giyorgis (House of St George) in northern Ethiopia was hewn out of volcanic rock 800 years ago. The area in the Amhara region, 600 km (370 miles) north of Addis Ababa, is named after King Lalibela (r. c. 1181–1221). Eleven rock-hewn churches were built there during the Zagwe dynasty – and according to legend, all built during Lalibela's reign. Their names recall those of the biblical Jerusalem: House of Golgotha and House of St Michael and Bethlehem, for example. Bete Giyorgis is cruciform in shape and, like all the churches, was carved from the top down using chisels, axes, and other types of blades.

The Ayyubids, Mamluks, and Ottomans

Three major empires in Egypt

A succession of great empires ruled medieval Egypt. The Ayyubids made Cairo the capital of the Arab world, before the Mamluks rose in the 13th century, and the Ottomans expanded Egypt's borders and strengthened its economy.

△ **Muhammad Ali**
This oil painting of Ottoman *pasha* Ali from 1841 is by French artist Auguste Couder. Regarded as "the great modernizer" of Egypt, Ali took power from the Mamluks and brought in economic as well as military reforms.

The Fatimid Caliphate, which followed Shia Islam, had conquered Egypt in 969 CE. However, by the 12th century it was riven by internal disputes and weakened by campaigns against Christian Crusaders, paving the way for its fall to the Ayyubid dynasty.

The Ayyubids

Syrian general Salah al-Din Yusuf ibn Ayyub, known in English as Saladin, joined a military expedition to Egypt led by his uncle Shirkuh. Saladin assassinated the Fatimid caliph, prevented the Frankish rulers taking Egypt, and on the death of Shirkuh was appointed vizier in 1169. He abolished the Fatimid Caliphate in 1171, established the Ayyubid dynasty, and announced that the region would return from Shia to Sunni Islam. Saladin enjoyed great military success, defeating the Crusaders in 1187 and reclaiming Jerusalem for Islam. He united Muslim-controlled territories in Egypt and the Middle East into an Ayyubid empire, declaring himself sultan, a secular title, rather than caliph. Under Ayyubid rule, canals were dug to irrigate farmland, the profitable Red Sea trade grew, and banking developed. In Cairo, *madrasas* (Islamic schools) and hospitals were built, science flourished, and the city became the intellectual centre of the Islamic world.

Saladin was succeeded by his brother al-Adil, who largely continued his policies, in 1198. The Ayyubid Empire was not a centralized state: instead, it was a

Cupola of the great Ummayad Mosque

▷ **A Mamluk welcome**
This Italian painting shows an unnamed Mamluk governor (seated) receiving a Venetian consul – Niccolò Malipiero (wearing red) – and his retinue in Damascus in 1511.

coalition of principalities, ruled by family members. Under Sultan al-Kamil (r. 1218–38), the Ayyubids ceded Jerusalem to the Crusaders and made a peace in 1229, which lasted for 10 years. However, remaining an independent state required a strong military, and the sultanate relied on Mamluks, enslaved people from the Eurasian steppe who had converted to Islam and trained as professional soldiers. As their numbers grew, Mamluks became an increasingly powerful caste.

The Mamluks

Ayyubid sultan al-Salih Ayyub was killed in another crusade and by 1250, a rebel group of Mamluks had set their own sultan, a general named Aybeg, on the throne. Over the next decade, armies of the Mongol Empire (which reached across Asia into northern Europe) swept through the Arabian Peninsula, sacking Baghdad in 1258, but in 1260, an Egyptian Mamluk army defeated them, bolstering Mamluk legitimacy. The Mamluks would rule Egypt for almost 300 years. Artisans and scholars who had fled Mongol attacks came to Egypt, and mosques and *madrasas* were built, cementing Cairo's status as an Islamic cultural centre.

Egypt prospered as the leading power in the Arab world. Islam continued to spread, and Egypt's substantial Coptic Christian minority were persecuted, although many Copts continued to hold key roles in government bureaucracy. However, the transition of power from one Mamluk sultan to the next was often violent, and by the 15th century, plagues and poor governance took their toll on the kingdom.

The Ottomans

Relations between Turkey's Ottoman Empire and the Mamluks had long been adversarial, with both states vying for control of the spice trade and the holy cities of Islam (Mecca, Medina, and Jerusalem). In 1517, the ascendant Ottomans conquered Egypt, as well as Mamluk territory in the Middle East (Syria). Mamluk culture and social organization persisted at a regional level, but the ruler of Egypt was a viceroy or *pasha* appointed by the Ottoman sultan in Istanbul and answerable to him. Turkish rule seems to have improved administration and the economy, and Egypt became a

major source of revenue for the Ottomans, although its cultural achievements faded. In the 1550s, its southern boundary was pushed into Nubia (in modern-day Sudan), and the port of Massawa (now in Eritrea) was taken from the Portuguese, helping to ensure Ottoman dominance of Red Sea trade.

While most early *pashas* were Turks, the Mamluks continued to be an elite within Egyptian society and grew to wield increasing power. By the early 18th century, Ottoman authority was limited to recognizing the autonomy of the ruling Mamluk faction in exchange for a guarantee of annual payments to Istanbul.

In 1798, the French seized Egypt, but were ejected by British and Ottoman troops, and in 1805 Ottoman commander Muhammad Ali seized power. He reformed the civil service and expanded Egyptian territory. The state was only nominally Ottoman but Ali believed he was powerful enough to challenge the sultan, and he conquered Ottoman Syria in 1831. Ali's successors became increasingly subject to European interventions, and in 1882 Egypt became a British protectorate.

The central emblem shows an eagle

▷ **Eagle chalice**
This 13th-century chalice probably dates from the late Ayyubid or early Mamluk period. Its heavy gilding and fluted body are typical of the time.

"So many of the **high-ranking** about me have discarded **mercy** as a **weakness**."

SALADIN

Nomads: the Bedouin, Tuareg, and Maasai

Nomadic peoples of the Sahara and East Africa

The Bedouin and the Tuareg made the Sahara their own, while the Maasai dominated the dry savanna of the Great Lakes. Together, these roaming pastoralists have helped shape African history and cultures.

The Sahara has not always been an arid desert (see pp. 20–21). Around 10,000 years ago, lush, green conditions supported Stone Age cultures, with a large population of nomadic pastoralists and sedentary agriculturalists. Around 5,000 years ago, as the climate grew drier, the desert expanded and the population decreased. However, in the thousands of years since, several peoples – including the Tuareg and Bedouin – have adapted to life here. These nomads were primarily pastoralists, relying on their herds of livestock to provide them with food and income. They also practised some forms of agriculture, such as growing dates and other fruits, and vegetables including okra and aubergines.

Mobile populations

The Tuareg are descended from Amazigh (Berber) peoples who have inhabited North Africa for thousands of years. In the first few centuries CE, the Tuareg are believed to have spread south from what is now Morocco into the Sahara. As Arab peoples arrived from the Middle East from the 8th century onwards, the Tuareg converted to Islam and moved deeper into the desert and the Sahel that borders it to the south. Many lived in tents or small villages as semi-nomadic pastoralists, with groups controlling trade routes across the desert and raising cattle such as zebu.

From around the 11th century, the Bedouin migrated from the Middle East into North Africa; today, they inhabit a wide region stretching from northern Mauritania to Egypt. Their herd animals – goats, sheep, cattle, and camels – shaped their movements, with many moving from farmland into the desert in the winter. The Bedouin fought the existing Amazigh population, occupying crucial desert oases and spreading Arabic and Islam.

To the east, the Maasai are believed to have originated in the Nile Valley of what is now South Sudan, on the Sahara's edge. They spread throughout the semi-arid plains of the Rift Valley region of Tanzania and Kenya, using spears and *orinka* (throwing clubs) to dominate the area of fertile grasslands. They shared a language, *maa*, with some local groups living as semi-nomadic pastoralists and hunters, and others following their cattle in a fully nomadic life, travelling long distances in search of pasture and water.

Trading cultures

The Bedouin, Maasai, and Tuareg have played a major role in the histories of North and East Africa, thanks in part to their ability to survive in arid environments. The Bedouin and Tuareg were integral to the trans-Saharan trade in gold, spices, salt, ivory, kola nuts, and cowrie shells, as well as enslaved people (see pp. 88–89). Camels were introduced from the Middle East in antiquity and became increasingly common after the 5th century CE. These animals can carry

△ **Tuareg cross**
These crosses, also known as Agadez crosses after the Nigerien city of the same name, are made by the Tuareg people. This example bears Arabic inscriptions from the Qu'ran.

◁ **Desert nomad**
The cartographer of the 1375 "Catalan Atlas" depicts a turbaned nomad, possibly a Tuareg, on a camel. Next to him is a tented encampment.

heavier loads than horses, and their adaptations to arid conditions allowed the nomads to travel further, as well as exploit camel milk and wool. As empires rose, particularly in West Africa, the nomads of the desert opened up new routes across the Sahara.

The cultures of these nomadic peoples have also enriched Africa. The Bedouin are known for their oral poetry, *nabati*, which dates to at least the 14th century and addresses a wide range of subjects including history, eulogies, social commentary, and riddles. Maasai culture maintains a focus on cattle and martial pride, with its acrobatic *adumu*, or jumping dance, performed at weddings, religious rites, and other significant occasions. The Tuareg are famous as makers of weapons and jewellery, such as Tuareg cross pendants, as well as music, which has found modern expression through the "desert blues" of acts such as Mali's Tinariwen.

Nomads in the modern age

The desert peoples have faced many challenges. European maritime dominance reduced the importance of trans-Saharan trade, and successive governments have sought to increase their control of once-remote regions. Some Tuareg groups have long argued — and fought — for independence from Mali, while, in Tanzania, Maasai are resisting their peoples' eviction from lands now used as private game reserves.

The nomads of the desert remain a significant presence — several million Bedouin live in Africa and the Middle East, the Maasai number almost a million, and over two million Tuareg live in nations including Niger, Mali, and Burkina Faso. But they often find themselves marginalized, as governments struggle to integrate seasonal herders into economies that depend on urban areas and settled agriculture.

△ **Bedouin tents**
This 19th-century image shows a Bedouin family and their tents in the Sahara. Tents, constructed from fabric made of camel hair and vegetable fibres, were designed to be easily erected, dismantled, and transported.

▷ **Maasai jumping**
Maasai men in the Maasai Mara, Kenya, demonstrate the *adumu*, a jumping dance that may have its origins in training drills for hunting and combat.

The Kingdom of Benin

Rule of the *obas*

One of the most prominent West African empires from the medieval period, the Kingdom of Benin was a resource-rich trading giant and military powerhouse in a region of fiercely competitive rivals.

△ **Absolute monarch**
This Italian lithograph from c. 1820 is a European view of an *oba* riding among his people. The *oba* was a revered figure who personally owned everything of value in the state.

The Edo people who populated the Kingdom of Benin originally called it "Ubini", which the Portuguese corrupted into "Benin". According to Yoruba history, Oranmiyan, a prince from Ilé-Ifè (see pp. 110–11), founded the kingdom in the 12th or 13th century. He and his descendants established themselves in what became Benin City (in modern Nigeria), a metropolis encompassing some 500 small settlements within high walls.

An entrepreneurial empire

The kingdom was ruled by a powerful king, or *oba*, although chieftains and local rulers were permitted to exercise self-rule so long as they paid tribute (in the form of goods or enslaved people) to their monarch. In 1440, the royal prince Ewuare (see pp. 130–31) seized power, becoming the first warrior-ruler who established Benin as a major force in West Africa. He and his successors extended the kingdom's territory further east towards the borders of modern Cameroon and west as far as Ghana.

One of the main motivating factors for the kingdom's expansion was economic. The state's kings realized that dominion over large sections

▷ **Queen Mother**
This bronze head depicts Idia, the powerful mother of King Esigie (r. 1504–50). Idia raised an army to ensure her son became king.

of West Africa's coastline enabled them to control Africa's Atlantic trade routes, through the imposition of taxes, tolls, and other levies on the ports that did business with other African nations and with Europe. In particular, Ewuare's son and successor, Ozolua, expanded Benin's trade with Portuguese merchants in the 1480s, trading glass beads, cotton, ivory, rubber, palm oil, and, most importantly, gold and pepper.

The Kingdom of Benin also participated in the slave trade, though not as extensively as Portugal would have liked. From 1516, for example, the king prohibited the sale of enslaved males to Europeans, as he needed them for his own army. At its height, Benin was able to put 100,000 armed men in the field and, around 1590, it expanded to the coastal city of Lagos, built a military base, and took over the control of a major port.

Masters of metalwork

The kingdom's wealth and military might gave it the economic power and access to valuable minerals to develop a rich material culture. Pottery-making and textile manufacture were two areas of expertise, but by far the Kingdom of Benin's most abiding – and contested – artistic legacy came in the form of its metallurgical acomplishments, particularly the "Benin Bronzes" (see pp. 132–33). Created from the 13th to the 18th centuries, they comprise thousands of expertly worked bronze and brass pieces, mostly in the form of reliefs, plaques, and sculptures made to decorate the royal palace in Benin City and in many cases showing the military prowess of ancient Benin and its trading activities with the

"Great Benin, where the king resides, is larger than Lisbon."

PORTUGUESE SHIP CAPTAIN
LOURENÇO PINTO, 1691

Portuguese. The kingdom's expertise in crafting beautiful items in metal also included jewellery and other ornamental objects.

A change in the balance of power

The golden age of the Kingdom of Benin lasted around 150 years, from the accession of Ewuare until the death of the last of the "warrior-kings", Ehengbuda, in 1601. From here, the state was weakened by a series of civil wars and succession disputes and went into a decline that was initially gradual but accelerated rapidly at the end of the 19th century, when British forces invaded the kingdom.

For centuries, the kingdom had accrued its wealth by acting as an intermediary between European traders and African vendors. But by the 19th century, Britain had replaced Portugal as the main European nation involved in West Africa, and the power dynamic began to change. Whereas Portugal's interests in the region were primarily commercial, Britain's were overtly imperial – at least, that is what the *oba* Ovonramwen believed when he cut off all trading links with the British in the mid-1890s and, as the dominant power broker for all trade in the region, blocked Britain from doing business with Benin's neighbours. Britain sent an allegedly peaceful but nevertheless provocative diplomatic mission to assert the country's "right" to trade. When Benin soldiers attacked and killed several members of the mission at the kingdom's borders on 4 January 1897, London used the attack as a pretext to invade.

The following month, more than 1,000 British troops entered the capital and in just under three weeks they deposed the king, razed Benin City's royal palace to the ground, and killed hundreds of citizens. Britain then forcibly incorporated the state into its empire, first as part of the British Niger Coast Protectorate and later as part of colonial Nigeria. In retaliation for "provoking" Britain's incursion, the British expeditionary force ruthlessly looted the

kingdom's treasures, particularly the Benin Bronzes. Today, many of them are still held in Britain, the US, and Germany, though in recent years progress has been made in repatriating some of the items from a number of museums.

By the turn of the 20th century, British colonial adminstrators had eliminated the last pockets of resistance and rebellion against British rule, and the former Kingdom of Benin would remain under imperial control until Nigeria's independence movement restored the country's freedom in 1960.

△ **King of Benin**
This photograph shows King Eweka II in c. 1920. The British did not abolish the Kingdom of Benin's monarchy and today *obas* sit on the throne in Nigeria.

Oba Ewuare

Benin's greatest warrior-king

A transformative ruler, Ewuare boosted the monarch's power in the Kingdom of Benin, expanded the state's territory at the expense of its neighbours, and achieved godlike status among his people.

The third son of the *oba* ("king") Ohen, Prince Ogun seized power after his father's death, defeating his own brother Uwaifiokun in a violent coup and taking the regnal name Ewuare, meaning "the trouble has ceased". He became the first – and greatest – of his country's so-called "warrior-kings".

Before his rule, monarchs in the Kingdom of Benin (see pp. 128–29) shared power with local chiefs; under Ewuare, the king became the sole authority – although Ewuare was also careful to appoint a council of advisors made up of both royal officials and local leaders (including some representing areas with a history of rebellion and resistance). To emphasize his power, Ewuare made the monarchy hereditary, removing the local leaders' right to select the new king on the death of the old one. Ewuare also changed the name of the kingdom from Ubini to Edo (although the old name persisted in some quarters, especially among European traders who corrupted "Ubini" into "Benin" and inadvertently gave the kingdom the name by which it is known today).

From king to god

Having remade the kingdom's politics, Ewuare revamped its army. He increased its size and organization, and used it to win territory from Igbo-controlled lands to the east and Yoruba-dominated regions to the west. Internationally, Ewuare began to agree trade deals with Portuguese merchants. At home,

he became a patron of the arts, especially ivory- and wood-carving, and the creation of bronze statuary (see pp. 132–33). The earthworks and defensive walls and ditches he constructed around Benin City's royal palace are among the finest building projects of the age. For his achievements, the king became "Ewuare the Great", and was said to possess magical, semi-divine powers – so too was each subsequent *oba*.

It is not known how Ewuare died, but by the time of his passing the kingdom of Benin had become perhaps the main regional force in West Africa. After a few years of tumult – one of Ewuare's sons was assassinated, the second deposed – Ewuare's third son, Ozolua, became *oba* in 1480 and carried on his father's expansionist policies.

▽ **Ceremonial cleansing**
The kingdom of Benin's rulers used this bronze water container in the form of a sacred leopard to wash their hands in purification rituals at court.

△ **Emblem of authority**
Kings and local leaders wore artfully carved ivory or brass bracelets like this one from c. 1550–1680 to symbolize their power and status.

---

c. 900s Area around Benin City first settled

c. 1180 Eweka I becomes the first *oba*

c. 1434 Ewuare's brother Uwaifiokun becomes *oba*

1440 Ewuare seizes power

c. 1470 Ewuare renames his kingdom Edo

1472 First contact between the Portuguese and the *oba*

1473 Death of Ewuare

1601 Death of Ehengbuda, the last of the warrior-kings

Head of state

A brass likeness of an *oba*. This sculpture dates from the 16th century, but is typical of the way in which Benin's kings were represented.

Woven cap accessorized by coral beads

Eyes and other facial features are stylized and symmetrical

Decorative coral strands hang from each ear

Attendant
shelters the
oba's head

Armed guard
flanks the *oba*

Horse wears
decorative bridle

> "These artefacts speak to **who we are** and speak to **our history**, our religion, our **values and ethics**."

LAL MOHAMMED, NIGERIA'S CULTURE MINISTER, 2022

Benin Bronze with oba and attendants

A West African portrait of power

The Kingdom of Benin (in modern-day Nigeria) was a powerful West African state between the 12th and 19th centuries (see pp. 128–29). Among the kingdom's most important cultural legacies are the thousands of artefacts known as the "Benin Bronzes". Produced between the 13th and 16th centuries, they include jewellery, ornaments, ritual artefacts, and decorative items. However, they are best known for the plaques and sculptures that mainly depict the kingdom's *obas* (kings), royal family, and important state figures.

Production of the artworks

It was probably during the rule of *Oba* Oguola (r. 1274–87) that production of the pieces began. The most distinctive works were created in the era of *Oba* Ewuare (see pp. 130–31), who came to power in 1440. He commissioned pieces to be hung exclusively in the royal palace in the capital city of Edo (also called Benin City). These would reflect the ruler's power and authority, as well as display his state's culture, traditions, and religious practices. They were made of bronze, brass, or a copper alloy. The earliest artefacts were produced by heating, hammering, and

manipulating the metal, but over time this evolved into the more technically complex "lost wax" process. In this method, a model of the sculpture or plaque is made in wax – which is easier to work and allows for more elaborate designs – that is then coated in clay. When the clay is fired in a kiln, the wax melts, leaving behind an impression of the object on the clay's hollow interior. Molten bronze or brass poured into the hollow cools and solidifies into the metalworks.

Many of these pieces were looted by colonial powers in the 19th and 20th centuries; some have eventually been repatriated to Nigeria from museums and collections outside Africa. The issue of their acquisition and return remains controversial (see pp. 128–29).

Representation of majesty

The c. 16th-century copper alloy plaque shown here is of an unnamed *oba*, identifiable by the beaded coral regalia worn by Benin's rulers from this period. His high status is also indicated by him being the only figure on horseback. He is surrounded by attendants and officials, their differing sizes representing their relative importance. This item shows Portuguese influences – horses were transported to the kingdom by Portuguese traders, as were the coral beads around the *oba*'s neck. The cross-shaped rosettes in the background may indicate the influence of Christianity, also imported to the country by the Portuguese.

◁ **Royal procession**
The *oba* is deliberately shown larger than his subjects and attendants, as a sign of his royal power. He holds the hands of his subjects in a fatherly, inclusive gesture.

△ **Palace performer**
This 14th- or 15th-century bronze figure of a court musician is shown playing a horn and wearing a leopard print – an animal associated with an *oba*.

Royal power

Rulers with divine powers or military might

More than 5,000 years have passed since the reign of the earliest African monarchs – the first pharaohs of a united Egypt c. 3100 BCE. Royal power in African societies has been expressed in diverse ways, usually by male rulers, though Queen Njinga of Ndongo ruled in her own right, while Nefertiti, the wife of the pharaoh Akhenaten, and the *iyoba* or queen mother in Benin, both had a major influence over their state's affairs.

A sacred leader

Common to many rulers is the idea of sacred kingship, where the head of state acts as a mediator with the gods, or is himself divine. In ancient Egypt, pharaohs were deemed earthly manifestations of the god Horus (shown as a falcon and representing power). Among

the Bunyoro people of what is now Uganda, the ruler depended on his control of sacred shrines, and his ancestors had to pass a test set by a deity. Divine kingship, however, encompassed great differences in the practical power of rulers. The Luba people of Central Africa believed that the king's power should not be absolute, so a council – the *bambudye* – acted as an intermediary between the king and the people. The vast Oyo state had layers of government. Its ruler, the *alaafin*, could not act without the consent of the *Oyo Mesi*, a council of seven leaders (see p. 112). In the Nri Kingdom of the Igbo, the idea of a divine king remained: the *eze nri* was a priest-king who held religious but not political power in a system that lasted until British conquest in 1911.

△ **Nefertiti**
The wife of pharaoh Akhenaten, and queen from 1353 to 1336 BCE, Nefertiti was one of the most powerful women in Egyptian history, ruling at a time of huge artistic and religious changes and elevated by her husband to be virtual co-ruler.

△ **Saladin**
Beginning as a lowly army officer, Saladin became vizier of Egypt and, after deposing the last Fatimid caliph in 1171, sultan. He united Muslim forces and conquered an empire, his power dependent not on birth or divine powers, but on the might of his armies and his political skills.

△ **Lalibela**
According to Ethiopian tradition, Emperor Gebre Meskel (r. 1181–1221) ordered the building of 11 rock-cut churches in northern Ethiopia to show the power of the Christian Church, which underpinned his rule. They are known by the emperor's birthname, Lalibela.

"I warn you against **shedding blood**… **blood never sleeps**."

SALADIN, SULTAN OF EGYPT

Power and wealth

Medieval rulers, such as Saladin, the founder of the Ayyubid dynasty (see pp. 124–25), were warriors who commanded great armies. The kings of Wagadou (ancient Ghana) and *mansas* of Mali, such as Musa, enjoyed resources greater than those of European royalty. The Asante Empire, which covered a large area, created a system from the reign of Osei Kwadwo (1764-77) onwards with ministers, provincial governors, and a treasury into which taxes flowed.

The coming of Europeans undermined many African rulers, but for others it cemented their status, as they derived new wealth from trade. The Zulu State built power from its military successes and conquests. Religions also acted as potent sources of authority:

the kings of Ethiopia from the 13th century claimed descent from the Biblical king Solomon, and dynasties in North Africa, including the Fatimids of Tunisia in the 10th century, and the Almoravids in northwest Africa from the 12th century, based their authority on their rulers' adherence to Islam.

As colonialism progressed, local rulers were often the only recognized source of the continuation of a tradition and acted as mediators with colonial powers. Monarchs such as the *kabakas* of Buganda (in Uganda) and the *shehus* of Borno survived centuries of foreign control to re-emerge as figures of authority and, in Morocco and Eswatini, as ruling heads of state. King Mswati III in Eswatini still reigns as an absolute monarch today, and is part of an almost 300-year-old dynasty.

△ **Iyoba**
This 18th-century bronze statue of an *iyoba* or queen mother is from the West African state of Benin. The *iyoba* acted as the chief advisor to the *oba* (her son), and commanded her own regiment in wartime, the only woman permitted to do so.

△ **Prempeh II**
Asantehene (king) from 1931–70, Prempeh was four years old when the British conquered Asante in 1896. After 40 years in exile he returned, and as the power of local rulers grew, he became the first president of Ghana's National House of Chiefs in 1969.

△ **Mswati III**
King since 1986, Mswati III is a member of the Dlamini dynasty that has provided all Eswatini's kings since Ngwane III founded the state in 1745. He is Africa's only remaining absolute monarch and representative of a pattern of rule once widespread throughout the continent.

Great Zimbabwe

The mighty walled cities of a lost Shona empire

Great Zimbabwe was the architectural and artistic high point of a powerful Shona civilization that endured for six centuries. Its people traded gold and ivory across the Indian Ocean and built vast fortified complexes whose ruins still stand today.

The Zimbabwe culture was centred on large settlements, including the city we now know as Great Zimbabwe, which was founded around the 9th century in modern-day southeastern Zimbabwe. In the 13th and 14th centuries, the city supported more than 10,000 people, and became the grand capital of a kingdom of the Zimbabwe culture that reached as far as present-day Mozambique. In Shona, the name Zimbabwe means "big stone house" and Great Zimbabwe was a city of immense scale – the largest in Southern Africa at the time.

The earliest origins of the Zimbabwe culture date to 2,500 years ago, when Bantu-speaking peoples from Central Africa migrated to Southern Africa (see pp. 36–37) and met the Indigenous San hunter-gatherers. Bantu-speakers known as the Shona settled in the plains and forests of the Shashe-Limpopo Basin around 500 CE. They grew crops and herded cattle, gradually displacing the San. The area, where modern-day Zimbabwe, Botswana, and South Africa meet, was not immediately prosperous, and the population declined after 700 CE, but around 900 CE settlement resumed, and the region became a hub.

Cattle were the principal form of wealth in this Iron Age society, representing power and status. The region's grassland made good grazing, and the Shona began to exchange goods along the Limpopo River with the Swahili, fellow Bantu-speakers who lived on the coast of what is now Kenya, Tanzania, and Mozambique. The Swahili kingdoms were part of a commercial network that crossed the Indian Ocean, connecting East and North Africa with the Arabian Peninsula, India, Indonesia, and even China. As trade links grew stronger, iron, salt, ivory, cattle, fish, snail and mussel shells, chert (a rock used for tools and to create sparks for fires), and beads made from ostrich eggs travelled up and down the great river.

Great Zimbabwe's rise

The Shona population grew through the 11th and 12th centuries, and the cattle economy evolved into what became known as the Zimbabwe culture. A class-based society, centred on Great Zimbabwe, emerged in which the ruling elite profited from the labour of traders, food producers, and artisans, and acquired new luxury trade goods such as Chinese porcelain and glass beads.

Great Zimbabwe was not yet dominant, though. Its predecessor as the capital was Mapungubwe, some 270 km (170 miles) to the south in what is now South

◁ **Prestigious complex**
The Great Enclosure may have been used as a royal palace or a grain store, while the plains that surround it supported large numbers of cattle.

Africa. In the 12th century, the population of Mapungubwe may have reached 5,000 people. By the 13th century, the Mapungubwe people were mining gold, which they traded and used to make objects such as sceptres, bowls, headdresses, and animal figures.

Great Zimbabwe was also growing increasingly sophisticated, with tall walls and elaborate buildings. When the Little Ice Age changed the climate in the 12th century, the interior of Southern Africa became colder and dryer, leading to Mapungubwe's decline and eventual abandonment in the early 13th century. This increasingly arid climate also presented challenges to the inhabitants of Great Zimbabwe, who took care to preserve water. Huge pits on the site are believed to have been used to harvest surface water and store groundwater, which was used during dry seasons. These measures may have contributed to the city's rise to replace Mapungubwe, since Great Zimbabwe was able to sustain a significant population, as well as livestock and agriculture.

Towering walls and soapstone birds

Today, archaeologists divide Great Zimbabwe into three key areas. The Hill Complex, which began to be constructed in the 10th century, was probably either the home of the king or a ceremonial site – it may have been used for rain-making rituals. Both it and the 14th-century Great Enclosure were surrounded by huge mortarless walls, with the Hill Complex's up to 6 m (20 ft) thick and over 10 m (33 ft) tall. The nearby Valley Complex, which dates from between the 14th and 16th centuries, included many stone buildings. Avian soapstone sculptures, known as "Zimbabwe birds", stood on columns in the city, and may represent totem animals. The presence of 15th-century potsherds, beads, woven goods, and golden artefacts show that the empire continued to thrive, and Portuguese traders were aware of its existence. However, by the mid-15th century Great Zimbabwe was declining, possibly due to shortages of food, water, or gold. It was eventually abandoned, with a new city at Khami, near Bulawayo in what is now southwestern Zimbabwe, rising to prominence in the 16th and 17th centuries. Other migrants from the city are believed to have founded the Kingdom of Mutapa, which became the main power in Eastern Zimbabwe and Mozambique between the 15th and 17th centuries.

After Great Zimbabwe's collapse, different Shona groups used the ruins for religious purposes. By the late 19th century, white colonists had begun to arrive in Zimbabwe, and the ruins' history was disputed, with some Europeans suggesting they could not be the work of Black Africans and might instead have been built by the Phoenicians or the Biblical King Solomon.

In 1931, the British archaeologist Gertrude Caton-Thompson described Great Zimbabwe as of "Bantu origin and of a medieval date", but the white minority government of Rhodesia (see pp. 252–53) continued to downplay the ruins' Bantu connection. Modern archaeology has confirmed that the Shona constructed the city, which is now a UNESCO World Heritage Site. It gave its name to Zimbabwe, which became independent in 1980, and Great Zimbabwe sits at the centre of the nation's coat of arms, while a Zimbabwe bird adorns its flag.

Rim is decorated with symbols

△ **Divination bowl**
This plaster cast of a wooden platter, decorated with a crocodile, was found near Great Zimbabwe in the late 19th century. It is thought to be a divination bowl.

Thin sheets of gold covered wooden carving (now decayed)

Holes where tiny gold nails once held covering in place

△ **Luxury item**
Found in a grave in the ruins of Mapungubwe, the 800-year-old Golden Rhinoceros of Mapungubwe shows the Zimbabwe culture's wealth and sophistication.

" … there is **a fortress** built of stones of **marvellous size**, and … no mortar joining them."

PORTUGUESE CAPTAIN VICENTE PEGADO, 1531

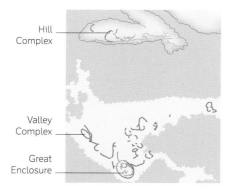

Hill Complex

Valley Complex

Great Enclosure

◁ **The site**
Great Zimbabwe comprises three main groups of ruins: the Hill Complex, which shows the earliest evidence of settlement; the Great Enclosure, where the masonry reaches its zenith; and the Valley Complex, a collection of smaller-scale stone enclosures where artefacts from Central Africa and Asia have been found.

◁ **Zimbabwe birds**
Among the most famous finds from Great Zimbabwe are eight distinctive bird figures carved from soapstone. While each is unique, several blend avian features with human features such as toes and lips. It is thought they may represent significant ancestors of Great Zimbabwe's people.

Chevrons appear on all eight bird monoliths

◁ **Masters of masonry**
The smooth, curving walls were constructed from local granite. No binding mortar was used: instead, the masons carefully positioned rectangular blocks in even layers, tapering gently upwards for maximum stability. A stonework chevron frieze, the significance of which is unknown, spans a 52-m (171-ft) length of the outer wall.

The core is packed with irregular blocks

The solid 10-m (33-ft) conical tower is thought to be symbolic

The *daga* platform may have had ritual significance

The Great Enclosure

Great Zimbabwe, Masvingo, Zimbabwe

The monumental dry stone ruins at Great Zimbabwe are the largest south of the Sahara. Built by ancestors of modern-day Zimbabwe's Shona people, the site is one of many stone settlements in the region, but its relative scale suggests it served as the capital of a kingdom. Among the ruins, the most imposing is the Great Enclosure, an enormous elliptical structure 250 m (820 ft) in circumference, within which lower walls interconnect to form a series of courtyards around individual homesteads. Archaeologists are still working to understand exactly how this enclosure was used. One theory is that it was a royal residence; another is that it served as a site for ritual ceremonies.

At its thickest, the outer wall is 5.5 m (18 ft) at the base and 3.6 m (12 ft) at the top

The outer wall is 250 m (820 ft) long and around 10 m (33 ft) high

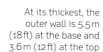

△ Typical dwelling
Homesteads had separate huts for cooking and sleeping made of *daga* (a mix of clay and gravel). *Daga* was also moulded to create hearths and raised surfaces for sitting, sleeping, and storage.

▷ **Great entrances**
The Great Enclosure's monumental entrances originally had lintels, at least two of which were wooden. No evidence suggests the immense walls were built to be defensive; they may have been intended to protect the privacy of an elite group.

Open communal area

Individual homesteads are separated by stone walls

The entrance buttresses are not structural but restrict the view into the enclosure

Buttresses may have provided privacy, or controlled movement

The height and thickness of the walls is uneven

A narrow passageway leads to the conical tower

Huts had conical thatched roofs

Huts and *daga* walls may have been painted

△ Use of the Great Enclosure
This reconstruction depicts the Great Enclosure as it may have looked in the 14th century, when Great Zimbabwe flourished. Archaeological finds indicate that metalworking, weaving, pot-making, and soapstone-carving were important activities.

The Mossi States

Powerful nations united

A shared ancestry, ethnicity, religion, political system, and social hierarchy allowed the Mossi States – a West African confederation of nations – to survive and thrive for at least 500 years, until the end of the 19th century.

The Mossi States were a collection of kingdoms in West Africa whose territory encompassed parts of modern-day Burkina Faso, Côte d'Ivoire, and Ghana. Many details of the states' origins and histories are lost, but most sources agree there were up to 20 states, of which five were particularly influential: Ouagadougou, Tenkodogo, Fada N'gourma, Zondoma (replaced eventually by Yatenga), and Boussouma. Although each kingdom was independent, they acted collectively in areas such as foreign affairs, trade, and war. This made the Mossi Empire, as it is sometimes known, one of Africa's strongest forces.

Beginning and growth

According to historical records, anthropological study, archaeology, and Mossi legends and stories, the Mossi originated some time between the 11th and 14th centuries. The culture's foundation myth tells how the Mossi people emerged from the union of a fugitive princess named Yennenga and an elephant hunter called Rialé (see box, opposite). Their son Ouédraogo is said to have founded Tenkodogo, which was then ruled after his death by his son, Zoungrana. His two other sons, Diaba Lompo and Rawa, founded Fada N'gorma and Zondoma respectively. Ouédraogo's grandson Oubri founded the Ouagadougou dynasty, supposedly around 1050. It was the actual or imagined existence of these ancestral and ethnic links that allowed the Mossi States to collaborate effectively.

Over the next several hundred years, the Mossi States concentrated on strengthening their economic and military power. By the 15th century, this empire was one of the most effective in West Africa. It successfully resisted the neighbouring Songhai Empire (see pp. 104–105) to the north, and from the early 18th century onwards formed trading links with powers including the Mali and Massina empires, as well as the Sokoto Caliphate (see pp. 194–95) and the nearby states and kingdoms of the region's Fula

Scarification patterns mark passage to adulthood

▽ **House of worship**
In a largely Muslim region, the Mossi kingdoms resisted becoming Islamic states, although many Muslims lived here and mosques, such as this one in Ouagadougou, were built.

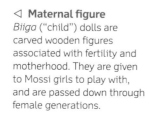

◁ **Maternal figure**
Biiga ("child") dolls are carved wooden figures associated with fertility and motherhood. They are given to Mossi girls to play with, and are passed down through female generations.

Realistically depicted antelope horns

Raised forehead ridge

Geometric patterns in mineral-based pigments

△ **Animal mask**
Masks were worn at important Mossi events, such as funerals. Each local group had its own representative spirit animal. This one is *wan-nyaka* ("the little antelope").

people. Disputes over matters such as religions, borders, or resources sometimes broke out into violence, but in general most of West Africa's states were evenly matched enough to avoid upsetting the area's balance of power. The Mossi States, for example, were not actively expansionist and preferred to defend the territories they already controlled.

The Niger and Volta rivers ran through Mossi lands, and this allowed the states to grow wealthy by controlling the flow of goods along these important trading waterways. Mossi farmers exported cattle and crops such as millet, sorghum, and cotton. The main imports were salt and highly prized, caffeine-containing kola nuts. The Mossi were also renowned as skilled ironworkers and produced both weapons and decorative items for domestic use and export. Unlike most of their neighbours, the Mossi States were not involved in the slave trade.

Power and belief

Despite each of the Mossi states being autonomous, Ouagadougou (in modern-day Burkina Faso) was preeminent among its peers. Ouagadougou's capital city, also called Ouagadougou, was the seat of the *morho naba* ("great king") of the Mossi people. More a spiritual figure than a ruling monarch, the *morho naba* was believed to channel a supernatural force – known as *naam* and derived from the Mossi's creator-god Wende – that gave him the power to lead other people. The *morho naba* oversaw the Mossi people in their rites and ceremonies that included the sacrifice of animals to appease Wende and the spirits they believed inhabited the natural world. The Mossi also practised ancestor veneration. Other belief systems such as Islam and Christianity had only limited success in converting the Mossi.

Mossi society was strictly stratified. The *nakombse* were the elite few who could trace their lineage back to the states' founders and who therefore possessed *naam* and enjoyed a divine right to rule; the *tengbiise*

were the people whose forebears had been the first inhabitants of the lands the *nakombse* first conquered and had become assimilated into the Mossi States.

During their height, the Mossi States ensured mostly peace and prosperity, as a result of their strong economy, stable social structure, ability to cooperate with each other, and the relatively settled balance of power in West Africa. This ended in 1896, when French forces invaded the Mossi States and incorporated them into France's Upper Volta colony. The last king of Ouagadougou, Wobgo, died in exile in the Gold Coast (modern-day Ghana) in 1904, and the regions of West Africa that France had colonized would not gain their independence until 1960.

LEGENDARY **PRINCESS**

Princess Yennenga – the legendary "mother of the Mossi" – embodied two important aspects of this West African culture: the martial and the maternal. She was trained in combat by her father Nedega, ruler of the Dagbon Kingdom in possibly the 11th or 12th century. She fought her first battle at 14, and was so skilled a fighter that her father barred her from marrying, fearing that family life would deprive his kingdom of a great warrior. This caused Yennenga to flee the kingdom in disguise on horseback. In Mandingo (Malinke) territory to the north, she married a local hunter, Rialé, and they had a child, Ouédraogo, whose descendants and kinship groups would go on to found the Mossi nations.

BRONZE FIGURINE OF PRINCESS YENNENGA

Kingdoms of the Luba, Lunda, and Lozi

Central Africa's most renowned trio of states

From the late 16th century, much of Central Africa was under the sway of the neighbouring Luba, Lunda, and Lozi kingdoms. All three coexisted more or less peacefully for around three centuries.

The Luba people emerged from what is today the southeast of the Democratic Republic of the Congo (DRC), in a marshy region of lakes and rivers known as the Upemba Depression. The first Luba leader of note was the semi-mythical Konglo Mwamba, who is said to have established a kingdom in 1585. His nephew and successor, Kalala Ilunga, conquered vast lands to the west and inaugurated many of the Kingdom of Luba's traditions. From his time on, the kingdom had a political culture of a king (or *mulopwe*), revered as a living god, who ruled alongside an advisory council. A fair and balanced governance was ensured by a committee-based decision-making process, a respect for authority (embodied in the person of the king), and adherence to the Luba religion's values of ethical conduct.

The Kingdom of Luba flourished for 300 years, and was known for its arts, especially wood carving and – often accompanied by music – poetry. Weakened by a succession dispute in the 1880s and the depredations of slave traders from East Africa raiding its lands, the kingdom finally succumbed to the imperial ambitions of

◁ **Ornamental instrument**
Cowrie shells were used as currency throughout West and Central Africa, and as decorations symbolizing wealth and status – as on this late 19th-century Lunda whistle.

Belgium. In the mid-1880s, Belgian colonization fragmented and split the Kingdom of Luba, forcing it into the Congo Free State, a colony established as the personal property of the Belgian king, Leopold II (see pp. 212–13).

Lunda Kingdom

The histories of the Lunda and the Luba kingdoms are inextricably linked. The Lunda people originated in an area along the Kalanyi River in the south of the DRC, close to the homelands of the Luba. The kingdom was founded some time in the mid-17th century after an exiled Luba prince named Ilunga Tshibinda took up residence in a region to the south called Ba Lunda. His son, Yao Nawedji, became the first Lunda ruler. The kingdom adopted a governmental model of monarchy supported by an advisory council similar to that of the Luba. This gave the state political stability. Economically, Lunda benefited from the highly profitable trade in enslaved

▽ **Domestic art**
This food dish is typical of the zoomorphic, or animal-themed, pottery, ironmongery, and wood-worked items produced by the Lozi.

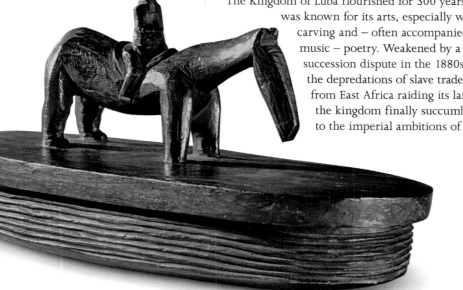

"I am the **great rock** that spreads all over **the lands**."

MULOPWE KALALA ILUNGA, 16TH-CENTURY LUBA KING

Seat is not intended
to be sat on

people, salt, ivory, copper, and forestry products such as timber. The wealth this generated allowed Lunda's rulers to commission a variety of artworks, particularly carved wooden sculptures.

The Kingdom of Lunda collapsed in the late 19th century, when it was invaded by the neighbouring Chokwe people. A much-diminished rump kingdom survived for a few more years, but this came to an end in 1887, when the Congo Free State took over the remaining Lunda lands.

Power-sharing in the south

The southern part of the Luba-Lunda states were occupied by the Lozi (sometimes called the Silozi) people in an area known as Barotseland. The name Lozi means "plain" and refers to the floodplain of the Zambezi River, along which most of the people lived. Each Lozi village had its own leader and ruling council, but the state was nominally a kingdom with a powerful and revered monarch, or *litunga*, whose court was based in the dry season at Lealui, close to the Zambezi, and in the wet season at Limulunga on higher ground. The annual decampment of the king and his court from Lealui to Limulunga was marked by a festival known as the *Kuomboko* (literally, "to get out of the water").

The British maintained an interest in Lozi lands from the late 19th century, but, as the region proved to be a poor source of valuable minerals such as gold and copper, imperial interference was minimal. In 1964, the Lozi heartland of Barotseland was incorporated into the newly independent Zambia.

◁ **Seat of power**
This stool was intended for a Luba chieftain. It was carved for ceremonial use and was highly symbolic: the female figure represents divine motherhood as the origin of royal authority.

Coloured beads signify high social status

Elaborate skin ornamentation symbolizes refinement

Kneeling posture provides base to support the stool

△ **Cultural crossover**
Lunda rulers commissioned skilful artists from client peoples such as the Chokwe to create artworks, such as this figure of the mythical Lunda hero, Chibinda Ilunga.

> ## "**Wakupile luzi bipa** [A person holding flies with clenched fists]."

LUBA PROVERB DESCRIBING THE *BANA BALUTE*
AS KEEPERS OF SECRET KNOWLEDGE

Luba "memory board"

History in your hands

The Luba people of what is today the Democratic Republic of the Congo (DRC) had a unique means of recording their history, laws, and customs. Known as *lukasa* ("the long hand", or "claw"), these hand-held wooden boards were crafted in an hourglass shape that represented, all at once, the Luba landscape, the royal court, the human body, and a turtle (the Luba monarchy's symbolic spirit animal). Each *lukasa* was studded with coloured beads, shells, and metal, and scored with lines and symbols. This arrangement of shapes and objects was a sophisticated narrative device – a "memory board" – encoding vital information.

The people charged with interpreting *lukasa* were members of the Mbudye (or Bambudye) Society, an elite organization of mostly male diviners, storytellers, and spiritual teachers known as *bana balute* ("memory men"). The *bana balute* had to master successive levels of specialist knowledge before they were permitted to decipher and interpret the *lukasa*'s intricate designs and motifs. To do so, they ran their right hand over the board's beads, shapes, and ridges while declaiming aloud its stories and instructions. The arrangement of items on a *lukasa* was more a guide than a set narrative. No two memory men read the same *lukasa* in the same way; indeed, an individual *bana balute* would read the same memory board differently on different occasions, depending on where and to whom he was giving his recital.

The information on a *lukasa* was displayed in one of three styles. *Lukasa lwa nkunda* ("the long hand of the pigeon") record, among other things, the history of the Luba kings and the society's myths and legendary heroes; *lukasa lwa kabemba* ("the long hand of the hawk") feature information on the structure of the Mbudye Society alongside political, cultural, and social instructions for the Luba people; and *lukasa lwa kitenta* ("the long hand of the sacred pool") were made for individual Luba rulers and, it is said, contained secret spiritual information shared only with the king. None of this last style of *lukasa* remain in existence.

Partial interpretation

As with most surviving *lukasa*, the style of the one shown here and its precise meaning are not entirely known. What is clear is the significance of some of its symbols and their patterns of arrangement. Human faces, for example, represent Luba chiefs, kings, and Mbudye members; coloured beads organized into rectangles, lines, ovals, and circles describe the layout of a chief or king's household, or the configuration of the Mbudye Society's meeting places, with lines also representing significant roads or migration routes. The carved and incised edges of the *lukasa* supposedly echo the shell markings of a turtle.

◁ **Memory man**
A Luba *bana balute* recites from a *lukasa* in this 1989 photograph taken in the DRC, showing that the practice of oral storytelling and instruction by this elite group continues.

▽ **Story board**
This late 19th- or early 20th-century *lukasa* is 25 cm (10 in) long and about 14 cm (5.5 in) wide. A row of carved mounds called *lukala* divide the board into female (left) and male (right) sides.

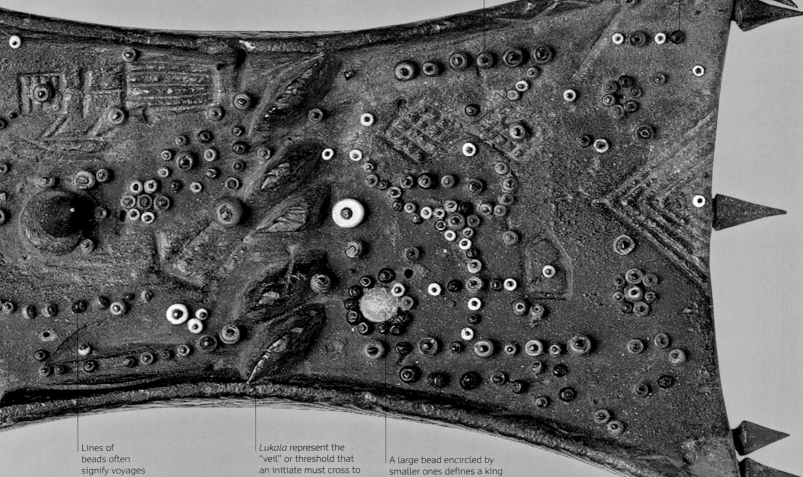

Beads and shells are attached to the board by slivers of wood or handmade iron wedges

Colours denote specific historical figures or events

Tapered ends represent stylized crocodile heads

Lines of beads often signify voyages

Lukala represent the "veil" or threshold that an initiate must cross to become a *bana balute*

A large bead encircled by smaller ones defines a king or chief within a court

△ **City of Kilwa**
The island of Kilwa was developed by Persian traders and later taken over by the Portuguese, who built this fort at Gereze. Despite its wealth, the Islamic city was not well defended.

The East African Sultanates

Trade with Persia, India, and Asia

Between the 8th and 15th centuries, much of East Africa became a trading hub for Islamic settlers who were based in powerful city-states known as the East African Sultanates.

Communities along the coast of East Africa where the modern-day countries of Somalia, Kenya, Tanzania, and Mozambique lie became significant trading posts for Islamic merchants who arrived by sea from Arabia and Asia. The Indigenous Bantu-speakers living in the region practised pastoralism and their attention had been pointed more towards the African interior. When merchants from the Islamic world, as well as from India and further afield, began arriving and settling along the coast, the focus of life in the region shifted outwards and transformed this part of the continent into one of the most diverse in Africa for its time.

Influences from the east
Transoceanic trade became part of East African life, its activity dictated by the prevailing winds that blew across the Gulf of Aden and the Indian Ocean. From November to March, west-to-east monsoon winds brought Asian merchants to East Africa, their wooden

▽ **Attractive items**
Merchants from Asia traded their jewellery, such as this beaded necklace found at Kilwa Kisiwani, textiles, spices, and porcelain for African gold and ivory.

dhows laden with cotton, silk, porcelain, glassware, and spices. When the winds changed direction from April to October, traders set sail for the east, their hulls filled with gold, ivory, tortoiseshell, ambergris (a substance excreted by sperm whales, which is used in perfume manufacture), incense, spices, iron, animal hides, and enslaved people. These journeys took several months, and sailors and travellers often put down roots in the port cities they visited, getting married, forming friendships, and bringing new ideas, cuisines, languages, and ways of life along with them.

Islam reaches East Africa

One major import the visitors brought was Islam, possibly arriving with Shia Muslim refugees from Oman, which was Sunni-Muslim dominated, in the 8th century. Between 1050 and 1200, people from the city of Shiraz (Shirazi) settled in the region around modern-day Mogadishu, in Somalia. Some scholars dispute that the settlers came from Persia – however, they were certainly Muslim and helped to spread the faith along the East African coast.

By the 12th century, the Shirazi had reached Kilwa, an island off Tanzania. It became the centre of an empire that a century later extended along the East African coast from Somalia in the north to Tanzania in the south. The Kilwa Sultanate, as it was called, dominated East Africa's lucrative trade in gold for 200 years. Its capital, Kilwa Kisiwani, boasted stone-built houses and the empire minted its own copper coins – one of the first places in Africa south of the Sahara to do so.

Islamic sultanates

With the success of Kilwa acting as encouragement, other, mainly Arabic, incomers set up commercial outposts along the East African coast, and these city-states came to be known as the East African Sultanates. Shanga, on the Kenyan island of Pate, was an early Islamic centre (its first mosque was built in the 8th century), followed by Kizimkazi on the Tanzanian island of Unguja (also called Zanzibar), and Mogadishu in Somalia, along with other city-states. Apart from the unquestionably powerful Kilwa, none of these places were "sultanates" in the traditional sense. The term really only indicates that they were all predominantly Arabic-Islamic in origin.

QVILOA

◁ **Wealthy city-state**
This illustration from 1572 shows the thriving city-state of Kilwa. By the 15th century, it was the most powerful city on the East African coast.

Trade continued along the coast and across the Persian Gulf and Indian Ocean, but now the commercial relationships between merchants and city-states were subject to taxes and tariffs that paid for the mosques, royal palaces, and other impressive Arab-style buildings that still decorate East Africa's coast.

Although the Sultanates were wealthy, they were not militarily strong. The first Portuguese explorers arrived offshore in the late 15th century and within a century had plundered the Sultanates' cities and destroyed their trade. Despite their collapse, however, the Sultanates had changed East Africa irrevocably. The merging of Islamic and other non-African people with local Bantu-speaking populations had created a new language and culture known as Swahili. In essence, Swahili is a Bantu tongue but written in Arabic script (and including some Arabic vocabulary). "Swahili" derives from the Arabic *sahil* ("coast"), so it can be translated as "people of the coast". Today Swahili, or, more accurately, Kiswahili, is the most commonly spoken language in East Africa, and Islam is widely practised among the people of the coast.

▷ **Establishment of Islam**
An 1882 illustration of the Fakhr al-Din Mosque in Mogadishu, Somalia, indicates the presence of Islam in the African city. The mosque was built in the 13th century.

وكنت احسبه سنبط سنظر سرورا الى ويعلى السنة على فاحلق الحين خلقت بما اغلفت

بل قال ان العبد اذا نزر تمنه وخفت مؤنه ترك بمولاه والتحف عليه مولاه فان

لا او تنجنب هذا الغلام النك بان اخفف نمه عليك من مائتي دهمان شيء

واشكرى ما حبيت فنقلته المبلغ في اكال كما انقد في ارخص الغال ولم

Visitors to the market

Enslaved people put on sale in the marketplace

△ **Slave market**
This page from the *Maqamat* of Al-Hariri, a 13th-century illustrated manuscript, shows traders and enslaved people at a market in what is now Yemen. Enslaved Africans in the Middle East were forced to work in homes and as labourers, concubines, or soldiers, though some rose to positions of power.

The Eastern slave trade

A trade that prospered in the face of abolition

Enslaved people were transported across the Sahara and the Indian Ocean for centuries. Like its transatlantic equivalent – which it outlasted – this slave trade changed societies and tore many Africans from their roots.

Slavery in Africa dates back at least 3,000 years, to ancient Egypt. Later empires such as the Romans, the Byzantines, and the Sasanians of Iran also enslaved Africans.

As the caliphates of the Middle East and North Africa grew in the 8th and 9th centuries CE, Muslim merchants began to buy enslaved people along a commercial frontier that stretched across the Sahara and into the Horn of Africa. Empires such as Wagadou (see pp. 84–85) and Kanem-Bornu (see pp. 108–109) enslaved people in raids, while Amazigh (Berber) and Arab enslavers led captives on gruelling marches across the Sahara. On the east coast, Arab and Swahili enslavers used the Indian Ocean and Red Sea to ship people, as well as commodities such as gold, to North Africa, Europe, the Middle East, and Asia, in exchange for spices, textiles, precious stones, and other goods.

The trade in enslaved people shattered communities and was used to build powerful empires, especially in West Africa. The Atlantic slave trade (see pp. 162–63) intensified these pressures but also rerouted the trade so that while Atlantic ports were busier than ever, trade across the Sahara declined.

Indian Ocean trade
By the late 18th century, the transatlantic trade was under pressure from abolitionists, and it was banned by the British Empire in 1807. But in East Africa the slave trade thrived as never before. French sugar and coffee plantations across the Indian Ocean relied on the labour of enslaved people, while Brazilian enslavers wary of British patrols off the coast of West Africa

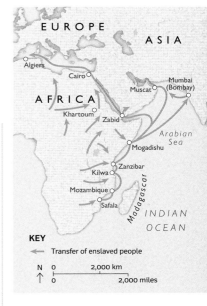

◁ **Tippu Tip**
Trader Tippu Tip worked for several Zanzibar sultans. Born around 1832, he became one of the most notorious enslavers in Africa before his death in 1905.

switched to East Africa, transporting enslaved people, mainly of Bantu-speaking origin, from modern-day Mozambique. Zanzibar became the richest sea port in tropical Africa, and enslaved people laboured in its clove plantations and were shipped to date plantations in the Persian Gulf. However, the days of large-scale slave trading were drawing to a close. In 1873, the British shut down the slave market in Stone Town, Zanzibar's capital (see pp. 188–89), and banned slave shipments by sea.

The impact of the trade across the Sahara and the Indian Ocean was immense. Huge numbers of people were taken from their communities and forced into servitude. While individual traders and rulers became wealthy, the suffering of some populations was horrific. Meanwhile, the persistence of slavery, and the dislocation of people caused by it, provided European colonialists with an opportunity and an excuse to intervene across Africa.

△ **Routes to slavery**
Slave-trading networks connected Africa south of the Sahara with the powerful states of the Middle East and the spice trade ports of Asia.

KEY

← Transfer of enslaved people

N 0   2,000 km
0   2,000 miles

▷ **Camp in the Congo Basin**
This 19th-century engraving shows a camp at Boyoma Falls, in the modern-day Democratic Republic of the Congo. Raids into the interior targeted enslaved people and ivory.

Textiles

The threads of a continent

Textiles in Africa have a rich history. Fabrics have been used for clothing, decoration, and trade, while different motifs, textures, and dyes often signify the individual wearer's ethnicity or status. There are many African textile traditions, but some common threads can be seen across the continent.

Most textiles have historically been handmade, by curing animal hide or using looms and shuttles to weave materials such as cotton, silk, hemp, wool, palms, tree bark, and bamboo. Decorative touches include introducing intricate sewn or drawn designs, adding beads, or dyeing and printing with colours derived from plants such as chilli peppers, indigo, and cashew bark. Roles differ by region: men are the main weavers among the Asante of Ghana, while among the Kuba people in the Democratic Republic of the Congo (DRC), men weave the cloth and women transform it into garments, baskets, and other items.

Fabrics and decoration

Historically, the availability of local materials shaped production. In North Africa, flax was a key crop for the ancient Egyptians, and was used for clothing (alongside linen and wool), sails, and the strips used to wrap mummies. Amazigh (Berber) herders used their flocks' wool to produce clothing and rugs, and Amazigh rugs and carpets remain a major export.

In West and Central Africa, the leaves of palm trees have been used to produce raffia cloth. In forested regions of East, West, and Central Africa, meanwhile,

△ **Yoruba shawl, Nigeria**
Aso-oke is a Yoruba fabric that dates back to at least the 15th century. There are several main types, based on their colours. This shawl is a magenta cotton and silk weave called alaari. Aso-oke is worn on special occasions, such as festivals and weddings.

△ **Kuba raffia, Democratic Republic of the Congo**
The Kuba people of the DRC make a unique, velvet-like cloth using fibres of the raffia palm. Women artists embroider the surface of the cloth with geometric patterns (shown here). They also use the appliqué process, by which patterns are cut from one piece of cloth and sewed onto cloth of a different colour.

△ **Shweshwe prints, South Africa**
Shweshwe is a cotton fabric characterized by bright colours and geometric patterns. It is mainly used for Sotho (South Africa and Lesotho) clothing, and takes its name from Moshoeshoe I, the first ruler of Lesotho, who popularized its use in the 19th century.

"Every piece [of *kente* cloth] has a **name and a meaning**. The cloth **speaks**."

KWASI ASARE, GHANAIAN MASTER WEAVER, 2020

bark was stripped from a range of trees and boiled to make it malleable, then beaten with wooden hammers and dried in the sun. The Baganda people of Uganda are particularly well known for mutuba-tree barkcloth, which continues to be worn on formal occasions.

Patterns of trade also shaped fabrics and decoration. Around 2,000 years ago, Arab merchants introduced cotton to Ethiopia: the long, cotton *shamma* robe is a popular item of clothing in the country today. In Madagascar, silk and cotton, introduced by the sea trade with Asia, joined materials such as raffia, wool, and bark. For much of their history, the Maasai of Tanzania and Kenya mainly wore leather from sheep and cattle, but they are now known for striped and chequered *shuka* cloth, which became popular after

trade with Europe brought cotton in the 19th century. In West and Central Africa, Dutch merchants during the 19th century introduced a colourful fabric with *batik*-inspired printing, which is known as *ankara*.

Many of the continent's best-known textiles are from West Africa. Nigeria's Yoruba use resist-dyeing (in which parts of the fabric are marked with substances such as wax so they resist the dye) to produce *adire*, a patterned indigo cloth. The Akan of Ghana began interlacing strips of silk and cotton around the 17th century to make *kente* cloth, which was used for royal robes. These fabrics are often used to communicate: *adinkra* cloth of the Asante, for example, carries symbols that represent proverbs, historical events, and cultural values.

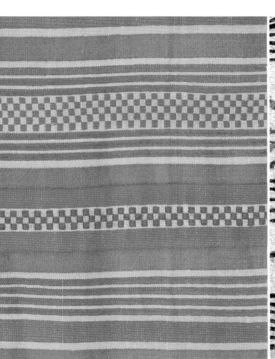

△ **Dorze cloth, Ethiopia**
Weaving is an important trade for the Dorze people of southern Ethiopia. Huts and fences are made from interlaced local bamboo, while the borders of bright cotton clothing and blankets often feature intricate patterns.

△ **Mbuti barkcloth, DRC**
The Mbuti people make barkcloth, used for clothing and bedding, by beating and soaking bark until it becomes soft enough to work with. The Mbuti are hunter-gatherers from the Democratic Republic of the Congo's northeastern rainforests and the fabric's patterns sometimes show forest maps or song structures.

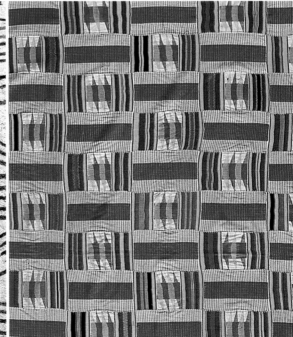

△ **Kente cloth, Ghana**
Traditionally made from handwoven strips of silk and cotton, *kente* cloth has long been worn by the Akan royalty of West Africa. The fabric is often used for special occasions and celebrations and, as machine-made *kente* print, is popular across the globe.

Pastoralists and hunter-gatherers

The San, Khoikoi, Nuer, and Oromo

Across Southern and East Africa, peoples hunted, foraged, herded livestock, and developed unique cultures. These groups have lived off the land for generations, but clashed with African and European empires.

Several semi-nomadic peoples have lived for centuries in the grasslands and deserts of Southern and East Africa. Their resourcefulness and perseverance is reflected in their long histories. One group, the San, are believed to be the oldest surviving culture in Africa, and their rock art stretches back over 20,000 years.

The San and Khoikhoi

The San people are Indigenous hunter-gatherer groups, whose origins can be traced back to the region that is now modern-day Botswana, as well as parts of Namibia, Angola, Zambia, Zimbabwe, and South Africa; their populations are still spread across these regions today. The various San communities speak different languages and practise different religions, but have much in common. The San way of life is based on hunting animals such as antelope with

△ **Leather bag**
San bags are used to carry hunting equipment, food, charms, and tobacco. Animals are usually hunted and skinned by men, before the hide is sewn and decorated by women and men.

bow and arrow and gathering edible plants and insects. These peoples are customarily mobile, with small, egalitarian groups staying in lightweight shelters as they forage or gathering in longer-term habitations, especially near waterholes during the dry season.

The Khoikhoi are another Indigenous group from Southern Africa, with a distinct cultural and linguistic heritage from the San. They are believed to have originally inhabited the southwestern region of Africa, which includes modern-day South Africa, Namibia, and northern Botswana. Today, Khoikhoi communities live mainly in Namibia and South Africa. This people's way of life is based on herding and trading cattle, sheep, and goats.

In the last few thousand years, waves of Bantu-speaking peoples (see pp. 36–37) spread into San and Khoikhoi lands in Southern Africa. However, both peoples remained widespread until European colonization intensified in the 18th and 19th centuries, when many were killed or displaced from the most productive lands. Some San and Khoikhoi remain dedicated to pastoral ways of life, while others work on farms or in cities.

△ **San village**
San gather outside a hut in Nyae Nyae Conservancy. This community-managed area in Namibia is a San ancestral heartland, home to several San villages.

△ **Hunting bow**
This San bow would be used in conjunction with arrows sometimes tipped in diamphotoxin, a poison derived from beetle larvae.

The Nuer and Oromo

Like the Khoikhoi, the Nuer, who are believed to have originated in what is now central Sudan, built their society around cattle. Cattle products were used in everything from clothing to shields, with dung used as toothpaste and burned to keep away pests. As Arab peoples expanded into their homeland, the Nuer moved into the grassland and marshes of South Sudan and western Ethiopia, defeating and absorbing communities of a local people, the Dinka, as they went. In the early 20th century, the Nuer faced the imposition of British colonial control in northeast Africa. Since Sudan gained its independence in 1956, Nuer forces have been involved in the conflicts for South Sudan's independence (gained in 2011).

The Oromo are fellow East African pastoralists. In the 16th and 17th centuries, they migrated from southeastern Ethiopia, conquering territory until they occupied much of southern and central Ethiopia. While most Oromo in the south remained cattle herders, more settled agriculture was increasingly widespread in other parts of the country. Today, the Oromo are the largest ethnic group in Ethiopia, mostly practising Islam or Christianity.

▽ **Village scene**
An 18th-century Dutch depiction of a Khoikhoi village shows a group of dancers and musicians.

Mundari cattle camp, South Sudan
The Mundari people from South Sudan are descendants of the original settlers of the Nile Valley, who first domesticated animals and practised agriculture at least 5,000 years ago. A species of long-horned cow called Ankole-Watusi forms the central focus of the Mundari people's lives, their culture, and their religion. Regarded as sacred, these animals bring social status and the possibility of getting married and starting a family, since dowries are fixed in units of cattle. While older people and maternal relatives often live in towns, younger members of the community usually reside in camps with the cattle, where they care for and graze the flock.

Mythology and folklore

Beliefs and legends in African cultures

In African societies — as in most cultures — mythology, stories, and ancient beliefs reveal much about how people viewed the origins of their world, and their place and role within it.

Anansi sits at the centre of the web

Shaft is intricately carved

Wood covered in gold leaf

Myths can encode a civilization's values and contain profound symbolism, which is of deep importance to the society where they originated. This makes them much more than colourful stories documenting old beliefs and superstitions. Africa's history contains many mythologies formulated across different eras by widely diverse cultures.

Origin stories and supreme beings

Many cultures have their own narrative that explains how life began. It may involve a pantheon of gods or one supreme being. Ancient Egypt's origin stories describe the world as created from the tears, saliva, and other bodily fluids of the gods. These tales clearly symbolize fertility, birth, and growth. In the Egyptian pantheon of deities, gods and goddesses embody qualities, physical objects, or important moments in life such as war, death, love, fertility, the harvest, and wine.

The creation mythology of the Yoruba of West Africa involves a supreme being, Olodumare, who empowered a lesser deity named Obatala to create humans. In some versions of the myth, only Olodumare could animate Obatala's humans with the breath of life. Yoruba religion also recognized other deities (known as *orisha*). These include: Orunmila, counsellor of the gods and god of wisdom, knowledge, and divination; Eshu, a trickster figure; Ogun, a god of war and iron; and Shango, a god of thunderstorms.

◁ **Symbol of office**
On this palace official's staff from West Africa, the spider's web represents the trickster god Anansi. The spider is considered wise and cunning.

In Southern Africa, the mythology of the San people of the Cape region included belief in shape-shifting figures such as IKaggen, a kind of divine artisan responsible for creating and maintaining the universe. IKaggen could assume many forms, including an eland bull, a snake, and a caterpillar, but was usually a praying mantis. In one telling of his story, he created the moon by throwing one of his shoes into the sky.

Bantu-speakers inhabit much of Africa south of the Sahara. While Islam and Christianity are the dominant religions among them today, their faith was once based around ancestor veneration and the worship of tutelary deities (protector gods of specific places or professions). These Bantu-speakers believed in a supreme being, whose name varied from place to place, but they also consulted diviners for advice and help in spiritual matters.

Like the Bantu-speakers, the Asante of what is now Ghana also worshipped a supreme deity. His name was Nyame, though he was also sometimes called Onyankopon. He created all things and then separated himself from the human world, ascending heavenwards in the tradition of sky-gods found in many other religions worldwide.

Animal legends

A variety of animals also play important roles in beliefs across African cultures. A common tale across the continent involves two creatures, often a lizard and a chameleon but sometimes a dog and a goat,

◁ **Spirit of the water**
This painted wooden figure shows Mami Wata, a water spirit who is feared and venerated in West, Central, and Southern Africa. The spirit represents wealth and success.

◁ **Brass fan**
Priestesses of Osun, the Yoruba goddess of beauty and fertility, carried brass fans in their rituals celebrating her power and authority.

Different birds are depicted

Snakes decorate the rim

Stylized palm leaves

Decorative carved handle

THE DOGON **CREATION STORY**

The creation myth of the Dogon people of Mali says that the supreme deity, Amma, created the first living creature, Nommo. Not content with being the sole living person, Nommo divided himself into four pairs of twins, from which the human race descended. In Dogon tradition, when a person dies their spirit returns to Amma after a ritual known as a *dama* is performed by masked dancers on stilts.

"**Anansi**, the child of Nsia, the mother of Nyame, the **Sky-god**."

AKAN/ASANTE DESCRIPTION OF ANANSI

and explains why humans are not immortal like the gods. The chameleon was sent to tell people that they would be allowed to live forever. But he was too slow and was overtaken by a lizard, who informed humans that the gods had decided to make them mortal after all. This was why the Zulu of Southern Africa regarded seeing a chameleon as a bad omen. Other animal-based fables involve trickster rabbits, gullible hippos, and helpful elephants delivering homilies on how to live good lives. In West Africa, the trickster spider god Anansi was the protagonist of a great many myths and legends.

Human spirits

Occasionally, real humans achieved legendary status. Chaminuka was a holy leader among the Zezuru, a branch of the Shona people of modern-day Zimbabwe. When he died in 1883, Chaminuka's spirit reportedly "spoke" through the mediums Mutota and Pasipamire. One of his prophecies that they channelled was the building of a large settlement "at Harare" — the city that is today Zimbabwe's capital.

Africa's myths and folklore bear witness to world views where the sacred and the secular are intertwined. Even today, old beliefs and mythologies continue to exert much power and influence.

◁ **Asante gold**
This pectoral badge, called an *akrafokonmu* ("soul washer's disc"), was worn for protection by members of the Asante court in modern-day Ghana. The Asante Empire became wealthy through the trading of gold mined from its territory.

4

European encounters

1440–1914

European encounters

Aside from the northern Mediterranean coast, large areas of Africa remained unknown to the rest of the world until the arrival of Portuguese explorers in the 15th century. Henry the Navigator and Bartolomeu Dias were among the first Europeans to sail along Africa's west coast, ushering in an era of European exploration that saw Portuguese mariners mapping the coastlines and hinterlands of Senegal, the Gambia, and Guinea between 1444 and 1447. In 1497–98, their compatriot Vasco da Gama rounded the Cape of Good Hope and sailed along the eastern coast of Africa to India – looting Arab merchant ships and attacking the island of Mozambique along the way.

An unfair exchange of resources

The Portuguese, and the other Europeans who followed, were not interested in exploration for its own sake. What drew them to Africa – and convinced them to stay and establish settlements and set up trading agreements – was the continent's wealth of resources. Gold and rubber were especially sought after, but it was one "commodity" above all that defined the complex relationship between Europe and Africa: people. With Portugal, Spain, and Britain establishing empires in the Americas from the early 16th century, people were needed to work the farms and plantations. West Africa in particular (but also East Africa and the Sahara) had a plentiful supply of enslaved people who had been captured in intra-African conflicts and could readily be bought in exchange for

weapons, gunpowder, iron, textiles, and other items. States such as the Dahomey and Asante empires in West Africa and the Sakalava Empire in Madagascar grew wealthy from the 16th to the 18th centuries based in part on slavery.

Further south, in 1652 Dutch navigator Jan van Riebeeck set up a fresh food supply station in what would become Cape Town. When Britain seized the Cape Colony from the Dutch in 1806, replacing one foreign power with another, the tone was set for future European actions. Europeans became less interested in trading with Africans or building relationships with local leaders: the emphasis now was on appropriating resources and assuming political and military control of territory. Commerce gave way to colonialization.

At the Berlin Conference of 1884–85, the main colonial nations met without the involvement of any African nations and agreed their spheres of influence on the continent. The resulting "Scramble for Africa" allowed imperialists such as King Leopold II of Belgium and Britain's Cecil Rhodes free rein to expand and exploit their nations' colonial holdings. Religion, too, became a tool of empire building, with missionaries criss-crossing the continent in order to spread a faith that sought to replace local beliefs with a "Europeanized" version of Christianity. The colonizers attempted to justify their actions – and their success in colonizing most of Africa – by claiming that they were bringing "civilization" to people they saw as "inferior". Consequently, between 1884 and 1914, the African continent was partitioned into protectorates, colonies, and free-trade areas, with the Europeans' control imposed by their superior weaponry and industrialized military might.

1444 Portuguese explorers round Cap-Vert, Africa's westernmost point

1488 Bartolomeu Dias becomes the first European to round the Cape of Good Hope

1560 Jesuit missionaries sail up the Zambezi River

◁ **Portuguese traders depicted on a bronze plaque from Benin, 16th/17th century**

1456 Portugal's Luis Cadamosto reaches the Cabo Verde Islands, off Senegal

1497–98 Vasco da Gama sails around Southern Africa to India

Africa colonized

The inset map (right) shows the routes of the Portuguese explorers in the 15th century and areas of colonial presence in 1878 (see key, below). The map below shows the extent of colonialization in 1914, less than 40 years later.

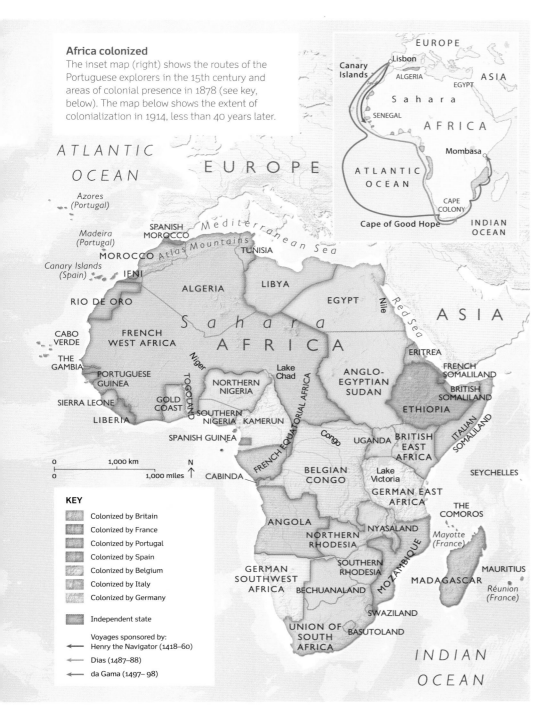

KEY

Colonized by Britain
Colonized by France
Colonized by Portugal
Colonized by Spain
Colonized by Belgium
Colonized by Italy
Colonized by Germany

Independent state

Voyages sponsored by:
← Henry the Navigator (1418–60)
← Dias (1487–88)
← da Gama (1497–98)

▲ Portuguese explorer Vasco da Gama

▲ Map of West Africa, 16th century

▲ South West African queen Njinga (c. 1583–1663)

1652 Dutch mariner Jan van Riebeeck establishes a settlement on the site of Cape Town

1806 Britain seizes the Cape Colony from the Netherlands

1884–85 Berlin Conference partitions Africa between the European nations

1908 Belgium annexes the Congo Free State from its own king, Leopold II, due to his misrule

1790 Scottish explorer Mungo Park travels up the Niger River

1871 Missing Scottish missionary and explorer David Livingstone is found alive at Lake Tanganyika

1879 The Zulu of Southern Africa defeat British forces at the Battle of Isandlwana

1914–18 World War I and its aftermath lead to weakening of some colonial powers in Africa

The Atlantic slave trade

The largest-ever forced transoceanic migration

Between the 16th and 19th centuries, European traders and merchants transported 12–15 million enslaved Africans to a life of hardship and forced them to labour on sugar and tobacco plantations in the Americas.

In the mid-15th century, European mariners began to explore the world. The west coast of Africa was an early port of call, merchants and adventurers drawn there by tales of vast gold reserves and the potential riches of unknown lands. By 1488, Portugal's Bartolomeu Dias had rounded Africa's southernmost tip, the Cape of Good Hope, opening for the first time a sea route from Europe to Asia; four years later, Christopher Columbus crossed the Atlantic to the Americas. The world was connected as never before, with unmapped territories opened up for commerce, settlement, development – and exploitation.

Origins of the slave trade

In this age of inter-connectedness, West Africa emerged as a vital maritime hub between Europe, Asia, and the Americas. West Africa had ports, gold mines, supply stations – and what traders of the time saw as another valuable resource: people. As early as

the 1480s, Portugal and the Kingdom of Kongo (see pp. 182–83) had been exchanging guns for enslaved prisoners of war, who were then transported to the sugar plantations that Portugal had established on the island of São Tomé (off Gabon). Along with the Cabo Verde Islands (off Senegal), São Tomé became both a testing ground for the viability of a slave-labour-based agricultural system and a way-station for the transport of enslaved Africans.

When the huge territory of Brazil became a Portuguese colony in the 1530s, the demand for enslaved Africans increased. In addition to Kongo, West African states including Luanda, Benguela (both modern Angola) and Dahomey (modern Benin) began to trade enslaved Africans – mostly captives from local wars – for European luxuries, clothing, and weapons.

The trade in enslaved people intensified from the 1650s. Export crops, such as sugar and tobacco, were in high demand and the owners of plantations in the Americas and the Caribbean had a limitless need for enslaved African labour, especially after it was discovered that the Indigenous people the colonizers intended to enslave had no natural immunity to "Western" infections such as flu and scarlet fever. Some sources estimate that 95 per cent of the Indigenous population died in the decades after the Europeans arrived.

Horror and abolition

West African coastal states contributed to the Atlantic slave trade, playing an important role in its structure. African leaders decided how many people they wanted to sell and their sex and age, compelling European traders to take often high quotas of women and children, despite their preference for men, viewed as the most profitable workers. Some 70 per cent of women and 90 per cent of children who entered the Americas between 1500 and 1800 were shipped from Africa. The journey from Africa to the Americas, known as the Middle Passage, was notoriously

▽ **Uprooted peoples**
The largest numbers of Africans were trafficked to the Americas, with smaller, but significant, numbers to the Middle East, Asia, and Europe.

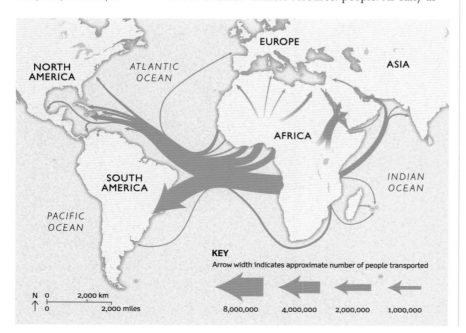

KEY
Arrow width indicates approximate number of people transported

N   0   2,000 km
↑   0   2,000 miles

8,000,000   4,000,000   2,000,000   1,000,000

△ **Life below deck**
A watercolour of a Spanish slave ship captured by a British anti-slavery patrol in 1846 provides an eyewitness view of the cramped conditions on board.

dangerous. Enslaved Africans were shackled and packed in confined and squalid conditions. The voyage took between six and eight weeks and mortality rates were high, with frequent outbreaks of dysentery, smallpox, measles, flu, and scurvy.

By the early 18th century, religious groups, including Quakers, Methodists, and Baptists in the US and Britain, had begun to call for the slave trade to end. Enslaved people also put pressure on the colonial system by staging revolts both on ships and in the Americas. In 1803, Denmark abolished the trade,

followed by Britain in 1807, the US in 1808, and most other countries by the 1830s. Although British, French, and American ships would patrol coasts to enforce the ban, compliance was not strict since slavery itself was not abolished until the 1860s.

While the end of the slave trade was a welcome development, it would ultimately lead to a new set of geopolitical dynamics. In 1884, the European powers met in Berlin to arrange the partitioning of Africa among each other (see pp. 210–11). By 1914, these imperial powers had fully colonized the continent.

Women's quarters at the back

Children in the middle

Men at the front

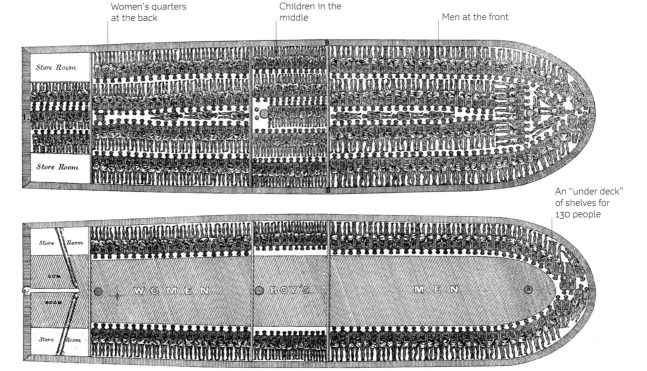

An "under deck" of shelves for 130 people

▷ **Ship plan**
This diagram of the *Brookes*, a British slave ship, was published by abolitionists in 1787. It shows how 454 enslaved Africans were crammed into the hold and transported to the Americas.

West African griots

In West Africa, *griots* are chroniclers of history, who for centuries have preserved the oral history, genealogies, and stories of people such as the Mandingo (Malinke), Fulani, Hausa, Songhai, and Tukulor. In African languages, they are known by many names, including *jeli* or *jali* in Mande (the Mandingo language) and *arokin* in Yoruba. Many *griots* sing their narratives, often providing their own instrumental accompaniment. Historically, they formed a specialized group, with marriage taking place only with other *griots*, and families of *griots* acting as advisors to kings and emperors. *Griots* would be called upon to settle disputes, and each village had its own own *griots* to relate local histories.

Europe in Africa

Early intervention on the continent

European interference in Africa did not begin with 19th-century colonization. Initially based on trade, Europe's earlier presence in the continent developed into something more sinister and exploitative.

The first Europeans to reach Africa south of the Sahara were Portuguese mariners in the 1440s. Over the next four centuries, virtually every corner of the continent was mapped and studied by European explorers, merchants, and missionaries. In the process, they opened up Africa – not always willingly – to the trade in goods and humans, foreign settlement, the exploitation of its resources, the spread of Christianity, and, ultimately, imperialism.

The huge plantations in the Americas established by Europeans in the 16th century, growing crops such as sugar and cotton, required vast amounts of labour. By the late 19th century, 15 million Africans had been enslaved and shipped across the Atlantic (see pp. 162–63) to work on these plantations. In the 19th century, the end of feudalism and the agricultural and industrial revolutions that followed saw the economies and the populations of Europe's nations grow, along with their need for new markets, products, raw materials, and resources. All were in plentiful supply in Africa.

European routes into Africa

The wealthy and hugely influential *Vereenigde Oost-Indische Compagnie* (VOC, or Dutch East India Company) was set up in 1602 to carry out trade activities in Asia. To make the journey from Europe to Asia easier, in 1652 the Dutch navigator Jan van Riebeeck established a supply and maintenance station for the VOC's ships at what would become Cape Town (see pp. 168–69). This marked the beginning of Dutch involvement in South Africa that would spread from a small fortified settlement to subjugation, wars, land expropriation, and colonization across the country.

Although Britain's entry point into African affairs was via its active participation in the Atlantic slave trade, by the early 19th century it was using its opposition to the slave trade – which it had abolished in its own empire in 1807 – as an excuse to increase its interference in Africa. To give the Royal Navy the bases it needed to stop British commercial vessels

▽ **Cultural exchange**
This 16th-century ivory salt cellar was carved in Benin, West Africa. It is possibly a depiction of the Portuguese merchant for whom it was made as a gift.

KEY
← Enslaved people
← Colonial products:
  Sugar, tobacco, dyestuffs, cotton, cacao, coffee, furs, silver
← Manufactured goods:
  Armaments, textiles, wine

△ **Triangular trade**
From the early 16th century, enslaved Africans were taken to the Americas to produce materials that were in turn transported to Europe and manufactured into goods. These goods were then transported to Africa and exchanged for more enslaved people.

collecting enslaved people from West Africa, Britain took over parts of Sierra Leone, the Gambia, and the Gold Coast in 1808, 1816, and 1821 respectively. In addition to this, Britain had seized the Cape Colony, around the Cape of Good Hope in South Africa, from its trading rivals the Dutch in 1795. Within a century, Cecil Rhodes, a British mining magnate, had formed the British South Africa Company (BSAC) and pushed north from the Cape into what would become Rhodesia (modern-day Zimbabwe). In doing so, he took control of the region's rich reserves of gold, diamonds, and other minerals, and ultimately paved the way for the British government to exploit these resources.

Other European nations followed similar routes to greater involvement in Africa. France's trading relationships with North Africa began in the early 16th century, bringing the region within its sphere of influence by the start of the age of imperialism in the

19th century. French merchants in West Africa set up similar arrangements. In Senegal, the trading post of Saint-Louis, established in 1659, gave France a foothold in Africa south of the Sahara. From here it extended its interference into Mauritania, Côte d'Ivoire, Niger, and elsewhere two centuries later.

Germany's presence in Africa began in 1682, when the then-independent state of Brandenburg-Prussia (Germany was not unified until 1871) founded two small settlements in modern-day Ghana, and established the Brandenburg African Company to explore business opportunities in the region.

Impact on African life and society

The Europeans' arrival in Africa had far-reaching consequences. European-introduced diseases such as cholera, yellow fever, meningitis, TB, measles, and smallpox decimated African populations. States unwilling or unable to trade produce for Western weaponry declined faster than those that did. South Africa's Zulu, for example, actively rejected the use of guns and rifles in favour of their habitual, but ultimately ineffective, spears and shields (see pp. 206–207). Christian missionaries converted Africans from their Indigenous belief systems (see pp. 204–205) by the millions, irrevocably changing the continent's religious landscape.

Europe's relationship with Africa before colonization saw many of the unequal power relationships, social changes, economic exploitations, and military interventions put in place that made imperialism, when it came, easier to impose and longer-lasting.

ENGLAND'S SLAVE-TRADING COMPANY

Set up in 1660, England's Royal African Company (RAC), whose emblem is shown here, was an early example of a state-endorsed commercial enterprise. It transported 187,697 people to the Americas, branding on the chest of each one the organization's initials.

TOP VIEW

Coat of arms of William IV

Ornamental *rocaille* carving in gold

Mercury, the god of trade, shown holding the company logo

Map of West African coast between Senegal and Angola

VIEW OF BASE

Enslaved people at a market

Figure representing the ivory trade

Real gold nugget embedded in lid

Figure representing panning for gold

△ **Commemorative box**
William IV, *Stadtholder* (leader) of the Dutch Republic, was given this presentation box by the Dutch West India Company (WIC) in 1749. It contained his letter of appointment as the WIC's Governor. Each finely carved detail depicts an aspect of the WIC's activities in Africa.

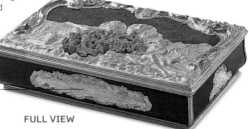

Side plaque depicts Dutch forts in West Africa

FULL VIEW

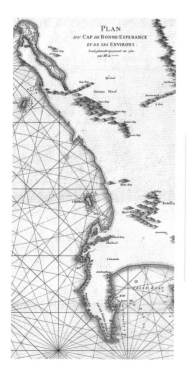

△ **New arrivals**
This 1680 work shows the Dutch fleet sailing into Table Bay – a far cry from the two ships Jan van Riebeeck arrived with in 1652.

Cape Town

One of South Africa's most historically important cities

South Africa's oldest and second-largest (after Johannesburg) city was founded in the mid-17th century. It grew from a humble Dutch naval supply station into a vibrant metropolis, albeit one with a troubled and contested history.

The Indigenous inhabitants of southern Africa were the Khoisan, an umbrella term covering the Khoikhoi and San people. As nomadic herders and hunter-gatherers, they moved with the seasons, their migrations based on a deep understanding of the land, its climate, water sources, vegetation, and animals. Their way of life was founded on a strong sense of community, with extended families often living together and an emphasis on the well-being of the group over the individual – important elements in

◁ **Maritime map**
This nautical chart of 1752 shows the Cape of Good Hope region. The fort that would eventually evolve into Cape Town is indicated just north of Table Mountain.

furnishing feelings of belonging among people who were always in motion, rarely settling in towns or villages. Their vast territory covered modern South Africa, Namibia, Botswana, Zimbabwe, and Angola.

The Khoisan way of life would change forever on 6 April 1652, when the Dutch navigator Jan van Riebeeck arrived. The Dutch East India Company (see pp. 166–67) had commissioned Van Riebeeck to establish a resupply station halfway along the route for ships making the long voyage between Europe and the East Indies. The Suez Canal would not be built until 1869, so European ships heading for Asia had to sail around Africa, navigating in the process the treacherous Cape of Good Hope, some 60 km (37 miles) along the coast from Cape Town.

"!ke e: /xarra //ke [diverse people unite]"

MOTTO ON THE COAT OF ARMS OF SOUTH AFRICA, WRITTEN IN THE EXTINCT KHOISAN LANGUAGE, |XAM

Van Riebeeck set up a small market garden with the intention of supplying fresh fruit and vegetables to passing ships. In doing so, he founded the first permanent European settlement in South Africa. Before long, the Khoisan were trading their livestock in return for European products, including tobacco, alcohol, and worked iron. Local figures such as the Khoi chieftain Autshumao acted as translators and intermediaries — and, in the case of his niece, Krotoa, served as ambassadors and even peace negotiators in times of conflict.

By 1654, several Dutch farmers had built farms, van Riebeeck's small market garden expanding into something much larger and commercially focused. Instead of only looking outwards, seeing their small harbour colony as a stopover en route to Asia, the Dutch turned inwards, looking for the ways and means to exploit the territory inland from the Cape.

A disputed land

The encroachment of Dutch farmers and settlers into Khoisan pastures and hunting grounds restricted these nomadic people's lifestyle and made conflict inevitable. This came in 1659, when the Khoisan stopped trading cattle with the Dutch and trebled the price of other livestock. In retaliation, the Dutch confiscated Khoisan cattle — initiating the First Khoi-Dutch War, which ended the following year with defeat for the Khoisan. In 1670, the Khoisan chieftain Gonnema, whose people were known as the Cochoqua, attacked Dutch settlers who had looted the Cochoqua's cattle. This became the prelude to the Second Khoi-Dutch War (1673–77), resulting in another Khoisan defeat. Both conflicts had disastrous consequences for the Khoisan. The Dutch disempowered influential clan chiefs and forced the Khoisan people into the less productive lands of the interior.

This "internal exile" of the Khoisan paved the way for further Dutch settlement and intensive agriculture, which was sustained by slavery. Britain temporarily annexed the Cape colony in 1795, and again more permanently in 1806. The British ended the slave trade the following year and this, along with the large influx of British settlers into the region, antagonized the Dutch. In 1836, the Cape's Dutch inhabitants embarked on the Great Trek, a mass migration north to escape British rule. In doing so, they intruded on both Khoisan and Zulu lands, displacing Indigenous peoples and fomenting unrest. Cape Town, meanwhile, thrived. Between 1891 and 1901 its population grew from 67,000 to 171,000, and on 31 May 1910 Cape Town became the capital of the new Union of South Africa.

As a result of its location and the circumstances of its foundation, Cape Town became a highly cosmopolitan city. Intermarriages between European settlers, enslaved people, the Khoisan, and other, smaller groups such as the Xhosa people of the Eastern Cape region, produced what, for its time, was a multiracial and uniquely heterogeneous population.

▷ **Settled community**
Not all Khoisan were migratory. Some lived in *kraal* (small villages), as captured in this c. 1835 lithograph. Note the tethered giraffe in the foreground.

Madagascar

An island at the crossroads

Lying off the coast of modern-day Mozambique, the island of Madagascar was well situated in the Indian Ocean to facilitate trade between East Africa and Asia from medieval times onwards.

First settled in the early Middle Ages, Madagascar had a population of ethnically mixed Austronesian (Asian) and Bantu-speaking (African) peoples divided into distinct groups. Among these were the Sakalava ("people of the long valley") from western Madagascar. Semi-nomadic pastoralists, they kept large zebu (humped cattle) livestock before developing into skilled seafarers and, by the early 16th century, they emerged as the island's dominant group under their king, Andriamisara.

Sakalava dynasties

The source of Sakalava power was the cattle and enslaved people they exchanged for guns with Omani and European traders. These weapons, which no other Madagascan peoples possessed, allowed Andriamisara, and later his son Andriandahifotsy, to assert Sakalava dominance across the island. But the Sakalava did not favour a centralized power structure. Instead, they divided areas into separate kingdoms. Some, like Menabe and Boina, ruled by Andriandahifotsy's sons Andriamanetiarivo and Andriamandisoarivo respectively, were relatively strong. Others, however, proved too small and weak to withstand the attentions of peoples that emerged as rivals

▽ **Men at arms**
The Sakalava, photographed here c. 1900, dominated Madagascar for around 150 years. They were superseded first by the Merina and then the French.

◁ **By royal appointment**
Also known as "the Great", Radama I, depicted in a painting from 1905, was the first king of Madagascar recognized by a European state.

around the mid-1750s. These peoples included the Betsimisaraka and the Merina – who had begun to transact with overseas traders, giving them access to firearms.

Under their leader Ramaromanompo (r. 1712–54), the Betsimisaraka ("the many inseparables") from eastern Madagascar gained strength through alliances with local leaders and conquest of rivals. But they – and the Sakalava – would be subdued by the Merina ("the elevated ones"), who emerged out of the central highland plateau. Their regional power base grew in the 16th century, led by their queen, Rafohy. This growth continued until King Andrianampoinimerina (r. 1787–1810) established the Merina as a preeminent force.

European intrusion

Merina power reached its greatest extent under Andrianampoinimerina's son, Radama I. Aged just 18 when he came to the throne in 1810, Radama introduced Westernizing policies and welcomed in Christian missionaries. His skeptical attitude towards his people's religious practices, especially their devotion to rituals involving *sampy* (sacred amulets), angered the Merina's conservative elites.

"**Ny ranomasina no valapariako** [The border of my rice fields **is the sea**]."

KING ANDRIANAMPOINIMERINA ON HIS AMBITION TO UNITE MADAGASCAR

Elongated
wooden poles,
called
tandotrano,
indicate
aristocratic
houses

Steep hillside
on which
Antsahatsiroa,
a wealthy suburb
of the capital,
Antananarivo,
is built

Keen to extend his kingdom, Radama embarked on
several wars of conquest, on some of which he was
accompanied by James Hastie, a British government
civil agent in Madagascar. Radama's willingness to
involve Britain in his country's affairs was not
universally popular among his people. Nevertheless,
Radama's pro-Western, Anglophone stance led to
Britain recognizing him as king of Madagascar in
1817, when the two nations signed an alliance. Britain
then supplied Radama with the arms and military
training that allowed him to conquer two-thirds of

the island. He abolished the slave trade, established
schools and churches, and codified the Malagasy
language in writing for the first time.

Radama died in 1828, aged 36, revered as a military
genius and great nation builder. He was succeeded
by his wife, Ranavalona I (see pp. 172–73), whose
opposition to Radama's Westernization was met with
aggressive European interference, especially from
France. In 1896, the French suppressed the last
remnants of Indigenous power and Madagascar
became a French colony until 1960.

△ **Iconic construction**
Madagascar's architecture
of tall sloping roofs, shown
here in a photograph from
1856, during the reign of
Queen Ranavalona I,
is unique in Africa. It
resembles styles in Borneo,
from where Madagascar's
earliest settlers arrived.

Ranavalona I

Powerful absolute ruler of Madagascar

Ranavalona I (r. 1828–61) was a ruthless and autocratic leader who suppressed her own subjects and made use of forced labour. But she presented a fierce and effective resistance to colonial interests in Madagascar.

Little is known for certain about the early life of Ranavalona I, but most sources agree she was born Rabodoandrianampoinimerina in 1778 in Merina (see pp. 170–171). Her father saved the life of King Andrianampoinimerina (r. 1787–1810), whose uncle plotted to kill him. In gratitude, the king adopted Ranavalona into the royal family and she later married his son, the future king Radama I. Their marriage was childless – although Ranavalona later had a child with Madagascar's prime minister – so when Radama became king, he had no children to succeed him.

△ **Trial of the conspirators**
This French engraving from 1861 depicts the trial of those who plotted Ranavalona's overthrow. The Queen executed many of the locals who were involved and banished the Europeans.

After Radama's early death in 1828, Ranavalona seized power from the rightful heir, the son of Radama's eldest sister, and became the absolute ruler of most of Madagascar and the first female ruler of the kingdom of Merina since its founding in 1540.

Sovereignty and independence

Ranavalona's reign was marked by efforts to protect Madagascar from European encroachment. In 1829, she repelled a French naval attack in the north of the island, albeit assisted by an outbreak of malaria among foreign forces. Thereafter, she stepped up her policies of self-sufficiency and isolationism. She also restricted missionary activities, banned her subjects from practising Christianity, and engaged in wars to expand her realm over the island. According to some scholars, she made significant use of the practice of *fanompoana* (forced labour). In 1857, she foiled a plot by her son, Rakoto, among others, to topple her from power.

Following Ranavalona's peaceful death in 1861, aged around 83, Madagascar was governed by a series of weak rulers and entered a period of decline. It was declared a French colony on 6 August 1896.

△ **Coronation gown**
Despite her hostility to European influences, Ranavalona's striking coronation gown is believed to have been designed by a French tailor.

> "I will **not cede** the **thickness of one hair of my realm!**"

RANAVALONA I

1778 Ranavalona is born in the kingdom of Merina

1829 French forces launch an unprovoked attack on Madagascar

1835 Ranavalona bans her subjects from practising Christianity

1857 Ranavalona thwarts a plot by her son Rakoto to dethrone her, but pardons him

1828 Ranavalona ascends to the throne following the death of Radama I

1831 A ban on Christian baptism and marriages is introduced

1840 Persecution of the Christians begins

1861 Ranavalona dies and is succeded by Rakoto (Radama II)

Kingdoms of the Great Lakes: Bunyoro and Buganda

Power and privilege in East Africa

Among the many kingdoms in the region of the Great Lakes, Bunyoro and Buganda were the two most significant. These two powerful states dominated the region through trade and their absolute rulers.

The Great Lakes are scattered across the East African Rift, a huge geological scar that first appeared 25 million years ago. The region contains some of the world's largest and deepest lakes, including Lake Victoria, Lake Tanganyika, and Lake Malawi, and its abundance of water, fertile volcanic soil, and good climate made it an excellent incubator for emerging civilizations. These include the Kitara Empire of c. 1200 BCE–900 CE from which successor states including Bunyoro and Buganda emerged. Today, the area comprises Uganda, Burundi, Rwanda, the Democratic Republic of the Congo, Ethiopia, Kenya, Tanzania, Malawi, Zambia, and Mozambique.

The kingdom of Bunyoro

One of the most successful Great Lakes civilizations was the kingdom of Bunyoro, northwest of Lake Victoria in present-day Uganda. Founded around the 12th century, Bunyoro was at its height from the 16th to the 19th centuries, dominating the region's lucrative salt trade through its control of the extensive Kibiro saltworks on the shores of Lake Mwitanzige

△ **On parade**
This European woodcut from 1864 depicts *Kabaka* Mutesa I. Under Mutesa, Christian missionaries, Muslim preachers, and Western commercial interests made inroads into Buganda.

(formerly Lake Albert). Bunyoro's metallurgy was also highly sought after and it traded heavily in ivory, cattle, and crops. Politically, Bunyoro's kings held absolute power and they personally appointed the chiefs that governed each of the state's provinces.

The state went into decline from the late 18th century, when the neighbouring kingdom of Buganda occupied two of its provinces, while another province, Toro, seceded and took the money-making saltworks with it. Bunyoro also lost its dominance of the ivory trade in the mid-19th century. A few decades later, when Bunyoro's *omukama*, or king, Chwa II Kabalega tried to resist imperial incursions by the British and

◁ **Royal resting place**
The Kasubi Tombs, in Kampala, Uganda, contain the remains of four Bugandan 19th- and 20th-century kings. The site is an important religious centre for the Buganda people today.

△ **King of Bunyoro**
In this photo from 1922, Bunyoro's king Duhaga II is flanked by two chiefs. The chinstraps of their ceremonial beaded caps are fringed with "beards" of colobus monkey fur.

the Ottoman Empire, he was overthrown and, in 1899, exiled to the Seychelles. Bunyoro was forcibly incorporated into the British Empire, subjected to what has been called a "scorched earth" policy. The guerilla war against the British, which had begun in 1894, led to widespread famine and the deaths of an estimated three-quarters of Bunyoro's population.

Power struggles in Buganda

Bunyoro's neighbour Buganda was located along the northern shore of Lake Victoria. A powerful local chief named Kato Kintu founded it in the 14th century and became the first *kabaka*, or king. Rulers relied on a first minister, or *katikkiro*, to administer the state. On the death of each *kabaka*, Buganda's clans would often battle for the throne. It was not unknown for a *kabaka* to murder his brothers and other potential rivals in order to secure his position.

Despite Buganda becoming the Great Lakes region's largest state and strongest military power, its constitutional instability would ultimately contribute to its decline. When in 1884 the *kabaka* Mutesa I died, Britain took advantage of the resulting political infighting to impose its authority. It forced through the Buganda Agreement of 1900, which formalized British control and made the kingdom a British protectorate. Buganda's economy expanded during the colonial period when it became a producer of coffee and cotton – although most of the resulting wealth was exported to the UK.

After Uganda won its independence in 1962, four monarchies in the country – Bunyoro, Buganda, Toro, and Busoga – were abolished in 1967, but were reinstated in 1993 following civil unrest. The kingdoms still exist, albeit in reduced states and with their monarchs occupying largely ceremonial roles.

Rwanda and Burundi

Countries with a shared history

The Hutu and Tutsi have coexisted in Africa's Great Lakes for centuries. Both groups were part of the kingdoms of Rwanda and Burundi from about the 15th to the 17th century, but colonialism stirred tensions that lasted into independence.

The first known inhabitants of the landlocked nations of Rwanda and Burundi, the hunter-gatherer Twa people, settled in the forests of the Great Lakes region before 3000 BCE. From around the 5th century CE, the hills and high plains of Rwanda and Burundi received waves of southbound Hutu migrants, most of whom were small-scale farmers. The Twa were pushed to the margins when minor Hutu kingdoms began to emerge in the 12th century, before the Tutsi arrived from the

◁ **Inyambo cattle**
Prized in Rwanda and Burundi, long-horned ankole cows are referred to as *inyambo*, "the cattle of kings", because of their close ties and importance to royalty, wealth, and status.

north around the 15th century. The martial Tutsi, whose herds of distinctive long-horned ankole cattle grazed large areas of land, then began to dominate.

The Kingdom of Rwanda

A centralized state, the kingdom of Rwanda, emerged in the 15th or 16th century. Some believe its roots go back to the ancient godlike Tutsi leader Gihanga I. Over the years, a succession of kings, or *mwami*, expanded Rwanda from its beginnings near the modern-day capital, Kigali. The kingdom followed a broadly feudal system (the *ubuhake*) in which Tutsi landowners offered protection and land to Hutu farmers in exchange for food and labour. The Twa were mistreated and considered low status. This structure, with a Tutsi aristocracy and Hutu vassals, lasted for centuries, although there was social mobility, including marriages between Tutsi, Hutu, and Twa people. Over time, the state became more unified, with a justice system and a grain supply network controlled by the king. Under Kigeli IV (r. 1853–95), the kingdom reached its greatest extent – which still forms Rwanda's borders today.

Social relationships in Burundi

The kingdom of Burundi (or Urundi) was established by Ntare I in the late 17th century. His family became known as the *ganwa*, an ancestral group considered distinct from the Tutsi and the Hutu. Between 1796 and 1850, Ntare IV doubled Burundi's territory by conquering neighbouring states, and strengthened his power by punishing disobedient local chiefs. The Hutus and Tutsis shared a common language but the Tutsi also wielded power here, although the social contract (or *ubugabire*) that governed relationships seems to have been more equitable than Rwanda's *ubuhake*.

German and Belgian rule

The hilly terrain and relatively stable governance of Rwanda and Burundi meant incursions by Europeans were limited. However, the Berlin Conference of 1884–85 (see pp. 210–11) designated the region part of German East Africa. When King Kigeli IV died in 1895, there was a scramble for the throne, which the German colonialists took advantage of, increasing their influence over Rwanda. In Burundi, Germany forced King Mwezi Gisabo to sign a treaty submitting to its authority in 1903. During World War I, Germany was forced to cede both colonies to Belgium, which introduced a divide-and-rule policy, sponsoring the dominant Tutsi minority as allies who could

△ **Royal ceremony**
King Yuhi V of Rwanda (centre) is pictured in Kigali around 1930. In 1931, he was deposed by Belgian administrators and replaced by his son, Mutara III.

rule at the expense of the Hutu. In Burundi, Hutu farmers staged a series of uprisings, which Belgium suppressed. Relations between the Hutus and Tutsis had been largely peaceful in the precolonial era but, under increasing repression, the Hutu sought change.

Independence and conflict

Nationalist feelings grew and in a referendum in 1960, the Hutus elected Hutu representatives and rejected the Tutsi monarchy, leading to Rwanda and Burundi gaining independence in 1962. However, tensions mounted and Tutsi groups led attacks in 1964 and 1990 in Rwanda. In 1994, soldiers and militia murdered around 800,000 Tutsi, moderate Hutu, and Twa in the Rwandan genocide. Efforts at reconciliation have made progress, but the scars remain. In Burundi, Mwambutsa IV became the head of state in 1962 but after a coup in 1966, instability has continued. Burundi became a republic that was effectively a military dictatorship, and conflicts in 1972 and 1993 led to the genocide of thousands of Hutu and Tutsi. The tensions stoked by colonizing powers remain, and Burundi regularly ranks as the poorest nation in Africa.

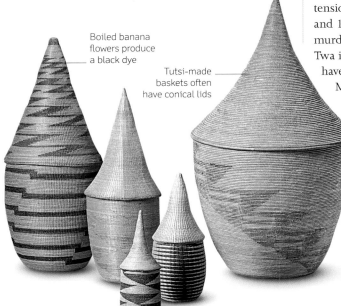

Boiled banana flowers produce a black dye

Tutsi-made baskets often have conical lids

◁ **Woven baskets**
These miniature grass baskets from Rwanda and Burundi were made in the first half of the 20th century. They were usually crafted by Tutsi women.

The Kingdom of Dahomey

Nation of the Fon people of Benin

Founded in about 1600 on the Abomey plain in present-day Benin, the Kingdom of Dahomey grew to become a major West African power, and an important centre in the Atlantic slave trade.

△ **King of Dahomey**
King Ghezo, who ruled from 1818–59, expanded Dahomey's military forces and won its independence from the Oyo Empire.

At the turn of the 17th century, a coalition of Fon peoples founded a nation on the inland Abomey plain of present-day Benin. However, the area lacked resources and was not on any trade routes. International trade along the coastal regions, by contrast, particularly in enslaved people, increased during the 16th century. West Africa provided European traders with a ready supply of labour for their colonies in the Americas. The Allada and Whydah groups on the coast prospered from providing enslaved people, captured from other groups. The Fon built a military force that could protect their people from exploitation and push south to profit from the lucrative Euro-American trade.

Expansion and interference

The Kingdom of Dahomey, as it became, developed a sophisticated, militaristic society, and over the next century expanded its empire: by the 1720s it had conquered the coastal kingdoms of Allada and Whydah, important ports for the Atlantic slave trade. As a major supplier of enslaved people, captured in its conquests and in raids on neighbouring countries, Dahomey had to defend itself from attack by the powerful Oyo Empire to the west. Unable to completely resist the Oyo forces, Dahomey remained an autonomous nation, but was made a tributary state of the Oyo Empire in 1730.

Nevertheless, the kingdom flourished, and its king, Agaja, instituted reforms to the administrative system, and introduced the Annual Customs, a festival with military parades and Vodun ceremonies, including human sacrifice. Dahomey expanded while the slave trade increased through the 18th century, but it was not until 1827 that King Ghezo freed his country from the Oyo Empire.

Soon, however, he faced British forces, who blockaded Dahomey's Atlantic ports to end the slave trade. Ghezo eventually gave in to some of Britain's demands, ceasing the supply of enslaved people and ending human sacrifice, but he resisted pressure to adopt Christianity and give up the Indigenous Vodun religion.

European interest in the region continued and in 1892 France invaded Dahomey and won control of the kingdom in 1894, incorporating it into the colony of French Dahomey in 1904. It finally regained independence as the Republic of Dahomey in 1960, later becoming the Republic of Benin.

▷ **Royal procession**
In this 20th-century copper and wood model, a Fon king is carried in his hammock in a procession of musicians and attendants.

Sun shade

Fon king

Large log drum

Royal attendant

Flintlock
musket

Child soldier

△ **Female fighting force**
The female soldiers of Dahomey, known as the *Mino*, are
pictured with male warriors in a French newspaper in
the 1890s. Originating as the King's bodyguard in the
18th century, the *Mino* were recognized as a permanent
fighting force during the reign of King Ghezo.

Njinga Ana de Sousa Mbande
Queen Njinga used her recently adopted Christian names to impress the Portuguese, but she also asserted her equality with them by proudly wearing the finest Ndongo clothing, jewels, and feathers – as this European portrait shows.

Njinga Mbande
A warrior queen

Regarded today as the "Mother of Angola", Queen Njinga led the Mbundu people of Ndongo and Matamba in resistance against Portuguese colonization from the 1620s until her death in 1663.

Born into the royal family of Ndongo, in present-day Angola, Njinga Mbande grew up at a time when European powers, notably the Portuguese, were seeking to expand their lucrative slave trade. Her father became *ngola* (the root of the name Angola and "ruler" in the local Kimbundu language) and ensured she was schooled in government, diplomacy, the military, and the Portuguese language.

In 1617, Njinga's brother Mbandi succeeded their father. Mbandi was a tyrannical ruler, killing anyone he suspected of being a rival, even members of his family. Njinga fled to neighbouring Matamba, but Mbandi, who was inept and lacked Njinga's diplomatic skills, recalled her to Ndongo in 1621, to act as ambassador to the Portuguese Governor in Luanda. With her Portuguese, and having been baptized as a Christian to gain respect from the Europeans, she asserted Ndongan independence, and negotiated an end to hostilities.

Ngola Njinga
After Mbandi's death in 1624, Njinga became *ngola*, despite opposition to the idea of a female ruler. The Portuguese took advantage of this unrest, renewing the fight for control of Ndongo. Njinga had hoped to regain the territory lost by her brother to neighbouring

states and the Portuguese, but instead was forced out of Ndongo, and replaced by a Portuguese puppet ruler. Undeterred, she returned to Matamba, where she became ruler, and consolidated her forces.

Meanwhile, Portugal was at war with the Dutch, who took Luanda in 1641. Njinga saw an opportunity, and entered an alliance with the Dutch, which enabled her to regain much of Ndongo. However, the Portuguese retook Luanda and the Dutch withdrew. In 1656, Njinga negotiated a peace treaty with the Portuguese that recognized Njinga as *ngola* of Matamba and Ndongo in return for concessions to the Portuguese for their slave trade. Njinga set up trade routes into Central Africa, welcomed formerly enslaved people, and set a precedent for Angolan resistance to colonization.

△ **Leading an army**
Queen Njinga is shown at the head of a Matamban military unit, armed with a bow and arrow. This was during her campaign to regain Ndongo from the Portuguese.

▷ **A powerful diplomat**
Njinga is negotiating with the Portuguese Governor in this engraving. She is shown using one of her servants as a seat to avoid the humiliation of standing throughout the meeting.

1621 Njinga appointed ambassador to the Portuguese by her brother, *Ngola* Mbandi

1624 After the death of her brother, Njinga becomes *ngola* of Ndongo

1626 The Portuguese declare war on Njinga

1628 Njinga forced to retreat from Ndongo

1631 Mbundu invade neighbouring Matamba

1641 Njinga makes an alliance with the Dutch after they oust the Portuguese from Luanda

1656 Njinga signs treaty with the Portuguese, who recognize her as the ruler of Ndongo and Matamba

1663 After Njinga's death, her sister Mukambu assumes the throne

The Kingdom of Kongo
Rise and fall of an African superpower

One of premodern Africa's largest and wealthiest states, Kongo dominated much of western Central Africa for centuries, before succumbing to internal tensions in the face of Portuguese imperial interest.

△ **A Catholic king**
King Afonso I (r. 1509–42), depicted in an 18th-century Portuguese illustration, opened Kongo to Portuguese and Christian influence.

The Kingdom of Kongo was a collection of states that came together around 1390 under the chieftain Lukeni lua Nimi. The territory he and his successors ruled over covered much of present-day Angola, the Republic of Congo, and the Democratic Republic of the Congo. Although he was advised by a council of aristocratic elders known as the *mwisikongo*, the king, or *mwene*, exercised absolute power. Authority was administered across his vast domain by local governors, part of whose role it was to collect tributes to the king in the form of ivory, grain, palm wine, and animal skins.

This system of government helped to guarantee Kongo's stability, as did its trade in ivory, cow skins, salt, raffia cloth, gold, copper, and enslaved people. The common currency in Kongo and other African nations was cowrie shells, known as *nzimbu*. Neighbouring states, such as Ndongo and Matamba (in modern Angola), were not part of Kongo but very much within its sphere of influence.

Christianity, culture, and conquest
A new era began when the Portuguese explorer Diogo Cão arrived in 1483. Within 10 years, Kongo's king Nzinga a Nkuwu had converted to Christianity, taking the name João I. This "Europeanization" continued when the Kongolese titles for regional leaders were abolished in favour of labels such as "Duke", "Marquis", and "Count". João I's son and successor Afonso I established Christianity as the state religion. He claimed that a heavenly vision of the cross, St James, and the Virgin Mary had inspired him to victory at the Battle of Mbanza Kongo in 1509, in which he defeated his brother and rival claimant to the throne, Mpanzu a Kitima. Kongo's version of Christianity fused Catholic beliefs with Kongolese

◁ **Cultural cross-currents**
The central section of this triple crucifix dates from the 16th–17th centuries. The Jesus figure displays the "Africanized" features characteristic of Kongolese Christianity.

cosmology, such as using the Kongolese term for the supreme being, Nzambi a Mpungu, instead of "God"; in devotional art, too, Jesus was often represented as an African. At the same time, local beliefs remained, and some Kongolese rejected Christianity, seeing it as the means by which the Portuguese exercised social control.

Afonso I's death in 1542 initiated a period of disputed successions and instability. This ended with the accession of Alvaro I in 1568, supported by the Portuguese who, in return, were granted concessions and land in the province of Luanda (modern Angola). This gave the Portuguese a base from which to pursue their imperial ambitions, most notably the seizure of Kongo's copper mines and greater access to the region's slave trade. European interference escalated over the next decades, leading to several Kongo-Portuguese wars – the first of which ended in defeat for Portugal at the Battle of Mbanda Kasi in January 1623.

> "**Each day**, traders are kidnapping **our people**."
>
> AFONSO I IN A LETTER TO THE KING OF PORTUGAL, 1526

Four figures at the top – two holding daggers, two clasping their hands in prayer

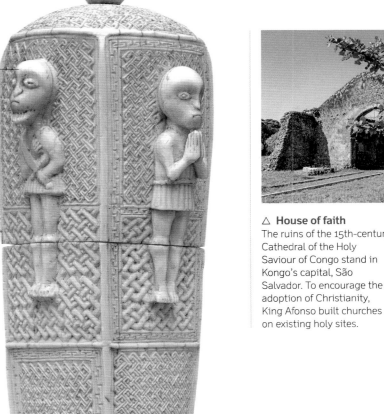

△ **House of faith**
The ruins of the 15th-century Cathedral of the Holy Saviour of Congo stand in Kongo's capital, São Salvador. To encourage the adoption of Christianity, King Afonso built churches on existing holy sites.

The fortunes of the Kongolese and the Portuguese fluctuated over the next half century, complicated by the arrival and interference of Dutch colonial adventurers from the mid-1620s. The three sides variously fought alongside and against each other in a series of shifting alliances – while Kongo's leaders were at the same time battling factional infighting between two branches of the royal family known as the Kimpanzu and Kinlaza. In 1670, Kongo's troubles came to a head when the Portuguese invaded Soyo, a powerful Kongolese province intent on declaring its independence. When the Soyo army defeated the Portuguese at the Battle of Kitombo in October that year, the consequences were far-reaching. Although the battle led to the Portuguese withdrawing from Kongo's affairs for 200 years, it only weakened the kingdom: Kongo was at that moment mired in civil war and did not welcome the emergence of a confident, militarily successful Soyo.

A disunited kingdom

By the early 20th century, Kongo was still nominally ruled by monarchs, but the kingdom had disintegrated into its constituent states, with local leaders and foreign trading corporations in control. In 1862, civil unrest in Kongo led its king, Pedro V, to ask the Portuguese for help. In return, he was forced to submit Kongo to Portugal as a vassal state. Following a rebellion in 1914, Portugal formally converted the state into a colony, its kings little more than figureheads. Portugal had already detached parts of southwestern Kongo as part of its Angola holdings in 1885, and that same year Belgium incorporated part of eastern Kongo into the Congo Free State (renamed the Belgian Congo in 1908). These developments saw the region subjected to a new phase of imperial entanglement (see pp. 212–13 and pp. 248–49).

Carved pattern echoes Kongolese textile designs

Four figures at the base form the "legs" of the knife holder

▷ **Ivory souvenir**
From the 16th century, Portuguese sailors commissioned Kongolese craftsmen to create objects to send home, like this skilfully carved ivory knife case, with lid, featuring a variety of figures.

Base identifies this as a display item

> "He who **spoke falsely** or bore **false witness** [before the *mangaaka*] **should die.**"

R.E. DENNETT, BRITISH TRADER

Mangaaka power figure

Divine protection – or retribution

In western Central Africa, *nkisi makondo* are wooden human-shaped sculptures imbued with spiritual power. When Europeans encroached into the Kingdom of Kongo in the late 19th century (see pp. 182–83), they posed a threat to the authority of Kongo's leaders, which led the Kongolese to respond in the form of *mangaaka*, or "power figures", an addition to the many types of *nkisi makondo*. Often over 1 m (3 ft) high, *mangaaka* represented a being with divine authority, able to impose social order and justice. Priests used them in rituals to resolve disputes and dispense punishments: to go against the judgement of the *mangaaka* was to invite terrible retribution.

Creation and preparation

To create *mangaaka*, carvers would work with a *nganga*, or spiritual specialist, who provided advice about the careful preparation that was needed before the figure could be activated, or imbued with its full power to protect or destroy. Made from weather-resistant hardwood, the figures were often placed outdoors.

The head was the most carefully carved part, its eyes usually inlaid with ceramic tiles with iron nails for pupils. The carvers used tools of hand-forged iron, with stone flakes, clamshells, and abrasive leaves to create the finishing touches. Hands on hips and leaning forward, the *mangaaka* was depicted with the attributes of a chief, such as a raffia *mpu* or headdress,

a long beard, and raffia armbands. The lower part was less well defined but a cavity was sculpted in the abdomen, coated with a layer of resin, into which sacred objects would be placed. Ritual objects were also hidden behind the eyes, and the figure coated in black pigment, with details picked out in red or white.

Symbol of resistance

Once the *mangaaka* was complete, the *nganga* activated it and pronounced its judgements. Each time a judgement was made, the *nganga* hammered an iron object, such as a nail, into the wood, most often near the abdominal cavity, the centre of the figure's spiritual power. These sharp objects included blades, and even fragments of bullets or musket parts.

The Yombe people from Kongo who created the *mangaaka* hoped the figures would protect them from intruders. The *mangaaka* became powerful symbols of resistance to the Europeans, who were therefore anxious to remove them, sending out expeditions for this purpose. A naval party from the British anti-slavery vessel HMS *Archer* was responsible for the first recorded seizure of a *mangaaka*, in 1865. Those *mangaaka* that survived ended up in foreign museums and private collections, but, before they were taken, the *nganga* seem to have ritually deconsecrated them, as none survive with the original sacred objects intact.

▷ **Striking artistry**
This 19th-century *mangaaka* is 118 cm (4 ft) tall. Its clothing and posture were intended to suggest divine power and strike fear into those who transgressed against the moral codes of Yombe society.

Nails are some of the 380 iron objects hammered into the figure

Mpu chief's hat

Ceramic eyes are inlaid
with a pupil made of iron

Abdominal cavity for
sacred objects

Remains of fixing
for long beard

Hands on hips and
forward-leaning
posture projects
fearless authority

Wooden base
carved with
power symbols

Armband carved in
imitation of raffia
adornments worn
by chiefs

The Sultanate of Zanzibar

An Arabian outpost in East Africa

From the 18th century, Zanzibar, now part of Tanzania, was controlled by the Sultanate of Oman. The island developed into such an important commercial centre that it eventually became the sultanate's capital.

△ **Visionary leader**
The Omani leader Sayyid Said recognized Zanzibar's potential as a commercial and trading centre. "I am nothing but a merchant," he once said – with approval rather than sorrow.

Situated on the southeast corner of the Arabian Peninsula, Oman was one of the key states plying the sea-trading routes between the Spice Islands of Indonesia and the coast of East Africa – off which lay the island of Zanzibar. Oman's control of Zanzibar fluctuated throughout the 18th century and into the early 19th century until, in 1806, Sayyid Said initiated a long and stable reign. Although he had only just turned 15, Said had already executed his cousin Badr bin Saif, who had briefly usurped the throne, and sidelined his brother, Salim bin Sultan, who their father had intended would reign alongside Said. The new sultan, it seemed, was a man of ambition.

Oman shifts its centre of gravity

In 1823, Said signed a treaty with Britain banning the trade in enslaved people between his Muslim subjects and any western Christian powers. Significantly, the treaty did not exclude slave trading along the East African coast, leaving Said free to invest in people-trafficking in Oman's sometime colony of Zanzibar. Once there, Said also helped make the island a hub for the lucrative trade in African elephant ivory and expanded Zanzibar's already large clove plantations so that the island became the world's largest source of the sought-after spice.

In 1840, Said transferred the Sultanate of Oman's capital from Muscat to Stone Town, in Zanzibar. Three years earlier, Said had conquered Mombasa, in

A BOLD **PRINCESS**

One of Sultan Said's 36 children lived a notably colourful life. Born in 1844, Sayyida Salme (below, in regal attire) learnt to ride and shoot, and taught herself to read, which was unusual for women in her culture at the time. In Zanzibar, she met a young German merchant and moved to Germany with him, where they married. Later in life, Sayyida wrote her autobiography – the first East African woman to do so. She died in 1924 and was buried with a treasured bag of Zanzibar sand.

Distinctive circular motifs

▽ **Double comb**
This beautifully carved wooden comb, dating from the 19th century, shows the skill and artistry of artisan makers in Zanzibar and surrounding coastal regions.

"[O]ur own **prosperity** dates from the time of **my father's conquest**... **of Zanzibar**."

SAYYIDA SALME ON HER FATHER, SULTAN SAYYID SAID

modern Kenya, on the African mainland, securing his supply lines of enslaved people and African goods such as ivory for export via Zanzibar; Oman had become peripheral to Said's needs.

As the state's ruler went, its religious culture followed. Omanis were followers of a branch of Islam known as Ibadism, and many Ibadi scholars migrated to Zanzibar with Said, turning the new capital into a centre of religious learning. Muslim academics from across East Africa followed suit.

From sultanate to independence

Said's death in 1856 was the beginning of the end of Zanzibar's golden age. Two of his sons quarrelled over the succession, resulting in the division of his territories. One son, Thuwaini, took control of Oman while another, Majid, became the first Sultan of Zanzibar. Britain's Viceroy and Governor-General of India, George Canning, mediated the dispute between the brothers, which led to Britain playing an increasing role in Zanzibar's affairs.

By 1890, Zanzibar had become a British protectorate; its sultans held office but no power. This was demonstrated in uncompromising fashion when a pretender to the throne, Khālid ibn Barghash, seized power from Britain's preferred candidate, Ḥamud ibn Moḥammed. After Khālid ignored an ultimatum to stand down, Britain declared war at 9am on 27 August 1896, sending in five Royal Navy ships to bombard Zanzibar's Royal Palace and Harem. Khālid surrendered within as little as 38 minutes, giving the Anglo-Zanzibar War the distinction of being considered the shortest conflict in history.

Ḥamud was installed as Zanzibar's sultan, but the Omanis' time was running out. Britain terminated its protectorship in 1963. A year later, the last sultan, Jamshid bin Abdullah Al Said, was deposed in the Zanzibar Revolution. Led by Ugandan John Gideon Okello, this socialist revolution saw the deaths of 20,000 people – mostly Arabs and Indians. In April 1964, Zanzibar merged with the recently independent mainland nation of Tanganyika to form what was later that year named Tanzania.

▷ **Grandee's chair**
This *kiti cha enzi* ("Chair of Power") dates from the 19th century, during Omani rule in Zanzibar. Unique to the region, such chairs were used by high-ranking officials on formal occasions and were offered to visiting foreign dignitaries as a sign of respect.

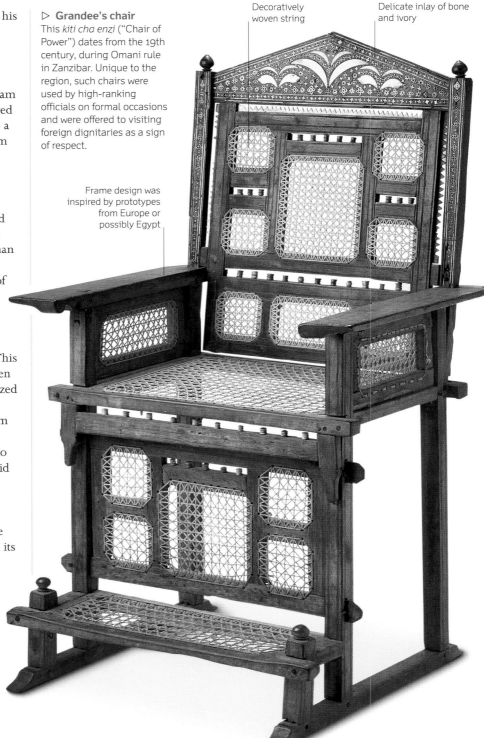

Decoratively woven string

Delicate inlay of bone and ivory

Frame design was inspired by prototypes from Europe or possibly Egypt

Stone Town

Capital of the Zanzibar Sultanate (present-day Tanzania)

From its humble beginnings as a fishing village, Stone Town developed into one of the most famous trading ports along the East African coast. Its location on the island of Zanzibar attracted competing foreign powers, which were eager to control a lucrative trade in enslaved people and commodities such as ivory between the African mainland, the Arabian Peninsula, Asia, and beyond. During the 19th century, the Omani sultan Sayyid Said moved his capital from Arabia to Zanzibar, recognizing its potential to extend the wealth and power of the sultanate. He encouraged local clove production and expanded international trade, transforming Stone Town into a thriving commercial hub with a multicultural population.

Distinctive architecture

Stone Town's buildings fused Swahili materials with the cultural traditions and tastes of its international residents. Behind the waterfront lay a dense maze of alleyways, characterized by townhouses of local coralline ragstone. Plain Arab-style frontages with decorative doorways neighboured narrow Indian shopfronts overhung by wooden balconies designed to catch sea breezes.

Sultan Said's Omani-style palace, the Beit al-Sahel, dominated the seafront, showing the sultanate's primacy. Successive sultans added extra palaces and embellishments, incorporating Indian-style elements. Under Sultan Barghash bin Said (r. 1870–88), a prolific builder and enthusiast for new technology, Stone Town acquired its iconic landmark: the Beit al-Ajaib or House of Wonders.

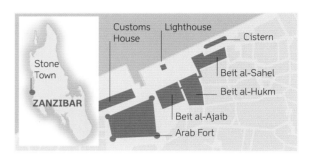

△ **Stone Town origins**
Stone Town developed on a peninsula offering safe anchorage on Zanzibar's west coast. Sultan Said encouraged the building of stone houses in his new capital, resulting in its name.

▽ **Waterfront palace complex**
This reconstruction depicts the sultan's palace complex as it appeared under Sultan Barghash in the mid-1880s, shortly after the House of Wonders was built. The architecture reflects the mix of Swahili, Arab, and Indian influences characteristic of Stone Town.

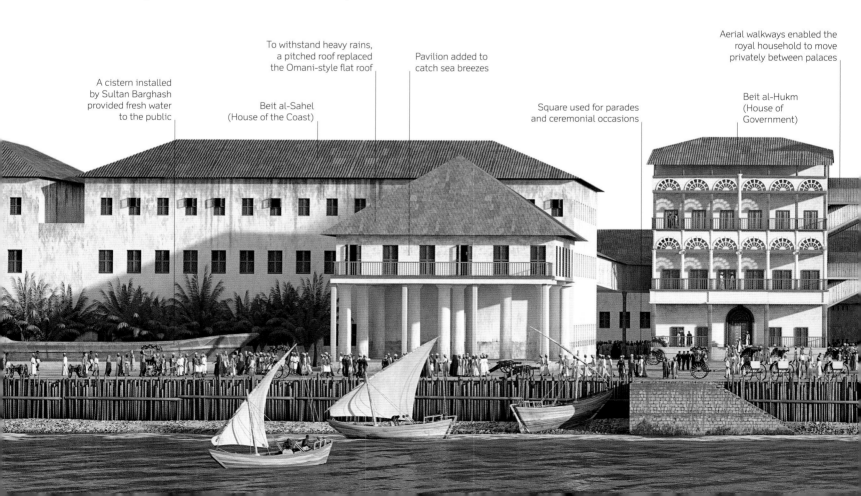

A cistern installed by Sultan Barghash provided fresh water to the public

To withstand heavy rains, a pitched roof replaced the Omani-style flat roof

Beit al-Sahel (House of the Coast)

Pavilion added to catch sea breezes

Square used for parades and ceremonial occasions

Aerial walkways enabled the royal household to move privately between palaces

Beit al-Hukm (House of Government)

1896: SULTANS **UNDER FIRE**

In 1890, Zanzibar became a British protectorate and the sultanate's independence and authority waned. In 1896, when the then sultan died suddenly, his cousin Khālid ibn Barghash (son of Sultan Barghash) tried to assume the sultanship. The British, however, had a different successor in mind: one more amenable to British interests. When Khālid refused to stand aside, the British Navy bombarded the palace complex, destroying Beit al-Hukm, the lighthouse, and much of Beit al-Sahel. In the following years, the area was relandscaped: Beit al-Sahel was rebuilt on a smaller scale, gardens were laid over the site of Beit al-Hukm, and the House of Wonders was remodelled to incorporate a clocktower with the original lighthouse clock. The waterfront was forever changed.

DAMAGED PALACE COMPLEX, 1896

▷ **Inside the House of Wonders**
The House of Wonders was an expression of Sultan Barghash's faith, modernizing instincts, wealth, and foreign influences, on a scale never before seen in Zanzibar. The sultan held court in panelled rooms arranged around a covered courtyard furnished with electric lights, European marble and silverware, and gilded doors inscribed with Qur'anic verses.

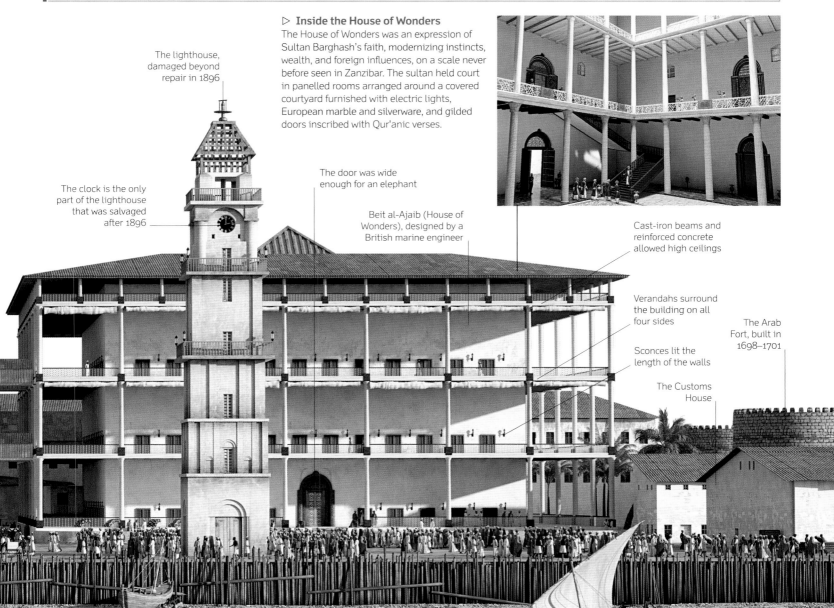

The lighthouse, damaged beyond repair in 1896

The clock is the only part of the lighthouse that was salvaged after 1896

The door was wide enough for an elephant

Beit al-Ajaib (House of Wonders), designed by a British marine engineer

Cast-iron beams and reinforced concrete allowed high ceilings

Verandahs surround the building on all four sides

Sconces lit the length of the walls

The Arab Fort, built in 1698–1701

The Customs House

The Asante Empire

West Africa's great imperial powerhouse

Growing from a small kingdom into West Africa's most significant state, the Asante Empire dominated Ghana's "gold coast", using its wealth and power to fend off British interference for almost a century.

△ **The Asante court**
Thomas Edward Bowditch's watercolour *Cape Coast Castle to Ashantee* (1819) captures the colour and pageantry of the Asante court at its imperial height.

The Akan people of what is now Ghana had long been divided into a number of autonomous groups when, in the late 17th century, war forced them together.

Denkyira was the wealthiest, strongest, and most actively expansionist Akan state. In 1694, its new leader, Ntim Gyakari, turned his attention to Denkyira's smaller but growing rival, the Asante

△ **Asante royal family**
Asantehene Prempeh I with the *Asantehemmaa* (Queen Mother). In 1900, the British exiled him to the Seychelles for 24 years.

Kingdom, which had been founded by the Okoyo of south-central Ghana. Shortly before Gyakari came to power, the Asante king, Osei Tutu, had seized territory from Denkyira and refused to give it back or pay the reparations Ntim Gyakari demanded of him. Unable to accept such a slight, Gyakari declared war.

In the conflict that followed, Osei Tutu put together an alliance of Akan peoples and states opposed to Denkyira's often tyrannical rule and, in 1701, the so-called "Kwaman Alliance" (named after the Asante capital) defeated Denkyira at the Battle of Feyiase. Ntim Gyakari died in combat and Denkyira became a member state of the new Asante Empire.

Establishing an empire

To establish the new order, the empire's capital was moved to Kumasi, in modern-day central Ghana, and Osei Tutu was ceremonially presented with the Golden Stool. This was a clever piece of political theatre organized by Tutu's trusted advisor, *Okomfo* (priest) Anokye, who, according to legend, summoned from heaven a golden seat, or stool, that landed in Tutu's lap – proof of his divine right to rule.

As *Asantehene*, or king, of the Asante Empire, Tutu was not an absolute monarch but was "first among equals". The empire he ruled operated along federal lines, with chiefs and regional leaders, or *Amanhene*, exercising a degree of local power and forming the membership of a law-making and advisory council known as the *Asantemanhyiamu* (which translates as the

▽ **Gold weights**
These brass figures were used to weigh gold. Rather than create simple round or square weights, the Asante cast decorative figures.

"When **a king** has **good counsellors**, his reign is **peaceful**."

ASANTE PROVERB

"Great Council") that met each year. Okomfo Anokye drafted "The Seventy-Seven Laws", which served as the codified constitution of the Asante Empire.

When Tutu died in 1717, the *Asantemanhyiamu* approved the accession of his successor – and this became the method by which all Asante kings were anointed (the nominee for kingship having been chosen from a list of candidates by the widowed queen). Once in place, the new king was acknowledged as the imperial leader and served as the empire's highest legal authority, chief executive, and military commander-in-chief.

It was in this latter capacity especially that the second Asante emperor, Opoku Ware I, excelled. By the end of his reign in 1750, he had expanded the empire's borders to their widest extent, defeating neighbouring peoples such as the Bono, Akyem, Akwamu, and Ga-Adangbe of present-day Ghana, Côte d'Ivoire, and other West African states. But empires that expand by conquest are often unsettled. The fifth Asante king, Osei Kwame Panyin, died by suicide in 1803 as a bitter civil war threatened the country. By this time, Britain was expanding its colonial control in West Africa, ultimately leading to the series of Anglo-Asante Wars that finally brought down the empire in 1901.

A golden age

Across its history, the Asante Empire was sustained economically by its large gold reserves (which were panned from rivers rather than mined), its trade in agricultural produce, and the manufacture of high-quality crafted goods. The empire was also involved in human trafficking, supplying enslaved people to British and Dutch traders in return for arms. As West Africa's leading precolonial power, the Asante Empire was blessed with a wealth of natural resources and a sophisticated, decentralized political culture that allowed it to thrive for two centuries.

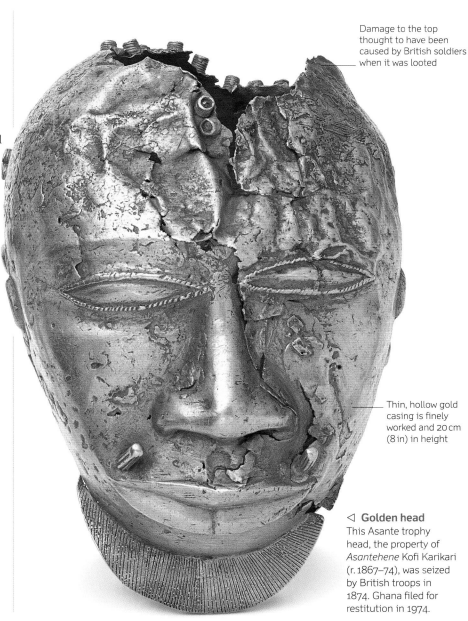

Damage to the top thought to have been caused by British soldiers when it was looted

Thin, hollow gold casing is finely worked and 20 cm (8 in) in height

◁ **Golden head**
This Asante trophy head, the property of *Asantehene* Kofi Karikari (r. 1867–74), was seized by British troops in 1874. Ghana filed for restitution in 1974.

Osei Tutu

The founder of the Asante Empire

In 1701, Osei Tutu led a coalition of states against the reigning kingdom of Denkyira. Tutu's inventive tactics helped him defeat the Denkyira and found the Asante Empire, which would dominate West Africa for centuries.

△ **Asante architecture**
This 19th-century engraving depicts houses in the Asante Empire's capital, Kumasi, which Osei Tutu founded.

In the late 17th century, the Akan states occupied the forested coastal regions of modern-day Ghana, Togo, and Côte d'Ivoire. They were dominated by Denkyira, which had become the largest and wealthiest kingdom after conquering several of its neighbours with the help of muskets bought from European traders. But the rulers of Denkyira became tyrannical, demanding ever-higher tributes (payments) from states they had conquered and executing rulers who couldn't pay.

Princely upbringing

Osei Tutu was a prince of Kwaman, an Akan state inhabited by the Asante. Born around 1660, he spent some of his youth in the nearby state of Akwamu and also served, probably as a page boy, in the court of Boamponsem, the ruler of Denkyira. In Akwamu, Tutu learnt about political and military tactics, and in Denkyira, he met a young man named Anokye – the son of an Akan noble – who became his chief advisor.

By the 1680s, Tutu succeeded to the throne of Kwaman, which had expanded its territory to become the heart of an Akan kingdom. When he defied the tribute demands of Boamponsem's successor, Ntim Gyakari, and conquered Denkyira lands, the rulers of the other Akan states agreed to back him. Open war broke out in 1699, with Tutu using nimble formations, pincer tactics, and firearms to gain an advantage. At the Battle of Feyiase in 1701, Tutu and his "Kwaman coalition" defeated the Denkyira, killing Gyakari and sacking the kingdom's capital, Abankeseso.

Tutu created a single state, the Asante Empire. Anokye, who had taken the title Okomfo ("priest"), used a stool – a traditional part of a king's regalia – to cement the union. In around 1717, Osei Tutu was at war with the rival Akyem state when a sniper's bullet hit him. It is said that he had believed the Akyem to be a lesser force so had not worn armour, and was killed instantly. Under his successor, Opoku Ware I, Osei Tutu's empire continued to flourish and expand.

> ## "Ankah me nim a [If only I knew]."
> OSEI TUTU'S LAST WORDS, APPARENTLY AT UNDERESTIMATING THE AKYEM IN BATTLE

Fine detailing, and all other parts, are carved from a single block of wood

◁ **Symbol of power**
For centuries, Akan rulers have used stools (*dwa*) as a symbol of royal authority.

c.1660 Born in the town of Kokofu Anyinam, modern-day Ghana

c.1680 Succeeds to the throne of the Akan Kingdom of Kwaman

1701 Battle of Feyiase, where Tutu's Kwaman coalition defeats the Denkyira

c.1717 Killed in battle against the neighbouring Akyem people

c.1678 Taken to Denkyira palace and meets Okomfo Anokye

1689 The Kwaman coalition is officially formed, and prepares for war with Denkyira

1695 Establishes Kumasi as capital city of Asante Empire

c.1701–02 Tutu and Anokye use the symbol of the Golden Stool to form a single state, the Asante Empire

Serene expression of
an idealized ruler

Head of a ruler

An 18th-century terracotta *nsodie*
(memorial head). These sculptures
were crafted to honour deceased
Akan rulers such as Osei Tutu.

The Sokoto Caliphate

Forging an Islamic state

One of Africa's largest 19th-century empires, the Sokoto Caliphate was founded by the devout Muslim scholar Usman dan Fodio and expanded to include much of West Africa.

A Sunni Muslim state established in the early 19th century in modern-day Nigeria, the Sokoto Caliphate was previously a collection of seven independent city-states forming the Hausa Kingdoms, which had been in existence for 700 years.

The city-state of Gobir was part of the Hausa Kingdoms and although it was culturally Islamic, its rulers did not demand strict religious adherence. Muslim cleric Usman dan Fodio, by contrast, had

an uncompromising faith. His preaching on the greed, corruption, and abuses of Sharia law by Gobir's elites brought him supporters, but also the enmity of his state's leaders. In 1802, a failed assassination attempt on Usman authorized by Gobir's king, Yunfa, drove him into exile. Usman took his supporters with him and two years later, when Yunfa declared war on Usman, he responded by declaring jihad – holy war – against Yunfa.

△ **Ceremonial head**
Sokoto's last independent caliph was Sultan Muhammadu Attahiru I. He was deposed after five months in power in 1903, and killed by the British at Mbormi five months later.

◁ **Hausa palace**
The royal palace in Bauchi, northeast Nigeria, is decorated with Hausa symbols. The Bauchi Emirate was established c.1810 by Yakubu, one of Usman dan Fodio's army commanders.

Beginnings of the caliphate

In the early 19th century, it was common practice in Islamic states for disaffected religious groups to declare jihad against rulers or countries whose beliefs they questioned. In Sudan, West Africa, for example, more than a dozen jihadi leaders displaced old rulers and established new states.

In the Hausa states, Islamic fundamentalism was strongest among the Fulani people, whose number included Usman dan Fodio. His jihad against Yunfa set off a chain reaction, with Muslim groups in the other Hausa Kingdoms also rising up against their political leaders. The groups acted independently, but all recognized the authority of Usman, the man his followers had anointed as *Amir al-Mu'ninin* ("Commander of the Faithful"). Usman and his supporters took control of the kingdom of Gobir in 1808, and by 1812 the other Hausa Kingdoms had also fallen. In their place the insurgents established the Sokoto Caliphate, named after its capital city in what is today northwest Nigeria.

The Sokoto Caliphate was not a unified nation but an association of 30 Muslim emirates. By 1812, Usman had retired from politics to return to teaching and a life of religious study and was succeeded by his son, Muhammad Bello. As caliph (supreme religious leader), Muhammad Bello and each of his successors would receive the annual visit of tribute from the ruler, or emir, of each of the emirates. Such was the authority of the caliph that – despite the large number of emirates that made up the Sokoto Caliphate and the diversity of peoples and ethnic groups comprising it – no caliph was ever deposed by his subjects.

A military and economic powerhouse

By the end of Muhammad Bello's rule in 1837, the Sokoto Caliphate was the most populous empire in West Africa, numbering up to 20 million people. Muhammed Bello and his brother Abdullahi were gifted military leaders and conquered new territories. At its height, the Sokoto Caliphate extended 1,600 km

(1,000 miles) from northern Cameroon in the east to Burkina Faso in the west. The caliphate became known as a centre of art and culture, as well as for Muslim scholarship. The city of Sokoto was endowed with two large mosques, the Masallacin Shehu and the Masallacin Bello, and a royal palace. All of this was paid for by the spoils of conquest and the profits from the trade in cotton cloth, sorghum, brassware, spices, kola nuts, salt, potash, and leather goods. The empire's agricultural economy was powered largely by enslaved labour.

Collapse of the caliphate

By the end of the 19th century, the Sokoto Caliphate had begun to fracture. Abdurrahman dan Abi Bakar became caliph in 1891 but he was thin-skinned and a poor decision-maker. He alienated his emirs, weakening the state when France, Germany, and Britain were seeking to extend their influence in West Africa.

By the time Abdurrahman died in 1902, the British had decided to act. On the pretext of helping to resolve trade disputes, and to protect its own interests in the region, Britain sent troops into the caliphate in January 1903. They defeated the emirates and, in March 1903, Abdurrahman's successor was deposed and replaced by a purely ceremonial caliph, Muhammadu Attahiru II. The Sokoto Caliphate's time as an independent empire was over – although Sokoto's sultans, each of them a direct descendant of Usman dan Fodio, continue to wield a degree of influence over their people to this day.

△ **Trading power**
This coloured engraving of Sokoto's market was produced in 1853. It shows a bustling market with livestock and produce near the Sokoto river.

"If the king is Muslim, **his land is Muslim**; if he is an unbeliever, his land is **a land of unbelievers**."

USMAN DAN FODIO

The Tukolor Empire

Conversion and conquest

The Tukolor Empire burned brightly but briefly in West Africa. Its founder, Al-Hajj Umar Tal, was a scholar and pilgrim who began a holy war, creating a 19th-century kingdom that survived for half a century.

△ **Resisting the French**
Umar Tal's son Ahmadu ruled much of the Tukolor Empire in the late 19th century. He coordinated resistance against the French colonizing forces.

By the early 19th century, the Islamic caliphates of the Fulani and Sokoto were expanding across West Africa. Meanwhile, European powers, once happy to trade with the kingdoms of the interior, were beginning to seek outright rule. Instability brought opportunity and, propelled by firearms and radical Islam, the Tukolor Empire took full advantage. This West African state began as the dream of one determined scholar and ended up stretching from Senegal to Timbuktu.

A pilgrim's empire

The Tukolor Empire was founded by Umar Tal, who was born in 1797 in Futa Toro, an arid region on the banks of the Senegal River. He studied at a *madrasa* (religious school) and took the pilgrimage to Mecca in his twenties, gaining the title "Al-Hajj".

Umar travelled for two decades, visiting Medina, Cairo, and Syria. In Mecca, an increasingly respected Umar was appointed the West African leader of the Tijaniyya, an Islamic order that foregrounded discipline and followed the mystic doctrine of Sufism. While a guest of Muhammad Bello, the sultan of the Sokoto court in modern-day Nigeria, he married the sultan's daughter and was groomed for leadership. In 1838, after Bello's death, Umar and a growing band of followers returned to Futa Toro determined to unite the Western Sahel under one ruler and one faith.

Wars, decline, and legacy

Umar initially failed to gain sufficient support in Futa Toro, and in the 1840s he established a *ribat* (sanctuary) in Fouta Djallon to the south, in what is now Guinea. He gathered soldiers, religious teachers, and European firearms for a holy war. His followers included members of the Tukolor people of Futa Toro and the Fulani people of Fouta Djallon. He even sought an alliance with the French, but they refused, wary of encouraging a potential rival.

During the late 1840s and 1850s, Tukolor troops struck at neighbouring kingdoms and skirmished with the French, who were augmenting their military with local troops, and had begun to construct roads and

> "**Do you not know** that **Al-Hajj**... has the capacity to **destroy you**... and **all your trade**?"

AL-HAJJ UMAR TAL IN A LETTER TO THE FRENCH, 1854

French-made blade

Sheath made of leather and brass

forts in the region. The Tukolor won victories against the Bambara — an empire weakened by clashes with the Fulani of nearby Masina — before defeating Masina in 1862. Umar's empire now covered much of modern-day Senegal, Guinea, Mauritania, and Mali.

The Tukolors occupied Timbuktu in 1863, but an allied force of Fulani, Tuaregs, and Moroccans eventually halted their wars of expansion. On Umar's death in 1864, his son Ahmadu and nephew Tidiani each governed parts of the empire, but struggled to hold the sprawling kingdom together. The French

encroached on Tukolor territory, building alliances with disgruntled local rulers, and eventually conquering cities. In 1893, Ahmadu fled to Sokoto, and the empire crumbled, with French West Africa taking control of Tukolor lands in 1897.

In West Africa, the Tukolor Empire is remembered for its heroic resistance to the French, but also for further dividing the region's peoples, making the French advance easier. Perhaps the empire's most significant legacy was to help spread Islam across the Sahel, where it remains the dominant religion.

△ **The Great Mosque**
In the 1840s, Al-Hajj Umar built the Great Mosque of Dinguiraye in what is now Guinea, photographed here in around 1900. The exterior of its impressive domed roof was thatched.

Handle in the shape of a bird's beak

△ **Prized weapon**
Often described as "the sword of Umar Tal", this blade actually belonged to his son, Ahmadu. The French took it in 1893, only returning it to Senegal in 2019.

West African art and craft

A wide range of artistic artefacts

West Africa has a rich and diverse artistic heritage. Its artwork is often intricately connected to the social and religious ceremonies of its many different peoples, and imbued with ceremonial or ritual significance. Its artefacts encompass sculptures in wood, ivory, metal, and stone, and include masks, headdresses, and figures.

Exaggerated high forehead

Naturalistic face

Simple carved figure

Bold, abstract patterns

Elaborate hairstyle

Tall, single plank of wood

△ **Sande helmet mask**
The women's initiation society of Liberia, Sierra Leone, Guinea, and Côte d'Ivoire – called the Sande – is probably unique in creating masks to be worn exclusively by women.

◁ **Kongo nkisi figure**
Materials and amulets are attached to the Kongo *nkisi* figure by a *nganga* priest, to add spiritual power to the work.

▷ **Bwa plant mask**
Representing invisible forest spirits, the plank masks of the Bwa people of Burkina Faso, known as *nwantantay*, are highly stylized and abstract.

Stylized facial features

Cast iron horns

Miniaturized legs

△ **Asante fertility figure**
The Asante *akuaba* figure with its distinctive disc-shaped head is for women hoping to conceive. The stylized features emphasize ideals of beauty and fertility.

Bare wooden figure

◁ **Dahomey sculpture**
A *bocio*, or power sculpture, from Dahomey depicts a member of the royal family. These wooden figures were adorned with cloth and various organic materials.

▷ **Fon silver buffalo**
This lavishly silver-plated wooden buffalo was commissioned by the 19th-century king Ghezo of Dahomey as a symbol of wealth.

Hammered silver sheet

△ **Head of an oba**
This cast bronze head depicts a recently deceased *oba*, or ruler, of Benin, and was commissioned by his successor.

Shells and beads form a design of a stylized spider, associated with wisdom

Beaded collar

△ **Guéré mask**
The masks of the Guéré people of Côte d'Ivoire typically include cloth, hair, and metal objects attached to a painted wooden base.

Carved mudfish

Stylized hairstyle

Elaborate necklace

Portraits of Portuguese traders

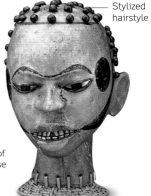

△ **Pendant mask**
This 16th-century representation of Idia, the first *Iyoba* or Queen Mother of Benin, was sculpted from ivory for her son, King Esigie.

△ **Ejagham headdress**
Made of antelope skin over a wooden form, this headdress was created by the Ejagham people of Nigeria and Cameroon.

Decorative painted band

Decorative zigzag border

Glass beads

△ **Helmet mask**
Richly decorated with shells and beads, this mask from the Bamum kingdom of Cameroon indicates the privileged status of its owner.

△ **Moon mask**
This Baule mask from Côte d'Ivoire depicting the moon is an example of masks representing natural phenomena worn during *gbagba* dance performances.

△ **Wan-balinga mask**
A central feature of the funeral ceremonies of the Mossi people of Burkina Faso, Wan-balinga masks are worn exclusively by dancers of the farming community.

European explorers
Into the African interior

Europe's trading interactions with Africa were at first confined to the coasts. By the 19th century, European explorers had spread deep inland and trade developed into a vastly more complex network of contested relationships.

The Greeks and then the Romans, respectively, gave the names "Libya" and "Africa" to the territory now known as North Africa (see pp. 70–71). However, their knowledge of – and interest in – Africa south of the Sahara was more limited. For Greek historians such as Herodotus, the interior was the "mysterious" source of the Nile, or, according to Homer, the origin of "the remotest of men", the Ethiopians. Later Roman writers such as Sallust portrayed Africa south of the Sahara as a "wild", "exotic", and "unknown" place.

Exploring a continent
Europeans' knowledge of Africa remained limited until the 15th and 16th centuries, when, primarily, Portuguese explorers began to chart its west coast.

Between 1444 and 1447, the Portuguese visited the seashores of Senegal, Guinea, and the Gambia, and mapped the Cabo Verde Islands in 1456 and the Bissau islands in 1462. This led, in 1488, to Bartolomeu Dias becoming the first European to sail around the Cape of Good Hope on Africa's southernmost tip, a journey that itself paved the way for Vasco da Gama's voyage to India via the Cape 10 years later. And with each point of contact came trade: European wheat, cloth, and weapons in exchange for African gold and enslaved people. In the 16th century, the Portuguese repeated a similar pattern of exploration followed by the trade in goods and humans along Africa's eastern coast.

Although mariners had charted Africa's full outline by the late 16th century, its interior remained largely unexplored by Europeans for another 200 years. (Muslim enslavers, meanwhile, established several trade routes traversing the desert kingdoms of the Sahara.) By the early 19th century, Europeans desired knowledge of Africa beyond its coast. British, French, Italian, German, and Belgian explorers ventured ever-deeper inland. This facilitated further trade and the spread of Christian missions, followed by more formal colonial control when Europeans began to use

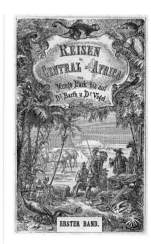

△ **Travels to the interior**
Scotland's Mungo Park (1771–1806), included in this German anthology of travellers' accounts, was one of the first Europeans to travel through Central Africa.

◁ **The river man**
In 1858, John Hanning Speke (1827–64) travelled to a body of water he named Lake Victoria – correctly surmising it was the source of the River Nile.

"Here at last I stood on the **brink of the Nile**; most **beautiful was the scene**…"

JOHN HANNING SPEKE, 1863

military force to protect the African lands they held. They believed that these tactics were necessary, seeing themselves as "opening" Africa to the emerging global trading economy.

During the 1830s and 1840s, Europeans made comprehensive explorations of regions south of the Sahara. They charted areas that had previously been shown as blank on their maps, including the Congo Basin, Burundi's Great Lakes region, and the territory of the modern Democratic Republic of the Congo, Kenya, Malawi, Mozambique, Rwanda, and Zambia. Explorers collected and preserved much important ethnographic data concerning languages, cultures, and customs – although racist bias and prejudice often undermined the accuracy of their interpretation.

Cultures and conquest

By 1875, men such as John Hanning Speke, Sir Richard Burton, David Livingstone, and Henry Morton Stanley (see box, right) had completed the European exploration of Africa, after which geologists surveyed the continent, chiefly to locate new mineral sites for exploitation. The revelation of the continent's mineral wealth led to conflicts between the Africans who possessed it and the Europeans who desired it.

During this period, European colonizers partitioned Africa into spheres of influence and colonies, often imposing ethnic and political divisions where there had been none before. This in turn resulted in

Africans' loss of political independence and the marginalization of Indigenous cultures. In short, cultural and political imperialism followed military imperialism, seeking to impose European customs onto African societies.

As well as military and police forces, imperial administrators, and commercial enterprises, Christian missionaries played an important role in the Europeanization of colonized African states. With the regions south of the Sahara less technologically advanced than Europe at this time, colonizing nations could easily portray Africa's people as "savages" in need of both God's salvation and the "civilizing" largesse of the West.

△ **Keeping a record**
Germany's Heinrich Barth (1821–65) was as much an ethnographer as explorer. He collected oral histories and made many sketches, such as this view of Kano, in Nigeria.

FROM GLORY **TO CONDEMNATION**

The shift in public perception of Henry Morton Stanley (1841–1904) symbolizes the changing reputations of all European explorers over time. Originally lionized as the man who found David Livingstone (see pp. 204–205) and as a successful explorer and colonial administrator, more recently Stanley (right, with his adopted African son, Kalulu) has been criticized as the archetypal "white saviour" figure, and as a cruel taskmaster and rapacious imperialist, not least in the ruthless land expropriations he carried out for King Leopold of Belgium in Congo Free State (see pp. 212–13).

"[Njoya] preserved… his kingdom's **physical boundaries** when **European colonialists** were erasing them…"

LANISA KITCHINER, CHIEF, AFRICAN AND MIDDLE EASTERN DIVISION, LIBRARY OF CONGRESS, 2022

Map of Bamum

Indigenous African cartography

During the German occupation of what is now Cameroon, Ibrahim Njoya, *fon* (ruler) of the Kingdom of Bamum from 1886 to his death in 1933, steadfastly defended his people's independence while working strategically with the colonizers to his advantage wherever possible. As well as devising an alphabet for writing the Bamum language and producing a written history of the people, he made a detailed map of the kingdom. He astutely realized that, in carving up the continent, the European colonizers laid claim to territory by making maps, and he set out to do the same to assert Bamum's existence as an independent nation – and to allow him to allocate land rights and resolve land disputes within his kingdom. In 1912, he established a group of surveyors to begin the task of mapping Bamun.

New mapping techniques

The first surveying expedition, consisting of around 60 individuals led by Njoya himself, made its way around the perimeter of the kingdom on foot, covering roughly two-thirds of the territory before the rainy season forced them to stop. In the absence of modern surveying equipment, they devised their own methods, timing their walks to estimate distances and gathering information from local guides. Interrupted by the death of the king's mother, followed by the turmoil of World War I, the survey was completed in 1920.

Njoya's surveyors created their own cartographic system. The map is oriented east–west rather than north–south, as indicated by the discs at the top and bottom, symbolizing the rising and setting Sun. Although the true shape of Njoya's kingdom was triangular, the mapmakers stretched the kingdom's western boundary to produce a rectangular shape, with a symmetrical river system, creating a sense of unity that projects the king's power, even over the landscape. The size and centrality of the capital, Foumban, is exaggerated to emphasize its importance. Towns, villages, and landmarks are marked with labels using Njoya's alphabet.

▽ **Royal city**
Njoya's palace, indicated by the grid of red squares, lies within the walled capital city, Foumban.

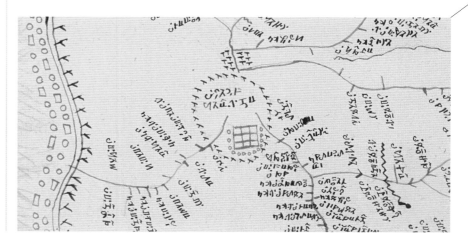

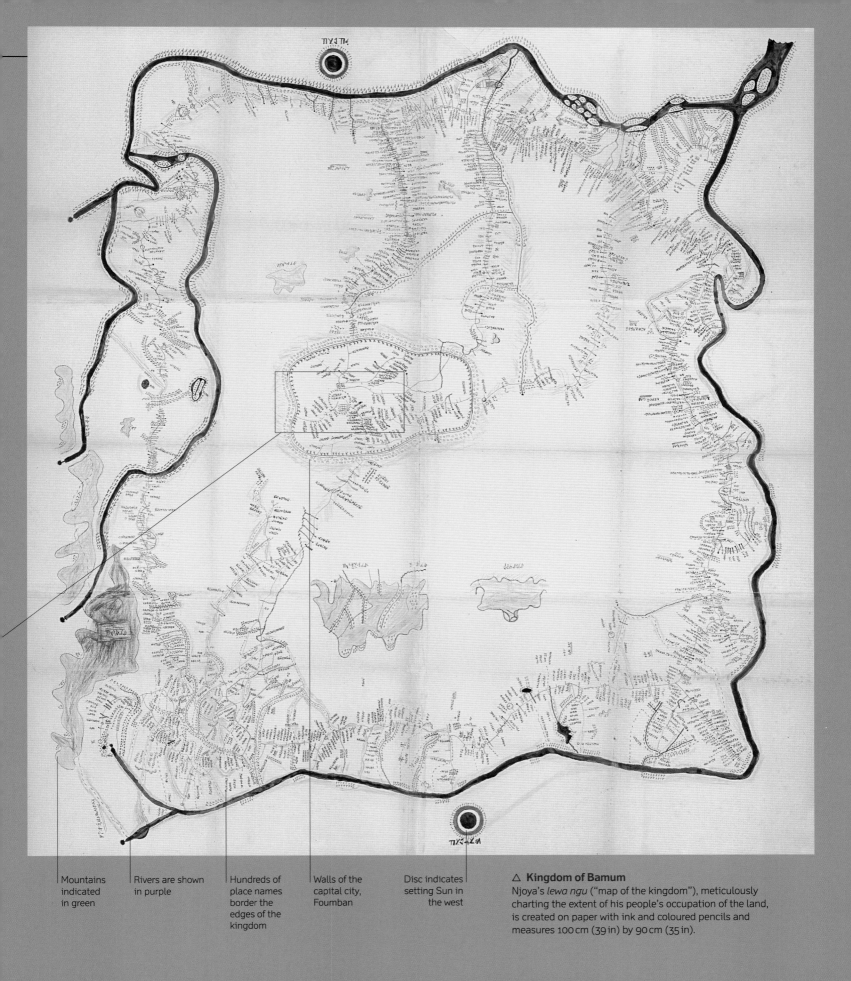

Mountains
indicated
in green

Rivers are shown
in purple

Hundreds of
place names
border the
edges of the
kingdom

Walls of the
capital city,
Foumban

Disc indicates
setting Sun in
the west

△ **Kingdom of Bamum**
Njoya's *lewa ngu* ("map of the kingdom"), meticulously
charting the extent of his people's occupation of the land,
is created on paper with ink and coloured pencils and
measures 100 cm (39 in) by 90 cm (35 in).

Text is mainly Visigothic, but contains notes in Latin and Arabic

Sacred bulls, shown here in the biblical story of the Adoration of the Golden Calf, appear in many cultures, including in ancient Egypt

△ **Mozarabic Bible**
Christianity had been established in North Africa and beyond before the rise of Islam in the 8th century. Mozarabs, who created this León Bible of 960, are Spanish Christians who lived under Muslim Amazigh (Berber) rule and adopted Arabic language and culture.

The illuminations are by a scribe and artist named Sanctus and his master Florentius

Christian missionaries

Conversion across the continent

Until the late 18th century, Christianity's influence in Africa had been limited to regions in the north. Christian missionaries in the 19th century transformed the continent's religious landscape – and had a profound impact on its history.

△ **Christian explorer**
Livingstone wrote about his extensive African travels in *The Life and Explorations of David Livingstone*, first published in 1870.

Some Africans embraced Christianity in its earliest days. The religion had spread to areas including Alexandria in Egypt, Cyrenaica in what is now Libya, and ancient Nubia by the 2nd century CE, and Aksum in Ethiopia by the 4th century CE. Yet the faith barely reached beyond these strongholds for centuries.

Christianity began to spread again as European influence increased. In the 15th century, Catholic Portuguese traders brought the faith to Kongo, in Central Africa. But it was the largely Protestant missionary enterprises of the late 18th and 19th centuries that had the greatest impact. Groups such as Britain's Church Missionary Society, which sent expeditions to the colony of Sierra Leone in the 1840s, emerged from growing evangelist movements in Europe and North America. Africans played a crucial role in missions founded by Europeans and also established missions on their own. For example, Samuel Ajayi Crowther, a formerly enslaved Yoruba man, opened a mission in the Niger Delta and became the first Black African Anglican bishop. From the 1880s, Africans began to found Africanized churches that incorporated local religious ideas, practices, and songs.

Religion and colonialism

Some missionaries, both European and African, struggled to convert local people. Others transformed communities via their faith and their encouragement of "legitimate commerce" in goods such as palm oil and sugar at the expense of the slave trade. Missionaries founded schools and orphanages, encouraging the rise of an educated elite. Today, around half of Africa's population practises Christianity. However, European missionaries discouraged Indigenous customs and divided communities. Education emphasized the achievements of Europe and North America. Indeed, religion and colonialism often went hand in hand.

David Livingstone, of the London Missionary Society (LMS), mapped wide areas of Central and Southern Africa for the British in the 1840s and '50s, and saw the Zambezi River as "God's Highway" – a route along which both Christianity and "civilization" could travel. Crowther urged that the British "pacify" the Niger Delta. In 1888, missionaries François Coillard and Charles Helm are said to have wilfully mistranslated treaties for the Lozi and Ndebele of Southern Africa, resulting in territorial losses to British colonial enterprises. Christian missionaries did not just change hearts: they reshaped nations.

"Spending so much of **my life** in Africa… is a privilege."

DAVID LIVINGSTONE, 1858

▷ **Mission school**
A nun teaches reading and writing to a group of Zulu children in an outdoor class at Mariathal Mission School in 1910, in what is now KwaZulu-Natal, South Africa.

Shaka and the Zulu Kingdom

A powerful southern force

In the early years of the 19th century, the Zulu Kingdom was one of several competing nations in Southern Africa; by the 1820s, under King Shaka, it had become a regional superpower.

The Zulus' ancestors arrived in the lands today known as South Africa around the 2nd millennium BCE, during the Bantu migrations (see pp. 36–37). They emerged from the Nguni branch of Bantu-speaking inhabitants of East Africa's Great Lakes region. The Zulu developed in the 17th century as semi-nomadic, pastoral groups, inhabiting the region now called KwaZulu-Natal on South Africa's east coast. These groups grew, consolidating into larger ones and establishing settled communities with powerful chieftains. They became wealthy on the cattle, grain, and goods gained by conquering nearby chiefdoms.

Creation of a kingdom

In the first decade of the 19th century, the Zulu competed with other local groups, such as the Mthethwa, Ndwandwe, and Swazi, for land and resources, which were in short supply after drought

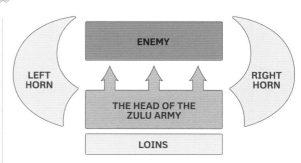

△ **Buffalo soldiers**
Shaka invented the immensely successful "Buffalo Horns" battle tactic. "Head" troops engaged the enemy's front and the "horns" attacked the flanks. The "loins" were reserves.

and famine affected the region from 1800–08. Under the leadership of Dingiswayo, who became king in 1806, the Mthethwa ruled a confederacy of local groups, which included the Zulu. One of his most able military commanders was a young Zulu man called Shaka. The illegitimate son of the Zulu king Senzangakhona kaJama, Shaka had lived among the Mthethwa from childhood with his mother, Nandi.

When Senzangakhona kaJama died in 1816, Dingiswayo helped Shaka to seize the Zulu throne, provided that he remained a vassal of the Mthethwa. Following Dingiswayo's death in 1817, however, Shaka embarked on a series of conquests that saw him assume control of the entire territory of South Africa. Under Shaka, all conquered peoples became Zulu, and Zulu customs, including the rule of law upheld by chiefs, were imposed throughout the kingdom, forging a national identity among what had been a diverse group of peoples.

From Shaka onwards, all power in the Zulu State was centralized under the king. Before this, the monarch had ruled in consultation with chiefs and

AN UNCOMPROMISING KING

Born c. 1787, Shaka kaSenzangakhona, known as Shaka Zulu, ran his state on martial lines. Boys as young as six were enrolled in his army, at first to carry supplies. When a warrior was unsuccessful in battle or showed cowardice, his family was executed. But it was not fear of failure alone that motivated Shaka's army. Soldiers were highly trained, and lived together in military stockades. Shaka introduced a variant of the long *assegai* throwing spear – the short *iklwa* stabbing spear used in hand-to-hand combat. A ruthless leader, Shaka became increasingly erratic in later life, and is said to have executed many people for not sufficiently mourning the death of his mother. He was assassinated in 1828 by two of his half-brothers.

STATUE OF SHAKA IN THE ZULU CAPITAL, ULUNDI

▷ **Communal life**
Most Zulu families and clans lived in *kraals*, defensible enclosures with room for livestock and several beehive-shaped huts called *iQukwane*, usually built by women.

advisors. Under Shaka, local leaders and the chiefs of conquered peoples were still allowed to administer their own areas and keep some powers – settling land disputes or overseeing local legal affairs – but had to pay tributes to Shaka and the kings that followed in the form of local produce. Dissent was not tolerated, and Zulu lands were dotted with military garrisons to ensure law and order was kept.

The end of an era
The Zulu Kingdom rose to power during a period known as the *Mfecane* ("the crushing"). Its wars of conquest, along with famine and regional conflicts among local peoples such as the Matabele, the Tsonga and the Ndwandwe, saw two million people lose their lives. This made Southern Africa highly unstable, a situation Shaka's successors were unable to rectify, especially as Boer settlers from Britain's Cape Colony and British imperialist forces began to encroach on Zulu lands from the 1840s. In 1879, Zulu king Cetshwayo (see pp. 208–209) attempted to drive the British from his territory. The British deposed him, and they and the Boers took over his kingdom.

During the apartheid era, South Africa's Zulus were confined to the KwaZulu homeland and denied civil rights – as were Black South Africans in the rest of the country's homelands (see pp. 254–55). Today, many of South Africa's 10–12 million Zulus still live in the region, now called KwaZulu-Natal, one of the country's nine provinces. Although part of the parliamentary democracy of South Africa, KwaZulu-Natal boasts its own Zulu king. While the monarch has no legislative power, he controls through a state-operated trust around 30 per cent of KwaZulu-Natal's land and exerts a considerable degree of political and social influence among his people.

▽ **Defensive weapons**
These Zulu warriors photographed c. 1875 carry ox-hide *umbumbolozo* shields. At 91 cm (36 in), they were shorter than the Shaka-era 152 cm (60 in) *isihlangu* shields.

Cetshwayo

The last great king of the Zulu Kingdom

Cetshwayo was a skilful negotiator and an uncompromising leader whose success and popularity brought him into direct conflict with Southern Africa's colonial occupiers at the end of the 19th century.

Physically imposing at more than 2 m (6 ft 6 in) tall, Cetshwayo literally fought his way to the throne of the Zulu nation: in 1856, the power struggle between Cetshwayo and his brother Mbuyazi for the right to succeed their father, King Mpande, was settled at the Battle of Ndundakusuka. Mbuyazi was killed, along with at least another five of his brothers. At this point, Cetshwayo became the Zulu Kingdom's de facto ruler for 16 years, until formally taking power in 1873, a year after Mpande's death (which was initially concealed).

Mpande had been a reluctant ruler, ceding some of his land to the British and Afrikaners rather than risk conflict with them. Cetshwayo took a different approach to kingship, adopting an anti-Western stance and encouraging other African rulers to do the same. At the same time, he negotiated skilfully with colonial powers over border disputes. Eager to avoid giving the British a reason to destroy his kingdom, Cetshwayo would strategically move his army away from the borders of British colonies.

Engaging with the enemy

Sir Henry Bartle Frere, the British High Commissioner for Southern Africa, decided to force the issue. In December 1878, after Zulu troops made minor border incursions into British-controlled Natal, Frere ordered Cetshwayo to disband his army and relinquish his sovereignty. Cetshwayo's refusal led to the first battle

◁ **Zulu shield**
In battle, the 20,000-strong Zulu army carried wooden and oxhide shields, like the one shown here, and *assegai* (spears), while the British used Gatling guns and rifles.

of the Anglo-Zulu War, at Isandlwana in 1879, which the Zulu won. After a Zulu defeat at the Battle of Ulundi later that year, the British exiled Cetshwayo to the Cape Colony and then, in 1882, to England, where he petitioned British politicians for his return. Britain annexed Cetshwayo's former realm and, in 1883, permitted him to return to "rule" a portion of it. He died the following year of a heart attack, though rumours persist that he was poisoned.

△ **Capture of Cetshwayo**
The British spent nearly two months searching for Cetshwayo after the Battle of Ulundi, finally capturing him in a remote *kraal* (village).

▽ **City of fire**
The British burned the Zulu capital Ulundi following Cetshwayo's defeat there in the final, decisive battle of the Anglo-Zulu War.

c.**1826** Birth of Cetshwayo in Eshowe, modern-day South Africa

1878 Negotiations with Sir Henry Bartle Frere

1881 Cetshwayo begins his campaign to reinstate the Zulu monarchy

1883 Cetshwayo returns to Zulu Kingdom

1873 Cetshwayo becomes king of the Zulu nation

1879 Anglo-Zulu War fought between the British Empire and the Zulu Kingdom

1882 Cetshwayo meets with Queen Victoria in England

1884 Death of Cetshwayo on 8 February

The scramble for Africa

Carving up a continent

As the 19th century ended, Africa became subject to Europe's increasing desire for imperial control. Without the involvement of any African leaders, rival European nations agreed the division of the continent between themselves.

By the mid-19th century, several European nations had established trading posts across Africa. Some, notably Britain and France, had already acquired colonies in South Africa, Algeria, and elsewhere. Christian missionaries and adventurers returned from Africa's interior with tales of its peoples, spectacular landscapes, and untapped riches of gold, timber, minerals, and resources. Explorers investigated and mapped the continent. In Europe's eyes, Africa had been "discovered" and now was ripe for exploitation.

Colonization and cooperation

The Industrial Revolution made the nations of the West wealthy and powerful. It also left them hungry for raw materials and new markets, both of which they saw in Africa. With the international slave trade abolished by the mid-19th century, Europe turned its focus to securing trading and territorial rights within Africa itself, often employing deceptive contracts that dispossessed African rulers of their lands. Other tools of colonization were quinine – introduced from the 1850s – which lowered mortality rates from malaria, enabling Europeans to live in areas where the disease was prevalent, and new weapons, such as the breech-loading repeater rifle and the Maxim machinegun.

European nations' biggest fear was competition from each other – and they tackled the issue through collusion. Convened by the German chancellor Otto von Bismarck, the Berlin Conference of 15 November 1884–26 February 1885 saw 13 European powers and the US meeting to agree between them spheres of influence in Africa. No African nations or peoples were represented at the conference – the Sultan of Zanzibar had requested to attend, but Britain refused.

As well as giving each country the right to claim a territory if it had treaties, flags, or people on the ground (a policy known as "effective occupation"), the European powers demarcated lands where future colonies could be established and set up free trade areas that mutually benefitted European interests.

Remaking Africa in Europe's image

The agreements made at Berlin had far-reaching consequences. The Belgian king Leopold II was handed sole ownership of a vast territory, the Congo Free State (see pp. 212–13). Today, as the Democratic

△ **European greed**
This French caricature from 1885 satirizes the Berlin Conference, showing Germany's chancellor Bismarck offering slices of Africa to his guests.

▷ **Camel Corps**
Britain's Egyptian Camel Corps stand guard, c. 1900. Many camel drivers were Egyptians, either hired or press-ganged into supporting and supplying British and imperial troops.

Republic of the Congo, it still bears the scars of his, and later the Belgian government's, misrule. Similarly, Britain's claim to the territories forming modern-day Nigeria joined together historically divided lands and ethnic groups such as the Hausa-Fulani, the Yoruba, and the Igbo. After Nigeria achieved independence in 1960, long-standing tensions between the three groups erupted into civil war in 1967. The arbitrary drawing of borders that separated peoples and forced together ethnicities was repeated across Africa, for example by the British in Somalia, Kenya, and Zimbabwe.

The Berlin Conference recognized French power in West Africa and Britain's primacy in East Africa, from Egypt to South Africa in an almost unbroken line. Germany's interest in what are today Tanzania, Togo, and Namibia was accepted, as was Portugal's right to Mozambique, Angola, and Guinea, among others. New players – notably Italy, with colonies in modern-day Eritrea, Somalia, and Libya – would seize other regions. Before the Berlin Conference, 10 per cent of the continent was under foreign control; by 1918 the figure was closer to 90 per cent. Only Liberia and Ethiopia maintained their sovereignty.

The Berlin Conference did not initiate the scramble for Africa, but it accelerated the process of imperial expansion already underway, giving it a formally

◁ **Unfair burden**
Europe's colonists routinely exploited their power. This pith-helmeted official in the French Congo makes four young men carry him.

approved structure in a published set of terms and conditions known as the General Act. By adopting Britain's tactic of using anti-slave-trade agreements to "justify" imposing their control on African affairs, and by claiming they were bringing the benefits of modern civilization to Africa, Europe's imperialists added a moral gloss to an immoral system that would endure for another 75 years.

Congo Free State

Colonial corruption in Central Africa

Leopold II of Belgium privately owned a huge, resource-rich region at the heart of the continent, which he named the Congo Free State. Having seized the region in 1885, Leopold ruthlessly exploited both its natural treasures and its people.

It was the writings of Welsh-American journalist Henry Morton Stanley (see pp. 200–201) that captured the imagination of the Belgian monarch Leopold II in the 1870s. Stanley had in 1871 famously "found" the Scottish missionary and explorer David Livingstone, who had gone missing while searching for the source of the Nile. Leopold hired Stanley to act as his agent in Central Africa, where he was interested in securing territory, resources, and trading agreements.

From 1879–84, Stanley travelled the region, setting up treaties with local leaders, who were not properly informed of their content or aware that agreeing meant handing over control of their land to Leopold. Stanley also oversaw the building of a highway connecting the Congo River to local trade routes, helping to make the area's economic potential easier to exploit. Leopold, meanwhile, had established organizations such as the *Association Internationale Africaine* and the *Association Internationale du Congo* to carry out nominally philanthropic, missionary, and anti-slavery work, but which mainly provided a respectable front for his activities.

This had the desired effect. At the Berlin Conference of November 1884 (see pp. 210–11), Leopold's claim to Central Africa was formally recognized; in 1885, he announced the creation of the Congo Free State.

Exploited land
Leopold treated the Congo Free State, 76 times larger than Belgium, as if it were his personal kingdom. It encompassed 2.34 million sq km (905,000 sq miles) of land and 15 million people – a large proportion of whom objected to Leopold's rule and the vast majority of which suffered oppression and expropriation during the state's two decades of existence. Leopold appointed only a small number of administrators, wanting to retain personal control. Instead, he formed the *Force Publique*, a private force of mercenaries notorious for their acts of torture, beatings, murder, and sexual assaults that caused millions of deaths.

Congo Free State was blessed with natural resources, including ivory and, most abundantly, rubber. Leopold soon saw opportunities for European corporations to exploit these resources within the country. When

△ **Threatened culture**
This *ndop* figure represents an 18th-century Kuba king. The Kuba people's culture was one of many to be suppressed under Leopold.

"Leopold's Congo state is **guilty of crimes against humanity.**"

BLACK AMERICAN BAPTIST MINISTER AND POLITICIAN GEORGE WASHINGTON WILLIAMS, 1890

◁ **Hard harvest**
Rubber tapping was labour-intensive and dangerous. Workers sliced into rubber vines, allowing latex sap to coat their bodies, which was later scraped off – taking skin and hair with it.

from 1887 Dunlop, and then Michelin, began mass-producing bicycle inner tubes and pneumatic tyres, the global demand for rubber skyrocketed, and Leopold granted companies such as the Anglo-Belgian India Rubber Company (Abir) concessions to run large swathes of Congo Free State in exchange for their investment in infrastructure, particularly road and rail. These concessionary companies' activities were unregulated. Extreme violence was meted out to those who refused to work or who did not collect enough rubber. With all resources devoted to rubber harvesting, agricultural production was neglected, resulting in crop failures and starvation.

By the turn of the century, the violence, coercion, and displacement suffered by the Indigenous people of the region became impossible for the international community to ignore: journalist E. D. Morel described Congo Free State as a "monstrous outrage". A 1904 report by British consul Roger Casement revealed the extent of Leopold's misrule and led to the arrest and punishment of several corporate figures and Congo Free State officials.

End of European rule

In 1908, Leopold was compelled to transfer control of the Congo Free State to the Belgian government, which renamed it the Belgian Congo. The economy gradually shifted away from rubber towards increasing investment in mining, but again there was forced cultivation of specific export crops such as cotton. Opposition to foreign rule continued, and many Congolese objected to – and resisted – paying taxes to Belgium. The colonial authorities met these acts of defiance with violence; a large number of inhabitants quit the country to work in European-run mines and farms in neighbouring states.

Belgium continued to administer the new state until it achieved independence in 1960, eventually becoming the Democratic Republic of the Congo.

△ **Ill-gotten gains**
This satirical image from c.1905 makes the point that Leopold II of Belgium built his fortune on the bones of the people in the Congo Free State.

ARMY OF **OPPRESSION**

The *Force Publique* was the paramilitary arm of the Congo Free State. It protected the exploitative activities of the concessionary companies and stamped down on protest. Established in 1886, it consisted of Belgian soldiers and European mercenaries commanding troops recruited or conscripted from the local region and further afield, including the West and East coasts. At its height, the *Force Publique* numbered 19,000 men. It was involved in many atrocities and its name was a byword for brutality.

△ **Coffee plantation**
Enslaved Africans pick coffee on a plantation in Brazil, where slavery was only abolished in 1888. Around 5.5 million Africans were transported to Brazil to work on plantations.

The African diaspora

People of African descent around the world

Africans have migrated from the continent since ancient times, but the 200-million strong diaspora of people of African descent was largely created by the enslavement and transportation of millions of Africans between the 15th and 19th centuries.

The African Union considers the African diaspora as "people of African origin living outside the continent, irrespective of their citizenship and nationality". In one sense, as human life began on the continent (see pp. 22–23), the whole world is filled with an African diaspora. However, the movements that forced millions of people of African descent away from the continent are mostly political and financial.

Africans first reached Europe in Roman times, when North Africa was part of the Roman Empire. Indeed, Septimius Severus, who was born in Libya, became Roman emperor in 193 CE. Other Africans

◁ **Sojourner Truth**
Born into enslavement in New York State (at that time a state where slavery still existed), Truth escaped in 1826 and became an outspoken opponent of slavery and an advocate of Black American and women's civil rights.

settled in the medieval Islamic world, often trafficked as enslaved people (see pp. 148–49). There was also a small African population in Tudor London and Renaissance Portugal. These people were musicians, skilled tradespeople, diplomats or part of wealthy households or the royal court.

The slave trade and the diaspora

The largest diaspora movement by far, however, was an entirely involuntary one: the transportation by Europeans of an estimated 11 million Africans across the Atlantic in the slave trade that devastated the African continent over four centuries. This was what led to a diaspora that today comprises over 200 million people of African or mixed descent, around 43 million of these living in the US and roughly 10 million in Europe. Many countries in the Caribbean now have a majority of their population of diaspora

"Africa is our **center of gravity**, our cultural and spiritual mother and father… no matter **where we live**…"

JOHN HENRIK CLARKE, AFRICAN AMERICAN HISTORIAN (1915–98)

descent. Smaller diaspora groups include the Siddi people of India and Pakistan taken there by the Arab slave trade, as well as the 100,000-strong Afro-Turk community in Turkey who were brought there in Ottoman times.

Impact of the diaspora

The forced migration of so many African people had a profound impact on many areas of society. The diaspora gave rise to political movements, especially in campaigns to abolish slavery, where works by formerly enslaved people such as Olaudah Equiano's *The Interesting Narrative* (1789) helped galvanize anti-slavery movements, and activists such as Sojourner Truth (1797–1883) and Frederick Douglass (1818–95) played a key part in its abolition in the US at the end of the Civil War.

Diaspora Africans, with their international connections, were key to the development of the ideology of Pan-Africanism (see pp. 232–33), with campaigners such as the Jamaican Marcus Garvey (1887–1940) and the American sociologist and historian W.E.B. Du Bois (1868–1963) laying the foundations for a movement that linked the diaspora with African politicians.

The end of colonial empires brought a further diaspora, as Africans moved from now independent colonies to the former colonial power. Some settled, others stayed for a while to study or work before returning to Africa. Often they were invited by the governments there to fill labour shortages. France, for example, received African migrants mainly from its former colonies in North and West Africa. While some diaspora Africans came voluntarily, others arrived as refugees from civil war, famine, or religious or political persecution.

New cultures emerge

Where Africans from many different cultures had been enslaved and forced to live together, this led to a loss of cultures and at the same time the emergence of new hybrid cultures. Religious systems such as Haitian Vodou, Cuban Santeria, or Brazilian Candomblé owed much to African origins, particularly from among the Yoruba people, but developed a vitality all of their own. In plantations where enslaved people had no shared language, creoles – adaptations of the colonial

language tinged with African influences – arose, such as Haitian Creole, which is today the national language of Haiti. Over time, diaspora Africans also had a strong influence on the arts and music in particular, with jazz developing from work songs of enslaved African Americans, and calypso and reggae emerging in the diaspora populations of the Caribbean.

△ **Frederick Douglass**
Shown here on a poster from c.1884, Douglass is in the centre, surrounded by other activists. The poster uses the language of the time, which today would be considered offensive.

Colonial wars

A continent in crisis

The 19th century saw unprecedented levels of European expansion into Africa, usually through war and conflict, followed by colonizing powers attempting to impose control over Indigenous populations.

△ **Stolen goods**
Following the British Army's attack of 1897, the colonial military looted the sculptures and other treasures from the razed Benin royal palace.

In the late 19th century, imperialist nations sought to exploit Africa's natural resources and establish strategically important military bases from which they could protect other territories that they had colonized around the world. This "Scramble for Africa" was formalized by the Berlin Conference of 1884–85, where the European powers agreed to partition Africa between them (see pp. 210–11). The colonial frontiers, however, might have been established on a map, but the colonial powers still had to occupy and take possession of lands by force. Across the continent, conflicts and wars broke out as European armies continued to meet African peoples who resisted European colonization.

The Anglo-Asante Wars had begun in 1824 when the Asante Empire (see pp. 190–91) in modern-day Ghana resisted British encroachment. In the first conflict, the Asante defeated the British forces and forced a retreat. The second conflict, from 1863 to 1864, ended in a stalemate, but the third, between 1873 and 1874, resulted in defeat for the Asante, when the British occupied and burned Kumasi, the capital. Seeking greater control of the region, the British attacked the Asante again in 1894 and overthrew King Prempeh I in 1896. A final conflict in 1900 resulted in the complete annexation of the Asante Empire, until Ghana achieved independence in 1957.

Resistance and defeat
In North Africa, France invaded the city of Algiers in 1830, initiating over a century of French rule in the region that would see hundreds of thousands of

▷ **Epic victory**
Zulu soldiers triumph at the Battle of Isandlwana, one of the British Army's worst colonial defeats – and a landmark moment in African opposition to imperialism.

Yaa Asantewaa (right, depicted in a statue in Ghana) was queen of Ejisu, a territory of the Asante Empire and an implacable opponent of colonialism. In the Fifth Anglo-Asante War in 1900, she led troops into battle against British forces in the Asante city of Kumasi, only to be captured and exiled to the Seychelles. She is revered as a Ghanaian heroine.

French settlers arrive and the attempted suppression of the Indigenous Muslim population. Armed uprisings against the French marked the period. Algerian religious and military leader Emir Abdelkader led a coalition of local peoples, and by 1839 controlled two-thirds of Algeria. By 1847, however, the French had brutally crushed his resistance.

In Southern Africa, the Anglo-Zulu War was fought in 1879 when the British invaded the Zulu Kingdom. At the Battle of Isandlwana in January, a large army of Zulu troops inflicted a heavy defeat on the smaller but much better armed British forces. By July, British reinforcements had deposed the Zulu king Cetshwayo (see pp. 208–209), ending the independence of the Zulu nation. Now Britain turned to the white Afrikaners, or Boers, of the Transvaal and Orange Free State republics, seeking overall dominance in a region rich in diamond and gold fields. The Anglo-Boer War of 1899–1901 resulted in Britain taking control of much of Southern Africa.

Like Cetshwayo, Samory Touré was the leader of a nation which resisted the colonizing armies. Touré's Wassoulou Empire (also called the Mandinka Empire), which encompassed parts of present-day Mali, Sierra Leone, Guinea, Côte d'Ivoire, and Liberia, fought France when it invaded in 1882. For several years, Touré held back the French in what would be known as the Mandinka Resistance Wars. By 1898, however, France's soldiers made a concentrated assault against Touré, capturing his lands and exiling him to Gabon.

A year earlier, Britain had used an army of 5,000 soldiers, armed with Maxim guns — weapons that could fire hundreds of bullets a minute — to destroy the 600-year-old Kingdom of Benin (see pp. 128–29). In this and countless other wars, Europeans used their superior firepower to impose military control, followed by civilian colonial government, on Africa. However, occupation would lead only to decades of uprisings and resistance from colonized peoples who demanded their freedom and independence.

△ **Resistant ruler**
Samory Touré's Sunni Muslim empire resisted French encroachment for almost 20 years. Samory was the great-grandfather of independent Guinea's first president, Ahmed Sékou Touré.

" ... the most dangerous antagonist the **Europeans have had to deal with**."

THE NEW YORK TIMES ON SAMORY TOURÉ, 1898

Resistance and uprisings

The fight for freedom intensifies

From the mid-19th century to 1914, Europe colonized the whole of Africa, except for Liberia and Ethiopia. Across the continent, Africans resisted imperial rule – through strikes, tax revolts, uprisings, and full-scale armed rebellion.

African reactions to the arrival of Europeans were mixed. Some groups, particularly the victims of internal warfare and intra-African slave raiding, welcomed the newcomers in the hope they would bring peace and protection. Others questioned the Europeans' motives for interfering in African affairs.

Confronting oppression

By the middle of the 19th century, it was clear the Europeans intended more harm than good – and that Africans would have to find effective ways to oppose

◁ **Hero in exile**
The Herero chief Samuel Maharero led the 1904 rebellion against Germany's control of Namibia. This 1907 image shows him in exile in Bechuanaland (modern Botswana).

them. The fates of the Asante Empire and the Zulu Kingdom (see pp. 216–17) after taking on British imperial forces in open warfare indicated that a directly confrontational approach would not always work. But sometimes it did. At the Battle of Adwa in 1896, for example, the Ethiopian army of Emperor Menelik II killed 4,000 Italian soldiers, thwarting the invaders' attempts to expand the territory they already controlled in Eritrea further into the Horn of Africa.

That same year, Mbuya Nehanda, a priestess of the Shona people of Rhodesia (modern Zimbabwe), led a revolt against the British South Africa Company's colonization of her lands. Another spiritual leader, Sekuru Kugavi, supported her, and both were inspired by the large-scale but unsuccessful uprisings by the region's Ndembele people a year earlier. The British captured and executed Nehanda and Sekuru, and Nehanda in particular became a folk heroine, memorialized through songs, novels, and poems.

In 1904, Namibia's Herero people revolted against their economic exploitation by Germany, and were suppressed in especially brutal fashion. The Germans summarily executed many Herero fighters, and tens of thousands of men, women, and children died from starvation and disease when they were herded into

△ **Spiritual leaders**
Mbuya Nehanda (left) and Sekuru Kaguvi (right) were *svikiro*, mediums said to speak with the gods. The British hanged both rebel leaders in 1898.

"**Let us die fighting** rather than… as a result of **maltreatment** [or] **imprisonment**."

SAMUEL MAHARERO IN A LETTER TO FELLOW CHIEF HENDRIK WITBOOI, 1904

△ **Ethiopian victory**
This painting depicts the Battle of Adwa that took place on 2 March 1896. Emperor Menelik II (top left, with umbrella) and the Empress Taitu (bottom left, on horseback) watch as their troops prepare to engage – and defeat – Italy's colonial soldiers.

concentration camps or fled the country to seek refuge. The following year, Germany crushed the Maji-Maji uprising in Tanganyika (modern Tanzania) organized by Kinjikitile Ngwale. A charismatic religious prophet, Ngwale supplied his followers with holy water instead of weapons to protect them from the Germans' bullets, with tragic results.

Pragmatic approaches

By the end of World War I, violent opposition to colonialism gave way to more measured and strategic responses: educated Africans demanded they be included in civic life; farmers resisted the colonial powers' attempts to control which crops they produced; and mine and port workers in Southern, West, and East Africa organized trade unions to fight for better pay and working conditions. In the Belgian Congo (today the Democratic Republic of the Congo) the Christian cleric Simon Kimbangu promised imperial liberation for the many followers of his new religious movement of Kimbanguism. The Belgians

arrested him in 1921 and, charged with undermining security, he spent the remaining 30 years of his life in prison. In southeastern Nigeria, the Aba Women's War of 1929 saw thousands of women engage in sit-ins and other demonstrations at their exclusion from economic and public life by British colonial administrators. When one of their rallies turned violent, soldiers opened fire and killed at least 50 people. Ultimately, their activism worked, and the British reformed the region's governance to include more Indigenous participation.

Resistance to colonial rule was clearly not just about violent confrontation. Africans practised countless acts of rebellion, large and small, on a daily basis. Sometimes this meant armed insurrection; on other occasions it meant something more mundane, such as deliberately giving visiting imperial officials wrong directions so that they would get lost. In all instances the intention was the same: to let the European colonizers know that their presence in other people's lands was not welcome.

Jaja of Opobo

The palm-oil king of the Niger Delta

Enslaved as a child, Jaja of Opobo founded a 19th-century city-state that dominated West Africa's palm oil trade. As well as wealth and power, it brought him into conflict with Britain's colonial ambitions in the region.

Jubo Jubogha was born into the Igbo community of what is now Nigeria around 1821, and was enslaved as a child. His enslaver controlled several trade routes in the Niger Delta, a network of swamps and creeks through which goods – chiefly palm oil, used as a lubricant for industrial machinery and in soap, as well as for cooking – passed on their way to the coast.

When his enslaver died, the young man, who would become better known as "Jaja", took control of the business. He soon led a merchant group called Anna Pepple House on Bonny Island, a kingdom on the Delta. After a clash with other traders, Jaja and his allies headed 40 km (25 miles) east to found an independent settlement named Opobo.

Palm oil and power
Jaja was a strong leader with an eye for opportunity, and grew to dominate the regional trade in palm oil. Jaja became Opobo's king, and was determined to maintain the independence of his rapidly modernizing operation. By the early 1870s, he was sending part of his stock directly to Liverpool and other British ports. He confined European traders to Opobo, away from markets further inland, and did not allow European missionaries in his kingdom.

Jaja embraced aspects of European culture. He sent his children to study in Glasgow, Scotland, and built a secular school in Opobo, staffed by white Europeans.

◁ **Palm fruits**
The yellowy-red pulp of oil-palm fruits is pressed to produce palm oil. Oil palms are native to West Africa.

During the Anglo-Asante Wars in what is now Ghana, he sent troops to aid the British. Yet the British would show no loyalty to Jaja. The Berlin Conference of 1884 (see pp. 210–11) imposed direct European control on many African nations, and Opobo was designated British territory. Jaja resisted, and refused to remove taxes on British traders. The British arrested him in 1887 and exiled him to the Caribbean. By 1891, Jaja had negotiated his return, but died on his way home.

▽ **Palm oil market**
Igbo traders show calabash gourds filled with palm oil to a European buyer in a market in Southern Nigeria around 1900.

(see pp. 210–11)

c. 1821 Jubo Jubogha, later known as Jaja of Opobo, is born

1869 After a clash with the established trading post of Bonny, Jaja founds the Opobo city-state

1873 Jaja's troops support the British army during the Anglo-Asante Wars

1884 Opobo is given to the British by the Berlin Conference

1885 Jaja's men use boom chains to limit access to the Opobo River

1887 Jaja is deposed and exiled to Saint Vincent and Barbados, in the Caribbean

1891 Jaja is finally granted leave to return to Opobo, but dies during the voyage

1903 A bronze monument honouring Jaja is erected in Opobo

Exploitation and administration

Governing the colonies

△ **Internment**
Suspected insurgents are held captive in a British concentration camp during the anticolonial Mau Mau rebellion (1952–60). Many suffered torture and abuse at the hands of British soldiers.

As colonial rule became firmly established in Africa, the European occupiers introduced various methods of administration of their colonies to best exploit the wealth of resources of the continent.

With improvements in communications in the late 19th century, the European powers began to explore the heart of Africa in search of tradable resources to fill the gap left by the ending of the lucrative slave trade, acquiring lands through means such as treaties with local leaders (see box, right). As they did so, they developed various forms of colonial governance. At the onset of colonialism, European nations permitted the establishment of private companies, such as the British South Africa Company formed in 1887, which were granted the administration of large expanses of land. The rationale behind this form of company rule was the need to administer the colonies while minimizing expense for the colonizing nation. However, many of companies proved unsuccessful as they generated only minimal profits for their stakeholders. By the mid-1920s, various forms of European governance had replaced company rule.

△ **Trading post**
Europeans established trading posts, called factories, on coasts or rivers, in order to influence and control trade, and generate profits for the metropole (imperial homeland).

The major colonial players were Britain (which took control of the lion's share of Africa), France, Germany, Belgium, Italy, Portugal, and Spain. In the main, these powers imposed their rule in order to extract resources with the minimum cost, but occupied only what was necessary for exploitation of the territory.

Systems of colonial rule

The French, Germans, Portuguese, and Belgians generally subjected their colonies in West and Central Africa to some form of direct rule, with a central colonial government that removed autonomy from Indigenous peoples. Britain, on the other hand, chose a form of indirect rule to govern its colonies in East Africa and Nigeria. Indirect rule granted African rulers some autonomy to choose their own leaders and local forms of government, but the colonizers had free rein to profit from exploring and exploiting the land, and from establishing trading posts.

In Southern Africa, a more common form of colonialism was by settler rule. This differed from other forms of colonial government in that migrants from Europe, who intended to make the colonies their permanent home, handled the administration. They established their status by direct rule, rather than by treaties with Indigenous peoples. Settlers from Britain, Germany, the Netherlands, and Portugal colonized regions in South Africa, Southern and Northern Rhodesia (present-day Zimbabwe and Zambia), Mozambique, Namibia, and Angola. Settler rule was also the model in the British colony of Kenya, and in the French colony of Algeria.

Under systems of colonial administration, communications from the interior to the coast were improved, with the building of roads and railways. But this was all to the colonizers' benefit, and achieved by oppression of the local people. In Togo, for example, German colonizers coerced local people

SIGNING TREATIES

In the late 19th century, European colonizers acquired territory through the signing of treaties with local African leaders – the French are pictured here signing an agreement with the Kingdom of Tamisso, in modern-day Guinea. Treaties offered "protection" from aggression or invasion in return for the right to carry out exploration and conduct trade, which ultimately gave the European power free rein to exploit the African state's resources.

to build railways and forced farmers to turn their land over to cotton rather than food crops. German administrators were authorized to punish by fines, whipping, and imprisonment, with little oversight.

Africans put up fierce resistance to all forms of colonial rule. This was especially violent in Kenya, where the British military forced the Kikuyu people from their territory in the central region. In the early 1950s, a secret society, the Kenya Land and Freedom Army, which the British called the "Mau Mau", stepped up attacks on European settlers and Kikuyus loyal to the government. Thus began the Mau Mau rebellion, lasting from 1952–60, the most prolonged and violent response to colonial rule, and a harbinger of the eventual withdrawal of the European powers.

"The colonial regime owes its legitimacy to force."

FRANTZ FANON, *THE WRETCHED OF THE EARTH*, 1961

◁ **Pretoria station**
Crowds greet the arrival in 1893 of the first train at Pretoria railway station, built to boost economic activities associated with the gold-mining industry.

◁ **Unique art form**
The craft of Zulu basketry, which had declined in the 1930s during colonization, has been revived as a symbol of national pride by South African artists such as Beauty Ngxongo, who wove this basket with *ilala* palm fibre.

5

The age of independence

1914–1994

The age of independence

The decolonization of Africa was a process that broadly took place from the early 1950s onwards. The first post-war independence movements took hold in North Africa, starting with Libya in 1951, and then spread to West Africa with the independence of Ghana in 1957, and from there eastwards and south. One year alone, 1960, called the Year of Africa, saw 17 nations gain their independence, including Mali, Senegal, and Madagascar from France, Somalia and Nigeria from Britain, and the Democratic Republic of the Congo from Belgium. While independence was more easily won in some places than in others, decolonialization was rarely anything less than a radical and multi-layered operation.

The seeds of independence
It is contested how much African decolonization was a top-down or bottom-up movement. It varied from place to place, but in all cases the role of educated African political elites was consequential. From around the 1880s, young African nationalists were able to travel and study abroad, exposing themselves to a cross-pollination of revolutionary ideas. Political impetus was provided by the freedom movements of earlier times, including the American Revolution of 1765–91, the French Revolution of 1789, and the Haitian Revolution of 1791–1804. African intellectuals also absorbed the newly emerging Pan-Africanism of figures such as the Jamaican activist Marcus Garvey (see pp. 232–33). The early years of the 20th century witnessed an upsurge of resistance to colonial rule, with educated African elites agitating the masses, initiating action against the colonists, and establishing nationalist political parties (see pp. 228–29).

World wars and decolonization
Millions of Africans' participation and sacrifice in World War I led to increased African calls for self-determination. The period saw revolts against colonial rule, such as John Chilembwe's armed uprising against the British in 1915. In World War II, many more millions of Africans fought for the freedom of the West and increasingly believed that they should share this freedom too. The Atlantic Charter, agreed in 1941 between Britain and the US (see pp. 230–31), asserted that all people had a right to self-government. This and the signing of the United Nations' Universal Declaration of Human Rights in 1948 further motivated Africans to demand independence. In the 1940s and 50s, grassroots nationalist movements sprang up across Africa, spearheaded by many inspirational figures, including Funmilayo Ransome-Kuti in Nigeria and Bibi Titi Mohammed in Tanzania.

The main era of decolonization coincided with the Cold War (see pp. 246–47), whose protagonists vied for influence among the emerging independent African nations. Meanwhile, the presence of entrenched white settlers in some states and long-standing rivalries between ethnic groups and peoples ensured that the process of decolonization was in several cases marred by violence, political turmoil, widespread unrest, and organized insurrections – though some nations also achieved independence through peaceful negotiations around the conference table.

◁ **Commemorative stamp from Ghana**

1900 Henry Sylvester Williams organizes the first Pan-African Conference, in London

1910 South African independence from Britain; power assumed by all-white government

1914 Marcus Garvey founds the Universal Negro Improvement Association

1915 Unsuccessful Chilembwe uprising in Nyasland (Malawi) against British rule

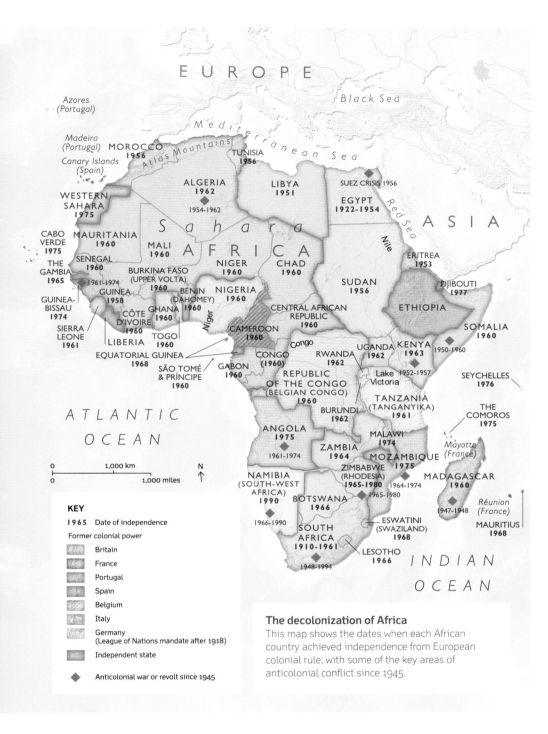

EUROPE

Black Sea

Azores
(Portugal)

Madeira
(Portugal)

Canary Islands
(Spain)

Mediterranean Sea

MOROCCO
1956

TUNISIA
1956

ALGERIA
1962

1954-1962

LIBYA
1951

SUEZ CRISIS 1956

EGYPT
1922-1954

Red Sea

ASIA

WESTERN
SAHARA
1975

Atlas Mountains

Sahara

AFRICA

Nile

CABO
VERDE
1975

MAURITANIA
1960

MALI
1960

NIGER
1960

CHAD
1960

SUDAN
1956

ERITREA
1953

DJIBOUTI
1977

THE
GAMBIA
1965

SENEGAL
1960

BURKINA FASO
(UPPER VOLTA)
1960

1961-1974

GUINEA
1958

BENIN
(DAHOMEY)
1960

NIGERIA
1960

CENTRAL AFRICAN
REPUBLIC
1960

ETHIOPIA

SOMALIA
1960

GUINEA-
BISSAU
1974

CÔTE
D'IVOIRE
1960

GHANA
1960

Niger

SIERRA
LEONE
1961

LIBERIA

TOGO
1960

CAMEROON
1960

Congo

UGANDA
1962

KENYA
1963

1950-1960

EQUATORIAL GUINEA
1968

SÃO TOMÉ
& PRÍNCIPE
1960

GABON
1960

CONGO
(1960)

RWANDA
1962

REPUBLIC
OF THE CONGO
(BELGIAN CONGO)
1960

Lake *1952-1957*
Victoria

TANZANIA
(TANGANYIKA)
1961

SEYCHELLES
1976

ATLANTIC
OCEAN

BURUNDI
1962

ANGOLA
1975

1961-1974

ZAMBIA
1964

MALAWI
1974

MOZAMBIQUE 1975

*Mayotte
(France)*

THE
COMOROS
1975

NAMIBIA
(SOUTH-WEST
AFRICA)
1990

1966-1990

ZIMBABWE
(RHODESIA)
1965-1980

BOTSWANA
1966

1964-1974

1965-1980

MADAGASCAR
1960

*Réunion
(France)*

SOUTH
AFRICA
1910-1961

1948-1994

ESWATINI
(SWAZILAND)
1968

LESOTHO
1966

MAURITIUS
1968

*INDIAN
OCEAN*

0   1,000 km
0   1,000 miles

N

KEY

1965   Date of independence

Former colonial power

Britain

France

Portugal

Spain

Belgium

Italy

Germany
(League of Nations mandate after 1918)

Independent state

◆   Anticolonial war or revolt since 1945

The decolonization of Africa
This map shows the dates when each African country achieved independence from European colonial rule, with some of the key areas of anticolonial conflict since 1945.

▲ Marcus Garvey (1887–1940)

▲ Funmilayo Ransome-Kuti, Nigerian activist

▲ Bibi Titi Mohammed, "Mother" of Tanzania

1922 Egyptian independence from Britain, following revolution in 1919

1951 Libya becomes first nation to win independence after the Second World War

1963 Kwame Nkrumah helps establish the Organization of African Unity

1967–70 Biafra War in Nigeria (independence 1960)

1919 W.E.B. Du Bois organizes the first Pan-African Congress, in Paris

1948 The Universal Declaration of Human Rights enshrines the rights and freedoms of all human beings

1954 Algeria's bloody war of independence from France begins (ends 1962)

1965 Rhodesia declares independence from Britain

1980 Rhodesia's independence formally recognized when the country becomes Zimbabwe

Early independence movements

Organized resistance grows

African peoples resisted the expansion of European colonial control from the 1870s and, after World War I, early nationalist movements emerged, seeking greater freedoms and ultimately independence.

Africans repeatedly challenged the increasing expansion into African lands by European powers from the mid-19th century, despite the Europeans' superior military might. There was organized military resistance against the French led by cleric Abd-al-Kadir in the Maghreb in 1847, and headed by Samory Touré (c. 1830–1900) of the Wassoulou Empire up to 1898. Similarly, the Asante Kingdom fought against the British up to 1901. However, all suffered heavy losses, though rebellions against the brutality of colonial governments continued. The *Chimurenga* Resistance in Zimbabwe in 1896–97 saw the Shona and Ndebele peoples rise up, provoked by the British South Africa Company's confiscation of the best land (see pp. 166–67). The Maji-Maji revolt against German colonial rule in Tanganyika in 1905 was sparked by the use of forced labour, and the Zulu leader Bambatha kaMancinza's rebellion against a poll tax in South Africa in 1906 was another manifestation of a continued will to oppose colonizers.

Impact of World War I

Following World War I, many European administrators left Africa, having been conscripted or co-opted into war work, and the colonial powers now decided to involve Africans who had had a secondary education in the running of the colonies. Hundreds of thousands of Africans were requisitioned as military labourers and soldiers, fighting in campaigns in East and West Africa, but also in the Middle East, and – particularly in the French forces – on the Western Front. Many

Africans resented the sacrifices being asked for little tangible reward and groups such as the Borgawa people in French Dahomey and the Egba in 1918 in British southern Nigeria rose up in revolt. Having pleaded in vain for a moderation of the cruel treatment of African labourers on plantations in Nyasaland (modern-day Malawi), in January 1915 the Baptist pastor John Chilembwe led an insurrection against the British. Although Chilembwe's revolt was brutally put down within weeks, it represented a new form of resistance, melding Christianity with the desire of Africans to have a nation-state of their own.

In the post-war period, Africans established a number of independent churches, such as the Kimbanguist Christian Church founded by Simon Kimbangu in the

△ **Algerian resistance**
Islamic scholar Abd-al-Kadir, shown here on an Algerian stamp, led the resistance to the French invasion of the Maghreb from 1830 until his surrender in 1847.

▷ **First party**
This photograph shows the founders of the South African Native National Congress. This was Africa's first Black political party, which in 1923 became the African National Congress.

◁ **African soldiers**
Members of the King's African Rifles stand to attention in this photograph from World War I. The regiment was raised in East Africa and saw service during the war in Somaliland.

modern-day Democratic Republic of the Congo in the 1920s, which acted as a focus for opposition to colonial governments. Up to and including the 1920s, when the continent's economies suffered a slump, workers became increasingly organized, with strikes in ports and mining towns and the formation of the first Black trade unions, such as the Industrial Workers of Africa in South Africa in 1917.

Colonial response and nationalist parties
In an attempt to find ways to hold on to the lands that they had colonized, European governments turned to an elite group of educated urban Africans for help. The French imperialist notion of the *mission civilatrice*, through which they expected African colonies to eventually be integrated culturally and politically into France, led the government to grant limited political representation to these groups. In 1914, the Senegalese Blaise Diagne became the first African elected to a post in the French government. The British adopted a different approach, establishing legislative councils, such as that set up in 1922 in Nigeria, which included a limited number of African members in an attempt to diffuse opposition from African nationalist groups.

The desire for independence, however, led to the founding of nationalist parties, such as the South African Native National Congress in South Africa in 1912 and the Nigerian National Democratic Party in 1923. A series of political organizations in North Africa, most notably the Destour in Tunisia in 1920, and the Wafd Party in Egypt in 1919, also became

prominent. While these parties made incremental improvements in conditions for Africans and gained a small say in colonial administration, their greatest impact was as forerunners of the mass-participation African political parties of the 1950s and '60s.

Pan-Africanism
In the UK, several activists were involved in setting up the West African Student's Union (WASU), which became a hub for anticolonial thinkers, including Ghanian Kwame Nkrumah (see pp. 242–43), Nigerian law student Ladipo Solenke, and Sierra Leonean doctor Herbert Bankole-Bright. Organizations like this that asserted Pan-Africanism (see pp. 232–33) helped build solidarity among colonized nations. The notion of *Négritude*, a cultural identity shared by every African, promoted by the Martiniquan Aimé Césaire (1913–2008), also fuelled the desire for independence. These ideas encouraged the next generation of nationalist parties, which built on the foundations laid by the early nationalist movements to create an irresistible momentum for self-rule.

▷ **Hat protest**
John Chilembwe, leader of the 1915 Nyasaland uprising, wears a hat in this sculpture. A colonial edict had forbidden Africans from wearing a hat in the presence of Europeans.

The figure of Chilembwe stands five times larger than that of Chorley

Chilembwe's friend John Chorley was a white missionary

Africa and World War II

The war that led to Africa's independence

World War II changed Africa. The participation in the war of up to one million Africans encouraged movements that pushed for colonial reforms and independence once the conflict was over.

World War II made a major impact on Africa in June 1940, when Italian forces in Ethiopia and Eritrea seized British Somaliland and moved into British Sudan and Kenya. Although Britain launched a successful counteroffensive, it was only achieved with the help of reinforcements from South Africa, East Africa, West Africa, and India.

As the war developed, human and material resources were mobilized across Britain and France's African colonies. Encouraged by Allied anti-Nazi recruitment campaigns, tens of thousands of Africans joined the war. They believed that they were fighting what the British called in their Swahili propaganda messages *vita vya Uhuru* ("a war for independence").

At the beginning of the war, in British West Africa, the Royal West African Frontier Force (RWAFF) grew from 8,000 to 146,000. Altogether, nine regiments came from the British West African colonies alone. These servicemen fought battles against the Axis Powers in East Africa, storming the

▽ **United nations**
In this poster from c. 1942, Allied troops – including those from the British Empire – march together in a "V for Victory" formation.

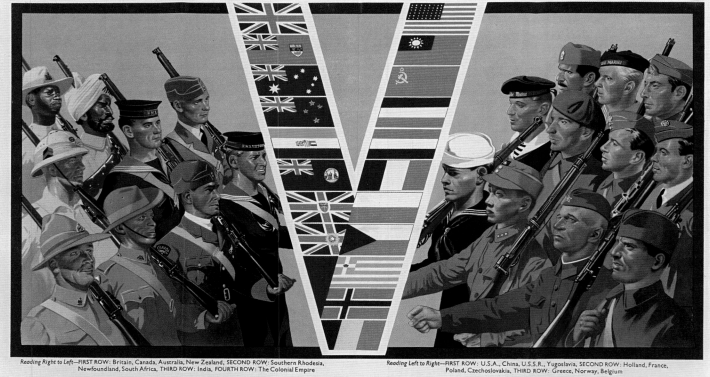

Reading Right to Left—FIRST ROW: Britain, Canada, Australia, New Zealand, SECOND ROW: Southern Rhodesia, Newfoundland, South Africa, THIRD ROW: India, FOURTH ROW: The Colonial Empire

Reading Left to Right—FIRST ROW: U.S.A., China, U.S.S.R., Yugoslavia, SECOND ROW: Holland, France, Poland, Czechoslovakia, THIRD ROW: Greece, Norway, Belgium

FREEDOM SHALL PREVAIL!

PRINTED IN ENGLAND BY FOSH & CROSS LTD., LONDON. (51-9956)

▷ **Commando emblem**
This is a badge of the African Commandos. Created in 1943, this division of the French army included riflemen from Algeria and Morocco.

Arab *lateen* sail and the crescent emblem of Northwest Africa

Italian divisions on the Juba River, in modern-day southern Somalia, and driving the fascists to complete defeat in Somalia and Ethiopia. They later went further afield, facing the Japanese in Burma and Ceylon (now Myanmar and Sri Lanka respectively).

Under duress, Africans donated cash, groundnuts, cotton, rubber, palm oil, palm kernel, food, and resources to support Allied forces. The war economy brought young people seeking opportunities to the cities to work and earn a living. The economic boom stimulated the rapid growth of communications facilities, and with it the spread of ideas and ideologies such as democracy, capitalism, communism, human rights, and self-determination.

Fighting for freedom

By presenting themselves as champions of equality and freedom against the racism and tyranny of the Axis powers, the Allies gave the colonies hope that they were fighting for their own freedom, too. This was encapsulated in the Atlantic Charter (see box, below) agreed by British prime minister Winston Churchill and US president Franklin D. Roosevelt.

By the end of the war, Britain and France had already backtracked from the principles of the Atlantic Charter, claiming that its terms only applied to Europeans, though the US affirmed that it believed all people had the right to self-determination. This led to the unusual situation in the 1950s and 1960s of British and French attempts to oppose or slow down independence

△ **Fighting for France**
African male and female soldiers of the Free French Army load a mortar in the Western Desert of North Africa in 1942.

movements being resisted by the US – supported by its Cold War enemy (see pp. 246–47), the equally anti-imperialist Soviet Union (USSR).

While many Africans believed they had earned the right to rule themselves, the war gave them the opportunity to fight for that right. The imperial powers recognized this; it is one of the reasons why they tried to restrict the freedom of movement of returning veterans to colonial cities such as Lagos, Nairobi, and Freetown in an effort to prevent them from influencing their fellow Africans. Nevertheless, Africans now had knowledge of military tactics, of strategy, and of working together. They saw the vulnerabilities of the white occupiers and realized that Africans had powerful allies in countries such as the US and the USSR (both of which wanted to gain influence in Africa).

Furthermore, after the war Britain and France – the two main colonial powers – were bankrupt and could no longer afford to maintain their empires. They held out for several more years, but by the mid-1950s Sudan and then Ghana had won their independence. By 1960, 17 African nations had followed suit.

THE ATLANTIC **CHARTER**

As a result of the Atlantic Conference of 1941, the US and Britain set out the principles they expected the post-war world to live by. Known as the Atlantic Charter, it declared that all subject peoples should have the right to self-determination – to choose the type of government they desired to live under. This led to the fall of the British Empire.

"**We have been told** what we fought for... nothing but **freedom**."

NIGERIAN VETERAN WRITING TO AFRICAN NATIONALIST HERBERT MACAULAY

Pan-Africanism

African bonds of solidarity

Pan-Africanism, a cultural and ideological movement to strengthen solidarity between Africans, including those in the diaspora, has deep historical roots. Its origins lie in resistance against enslavement and liberation struggles against European colonization.

African organizations had been campaigning against oppression for centuries. Abolitionist groups such as the Sons of Africa, led by Olaudah Equiano and Ottobah Cugoano in the 1780s, protested against the trafficking of enslaved people. The Haitian Revolution from 1791 led the French colony of Saint-Domingue to become Haiti – the first former colony in the western hemisphere to become slavery-free and independent – and inspired hopes for an independent political destiny. Activists such as Martin Robison Delany

(1812–85), the first African American officer in the Union army, and Edward Wilmot Blyden (1832–1912), an influential Liberian politician and writer, argued that Africans must return to Africa (in particular, Liberia) to attain real freedom.

Arguing for Pan-Africanism

The first formal Pan-African Congress met in Paris in 1919, bringing together delegates from Africa and the Caribbean to call for a global effort to end injustices against Black people. Among its key movers was the American academic W.E.B. Du Bois, who argued for the study of African history and cultures and the cultivation of a specifically African consciousness that colonialism had suppressed. In the 1920s, Jamaican

△ **Ottobah Cugoano (c. 1757–c. 1792)**
Born in present-day Ghana, enslaved and transported to Grenada, Cugoano gained his freedom after being brought to England in 1772. He became a prominent abolitionist, giving speeches and writing one of the earliest first-hand accounts of slavery.

△ **W.E.B. Du Bois (1868–1963)**
Sociology professor and founder of the National Association for the Advancement of Colored People (NAACP) in 1911, Du Bois was the prime mover behind the early Pan-African congresses and believed that improving the economic and educational status of Black people would help to bring about their liberation.

△ **Amy Jacques Garvey (1896–1973) and Marcus Garvey (1887–1940)**
Amy Garvey played a leadership role in her husband Marcus's Universal Negro Improvement Association (UNIA), which championed Black separatism and migration back to Africa.

"If **Europe** is for the **white man**… then surely **Africa** is for the **Black man**."

MARCUS GARVEY

journalist Marcus Garvey opposed the idea of equality through integration, arguing for self-reliance and economic development for Black people.

In the 1940s, the focus of Pan-Africanism shifted from the diaspora to the continent itself. Building on the arguments of Du Bois and Garvey, Senegalese poet Léopold Senghor developed the idea of *Négritude* — that Africans share a particular cultural identity and should reject assimilation and European cultural domination — which became very influential in Francophone colonies.

The Fifth Pan-African Congress in Manchester, UK, in 1945, attended by nationalist leaders including Kwame Nkrumah, Julius Nyerere, and Ahmed Sékou Touré, emphasized the importance of unity among Africans once they had won their independence. The 1959 Sanniquelle Declaration called for a "Community of Independent African States", leading in 1963, with Nkrumah's guidance, to the Organization of African Unity.

New movements

Disillusionment with failed projects for unity created other forms of Pan-Africanism. The Black Power movement that emerged in the US in the 1960s was led by Malcolm X (1925–65), who argued for mass action and assertive reclaiming of Black heritage and rights, and the Black Consciousness movement in South Africa, championed by radical Steve Biko (1946–77), focused on liberating the minds of Black people as a key weapon in their fight for freedom.

△ **African arts**
This poster advertises the First World Festival of Black Arts in Dakar, Senegal, in 1966 — an event that drew around 2,500 delegates from 40 countries.

△ **Léopold Senghor (1906–2001)**
President of the West African Students' Association in Paris in the 1930s, Senghor was a writer and theorist of the *Négritude* movement. He became a member of the French Assembly and the first president of independent Senegal in 1960.

△ **Aimé Césaire (1913–2008)**
A poet and playwright from Martinique, Césaire made the cultural identity of Africans a prominent theme of his poetry and coined the term *Négritude*. He was a member of the French Assembly for 48 years, always arguing passionately against colonialism and racism.

△ **Angela Davis (1944–)**
Philosopher, feminist, anti-war campaigner, and Black rights activist, Davis maintained that feminism needed to fight not only gender-based oppression but also race- and class-based oppression. She was *Time* magazine's Woman of the Year in 1971.

Independence from France

Breaking free from French control

The African countries colonized by the French pressed for independence, with France offering only limited reforms. Eventually, most were successful and the process was largely peaceful, though marred by the brutal Algerian War.

△ **Ahmed Sekou Touré**
Guinea's first president, Sekou Touré, shown on a stamp, headed a campaign to reject the French Community Proposals in 1958. Guinea was the only country to do so.

World War II had a profound effect on independence movements in France's African colonies. Around one million Africans fought in the conflict and the ordeal fostered a sense of their national identities and a commitment to free themselves of foreign rule.

Independence movements in North Africa
As early as 1943, Algerian politician Ferhat Abbas drew up his *Manifesto of the Algerian People*, calling for "the condemnation and abolition of colonization". When France failed to honour its promise of self-rule for Algeria after World War II, the FLN (*Front de Libération Nationale*, or National Liberation Front) vowed to win it by force. The Algerian War of Independence began in 1954 and would last for eight years.

To Algeria's west, Morocco's *Istiqlal* independence party took a different approach. The party persuaded Morocco's long-standing precolonial ally, the US, to support its case for independence in the United

Nations, putting international pressure on France to quit the country. Meanwhile, Tunisia's *Neo Destour* independence movement, with Habib Bourguiba among its leaders, organized strikes and demonstrations, and threatened armed struggle – adding to the fierce pressure also coming from Algeria on the colonial power. Morocco and Tunisia both gained their independence in 1956.

Reforms and decolonization
In 1946, France amended its constitution to create the French Union. This new political arrangement abolished France's colonies and incorporated them into the French state. It also allowed the former colonies to elect deputies to sit in France's parliament, the National Assembly. In response, the Côte d'Ivoire politician Félix Houphouët-Boigny formed the *Rassemblement Démocratique Africain* (RDA or African Democratic Rally), a coalition of West African nationalist parties that acted together to push forward their decolonization agenda. Houphouët-Boigny even held several ministerial posts in France's government, from 1957–59, as leader of the largest party in France's African colonies. He was the first Black nationalist politician to hold high office in France.

While the RDA was united in its opposition to colonization, its members were divided over aiming for total independence or retaining some links with France. In 1958, the new government in France reinvented the French Union as the French Community, offering its

◁ **Triumphant return**
Tunisian nationalist leader Habib Bourguiba is greeted by huge crowds in Tunis on his return in June 1955 following three years of exile imposed by the French government.

African territories investment funds and a degree of self-rule if they chose to remain in the Community. Only Guinea chose to leave, becoming independent on 2 October that year. This was just a small breach in France's colonial edifice, but it was significant. It came at a time when the war in Algeria was escalating and Cameroon's left-wing nationalist UPC (*Union des Populations du Cameroun*, or Union of the Peoples of Cameroon) was conducting a guerrilla campaign against colonial forces that left thousands dead.

It was becoming clear that France was losing control of its former colonies and the French Community's limited political reforms and promises of financial support were not enough. Although only Guinea had officially made the break from France, other RDA members began questioning their choice to remain. France's days as an imperial power in Africa were numbered. It had neither the will nor the resources to resist the mass defection of its former colonies. In 1960, Cameroon, Senegal, Togo, Mali, Madagascar, Benin, Niger, Upper Volta (Burkino Faso), Côte d'Ivoire, Chad, the Central African Republic, Congo, Gabon, and Mauritania gained their independence. Algeria followed in 1962, and Comoros and Djibouti in 1975 and 1977 respectively. The African states' independence was achieved largely peacefully, with most of the former colonies choosing to maintain some business, military, and political links with France.

△ **Victory parade**
FLN troops parade through Algiers on 3 July 1962, the day independence was declared, ending a bitter conflict that had lasted eight years and caused up to 1.5 million Algerian deaths.

Independence of Libya and Egypt

The long road to self-rule

Centuries of competing Ottoman, Italian, and British control led to distrust and growing resistance in Libya and Egypt. The leaders of their freedom movements had to act cleverly and determinedly to achieve their aims.

Since the 9th century BCE, the North African regions of Tripolitania, Fezzan, and Cyrenaica had endured Phoenician, Roman, Islamist, and Ottoman rule. The Italians arrived in 1912 and as imperialist occupiers, they renamed these territories "Libya" in 1934. The majority of Italy's time there was marked by fierce resistance, particularly in Cyrenaica, led by Omar al-Mukhtar, a teacher and prominent figure in the region's powerful Sufi Muslim clan, the Senussi.

A disunited state

The area was put under Allied control after World War II. Britain administered Tripolitania and Cyrenaica; France took Fezzan. Libyan nationalists, the US, and the United Nations put pressure on the British and French, forcing them to leave. When they did so, they invited the religious leader and former resistance fighter Muhammad Idris to become the first monarch of a united Kingdom of Libya in 1951. Knowing that his new state was extremely poor as well as disunited – "Libya" had never existed before as a single political entity – Idris reluctantly agreed. Few people in Tripolitania, Fezzan, and Cyrenaica had ever campaigned for a united Libya, and local leaders and chiefs in all three regions had no intention of giving up their power.

What little revenue the country received came from international aid provided by the UK and the US in particular, which were allowed to establish military airfields and naval bases in Libya in return.

Impact of oil production

The regime of King Idris limped along in this way until, in 1959, the country's first successful oil well went on stream. Commercial oil production would transform Libya from one of the world's most impoverished nations to among its wealthiest. Hundreds of thousands of Libyans migrated to the cities and ports in search of work and opportunities in the oil-rich state. When these failed to materialize, and the thousands of millions of petrodollars flowed instead into the coffers of Idris, unrest grew.

On 1 September 1969, a group of twelve junior army officers, led by a young captain whose name was Muammar Qaddafi, seized power in a bloodless coup that easily toppled Libya's corrupt and inefficient government. A new phase in the country's history was about to begin.

△ **National hero**
This Libyan 10-dinar note shows the Cyrenaican freedom fighter Omar al-Mukhtar, the "Lion of the Desert". He drew on his experience of desert warfare to resist Italian colonizers.

"We were under **trusteeship**; we were **colonized**; and now we are **independent**."

MUAMMAR QADDAFI, 2009

Egypt under foreign control

Part of the Ottoman Empire since 1517, Egypt fell under British dominion with the opening of the Suez Canal in 1869. Egypt built the waterway with France, but economic mismanagement, corruption and looming bankruptcy forced the country's ruler, Ismail Pasha, to sell all of his government's shares in the Suez Canal to Britain in 1875. By 1878, British and some French commercial and political representatives were sitting in on Egyptian government cabinet meetings.

The foreign control of a large area of Egyptian territory provoked widespread nationalist anger. Its first manifestation was the 'Urabi Revolt of 1879, an army mutiny that turned into an anti-British uprising. Britain suppressed the uprising and used the incident for its own ends, informally taking over the country in what has been called a "veiled protectorate".

Resistance builds

Egyptians across the country resisted. The middle classes flocked to support nationalist movements such as El-Nahda ("Renewal"), after being excluded by the British occupiers from high-level political and administrative roles. The general population also protested against Britain's heavy-handed approach to law and order, encapsulated by the Denshawai Incident of 1906, where four Egyptians were summarily tried and executed after allegedly attacking a British army officer.

Britain formally took over Egypt as a protectorate at the outbreak of World War I. At the war's end, Egyptian nationalists formed the Wafd ("Delegation") Party with the intention of attending the Paris Peace Conference and winning international support for self-rule. When Britain blocked this by exiling the Wafd leaders to Malta, Egypt rose up in the Egyptian Revolution of 1919. Its wave of riots, strikes, and demonstrations left at least 800 dead. Nationalist sentiment was too strong to be ignored by the British any longer. On 28 February 1922, the government of Britain unilaterally declared Egyptian independence.

Independence and the Suez Canal

The terms of the independence declaration that Britain had imposed – without consulting the Egyptians – meant that Britain retained control of the Suez Canal, as well as influence over the country's foreign affairs and defence. It was not until 1952 that the British were finally completely ejected from Egypt, when the military coup led by army officer Gamal Abdel Nasser (see pp. 238–39) seized power. He went on to remove British influence from the Suez Canal by nationalizing it in 1956.

△ **First king**
Formerly sultan of Egypt, from 1917, Fuad I became independent Egypt's first king (r. 1922–36) when Britain declared the country's independence in 1922.

▽ **Journey to freedom**
Students take over a trolley car in Cairo during the 1919 Revolution. This was Egypt's first nationwide rebellion against British control, and one in which women also played a vital role.

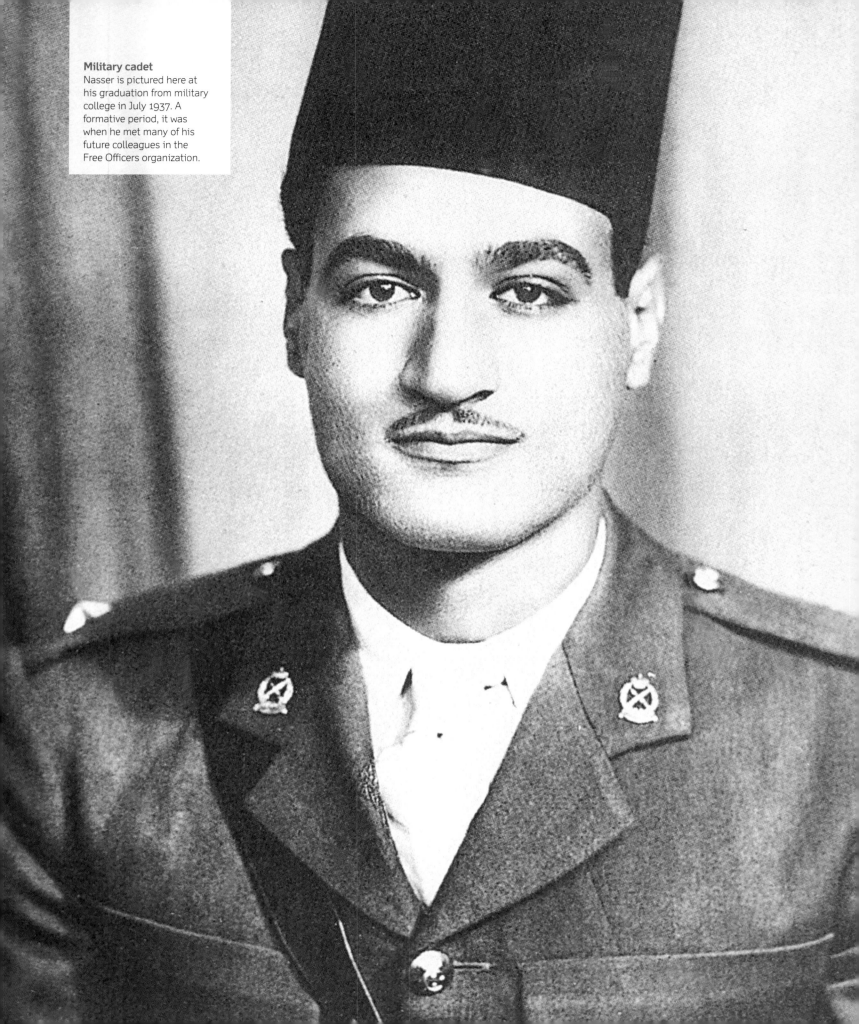

Military cadet
Nasser is pictured here at his graduation from military college in July 1937. A formative period, it was when he met many of his future colleagues in the Free Officers organization.

Gamal Abdel Nasser

Leader of an independent Egypt

A towering figure of Arab nationalism and one of the most important modern African politicians, Gamal Abdel Nasser steered an independent course for Egypt that often set it at odds with the West.

Gamal Abdel Nasser was born in Alexandria, Egypt, and became involved in politics early. When he was 18 years old, he joined a demonstration against Egypt's 1936 treaty with the British, which allowed British military bases to stay in the country. Graduating in law, Nasser joined the Military Academy in 1937, and saw service in Sudan, making useful contacts such as future Egyptian president Anwar el-Sadat. He also fought in the Palestine War against Israel in 1948, and was wounded.

Rise to power

Nasser became an instructor at the Military Academy but, dissatisfied with the peace Egypt had made with Israel and what he saw as a corrupt Egyptian monarchy that had lost touch with the people and alienated the military, he formed a secret group of dissident officers. On 23 July 1952, these Free Officers launched a coup against the nationalist party Wafd. They toppled King Farouk and installed a Revolutionary Command Council headed by Mohamed Naguib. Nasser was the coup's real instigator and he removed Naguib and installed himself as prime minister in 1954. He established a one-party state based on socialist ideals.

On 26 July 1956, now president, Nasser nationalized the British-controlled Suez Canal, sparking a military intervention by Britain, France, and Israel. This was a

◁ **Support for Arafat**
Nasser in 1969 with Yasser Arafat, leader of the al-Fatah faction of the Palestinian Liberation Organization (PLO). Nasser helped to promote Arafat to be the dominant Palestinian leader.

defining moment for Pan-Arabism, as the US forced the British and French into a humiliating withdrawal and made Nasser a hero.

Nasser promoted a Pan-Arab agenda, though he ruthlessly suppressed opposition at home. In 1957, he helped to form the United Arab Republic with Syria, though it dissolved following an uprising by dissatisfied Syrian army officers in 1961. Egypt became embroiled in Yemen's Civil War in 1962 and the devastating losses in the Six-Day War with Israel in 1967 led Nasser to attempt to resign, but public pressure persuaded him to stay.

Eventually, he began to loosen state security and enhance support for the Palestinian Liberation Organization. In 1970, he started negotiations with the US to reach a peace deal with Israel, but then suffered a heart attack and died. He was given a hero's funeral and was succeeded as president by his former colleague Anwar el-Sadat.

▽ **Funeral tribute**
A soldier stands guard in front of a photographic tribute and wreaths of flowers for Nasser at his funeral in 1970.

1918 Born in Alexandria to a postal worker father

1952 With Mohamed Naguib and other Free Officers launches revolution that topples the monarchy

1956 Elected president after inauguration of New Constitution; nationalizes the Suez Canal

1967 Defeat in Six-Day War and attempted resignation

1938 Graduates as a second lieutenant from the Military Academy

1954 An alleged assassination attempt galvanizes support for Nasser

1957 Forms the United Arab Republic with Syria

1970 Dies of a heart attack and is succeeded by Anwar el-Sadat

△ **Independence dance**
A crowd in Accra, Ghana, watches dancers rehearse for Ghana's Independence Day on 6 March 1957. Events were attended by foreign dignitaries, including Martin Luther King Jr.

Independence from Britain

Unstoppable momentum for change

After years of struggle by nationalist parties and liberation movements, the 1960s saw an acceleration in the pace of independence that left almost all of Britain's former African colonies free by the end of the decade.

By the middle of the 20th century, developments in Africa were key to the growing calls for freedom. Economic changes brought increasing prosperity for some Africans and demands from others for a share

◁ **Future president**
Nnamdi Azikiwe, the Governor-General of Nigeria, features on the cover of *Drum* magazine in March 1961. Azikiwe later became president of the newly independent Nigeria.

of it. For example, on the Gold Coast (later Ghana), cocoa exports rose from 1,000 to 240,000 tons annually between 1900 and 1951. Across the colonies occupied by Britain, railways and roads that the British instigated and local workers built increased economic activity and helped bind together disparate Indigenous peoples.

The emergence of a generation of young nationalist leaders, who had received an advanced education and were determined to put it at the service of the cause for independence, also played an important part. When World War II was over, the British government focused on improving Britain's domestic economy, with little left over to invest in its colonial empire. There were also growing international calls for the rights of colonized peoples for self-determination, while the meeting of African leaders at the Fifth Pan-African Congress in Manchester in 1945 (see pp. 232–33) added moral weight to calls for freedom.

The pace accelerates

Impatience with the slow progress of some existing organizations, such as modern-day Ghana's United Gold Coast Convention, prompted young, assertive leaders such as Kwame Nkrumah (see pp. 242–43) to form their own parties. Nkrumah's Convention People's Party, with its memorable slogan "self-government now", was founded in 1949. By 1951, he had led the CPP to victory in assembly elections. After he became prime minister in 1952, full independence was inevitable.

British concessions to African self-determination were initially timid, but once Britain had begun the process, its African colonies took control of it. In Tanganyika (later Tanzania), a legislative council was only established in 1945 and had just four African appointees out of 15 members, but the foundation in 1954 of the Tanganyika African National Union under Julius Nyerere created a political body with whom the British were forced to engage. Nyerere had huge support and he urged non-violence, so Britain's only hope for a peaceful transition to independence was via him. In Nigeria, divisions between Igbo and Yoruba hampered moves for self-determination, but the National Council of Nigeria and the Cameroon, founded in 1944 with Nnamdi Azikiwe as secretary, argued against parties based on Nigeria's ethnic groups and so created a common front against British rule. By 1957, Nigeria had a prime minister empowered to choose his own cabinet.

Once African leaders saw that the British would grant only limited additional rights, they demanded greater freedom and set the increasing pace of change. Nkrumah had won Ghanaian independence in March 1957, while Nigeria gained its independence in 1960 (with Azikiwe initially as governor-general). Tanganyika became independent in 1961, with Julius Nyerere as prime minister. Problems in Uganda with rival political groups based around the Baganda Kingdom and Bunyoro state delayed progress, but by October 1962 it too was independent. The vocal European settler lobby

impeded Kenyan independence, and the British fought a bloody anti-insurgency campaign against a group they called the "Mau Mau rebels", who led an anticolonial uprising from 1952 to 1960. Nationalist leaders united behind Jomo Kenyatta, and in 1963, the British flag was lowered and Kenyatta became prime minister, remarking, "We shall build a country where every citizen may develop his talents to the full."

During the 1960s, almost all Britain's African colonies became independent states. The Seychelles followed in 1976 and Zimbabwe (formerly Southern Rhodesia, see pp. 252–53) in 1980. By that point, Ghana was into its third decade of independence and Britain's substantial colonial empire in Africa had finally unravelled.

△ **First leader**
A Kenyan 10-cent coin bears the head of Jomo Kenyatta, who led the country to independence in December 1963.

COMPLETE INDEPENDENCE 1961

▷ **Tanzanian independence**
Julius Nyerere celebrates the granting of internal self-government to Tanganyika in 1960, with him as prime minister However, he makes it clear his objective is total independence.

Young leader
In this photo portrait of Kwame Nkrumah as a young man, he wears Ghanaian *kente* cloth. His considered choice of clothing sends a message to the world about his ambition for his country to be free from British rule.

Kwame Nkrumah

Ghanaian nationalist leader

A nationalist politician in the colony of the Gold Coast, Kwame Nkrumah led his country to independence from Britain and became the first prime minister and president of the newly formed Republic of Ghana.

The founder of the independent nation of Ghana, Kwame Nkrumah was born and brought up in the Gold Coast, then under British colonial control. He trained as a teacher, and took up various teaching posts, before moving to the US and then to London to study economics, sociology, and philosophy. At this time, Nkrumah also became increasingly involved in Black nationalist politics and Pan-Africanism (see pp. 232–33). His political ideas, like those of other African nationalist leaders such as Robert Mugabe and Samora Machel, were shaped by Marxism and Leninism, which he encountered during his studies.

Liberation movement

Upon his return to the Gold Coast in 1947, Nkrumah ran the United Gold Coast Convention (UGCC), the colony's first true political party, established that same year with the aim of effecting gradual constitutional change leading to self-government. In 1949, he founded his own party, the Convention People's Party (CPP). Making deliberate moves to reach people all across the country, especially in rural areas, he quickly gained support for his growing movement.

In 1950, the British authorities sentenced Nkrumah to three years in prison for his role in organizing mass strike action in Accra against the colonial

◁ **Memorial statue**
Nkrumah's statue stands in the Kwame Nkrumah Memorial Park in Accra and marks the spot where he declared Ghana's independence. A mausoleum houses the bodies of him and his wife Fathia.

government, demanding self-rule. He was released in 1951, after the CPP won a landslide victory in the election – the first in Africa to be held under universal suffrage.

In 1952, Nkrumah became prime minister, in an arrangement overseen by the British. Retaining his resolve to achieve total independence, he led the CPP to success in two more elections, in 1954 and 1956, putting additional pressure on Britain. In 1957, the Gold Coast attained independence from Britain, adopting the name Ghana. Three years later, Nkrumah became its first president.

Overthrow and exile

In 1966, amid wage freezes and tax increases, and with many workers on strike, Ghana's military and police forces overthrew Nkrumah's government in a violent *coup d'état*. Nkrumah was on a state visit abroad at the time of the coup, and never returned to his home country. Instead, he moved to Guinea where he lived until ill health prompted him to seek treatment in Romania, dying there in 1972.

△ **Bust of Nkrumah**
A 25-pesewa coin bearing the head of Nkrumah, with the inscription *Civitatis Ghanensis Conditor* ("Founder of the Ghanaian State").

1949 Founds the Convention People's Party (CPP)

1952 Appointed prime minister of Gold Coast

1960 Elected first president of Ghana

1972 Dies in Romania

1909 Born in Nkroful, Gold Coast

1951 CPP wins landslide victory in first free election

1957 Ghana wins its independence

1966 Exiled to Guinea following his overthrow in a *coup d'état*

Capturing the new mood
Photographs taken by Benin-born, Senegal-based Roger DaSilva epitomize the confident mood of African nations on the brink of self-rule in the 1950s and '60s. Primarily a portrait photographer, DaSilva also captured street scenes, nightclubs, and much else – in this image, an elegantly dressed man poses next to his car in front of DaSilva's studio in Senegal's capital, Dakar. With access to cheaper film and user-friendly cameras after World War II, photographers such as DaSilva, Seydou Keïta in Mali, and Lazhar Mansouri in Algeria began to document the optimism, modernity, and fashion consciousness of the era.

Africa and the Cold War

Caught between East and West

The post-war rivalry between the US and the USSR had a profound effect on Africa. Some African states profited from the Cold War, but many more experienced conflict and chaos.

The end of World War II saw one global conflict replaced by another. From 1945 to 1991, the US and the Soviet Union (USSR) faced each other in a state of political and military tension as they competed for power and influence around the world. In Africa, both the US and the USSR involved themselves in national politics, propping up supportive regimes and toppling uncooperative ones. However, the process was not entirely one-way. In the postcolonial period, some newly independent nations played on US–USSR rivalries to further their own interests.

Non-aligned stance

Having staged a military coup in 1952, Egypt's Gamal Abdel Nasser (see pp. 238–39) needed to secure his regime by seizing the British- and French-controlled Suez Canal. He managed this in 1956 by gaining the backing of the USSR and the US. Egypt had strong links with the USSR, and the US pointedly failed to support its ally Britain in order to win favour with pro-USSR Egypt. Over the next two decades, Egypt aligned itself with both the USSR and the US as its own needs – not theirs – dictated.

Like Egypt, other newly independent African states were intent on not becoming pawns of either the US or the USSR, mainly by practising a policy of non-alignment. The Non-Aligned Movement (NAM) was established in 1961 by anti-imperialist nations committed to maintaining a neutral position in the Cold War. The non-alignment of many of Africa's states made them an awkward prospect for the US and the USSR, both of which attempted to buy their favour through aid, trade, weapons, and development cash. Much of this funding was diverted into the bank accounts of corrupt leaders and kleptocratic bureaucracies, though neither Cold War superpower appeared to be very concerned about this. As most of Africa's liberation movements had been left-leaning, the US had to work harder than the USSR to win – or pay for – the support of African nations.

Left-wing African leaders such as Ghana's Kwame Nkrumah, Tanzania's Julius Nyerere, and Guinea's Sékou Touré became adept at manipulating this situation, playing off the two Cold War powers against each other by tempering their friendliness towards Moscow or Washington when they believed their backing for one state or the other was being taken for granted. This ensured that they received a constant flow of funds and support from both Cold War capitals – sometimes simultaneously.

Proxy wars

However, not all African states were able to use east–west rivalries to their advantage, and a number of them fell victim to US and USSR interference. There were a number of so-called "proxy wars" across Africa during the Cold War, when the US and the USSR acted out their

▷ **Cold War art**
Figures on the Tiglachin Memorial in Addis Ababa, Ethiopia, celebrate the 10th anniversary of the revolution in 1974, which brought the Marxist Derg regime to power.

◁ **On parade**
Soldiers of Angola's UNITA movement parade with a flag bearing the image of their leader Jonas Savimbi. He fought for 28 years against the Marxist MPLA movement until his death in 2002.

own aggression by backing rival sides in conflicts. This frequently led to bloody civil wars that left hundreds of thousands dead and states bankrupt and destroyed. Such wars included the Congo Crisis of 1960–65, the Namibian War of Independence of 1966–90, and the Angolan Civil War of 1975–2002 where the USSR sent in Cuban troops to back the Marxist MPLA. The Ogaden War of 1977–78 involved Ethiopia's pro-USSR, Marxist–Leninist Derg regime and the breakaway Somali Democratic Republic, which was backed by the US.

Lingering legacy

By the late 1980s, liberation movements that had drawn on Soviet help had secured power in Angola, Mozambique, Ethiopia, and Zimbabwe. However, with the collapse of the USSR in 1991, the Cold War came to an end.

Nonetheless, the effects of the period continue to be felt in Africa, particularly in the political and economic instability it engendered. Today, the US continues to pursue its interests in Africa, alongside Russia and an increasingly ambitious China.

△ **Luxor tour**
Egypt's President Nasser (centre) shows a group including Soviet leader Nikita Khrushchev (in the hat) around Luxor in 1964, at the height of the Egyptian-Soviet rapprochement.

Independence from Portugal

A violent struggle for freedom

△ **Skilful leader**
Amílcar Cabral adeptly ran PAIGC's campaign for independence for Guinea-Bissau. He was assassinated eight months before the country achieved its independence.

Nationalist movements in Angola, Mozambique, and Guinea-Bissau demanded freedom from their Portuguese occupiers. They each fought guerrilla wars against Portuguese forces, which led finally to independence.

The Africans of Angola, Mozambique, and the smaller territory of Guinea-Bissau on the coast of West Africa had had to deal with the Portuguese occupying power since the 15th century. The slave trade had ended in the 1860s and the Portuguese had more or less left the interior of the region and withdrawn to the coast. The meeting of colonial powers at the Berlin Conference of 1884–85 called upon Portugal to exercise "effective occupation" of its African colonies (see pp. 210–11), encouraging migration there and the exploitation of their land for cheap raw materials.

In the early 20th century, private companies backed by the Portuguese government took the most fertile lands and coerced Africans into forced labour. Africans paid high taxes and received low wages from the private enterprises using their land and this injustice built support for African leaders who wanted change.

The liberation movements that arose in the 1950s found ready recruits. In Angola, politician Agostino Neto formed the *Movimento Popular de Libertação de Angola* (MPLA) in 1956, and in 1961 activist Holden Roberto established the *União das Populações de Angola* or UPA (later *Frente Nacional de Libertação de Angola* or FNLA).

The fight gains momentum
Also in 1961, cotton plantation workers in Baixa de Cassanje began to protest against their poor treatment and nationalists attempted to free political prisoners in Luanda. The Portuguese army responded violently, killing as many as 20,000 Africans. At least 150,000 Angolan refugees were forced to flee to Congo, though the struggle against Portugal continued. Portugal called in 20,000 troops to control Angola's vast area. Angola's liberation armies continued to make progress, which was only hampered by the divisions between them. In 1965, rebel leader Jonas Savimbi split from the FNLA (the majority of whose membership were from the northern Bakongo people) and set up *União Nacional para a Independência Total de Angola* (UNITA) to represent the Ovimbundu people of central Angola. Despite the divisions, by 1970, the liberation forces had pushed back the Portuguese armies into the main towns.

In Mozambique, in 1960, Portuguese troops massacred pro-independence demonstrators in the town of Mueda. Armed resistance groups rose up and merged to form *Frente de Libertação de Moçambique* (FRELIMO) in 1962. Led by former anthropology

◁ **Mozambique's resistance**
FRELIMO fighters ride a truck in Mozambique's northern Cabo Delgado province in 1973 during the later stages of the war for independence.

professor Eduardo Mondlane, the group aimed to create a socialist society as well as gain independence. After FRELIMO launched a full-scale uprising in 1964, the Portuguese army detained and tortured civilians and forcibly relocated villagers. By 1967, FRELIMO controlled around a fifth of the country and Portugal had 50,000 troops involved in the war. The assassination of Mondlane in 1969 halted FRELIMO's advance. However, military commander Samora Machel replaced Mondlane and by 1971, FRELIMO's progress towards the capital Lourenço Marques (modern-day Maputo) had resumed.

In Cabo Verde and Guinea-Bissau in West Africa, the nationalist Amílcar Cabral formed *Partido Africano para a Independência da Guiné e Cabo Verde* (PAIGC) in 1952, to work for independence. These territories had been so neglected by the Portuguese that there was only one doctor for every 100,000 Africans. In 1961, Cabral announced an armed struggle, launching raids from bases in Guinea. PAIGC set up its own alternative state, which included over 125 primary schools.

In 1968, Marcelo Caetano replaced the Portuguese dictator António Salazar, though he also sought to hold on to the African colonies. In 1970, FRELIMO, the MPLA, and PAIGC issued a joint statement calling for policy change. In September 1973, PAIGC declared the independence of Guinea-Bissau, though fighting continued in Mozambique and Angola. In 1974, General Antonío de Spínola became president of Portugal and promised to transfer power to the African territories, bringing about a ceasefire.

Independence at last

Portugal's colonial empire now rapidly wound up. In January 1975, Portugal signed the Alvor Agreement with the MPLA, FNLA, and UNITA, giving Angola independence, though fighting broke out between the groups as they jockeyed for power. In Mozambique, a deal was signed with FRELIMO and 25 June 1975 was set as independence day. Similar agreements granted independence to Cabo Verde and São Tomé & Príncipe, where there had been no fighting. The departure of the Portuguese was chaotic, with hundreds of thousands of settlers fleeing the former colonies. In Angola, there was no recognized government to hand over to and a decades-long civil war broke out. However, West Africa had now freed itself of Portuguese control.

▽ **MPLA victory**
A poster commemorates the MPLA's 1976 victory in the Angolan War of Independence. The MPLA's flag is on the left and that of Angola on the right.

Samora Machel

East African opponent of colonialism

An army commander and anti-imperialist, Samora Machel became Mozambique's first president after securing the country's independence from Portugal. He nationalized key institutions and supported Africa's freedom movements.

Growing up in Mozambique's agricultural Gaza Province in the 1940s and '50s, Machel saw how the country's Portuguese rulers exploited Black farmers like his father, telling them which crops to grow and threatening their rights to their land. Machel also watched as many poor Mozambicans left the country for low-paid work in neighbouring South Africa's mines – some, like his own brother, dying in accidents there. While working in a hospital, Machel led protests against Black nurses being paid less than their white equivalents.

Committing himself to driving out the Portuguese, Machel journeyed to Tanzania and joined the independence organization FRELIMO (*Frente de Libertação de Moçambique,* or the Liberation Front of Mozambique), which the Portuguese had outlawed. He rose through the ranks, becoming head of the movement's guerrilla forces, then army commander, and finally, in 1970, the leader of FRELIMO itself.

Putting theory into practice

FRELIMO won Mozambique's independence in June 1975 and Machel became the country's first president. A self-declared Marxist-Leninist, he introduced wide-ranging socialist policies, nationalizing the land, health, rented housing, and the assets of the Catholic Church. He also supported the independence movement in Rhodesia and the anti-apartheid campaign in South Africa. In response, the leaderships of the two states established in 1977 a new political and paramilitary organization, RENAMO (*Resistência Nacional Moçambicana,* or the Mozambique National Resistance), which was diametrically opposed to FRELIMO. Violence between FRELIMO and RENAMO continues to this day.

Samora Machel died in a plane crash over South African airspace in 1986. A South African-established investigation declared the accident was due to pilot error, but many in Mozambique still suspected the apartheid regime of foul play.

△ **Tragic memorial**
The Samora Machel Monument marks the site in South Africa where Machel's plane crashed and contains several pieces of the wrecked aircraft. Steel tubes represent the 35 lives lost in the crash.

◁ **Brothers in arms**
Machel (left) with Eduardo Mondlane, his predecessor as FRELIMO leader. Mondlane was killed in 1969 by a parcel bomb. His assassin has never been named.

1933 Born in the village of Madragoa

1954 Studies nursing in the capital city, Lourenço Marques (now Maputo)

1962 Joins FRELIMO, founded that year in modern-day Tanzania

1964 FRELIMO begins its armed pro-independence campaign

1966 Machel assumes command of FRELIMO's armed forces

1970 After a disputed leadership campaign, Machel becomes FRELIMO's president

1975 Mozambique secures its independence from Portugal

1977 RENAMO is founded and launches a violent insurgency against Machel's regime

1980 Machel makes a state visit to the newly independent Zimbabwe (formerly Rhodesia)

1986 Dies in a plane crash in Mbuzini, South Africa

The fight for Zimbabwe

The armed conflict that created a new country

△ **Independence day**
On 18 April 1980, Zimbabwe became independent from Britain and crowds across the country celebrated.

A struggle that began with a 19th-century colonial war finally ended after a 20th-century war of liberation, as Zimbabwe's Black majority fought to free itself from the white-minority state of Rhodesia.

In the 19th century, the area now known as Zimbabwe was home to several ethnic groups, including the Shona and Ndebele. The Shona occupied Mashonaland, in the north, while the Ndebele had moved to Matabeleland, in the southwest, after splitting from the Zulu Kingdom. From the 1880s, European colonists, led by Cecil Rhodes's British South Africa Company, began to invade the region. They took land and cattle – crucial commodities on which both the Shona and Ndebele were dependent – and imposed taxes, leading to the First *Chimurenga* (meaning "uprising" in the Shona

language) in 1896–97, when the Ndebele and Shona revolted against the British administration. The British crushed the uprising and appropriated the region as a colony in 1898. The war marked the beginning of organized armed resistance in Zimbabwe.

Migrants from Britain settled in the colonies of Southern Africa. Southern Rhodesia, as Zimbabwe was then known, became self-governing in 1923, though rules surrounding property ownership meant that the vote was effectively restricted to white settlers. The settlers offered prime farmland to new arrivals, and restricted Black people to unproductive areas or

△ **First prime minister**
Robert Mugabe speaks to a crowd in Harare in the 1980s. Mugabe ruled Zimbabwe as prime minister (1980–87) and then president (1987–2017).

> "Africa **must revert** to what it was before the imperialists divided it. These are **artificial divisions** which we... will seek to **remove**."

ROBERT MUGABE, AT A SPEECH IN SALISBURY (NOW HARARE), 1962

forced them to work on white farms. Black people were economically marginalized, and some workers suffered from forced labour and settler brutality. Unrest bubbled in Black townships, and activists called for equal employment rights and the right to vote.

Second Chimurenga

After World War II, African nationalism grew (see pp. 230–31) and neighbouring Malawi and Zambia gained their independence in 1964. A year earlier, two rival revolutionary groups had formed in Southern Rhodesia. The Zimbabwe African People's Union (ZAPU), led by Joshua Nkomo, had primarily Ndebele members, while the Zimbabwe African National Union (ZANU), led by Robert Mugabe, was dominated by the Shona. The Second Chimurenga began in 1964, with ZAPU and ZANU forces fighting the Rhodesian army and clashing with each other.

Southern Rhodesia's white minority, which never made up more than around eight per cent of the population, offered little in the way of compromise. As the conflict intensified, fears that Britain would open the franchise to the Black majority led Prime Minister Ian Smith to declare Southern Rhodesia's unilateral independence from Britain in 1965. A new constitution that offered "non-Europeans" several seats in parliament failed to quell Black Africans' resistance to white-minority rule. Guerrillas disrupted transportation and communications in the cities, and neighbouring Zambia and Mozambique provided bases for anti-government forces.

Towards independence

Facing increasing international isolation and escalating internal resistance, the Smith regime announced a political settlement in 1978, on the condition that the police and army remained under white control. The elections in 1979 were still skewed towards the white minority, but resulted in a victory for the United African National Council (UANC) of Bishop Abel Muzorewa, which supported Black majority rule but had not advocated armed struggle. The new government failed to win international recognition,

and continued resistance led the warring parties to the negotiating table a few months later. The Lancaster House talks, between the British government, the Patriotic Front (a coalition formed by ZAPU and ZANU), the UANC, and Smith's Rhodesia Front began in London in October 1979. The parties agreed on new elections, a new constitution, and a ceasefire, ending the Second Chimurenga. But the burning issue in the negotiations was land, with the white minority holding the vast majority of fertile farmland. Robert Mugabe fought hard for radical change, but accepted the principle that white landowners would be compensated for any land sales.

In the 1980 election, ZANU-PF (ZANU Popular Front) won a majority, with Robert Mugabe as prime minister and clergyman Canaan Banana as president. The country, now known as Zimbabwe, finally had its independence. ZANU-PF increased its majority in the 1985 election, allowing for reforms such as the removal of the last "whites-only" seats in parliament. In 1987, the opposition ZAPU joined with ZANU-PF.

However, the issue of land reform has never gone away. White farmers, who continued to own a high proportion of arable land, increasingly began to be forced off their land in the early 21st century. This fed into wider economic and social instability, and an increasingly unpredictable Mugabe was finally forced out in 2017, with ordinary Zimbabweans hoping the new government could turn troubles such as ferocious inflation and corruption around.

THE ROLE OF WOMEN IN THE STRUGGLE

Women played critical roles in the war of liberation. One of their first roles was carrying arms, often at night, to the front lines. By 1977, they had been integrated into combat roles, and held training and leadership positions. Women also galvanized support for the struggle among rural villages. By the end of the war, women made up an estimated third of the ZANU fighting force.

South Africa and apartheid

Racism on a national scale

△ **Permit to travel**
A Black woman in Cape Town displays her "interior passport", showing that she is only allowed within the city limits during working hours.

South Africa's white leadership held out against sharing power or integrating with the country's majority Black population. Instead, it institutionalized ethnic discrimination and adopted white supremacy as official state policy.

The Union of South Africa was proclaimed in 1910 and from the beginning power rested with the country's minority white population, which was mainly Boer – settlers of Dutch, German, or Huguenot (French Protestant) descent. For the next eight decades, South Africa's leaders marginalized the country's majority Black population by introducing discriminatory laws. The Natives Land Act of 1913 and the Natives (Urban Areas) Act of 1923 between them prescribed where Black people could live, for example, while the tellingly-named Master and Servant Act allowed (white) employers to whip (Black) workers. The so-called Hertzog Bills of 1936 disenfranchised the few wealthy Black South Africans who had been qualified to vote.

By the late 1940s, white South Africa was enjoying a post-war economic boom, but millions of Black people remained poor. Hundreds of thousands lived on the fringes of major cities in illegal squatter camps,

in dismal conditions and working for low pay. When Black people began to campaign for their rights, South Africa's white electors reacted in 1948 by voting into power the uncompromisingly white supremacist National Party (NP). Once in office, the NP set about introducing its programme of state-sanctioned racial discrimination that it called apartheid ("apartness").

First acts of oppression

Apartheid legislation began with 1949's Prohibition of Mixed Marriages Act, followed by a law forbidding interracial sexual relations. To clarify what "race" meant, the Population Registration Act of 1950 established three categories: "Whites", "Coloureds" (multiracial heritage), and "Blacks". A fourth category, "Asian", was added later. A series of Land Acts put 80 per cent of South Africa's farmland under white control. Beaches, car parks, public toilets, restaurants, and even graveyards were segregated, and people of colour were forced to carry pass books – essentially internal passports – allowing them to enter certain areas. Only white South Africans could join a trade union or be elected to the country's parliament.

South Africa's people of colour reacted to apartheid in a number of ways. In 1949, the main anti-apartheid organization, the African National Congress (ANC), introduced a Programme of Action calling for resistance to white domination through active opposition. Inspired by a new generation of leaders such as Nelson Mandela, Oliver Tambo, and Walter Sisulu rising through its Youth Wing, the ANC grew increasingly

◁ **Enduring defiance**
Soweto protestors vent their anger in 1980 – showing how state repressions like the one that suppressed the earlier Soweto Uprising in 1976 failed to end public defiance.

confrontational as South Africa's governments became more oppressive. The "defiance campaign" it organized in 1952, for example, encouraged the burning of pass books. In 1955, a group called the Congress of the People drew up a Freedom Charter that declared "South Africa belongs to all who live in it, Black or white." At a public meeting to adopt the charter, 150 attendees were arrested and charged with high treason. Other groups such as the South African Indian Congress, the Coloured People's Organization, Trade Unions, and the Pan Africanist Congress also actively opposed apartheid.

Segregation and resistance

In 1959, the government of prime minister Hendrik Verwoerd passed the Promotion of Bantu Self-Government Act. It established 10 "Bantustans", or Black homelands, including QwaQwa, Transkei, and KwaZulu. These Black-only regions were allowed some self-government but were ultimately state-subsidized ghettos, with high rates of crime, poverty, ill health, unemployment, and disease. Each Bantustan was established as home to a particular ethnic or linguistic group (KwaZulu was the Zulu people's homeland, for example), deliberately emphasizing the differences between Black populations and making it difficult for them to work together. Between 1961 and 1994, some 3.5 million Black people were relocated to Bantustans. In 1970, Black people were stripped of

their South African citizenship by being defined as legal citizens of the homeland in which they lived.

In March 1960, 7,000 people protested against pass book laws in the township of Sharpeville. Police fired on them, and at least 67 were killed and 180 wounded, leading to national and international condemnation. The ANC was one of several resistance groups to set up military units in the aftermath of the "Sharpeville Massacre". Between 1960 and 1963, the ANC's *Umkhonto we Sizwe* ("Spear of the Nation") armed wing carried out almost 200 attacks, mostly bombings, against state buildings and institutions. No deaths were recorded in this period, at the end of which the *Umkhonto we Sizwe* leader Nelson Mandela was captured and imprisoned in Cape Town's Robben Island prison, becoming in the process an international figurehead of the anti-apartheid movement (see pp. 270–71).

By the end of the 1960s, many African states had fought for and won their independence, while South Africa's people of colour remained unfree. But the opposition to apartheid would only grow – at home and abroad. This ensured that the struggles of the 1950s and '60s were not in vain and ultimately contributed to the end of apartheid (see pp. 268–69).

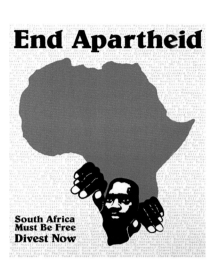

△ **International support**
This anti-apartheid poster was made by the American artist and activist Lincoln Cushing in 1985, displaying solidarity with the Black South African cause.

◁ **Homeland housing**
These homes are in eastern South Africa's QwaQwa homeland, established for the country's Besotho people. The single-storey houses were "self-built" by residents under supervision.

"The act of **creating art** should complement… **liberating the country for my people.**"

THAMI MNYELE, MEDU CO-FOUNDER

▷ **Imagining the future**
Made in 1981, this Medu Art Ensemble poster depicts and predicts both the end of apartheid and the election of Nelson Mandela as democratic South Africa's first president, an event that would happen in 1994.

Anti-apartheid poster

Art as a weapon of struggle in South Africa

In 1978, Black South African exiles in Gaborone, Botswana, founded Medu Art Ensemble. The aim of the group was to organize resistance to apartheid through literary, musical, and artistic works, as well as with conferences, workshops, and other events. Members of Medu – which means "roots" in the Sepedi-Sotho language spoken in northeast South Africa – called themselves "cultural workers", to emphasize that their activities were a necessary social, ethnic, and political task rather than merely art for art's sake, which they viewed as elitist.

At its height, Medu comprised 60 "cultural workers", campaigners whose works drew attention across the continent and beyond to South Africa's inequalities. In 1982, Medu held its most influential event, the week-long Culture and Resistance Festival and Symposium in Gaborone that attracted human rights activists, political agitators, and members of the public from Africa, Europe, and the Americas. The event included politically themed concerts, exhibitions, talks, and activities. Attendees explored aspects of life under apartheid, including censorship and land and labour policies, and promoted Pan-Africanism, civic education, and the role artists could play in bringing about social change in South Africa.

This symposium and Medu's other activities brought the group's message to a wider audience than ever before – convincing South Africa's government that it needed to take action against it. On 14 June 1985, up to 50 members of the South Africa Defence Force (SADF) crossed the border into Botswana and launched Operation Plecksy, a targeted search-and-destroy raid on anti-apartheid activists based in Gaborone, including members of the Medu Art Ensemble. SADF operatives murdered at least 12 people, four of whom were members of the collective, including one of its founders, the artist Thami Mnyele. A decimated Medu was disbanded in the aftermath of the attack.

Art and propaganda
An important aspect of Medu's output was its political posters, which usually displayed striking imagery and direct and inspiring messages and slogans such as "The People Shall Govern" and "Unity, Democracy, and Courage". As all Medu work was banned in South Africa, it took a dedicated and courageous network of sympathizers to smuggle posters across the borders and hang them in public spaces, much to the chagrin of the country's leaders.

US-born artist Judy A. Seidman made the poster shown here. Seidman lived and worked in Zambia and Swaziland (now Eswatini) before moving to Gaborone and joining Medu in 1980. This piece, like Medu's other output, shows how opposition groups inside and outside South Africa used art as a means of promoting and effecting change to help undermine the country's undemocratic apartheid regime.

Grouping of miners, mothers, students, and workers

White woven paper, on which artwork has been printed

Rare intact edges of poster (most posters from South Africa were confiscated or torn down by the authorities)

...and the people
e for Nelson Mandela

MEDU ART ENSEMBLE

Artists agreed to work under the collective imprimatur of the group rather than as individuals

The legacy of colonization

Far-reaching impacts of European misrule

European powers brought new infrastructure and trade to Africa – but they also exploited its resources. Communities were divided and African cultures and learning were sidelined, leaving independent states with a legacy of instability.

△ **Graduation ceremony**
Founded in 1960, the *École nationale d'administration* in Madagascar trained senior civil servants for the newly independent nation.

By the 1970s, most African nations had won their independence, but their colonial past shaped their development. These states were not organic nations, but lines on a map drawn by 19th-century European colonizers. The empires of Europe ignored the size, natural resources, ethnic mix, religions, and trading relationships that might make viable, long-term states. These arbitrary borders led to instability, civil wars, and the marginalization of some groups.

Many African nations have struggled to reconcile their territory and peoples. In Nigeria, which became independent from Britain in 1960, colonial borders had brought together over 250 ethnic groups. Clashes between the largest ones, the Hausa-Fulani, Yoruba, and Igbo, led to a conflict that ended the First Republic in 1966. In Sudan, also previously occupied by Britain, tensions between Muslim Arabs in the north and Dinka and other groups who practised Christianity and local religions in the south led to bloodshed and the 2011 secession of South Sudan.

▷ **Uganda railway**
This 1908 poster shows the railway that connected Mombasa and Lake Victoria. Constructed by mainly Indian workers, it consolidated British power over East Africa's Great Lakes.

Colonizing powers did not just divide Africa into different states. Missionaries converted numerous people to Christianity, while industries, from mining and agriculture to colonial administration, trained their staff. The positive impacts of this included increased literacy and numeracy, but colonial education and missionary work often spread European learning and faith at the expense of local cultures, religions, and crafts. Some taught entirely in languages

"[T]he struggle against colonialism does not end with **the attainment** of **national independence**."

GHANAIAN PRESIDENT KWAME NKRUMAH, 1963

such as English or French, and European writers and thinkers were held up as exemplars. Meanwhile, although European laws provided a framework for newly independent states, laws such as the British penal code that outlawed same-sex sexual acts in countries like Uganda institutionalized prejudice.

While colonial education introduced new ideas and prepared some Africans for nationalist agitation, most training was focused on the needs of the colonial administration, with Africans taking on less skilled or low-ranking jobs. On the eve of independence in 1959, Belgian Congo had no Congolese people in the senior grade of the civil service due to the paucity of colonial education policies.

Cash crops and transportation

European nations' use of colonies to supply raw materials resulted in a focus on cash crops such as groundnuts, palm oil, rubber, timber, coffee, cocoa, tea, tobacco, cotton, and spices; and minerals like copper, gold, and diamonds. Large farms and mines were established and infrastructure, such as railways, modern roads, telegraphs, electric power, bureaucracy, hospitals, and pipe-borne water and sewage systems, was set up around these resources. Many Africans were encouraged or forced to leave their lands to serve resource production, contributing further to uneven development and social instability.

Land transport connected these production hubs with ports that could export goods to Europe and beyond. In East Africa, great railways were built under British and German rule, but they were designed to help colonial nations exploit the Great Lakes region's immense resources and cement their power there, not to assist local communities.

Struggle for self-reliance

When states gained their independence, colonial infrastructure aided international trade, but had not been designed for self-reliance. Foreign influence, termed neocolonialism (see pp. 260–61), often continued to disadvantage African economies. European powers had little interest in encouraging the development of a manufacturing base or balanced agriculture. Long-standing crops such as sorghum, fonio, and millet were pushed off the land, leaving many African nations dependent on the large-scale import of wheat and maize. Meanwhile, skewed trade arrangements limited the profits and benefits received by African economies. Many nations emerged from colonization dependent on a limited number of exports (such as coffee in Kenya, oil in Libya, and copper in the Democratic Republic of the Congo) whose value can shift dramatically, creating instability.

Local elites, such as the Tutsi of Rwanda and Burundi, who worked closely with Europeans, often inherited power after independence, and fought to maintain it as marginalized groups struggled for equality. In parts of Southern Africa, white settlers who had grown used to superior farmland and political influence used a mix of legal tools and state violence to maintain their privileged position, as seen most notoriously in apartheid South Africa (see pp. 254–55).

△ **Ewe chiefs**
Colonial borders created an identity crisis among the Ewe of West Africa, whose homelands were divided between Ghana, Benin, and Togo. Since independence, some Ewe have campaigned for a consolidated state.

THE TEXTILE **TRADE**

Cotton is widespread in Africa, and is grown primarily as an export crop – this 1964 stamp celebrates Zambia's industry. During the scramble for Africa in the late 19th century, the availability of cheap cotton, which was required by an expanding European population, was a major reason for colonial investment in the continent. Today, price fluctuations and the subsidies enjoyed by European and North American competitors mean profits from the crop are often marginal.

△ **Liberation artwork**
Ethiopian artist Afewerk Tekle's stained-glass work *The Total Liberation of Africa* is situated in the headquarters of the United Nations Economic Commission for Africa in Addis Ababa.

A new political generation

Taking up the reins of power

The political leaders who came to prominence from the 1930s onwards – many of whom had been exposed to new political ideas via Western educations – went on to face the immense task of leading newly independent African nations.

European colonizers used education to produce workforces that could administer African colonies for colonial gain. But schools and colleges also helped shape a new elite that campaigned for self-rule and would govern new nations. These leaders were mostly men from privileged backgrounds, and their Western education differentiated them from the majority of the population, who had less access to schooling.

An influential early figure was Nnamdi Azikiwe (1904–96), who gained an education at religious schools before continuing his studies in the US. In 1937, he returned to his native Nigeria, where he published nationalist newspapers and grew

increasingly prominent, becoming president in 1960. Azikiwe was Igbo, but also spoke Yoruba and Hausa, helping him appeal to a multiethnic electorate.

Azikiwe's eloquence and mix of international and church-school learning was shared by other members of the new generation. While working as a newspaper editor in the Gold Coast colony (now Ghana), Azikiwe briefly mentored another leader-in-waiting, Kwame Nkrumah (see pp. 242–43). Nkrumah studied socialist literature in the US, before returning to the Gold Coast to become an impassioned campaigner for independence. Hastings Banda studied in the US and Britain before returning to his home country, Malawi (then British-ruled Nyasaland), in 1958 to advocate for independence, becoming prime minister in 1963 and, from 1966, an increasingly autocratic president.

Many of the new generation had strong cultural as well as political interests. Léopold Senghor (1906–2001), who became Senegal's first president in 1960, was a poet and one of the founders of the *Négritude* literary and artistic movement, which sought to foreground African and Black identities and experiences. The long-standing Tanzanian president Julius Nyerere (1922–99) translated several plays by William Shakespeare into Swahili and wrote widely on nationalism and liberation, while Kenya's Jomo Kenyatta (c. 1894–1978) authored a study of the culture and society of the Kikuyu people of Kenya.

Kenyatta's long career saw him campaign against colonial land seizures and endure jail as a suspected terrorist before becoming prime minister (1963–64) and president (1964–78) of Kenya. Not all leaders enjoyed such lengthy careers. The transition from colonies to independent nations proved challenging, thanks in large part to colonization's divisive legacy (see pp. 258–59). Nkrumah was forced from power by a coup, while Azikiwe was ousted by the Nigerian military. Other leaders, including Nyerere and Senghor, became increasingly autocratic.

New challenges

While this generation might not have all fulfilled their early promise, they played a pivotal role in the fight for independence and the development of ideas. They fused beliefs such as socialism and nationalism into African forms – stressing political and economic self-reliance – and used their colonial education to articulate the aspirations of the newly enfranchised electorates and drive their new nations forward.

However, while generations of leaders have upheld Africa's independence, regions such as Europe and North America still wield influence, while China's power increases. Neocolonialism has made the questions the postcolonial generation pondered as vital as ever. How can African nations stand on their own, tap into their wealth of science and culture, and indigenize democracy for political and social peace? And are African leaders – often wealthy and with elite educations – mere gatekeepers for neocolonialism?

These questions have a practical impact. In West and Central Africa, 14 nations that were formerly under French control still use the CFA franc and are required to deposit a percentage of their GDP in the Bank of France as a trust. Such issues are the responsibility of another generation of leaders, such as Macky Sall of Senegal, Alassane Ouattara of Côte d'Ivoire, Paul Biya of Cameroon, Paul Kagame of Rwanda, and Sahle-Work Zewde of Ethiopia. They face a struggle to live up to the intellectual weight of their predecessors, and a mighty challenge to build a better world.

△ **New leaders**
African heads of state gather in Kinshasa, Democratic Republic of the Congo (then Zaire), for the 1967 summit of the Organization of African Unity. Julius Nyerere (sixth from left) and Jomo Kenyatta (ninth from left) are among those pictured.

ORGANIZATION **OF AFRICAN UNITY**

The Organization of African Unity (OAU) was founded in 1963 to increase collaboration between its 33 member states, and to resist colonialism and neocolonialism. Its inaugural conference (pictured here) was held in 1963 in Addis Ababa, Ethiopia. Pan-African integration has been a major theme for the continent's leaders, and has also been encouraged through a series of meetings of the Pan-African Congress (see pp. 232–33), which first convened in 1919, and set itself against imperialism and discrimination. The OAU contributed to African unity on the world stage, but was criticized for doing little for ordinary Africans. In 2001, it was succeeded by the African Union, which has 55 members, covering almost the entire continent.

The rise of the military

Taking power by force of arms

In the decades after independence, military coups were a regular occurrence in Africa. The reasons behind these destabilizing events are complex and varied – not least the impact and legacy of colonization itself.

The end of European colonial rule had a profound effect in many African states. While the process of decolonization was mostly carried out peacefully, nations such as Britain and France did not always give up their imperial holdings willingly. In many cases, minimal preparation was done to ensure a smooth transition of power. Incoming political leaders, often with no experience of holding office, inherited countries riven with social, political, and economic problems. In many countries, the imperial power had provided a single focus for opposition groups; with the foreign powers gone, opposing factions turned on each other. Popular unrest followed, and military coups became a means of effecting regime change.

Numbers and causes

More than 200 coups have taken place in Africa since the 1950s. Around half have been successful. The most intense period of coup activity was during the 1960s and 1970s, with a coup or attempted coup every 55 days; 90 per cent of African states had some form of coup experience in this era. Geographically, West Africa had the highest proportion of coups, accounting for 44.4 per cent of them from 1958–2008.

It is, of course, not the case that Africa is simply predisposed towards military coups. The causes are multiple and complex, in large part arising as a result of how the colonial empires left the continent. Poverty, lack of economic development, political corruption, ethnic rivalries, and religious divisions are common factors. Additionally, what South African politician and strategist Joel Netshitenzhe has described as an ongoing "thirst for Africa's resources" (for example, for minerals and oil) from external powers has led to corruption and oppression. Added to this, from the Cold War onwards (see pp. 246–47), the US, the Soviet Union (USSR), the former colonial powers, and – from the early 2000s – China and Russia have sought to increase their influence in the continent. This has boosted the power of the military in many states, sometimes acting as proxies for non-African nations or as the beneficiaries of the political disruption they cause.

Coups across the continent

Africa's first post-war military coup took place in Egypt. In July 1952, a group of young army officers led by Mohamed Naguib and Gamal Abdel Nasser toppled the corrupt and incompetent regime of the country's hereditary ruler, King Farouk I. Naguib and Nasser's coup was backed by the anticolonial US and USSR – which trumped the opposition the insurgents faced from imperialist Britain and France.

As well as inspiring other independence movements throughout Africa, the Egyptian Revolution of 1952 showed that military coups worked as a means of seizing power, especially with help from abroad. The military coup that overthrew Ghana's president Kwame Nkrumah (see pp. 242–43) in 1966, for

▽ **Council of war**
Gamal Abdel Nasser (seated, third right) sits with his fellow coup plotters. Having ousted Egypt's king in 1952, Nasser would rule the country from 1956 until his death in 1970.

△ **Political ringmaster**
Zaire's dictator Mobutu Sese Seko makes political capital from a fight between boxers Muhammad Ali and George Foreman, with the line, "Ali and Foreman have confidence in Mobutu".

> "Everywhere that the **struggle** for **national freedom** has triumphed… there were **military coups** that overthrew their leaders."

AHMED BEN BELLA, PRESIDENT OF ALGERIA (1963–65)

Some argue that martial regimes stabilize (however temporarily) the states they take over because such regimes impose strict obedience, as well as fear and repression. However, the violent careers of Uganda's Idi Amin and Nigeria's Sani Abacha, to name but two, show how military dictatorships bring economic decay and corruption on their nations. More often than not, military rule only leads to autocratic rule and more governmental fragility. Sudan – plagued by corruption, civil unrest, and dire poverty – has experienced more than a dozen military coups since 1950, the most recent in 2023.

Coups in perspective

In fact, military coups are only a regular occurrence in around a dozen of the 54 countries that make up Africa. The development of strong civil institutions can make the overthrow of governments unlikely and unnecessary, as has been the case in South Africa since the end of apartheid. Some states, including Botswana and Senegal, have never experienced a coup at all. Countries such as Morocco, Kenya, and Cameroon have only ever experienced unsuccessful military coups; other states saw coups solely in the instability of the post-independence era. Ghana's series of coups, for example, took place between 1966 and 1984, the last successfully put down by Jerry John Rawlings's government. Rawlings was himself a military officer who had staged coups in 1979 and 1981. He led a military junta until 1992, after which he resigned from the military and founded the National Democratic Congress (NDC). He served his allotted two terms as president and oversaw the peaceful transfer of power to an elected member of the opposition. Ghana has since seen decades of stable democracy.

▽ **Military leader**
Mali's Moussa Traoré, pictured here in 1982, took power in a 1968 coup and was himself overthrown in a military takeover in 1991.

example, was backed by Britain and the US because of the African leader's communist leanings. Similarly, in the newly independent Republic of the Congo (now the Democratic Republic of the Congo), prime minister Patrice Lumumba was executed in 1961 in an army-led rebellion in part orchestrated by his country's former colonial occupier, Belgium. This happened after Lumumba tried to nationalize his country's lucrative (and Belgian-controlled) uranium, rubber, and copper industries. His replacement, General Mobutu Sese Seko, was a corrupt and murderous dictator. He became president in 1965 and held power until 1997, running his state – which he renamed Zaire in 1971 – as a kleptocracy and amassing a fortune as his country sank into poverty.

In Mali, when the first post-independence president Modibo Keïta began to advocate socialist-style policies, France secretly assisted the 1968 military coup led by Lieutenant Moussa Traoré that brought him down.

Civil wars

Power struggles across the continent

At least 20 African nations have experienced civil wars. Their causes include colonialism, religious or ethnic divisions, corruption, leadership failures, poverty, and foreign interference in domestic affairs. While no single factor explains the scale of Africa's armed struggles, the impacts of imperialism laid the groundwork for many of them. As foreign powers left, they were replaced by national leaders who had been afforded little to no experience in government, and who had inherited weak economies and undeveloped political institutions. In addition, large areas of Africa were rich in resources. The former colonial powers, as well as the US, the Soviet Union (USSR), and, later, Russia and China, used all means at their disposal, both fair and foul, to gain access to them.

The First Sudanese Civil War, which began in 1955, saw mainly Christian southern Sudan attempt to separate itself from the majority Muslim north. Britain, the USSR, and Egypt supported the north, while Ethiopia, Uganda, and Israel endorsed the south. After 500,000 deaths, the war ended in 1972 with the establishment of the Southern Sudan Autonomous Region. A second civil war from 1983 left two million dead before a peace deal was brokered in 2005. South Sudan gained its independence six years later, but remains a troubled region, while in Sudan armed conflict flared up again in 2023.

In the Nigerian Civil War (1967–70), the Igbo people of the country's southeast attempted to declare an independent Republic of Biafra. Once again, the

△ **Nigerian Civil War (1967–70)**
This soldier from the putative Biafran Republic carries an injured comrade in 1968. Igbo attempts to form a country of their own in the southeast of Nigeria led to civil war. The Nigerian government eventually mounted a food blockade to force Biafra's surrender.

△ **Ethiopian Civil War (1974–91)**
Eritrean women played a vital role in the Ethiopian Civil War, in which Eritrea won independence from Ethiopia. As soldiers, they made up over a third of the Eritrean People's Liberation Front (EPLF), a left-leaning nationalist organization that also supported women's rights and worked to improve literacy.

△ **Ugandan Civil Wars (1980–present)**
This "night commuter" is one of an estimated 30,000 young people in Uganda who, fearful of kidnap or worse by marauding rebel groups, leave their homes each evening to seek safety in NGO-run public shelters.

"Virtually all of **Africa's civil wars** were started by politically **marginalized** or **excluded** groups."

GEORGE AYITTEY, GHANAIAN ECONOMIST AND POLITICAL COMMENTATOR, 2010

triumvirate of Britain, the USSR, and Egypt supported the established government against the secessionists. One million citizens died in a conflict that lasted for three years and resulted in defeat for the breakaway republic and marginalization of the Igbo in the Yoruba- and Hausa-Fulani-dominated state.

Difficult path to peace

The misrule and state-sanctioned violence that have afflicted Uganda since independence in 1962 put the country into a 25-year-long tailspin of poverty, dictatorship, and societal breakdown. The result, in 1987, was the ongoing insurgency against the corrupt regime of Yoweri Museveni by the Lord's Resistance Army (LRA). Led by the self-styled Christian warrior

Joseph Kony, the LRA has no coherent aims, apart from a desire to destroy its opponents. LRA violence has dislocated 2 million Ugandans and Kony's militias have abducted 60,000 civilians — most of them turned into child soldiers and enforced sex workers.

The Somali Civil War began after a coup ousted the country's dictator, General Siad Barre, in 1991. The conflict has claimed a million Somali lives in violence, famine, and disease. The aims of its many competing forces (Islamic, socialist, nationalist, separatist) are so diverse that the prospect of peace appears distant.

The best antidote to war, as shown by countries like Botswana, Namibia, and Ghana, is to establish stable, democratic governments that effectively manage the socio-cultural diversity in African societies.

△ **First Liberian Civil War (1989–96)**
This masked militiaman is a member of the National Patriotic Front of Liberia (NPFL), the rebel group that won Liberia's first civil war in 1996. The NPFL leader Charles Taylor was himself ousted in a second civil war ending in 2003.

△ **Rwandan Civil War (1990–94)**
The civil war in Rwanda saw a brutal genocide take place among the Tutsi and Hutu people. At the war's end, two million defeated Hutus fled to neighbouring Zaire (now the Democratic Republic of the Congo) — many abandoning their machetes, as shown here. Tens of thousands of Hutus died in further civil conflicts in Zaire.

△ **South Sudanese Civil War (2013–20)**
Soldiers celebrate the 34th anniversary of the founding of the Sudan People's Liberation Army (SPLA) in 2017. South Sudan gained independence from Sudan in 2011, but a power struggle between its leaders erupted into ethnic violence and civil war.

Africa's Great War

The world's deadliest conflict since World War II

A year after the First Congo War (1996–97), the Second Congo War (1998–2003), sometimes called Africa's Great War, broke out. It involved multiple African countries and claimed around 5.4 million lives.

The African region known as the Congo has been troubled since at least 1885, when Belgium's king, Leopold II, assumed personal ownership of what was then called the Congo Free State (see pp. 212–13). Ever since, the country's changing name – the Belgian Congo, the Republic of the Congo, the Democratic Republic of the Congo, Zaire, and, from 1997, the Democratic Republic of the Congo (DRC) once more – has reflected its unstable and often violent fortunes.

The Second Congo War marked a particularly volatile period in the state's history. The roots of the conflict were in the First Congo War (1996–97), the civil struggle that ended the dictatorship of Mobutu Sese Seko, president of what was at that time called Zaire. The man who usurped and replaced Mobutu was Laurent-Désiré Kabila, a dissident, a revolutionary, and the leader of the Alliance of Democratic Forces for the Liberation of Congo (ADFLC). The state Kabila inherited was riddled with corruption, failures of leadership, poverty and institutionalized violence. Vested interests at home and abroad (mostly Belgium and the US) vied for control of the country's abundant mineral wealth.

Foreign influences

Kabila was swept to power in 1997 by an alliance of Mobutu's opponents that included the governments of neighbouring Uganda and Rwanda. Just as the US and Belgium had gained access to the DRC's natural resources in return for supporting Mobutu in power, so Uganda and Rwanda expected a similar quid pro quo from Kabila. They also wanted unrestricted freedom to take action against the Hutu militias that had fled to the DRC (then called Zaire) after perpetrating the 1994 genocide against the Tutsi people of Rwanda. When, a year after the end of the

◁ **All-powerful leader**
Mobutu Sese Seko seized power in 1965. With Western support, he was the DRC's president-dictator for 32 years and was one of Africa's most corrupt leaders.

First Congo War, Kabila made it clear that none of these concessions would be forthcoming, Uganda and Rwanda switched sides and began to support the new president's opponents. This development marked the beginning of the Second Congo War.

The main party against Kabila in the DRC was the Rally for Congolese Democracy (RCD). It was backed by Uganda and Rwanda, and headed a coalition of rebel factions, disaffected regional parties, and other groups that felt excluded by Kabila's rule. The war itself was not a single conflict but rather a series of contests, with multiple fronts and a shifting alliance of states and militias. At various times, Kabila's supporters included Angola, Chad, Namibia, and Zimbabwe, as well as the Allied Democratic Forces (ADF), an Islamic group, and the Lord's Resistance Army (LRA), a notoriously brutal Christian force. Most of these pro-Kabila countries and groups were motivated more by their mistrust of Uganda and Rwanda's territorial ambitions than their belief in the DRC's government. To complicate matters, Uganda and Rwanda's opposition to the DRC did not mean they fully supported each other: the two countries' forces came to blows over rival territorial ambitions more than once during the Second Congo War.

Ongoing challenges

Laurent-Désiré Kabila was assassinated by one of his bodyguards in 2001. He was succeeded by his 29-year-old son, Joseph, who agreed to take part in the South Africa-brokered peace talks of 2002–03 that ended the war. A transitional government was established in

◁ **Displaced people**
Up to 600,000 Hutu refugees fled the DRC (then Zaire) in 1996 at the start of the First Congo War, returning to their ethnically divided home nation of Rwanda.

the DRC and the UN deployed a peacekeeping force to monitor the fragile ceasefire between the conflict's many armed groups. In 2006, Joseph Kabila was named president in the DRC's first democratic elections since independence. He was re-elected in 2011 and stood down in January 2019 after losing the 2018 election to opposition candidate Félix Tshisekedi.

Despite these moves towards democracy, the DRC is far from stable and peaceful today. The issues that fuelled the war – foreign interference, corruption, economic inequality, ethnic differences, resource conflicts, ideological and religious schisms, and poverty – have not gone away. Armed factions and rebel groups, some backed by the DRC's neighbours, continue to fight. In pursuit of territory gains and control of resources, rebel forces have committed acts of alleged genocide, for example against the DRC's Twa (or Batwa) and Bambuti people, situated in the northwest and northeast of the country respectively. In 2005, the UN's International Court of Justice ruled that Uganda had violated the DRC's sovereignty and looted resources worth billions of dollars. The DRC demanded $10 billion in reparations from Uganda. This was arbitrated down to $325 million. In 2022, Uganda paid its first instalment of $65 million.

SHIFTING **ALLIANCES**

Citizens celebrated when soldiers from Laurent-Désiré Kabila's Alliance of Democratic Forces for the Liberation of Congo (AFDLC) marched unopposed into the DRC's capital Kinshasa in May 1997 (below). Formed less than a year earlier, in October 1996, the army was a loose coalition of mainly Rwandan, Ugandan, Burundian, and Congolese dissidents who opposed Mobutu Sese Seko. After a short-lived peace, many of these same soldiers turned against Kabila, initiating the Second Congo War.

The end of apartheid

Equality comes to South Africa

The steady growth of opposition to apartheid in South Africa from the 1970s onwards showed that "people power" – combined with international support – could bring down even the most oppressive of regimes.

△ **Men of the moment**
Nelson Mandela and F.W. de Klerk join hands in unity in 1994. A year earlier, both men were awarded the Nobel Peace Prize for their efforts to remake South Africa.

The first two decades of apartheid (see pp. 254–55) had been marked by largely peaceful protest and acts of defiance. The next 20 years, however, were marked by increasing levels of direct confrontation, violence, and an ever-more confident and organized anti-apartheid movement.

The people fight back

By the beginning of the 1970s, it was clear that the nature of South African resistance to apartheid was changing. Government crackdowns in the mid-1960s had seen many leaders of the outlawed African National Congress (ANC), the main anti-apartheid organization, arrested or exiled. These events opened the way for a new generation of activists, such as the charismatic Steve Biko (see box, below) and other figures in the Black Consciousness Movement (BCM). As a grassroots operation, the BCM preached the gospel of resistance in Bantustans and townships, convincing Black South Africans that they could be liberated through their own efforts. It was a way of thinking that influenced one of the anti-apartheid movement's defining incidents.

In June 1976, a series of protests by Black students in the Johannesburg township of Soweto escalated from a demonstration about their curriculum into a challenge against apartheid itself. Government troops opened fire on the "Soweto Uprising" demonstrators, killing at least 176 of them. In response, the ANC reactivated its armed wing, *Umkhonto we Sizwe* ("Spear of the Nation"), which had been unused since the imprisonment of its leader Nelson Mandela in 1963.

Support from around the world

With anti-apartheid groups within South Africa becoming more assertive, populist protest movements outside Africa joined the fight for freedom. In October 1970, around 10,000 people gathered in London's Trafalgar Square to protest against British arms sales to South Africa. Throughout the 1980s, activists in the UK, the Netherlands, and the US ran a concerted campaign to protest against the energy company Shell's activities in South Africa. In the UK alone, the "Boycott Shell" movement contributed to the company losing almost 7 per cent of its share of the petrol market – a deficit that was in part passed on to the South African government in the form of lost taxes and revenues.

Anti-apartheid agitation was not confined to protest groups and activist organizations. In 1973, the United Nations' General Assembly officially denounced apartheid, and in 1977 the UN Security Council introduced an embargo on arms sales to South Africa.

As the 1970s ended, South Africa's government was increasingly embattled. The anti-apartheid movement was not deterred by the white authorities' violent attempts to repress protest, and international pressure for change was mounting. From 1983, prime minister P.W. Botha began to introduce piecemeal reforms, including offering limited voting rights to Asian and "Coloured" (the apartheid-era term for people of mixed race) South Africans. But when the US and the British Commonwealth introduced damaging trade

THE "FATHER OF **BLACK CONSCIOUSNESS**"

Born in South Africa's Eastern Cape in 1946, Stephen Bantu Biko, or Steve Biko, rose to prominence in the late 1960s as an anti-apartheid student activist. He was a leading light of the Black Consciousness Movement, which rejected the support of white liberals (believing it paternalistic and condescending) and held that Black people alone should solve their own problems. Biko's uncompromising stance, combined with his grassroots activism in student, community, and health programmes, made him a target. After his arrest in September 1977, he was beaten to death while in custody. Biko's funeral (pictured here) became one of the defining moments of the anti-apartheid movement at home and around the world.

> "We are starting a **new era** of **hope**, **reconciliation**, and **nation building**. We are **one nation**."

NELSON MANDELA, 1994

△ **Democracy in action**
Citizens queue to vote at a Soweto primary school in April 1994. This was South Africa's first democratic election and the first one where all Black people were allowed to vote.

and business sanctions against South Africa in 1985, it was clear that apartheid's time was running out. Faced with economic, political, and even cultural isolation across the globe, South Africa's government began to acknowledge that only a constitutional revolution would work.

The birth of democracy

In 1990, President F.W. de Klerk lifted the 30-year ban on the ANC and other anti-apartheid groups and released political prisoners, notably Nelson Mandela after 27 years in jail. A dialogue was opened between the government and opposition parties, mainly the ANC, and De Klerk and Mandela drew up a new constitution as apartheid laws were repealed and Black people were given the vote. In 1993, Mandela and

de Klerk were awarded the Nobel Peace Prize "for their work for the peaceful termination of the apartheid regime, and for laying the foundations for a new democratic South Africa".

The country held its first democratic elections in April 1994. The ANC took 62 per cent of the vote and headed a new coalition government of national unity that also included the National Party and the mainly Zulu Inkatha Freedom Party. On 10 May 1994, Nelson Mandela was inaugurated as South Africa's first Black president.

▷ **Champion of change**
A committed Black rights activist, Winnie Mandela was Nelson Mandela's second wife (from 1958–96) and was known to her supporters as "the mother of the nation".

Peace advocate
Wearing his trademark colourful silk shirt and HIV/AIDS-awareness pin, Nelson Mandela appears in 2000 at peace talks for Burundi, which was then engaged in a bitter civil war. Even in his 80s, Mandela played an active role in world politics.

Nelson Mandela

South Africa's first Black president

Nelson Mandela was a lawyer, an activist, a prisoner, a president, and a celebrity. This transformative politician is still revered globally as a symbol of freedom and as a founder of modern South Africa.

Born into a powerful Xhosa family in 1918, Nelson Mandela attended Christian missionary schools, and trained as a lawyer in Johannesburg. As a young man, he became interested in the politics of African nationalism and joined the youth wing of the African National Congress (ANC) in 1944 (see pp. 254–55).

Mandela's rise up the ANC's ranks came as South Africa – then a self-governing dominion of the British Empire – moved towards apartheid. Mandela spoke at rallies and pushed for radical action. As repression intensified, he became an anti-apartheid figurehead, and was repeatedly arrested and imprisoned.

Hardship and triumph

Mandela grew increasingly determined to fight for freedom. In 1960, police killed 69 protesters in Sharpeville, near Johannesburg, and the following year Mandela co-founded *Umkhonto we Sizwe* ("Spear of the Nation"), the ANC's paramilitary wing. The group launched acts of sabotage, and in 1962 Mandela received military training in Morocco and Ethiopia. Later that year, he was arrested in South Africa. Mandela turned his trial into political theatre, declaring in a three-hour speech that equality was "an ideal for which I am prepared to die". He avoided the death penalty, but was imprisoned in 1962 and sentenced to life imprisonment in 1964.

By the 1980s, internal resistance was growing and South Africa was an international pariah. Mandela had remained popular throughout his imprisonment, and was finally released in 1990. He became president of the ANC in 1991 and negotiated the end of apartheid with President F.W. De Klerk (see pp. 268–69).

Elected the country's first Black president in 1994, Mandela prioritized the dismantling of apartheid through racial reconciliation. He appointed politicians from De Klerk's National Party to government roles and created a Truth and Reconciliation Commission to investigate crimes committed by government forces and the ANC.

Nelson Mandela served only one term in office, stepping down in 1999 to campaign and raise money for rural development and HIV/AIDS treatment. But the impact of this freedom fighter turned man of peace is unparalleled.

△ **Young activist**
A young Mandela wears a beaded necklace and a kaross (blanket) during his time in hiding from the police in South Africa in 1961.

▽ **A free man**
Mandela and his then wife Winnie greet crowds in Cape Town on his 1990 release from prison. Mandela spent over 27 years behind bars.

1918 Rolihlahla Mandela is born – he is given the name Nelson by a school teacher

1961 Co-founds *Umkhonto we Sizwe*, the ANC's military wing

1990 Release from prison, after massive global controversy at his imprisonment

1994 Elected president in South Africa's first election with universal suffrage

1944 Joins the youth wing of the African National Congress (ANC)

1964 Imprisoned for life for sabotage and conspiracy to overthrow the government

1991 Becomes president of the ANC and leads negotiations with the government

2013 Dies after a respiratory infection at home in Johannesburg

6

Contemporary Africa

1994–

Contemporary Africa

Huge strides towards African freedom and self-determination were made in the 20th century. In its closing decades, two events became beacons of hope: Zimbabwe's hard-won independence in 1980 and the 1994 victory of the African National Congress in South Africa's first free elections.

Many nations have thrived in the modern age. Countries including Botswana and Mauritius have been democratic for the entirety of their postcolonial history, and cities such as Lagos, Cairo, and Kinshasa (see pp. 284–85) have become global powerhouses. Organizations like the African Union have sought to increase collaboration between African nations, while major global events such as the 2010 World Cup, hosted in South Africa, have put the continent in the spotlight.

Growth and challenges

Progress has been remarkable. Child mortality across the continent has fallen consistently for 50 years, and healthy life expectancy has increased. The spread of internet access and peer-to-peer payment networks has helped drive growth. Dams, railway and bridge building, land reclamation, and new data centres and undersea internet cables have transformed physical and digital spaces. Some projects have been supported by foreign investment, particularly from China, indicating both the continued impact of neocolonialism and the recalibration of world power.

However, Africa's difficulties have not vanished. Rwanda suffered a genocidal conflict in 1994 and other nations have endured civil wars or long-standing insurgencies. Much of Central Africa remains under authoritarian rule. The Arab Spring of the early 2010s led to elections in Tunisia and Egypt, but popular movements have often met with mixed success, resulting in civil wars in countries like Mali and Libya. Diseases including malaria have wreaked havoc, although COVID-19 deaths in Africa have so far been among the world's lowest. Despite these ongoing challenges, and growing threats such as climate change – which brought severe floods to West Africa in 2022 and Libya in 2023 – Africa's power and potential continues to rise. By 2100, it is estimated that a third of the world's population will be African, as the continent takes centre stage.

New voices

Since the 1990s, African voices have been growing in prominence, with talented artists, film-makers, athletes, and leaders pushing boundaries and setting new standards. Musical genres such as Nigeria's Afrobeats, Senegal's *mbalax*, and Egypt's *mahraganat* (or electro-*shaabi*) are increasingly influential, while African artists are reinvigorating existing traditions, often combining African heritage with new technology, as in Nigerian Dennis Osadebe's pop art-inspired "Afrofuturist" paintings. In cinema, Nigeria's Nollywood is Africa's best known, but across the continent film-makers, performers, actors, and comedians are exploding into the global mainstream. Authors are exploring African identities and choosing to write in their own languages rather than English, while athletes have dominated sports including football and distance running – as the continent continues to nurture and celebrate African talent.

◁ **Magodi-Noxolo (2020) by South African ceramicist Zizipho Poswa**

1994 Nelson Mandela becomes South Africa's first Black president

1997 Zaire's long-standing President Mobutu is ousted and the nation becomes the Democratic Republic of the Congo

1999 Rwanda's National Unity and Reconciliation Commission is formed

2001 The African Union forms. It now has 55 member states across the continent

2002 The First Ivorian Civil War begins after a military rebellion

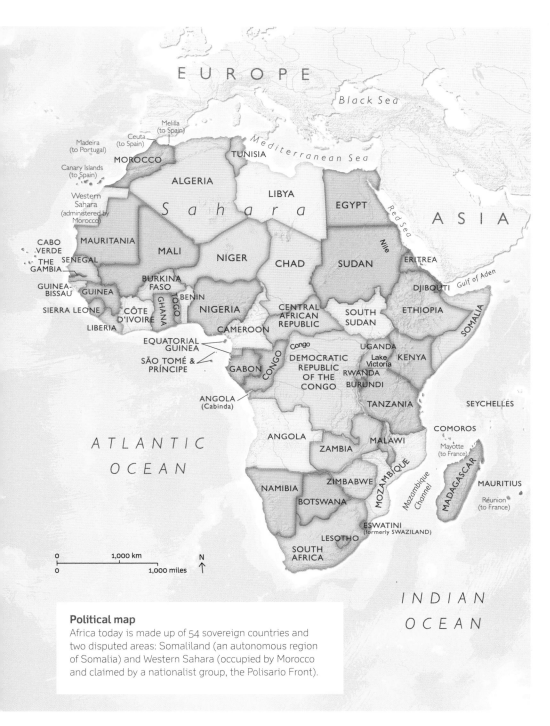

EUROPE

Black Sea

Madeira
(to Portugal)

Melilla
(to Spain)

Ceuta
(to Spain)

Canary Islands
(to Spain)

Mediterranean Sea

MOROCCO

TUNISIA

ALGERIA

LIBYA

EGYPT

Red Sea

ASIA

S a h a r a

Western
Sahara
(administered by
Morocco)

CABO
VERDE

MAURITANIA

MALI

NIGER

CHAD

SUDAN

Nile

ERITREA

THE
GAMBIA

SENEGAL

GUINEA-
BISSAU

GUINEA

BURKINA
FASO

DJIBOUTI

Gulf of Aden

SIERRA LEONE

CÔTE
D'IVOIRE

GHANA

TOGO

BENIN

NIGERIA

CENTRAL
AFRICAN
REPUBLIC

SOUTH
SUDAN

ETHIOPIA

SOMALIA

LIBERIA

CAMEROON

EQUATORIAL
GUINEA

SÃO TOMÉ &
PRÍNCIPE

GABON

CONGO

Congo

DEMOCRATIC
REPUBLIC
OF THE
CONGO

UGANDA

Lake
Victoria

RWANDA

BURUNDI

KENYA

ANGOLA
(Cabinda)

TANZANIA

SEYCHELLES

ATLANTIC
OCEAN

ANGOLA

ZAMBIA

MALAWI

COMOROS

Mayotte
(to France)

MADAGASCAR

MOZAMBIQUE

*Mozambique
Channel*

MAURITIUS

Réunion
(to France)

NAMIBIA

ZIMBABWE

BOTSWANA

ESWATINI
(formerly SWAZILAND)

LESOTHO

SOUTH
AFRICA

0   1,000 km
0   1,000 miles   N

INDIAN
OCEAN

Political map
Africa today is made up of 54 sovereign countries and
two disputed areas: Somaliland (an autonomous region
of Somalia) and Western Sahara (occupied by Morocco
and claimed by a nationalist group, the Polisario Front).

▲ The Hillbrow Tower, Johannesburg, South Africa

▲ Fans at the 2022 Africa Cup of Nations

▲ Runway show at Lagos Fashion Week, 2022

2009 Islamist militant
group Boko Haram begins
an insurgency in Nigeria

2013 The Ebola virus claims victims
in West Africa, particularly in Sierra
Leone, Liberia, and Guinea

2022 COP27 is held in Egypt, the
first time the UN climate change
conference has been held in Africa

2008 Africa's population
reaches a billion; by 2023,
it is nearly 1.5 billion

2011 After decades of
conflict, South Sudan gains
its independence from Sudan

2019 The largest-yet Africa
Cup of Nations, held in
Egypt, is won by Algeria

2023 African Union made a permanent
member of the G20 (or Group of 20) forum
for international economic cooperation

Reclaiming cultures

Preservation, renewal, and reinvention

During the colonial era, many European powers attempted to suppress the practices of African cultures. Today, people across the continent are reclaiming and reinventing cultures and values via politics, language, and art.

Oppressive colonial policies discouraged the use of African languages, technologies, and artistic expressions, and even after independence, Western cultures and customs continued to spread. However, African cultures have deep roots, and many people have increasingly sought to embrace and redefine these long-standing practices.

Some peoples have consciously chosen to use their own languages, with the Khoi and San languages added to the South African curriculum, and Kenyan author Ngũgĩ wa Thiong'o eschewing English for Gikuyu. In Kenya, the Maasai are creating a digital archive of their entire community's shared intellectual property and language. Other campaigns include the digtizing of the vast libraries of centuries-old documents that form the Timbuktu Manuscripts of Mali (see pp. 96–97).

The European occupation of African countries led to the theft of many ancient and valuable objects that hold cultural and historical significance for local communities, many of whom are demanding these objects back. Some museums in Europe have begun to return the bronze sculptures looted from Benin (see pp. 128–29) in modern-day Nigeria. Egyptian mummies have been sent back to Egypt from Ireland and the US, and efforts to return other great cultural works, including a Ugandan throne held by the UK, continue.

Elsewhere, art forms are being revitalized. In Bamako in Mali, the *bogolan* custom of producing and dyeing patterned fabric has been recreated and celebrated. In the north of Tanzania, Jita elders are working to restore their cultural heritage, in particular their dance styles. In Port Harcourt and Calabar in Nigeria, projects involving young people have reclaimed the art of mask-making and masquerades, blending historical practices with commentary on contemporary life and politics.

△ **Benin cockerel**
Okukor is one of the Benin Bronzes produced by artisans in the Kingdom of Benin. The British stole the work in 1897, and it was returned to Nigeria in 2021.

◁ **Zulu coronation**
Misuzulu ka Zwelithini is recognized as the king of the Zulu nation at a 2022 ceremony in Durban, the first such Zulu coronation since South Africa became a democracy in 1994.

New forms are also being born from older, existing traditions. Contemporary artists have been inspired by the geometric murals of the Ndebele people of South Africa and the sinuous abstraction of Nigerian uli art, while others have Africanized Western genres such as pop art. The music of nations across Africa has been revived in everything from Cameroonian *makossa* and Ghanaian highlife to Tanzanian *bongo flava*.

Political renewal

Pan-African collaboration is an important part of the reclaiming of the continent's cultures. The African Union (see pp. 304–305) gathers heads of state, but grassroots efforts to foster unity are just as vital. Zimbabwe's Pan African Women's Organization brings together women from across Africa, while events such as the Panafrican Film and Television Festival of Ouagadougou (FESPACO) gather creative voices. Youth movements, meanwhile, show a new generation eager to challenge the status quo, with the Ghana Youth Party (GYP) campaigning on unemployment and access to education, and *Y'en a Marre* ("Fed Up"), a group of rappers and journalists, mobilizing the young Senegalese to vote on issues such as land reform.

Campaigns for land rights and sovereignty strive to reclaim nations that vanished from the map when Europeans redrew African borders at the end of the 19th century. Numerous African peoples are advocating for the autonomy of their native land, with South Sudan's 2011 independence from Sudan a significant result. Groups such as the Oromo and Tigray (Ethiopia), Kabyle (Algeria), Igbo (Nigeria), and Tuareg (Mali) are pushing for independence via a mix of strikes, advocacy, and military means. The Canary Islands, one of a handful of territories still under European control, has an active nationalist movement. These efforts, and many other drives to preserve and renew African cultures, are ongoing.

△ **Uli-inspired tapestry**
The Beauty Within, a 2019 tapestry by Nigerian artist Jennifer Ogochukwu Okpoko, recalls *uli* art, in which Igbo women paint curves and other shapes on people and buildings.

▽ **Ndebele art**
Artist Esther Mahlangu is pictured in front of her home in Mpumalanga, South Africa. Her colourful, geometric works are inspired by Ndebele jewellery, clothing, and wall paintings.

Beadwork

Crafts from across the continent

In Africa, beadwork takes many forms. Beads can be sewn onto backings of fabric or leather to create tunics, collars, hats, stools, and aprons, or strung on thin wire for support, as in Maasai collars and Dinka bodices. The most intricate beading techniques are used to create free-standing pieces, such as Mfengu necklaces.

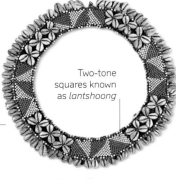

Two-tone squares known as *lantshoong*

△ **Kuba collar**
This collar, made by the Kuba people who live in the Democratic Republic of the Congo, utilizes glass beads and cowrie shells attached to a leather backing.

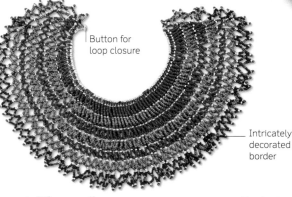

Button for loop closure

Intricately decorated border

△ **Mfengu collar**
Ingqosha (collar) necklaces are worn by the Mfengu people, a Xhosa-speaking group who live in southeastern South Africa.

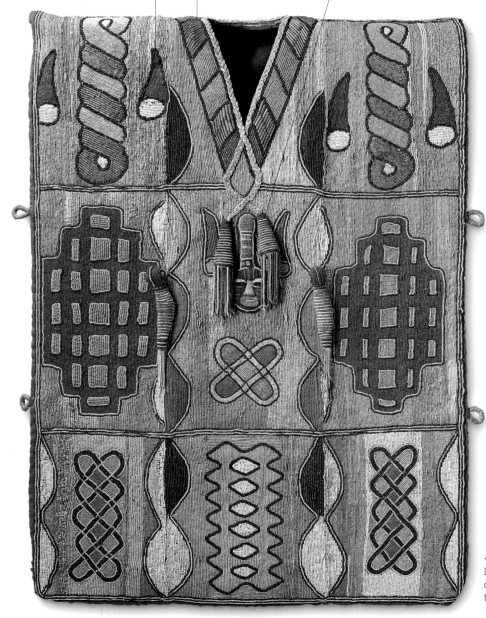

Animal horns said to give *oba* ability to speak with authority

Neck design uses rare African jasper beads and the tiniest seed beads

Crowns on either side of appliquéd face symbolize continuity of *oba*'s office

Geometric patterns symbolize balance

Face of Orunmila, deity of wisdom and divination

Top-knots often represent a town, city, or people

△ **Prestige cap**
Made by an artist from the Pende people of the Democratic Republic of the Congo, this *misango mapende* (royal crown) indicates high authority.

△ **Oba's crown**
This mid-19th century *oba*'s royal crown from Nigeria was created from a metal frame covered with printed cotton, onto which polished glass beads were embroidered.

◁ **Royal Yoruba tunic**
Dating from around 1900 and intended to be worn by the *oba*, or king, this Yoruba v-neck tunic from Nigeria is covered with thousands of glass beads, expressing the wearer's high status.

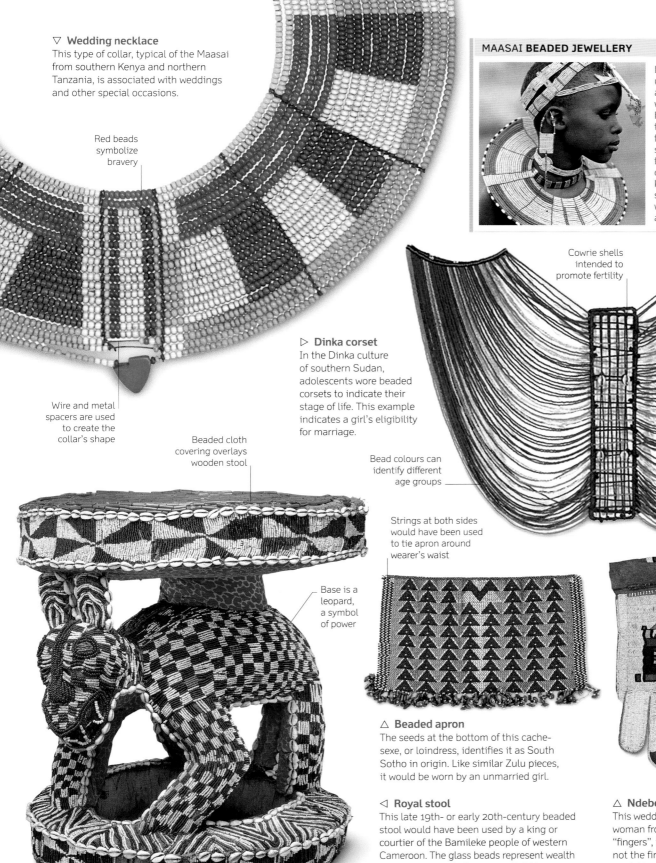

▽ Wedding necklace
This type of collar, typical of the Maasai from southern Kenya and northern Tanzania, is associated with weddings and other special occasions.

Red beads symbolize bravery

Wire and metal spacers are used to create the collar's shape

MAASAI BEADED JEWELLERY

Historically, the Maasai used local materials, such as shells, ivory, bone, wood, clay, copper, or brass, for their beadwork; today, glass beads are favoured. Colours have symbolic meanings derived from the Maasai's deep connection with cattle, a key source of wealth and sustenance; for example, white represents purity by association with milk.

Cowrie shells intended to promote fertility

▷ Dinka corset
In the Dinka culture of southern Sudan, adolescents wore beaded corsets to indicate their stage of life. This example indicates a girl's eligibility for marriage.

Bead colours can identify different age groups

Leather (goatskin) backing

Beaded cloth covering overlays wooden stool

Strings at both sides would have been used to tie apron around wearer's waist

Base is a leopard, a symbol of power

△ Beaded apron
The seeds at the bottom of this cache-sexe, or loindress, identifies it as South Sotho in origin. Like similar Zulu pieces, it would be worn by an unmarried girl.

Small additional finger

◁ Royal stool
This late 19th- or early 20th-century beaded stool would have been used by a king or courtier of the Bamileke people of western Cameroon. The glass beads represent wealth and the cowrie shells express fertility.

△ Ndebele apron
This wedding apron, made by a Ndebele woman from South Africa, has seven "fingers", indicating that the owner was not the first wife; a first wife's apron would include only five "fingers".

Religions

Africa's faiths, old and new

Scores, if not hundreds, of Indigenous belief systems exist in Africa. Their tenets vary greatly, but they share common elements. Chief among these is a belief in a supreme deity. Its name varies from place to place. The Yoruba of West Africa call it Olodumare, for example; the Ruvu and Kamba people of East Africa refer to it as Mulungu. As in the ancient Greek, Roman, and Egyptian religions, the supreme deity often oversees lesser gods of the harvest, fertility, war, and so on.

Like most faiths, Africa's Indigenous belief systems are intensely spiritual, their aim being for believers to connect directly with the divine. Ancestor veneration is widely practised, as are forms of belief in which rivers, trees, and other parts of the natural world are thought to be possessed by protective spirits whose favour is sought through offerings, prayers, and sacrifice. Often, contact with the divine or spirit world is made through intermediaries such as shamans, the *babalawos* ("medicine men") of West Africa, and the *Sangoma* healers of Southern Africa.

Fusion of beliefs

Today, fewer than 10 per cent of Africans practise Indigenous faiths, but research shows that up to half of the populations of some states look to ancestors or spirits for protection from harm. Many Africans have faith in the protective power of charms and amulets, or juju. Indigenous beliefs are embedded in African cultures and hugely affect the way the continent's two largest religions, Islam and Christianity, are practised.

△ **A celebration of creation**
Each October, the Yoruba of Ife, Nigeria, celebrate *Olojo* ("the day of the first dawn"). After a seven-day seclusion to commune with his ancestors for the welfare of the people, Ife's *ooni* (king) leads ritual processions through the city.

△ **Divine intermediaries**
Male and female priests, called *saltigues*, preside over the religious ceremonies of the Serer people of Senegal, such as at the *Xooy* ceremony, where they predict the future and commune with their creator-god, *Roog*. The *saltigues*' skills include casting cowrie shells and divining the meaning of the shapes they form.

△ **Woman of faith**
The dolls, beads, and carved stick carried by this priestess are totems in West Africa's Vodun religion. This faith's tenets of ancestor veneration and spiritualism (communicating with the spirits of the dead) reached the Americas as "Voodoo", via the slave trade.

"We may have **different religions**… but we all belong to **one human race**."

KOFI ANNAN, 2016

Of the two, Islam has been more accepting towards Indigenous beliefs. The *jinn*, a protective spirit revered by North Africa's Amazigh (Berber) people, became the "genie" of popular legend following the arrival of Arab Muslims from the 7th century. Islam has become the most popular faith in North and East Africa, with around 450 million followers. Devotees of both Islam and Christianity seek a personal relationship with their God and value the spiritual dimension, just as those who practise Indigenous beliefs do.

However, when Christianity spread in Africa during colonial times, its adherents openly disapproved of Africa's Indigenous belief systems. The hierarchy of the Catholic Church, in particular, disliked the more "democratic" approach of Indigenous beliefs, which allowed all followers to connect to the divine. But Indigenous beliefs persist, and an increasing number of so-called "breakaway" Christian churches have emerged to accommodate this. The Catholic Legio Maria Church and the Protestant Church of Christ in Africa both recognize ancestor veneration and polygamy among their congregations, for example. Pentecostalism, with its dynamic, energetic emphasis on the power of the Holy Spirit, is increasingly popular among Africa's 600 million Christians.

Africa's many religions and belief systems have developed in ways that are unique to the continent. Their differences are numerous, but it is their similarities, above all their shared spirituality, that is helping to ensure their continued success.

△ **Turning towards God**
Sudan has one of the world's largest Sufi communities. Sufism is a mystical branch of Islam. Its adherents achieve divine, spiritual ecstasy by spinning themselves into a trance-like state. These are the famous "whirling dervishes".

△ **A humble offering**
The *Irreechaa* is a ceremony performed by the Oromo people of Ethiopia and northern Kenya at the end of winter to thank the chief god, *Waaqa Tokkicha*, for the previous year's good fortune. Those who practise the *Waaqeffanna* faith believe lesser gods possess their bodies in order to communicate with them.

△ **A fusion of faiths**
South Africa's Nazareth Baptist Church fuses Zulu culture with Christianity. Founded around 1910 by the faith healer and preacher Isaiah Shembe, its roots in Indigenous beliefs are evident in its Pentecostal-like, ecstatic approach to worship.

Protecting environments
The challenge of climate change

Africa accounts for the smallest share of greenhouse gas emissions compared to regions such as the US, China, and Europe. Yet the continent has suffered some of the worst effects of climate change, and has begun searching for solutions.

Global warming from climate change is occurring across almost all the Earth's surface, causing extreme events, including flooding, heatwaves, and drought. Africa is responsible for less than 4 per cent of global greenhouse gas emissions, yet is the most vulnerable region in the world to the changing climate, according to the UN's Environment Programme.

Perhaps the most significant impact of global warming in the continent is desertification, the process by which vegetation in arid and semi-arid lands, such as grasslands or shrublands, decreases, degrading the productivity of the land. The most affected areas include the Sahel region to the south of the Sahara and the Congo Basin in Central Africa.

Desertification occurs as a result of multiple interacting causes. In addition to anthropogenic (human-caused) climate change, factors include natural fluctuations in climate, deforestation, over-grazing and over-cultivation of crops, poor irrigation, and resource exploitation. Desertification leads to hotter and drier conditions, and more frequent and more severe droughts and famines. These conditions exacerbate existing food security issues by negatively impacting crop yields and livestock health. To help combat desertification, the African Union (see pp. 304–305) adopted an initiative in 2007 known as the Great Green Wall. This mass planting of trees across the Sahel aims to prevent expansion of the Sahara and increase the amount of arable land.

Ecosystems and weather patterns

A serious issue in regions like the Congo Basin, where some of the largest rainforests in the world are found, is deforestation. Vast areas of this woodland have been cleared for logging, mining, agriculture, roads, hunting, and other purposes. This has resulted in the loss of habitat for many species and poses a global threat to the world's ecosystem, since rainforests are vital for trapping carbon that would otherwise be released into the atmosphere. The Democratic Republic of the Congo (DRC), home to the majority of the Congo Basin rainforest, has made commitments to

▽ **Great Green Wall**
The "greening" of a strip of land across Africa from the Atlantic Ocean to the Red Sea will help to slow the progress of desertification and mitigate the effects of climate change.

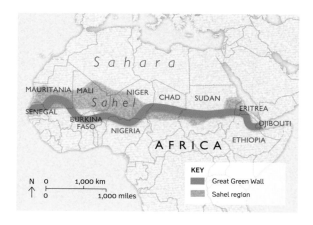

◁ **Sustainable agriculture**
Women tend to crops in Senegal near the Great Green Wall. The initiative includes not only planting new trees, but also improving soils and setting up community gardens.

protect its rainforests by replanting trees and banning the export of raw timber. In other schemes, the DRC's government has granted local communities large tracts of land to manage sustainably, helping to halt the decline of the forest and alleviating poverty.

Climate change also increases the risk of floods, storms, and other natural disasters, which can cause famines, poverty, and the displacement of populations, putting pressure on neighbouring lands. In Nigeria, which has experienced increasingly widespread flooding in recent years, the government has set a target to cut emissions by 45 per cent by 2030 and initiated measures such as tree planting and land reclamation. Farmers in countries including Kenya, Uganda, Senegal, and Ethiopia have adopted

solar-powered irrigation systems, which reduce power usage while increasing yields, while South Africa has invested in renewable energy production, especially solar and wind. Rwanda plans to connect households to solar mini-grids.

Battery minerals

As the world moves to electric vehicles, demand has grown for minerals used in their batteries, such as cobalt, lithium, and nickel. Africa is home to many of these minerals; the DRC, for example, produces over 70 per cent of the world's cobalt. The country has cooperated with neighbouring Zambia on a "Green Minerals Strategy". The aims of the agreement are to reduce the environmental impacts of mining and to benefit local communities by developing the capacity not just to extract the minerals, but to assemble the batteries as well.

△ **Eroded soil**
This landscape in Kenya shows the effects of soil erosion. Activities such as building terraces, planting trees, and installing grass strips can help to reduce the problem.

"Desertification... is the greatest environmental challenge of our time."

LUC GNACADJA, BENINESE POLITICIAN, 2010

▷ **Panning for minerals**
Miners wash metal bowlfuls of sandy earth in the Lukushi River in the Democratic Republic of the Congo, looking for black nuggets of cassiterite (tin oxide ore).

Lagos

An iconic African megacity

Nigeria's unofficial capital, Lagos, is one of the world's largest urban areas. This thriving metropolis is an economic and cultural giant – and is so populous that it has been deemed one of Africa's three megacities.

The greatest cities of Africa are so large that it can be hard to know where they end and their hinterlands begin. However, Lagos in Nigeria (with a population of around 16 million), Kinshasa in the Democratic Republic of the Congo (16 million), and Cairo in Egypt (22 million) all qualify as megacities – urban areas with a population over 10 million. Megacities like these attract people and investment, but their rapid growth has brought inequalities and challenges in infrastructure, health, and education.

Lagos, the largest city in Nigeria, is a prime example of an African megacity. It began as Eko, a Yoruba fishing village on Lagos Island. Portuguese traders called it Lagos, from the Portuguese word for "lakes", and from the 17th century it became an increasingly important port for the trade in palm oil and enslaved people (see box, opposite). It stayed under Yoruba rule until the British occupied it by force in the mid 19th century and made it the capital of the colony of Nigeria.

Lagos expanded further under British rule, and, by the time Nigeria won its independence in 1960, it was a sizeable coastal city surrounded by villages. Crude oil supercharged its development: in the 1970s, Lagos's role in oil exports from the Niger Delta saw its population reach two million as it expanded onto neighbouring islands and the mainland. Eager to spread Nigeria's development more evenly, the government moved the capital to Abuja in 1991, but Lagos continued to thrive, and today stretches for more than 1,000 sq km (386 sq miles).

Challenges and successes

The development of Lagos was rapid but often haphazard. The British were focused on extracting resources, rather than building a sustainable city. The 1970s crude oil rush saw hastily erected warehouses crowd the shore and unplanned suburbs link the city with the villages around it. As a result, Lagos's infrastructure is uneven, and has struggled to keep up with its growing population. Today, congestion is common, and despite recent bridge and motorway construction, *keke* motorized tricycles and yellow *danfo* minibuses crowd the streets, as pedestrians and street vendors weave through the traffic.

Neighbourhoods such as Ikoyi have skyscraping luxury apartments and expensive boutiques, and if Lagos were an independent nation it would have one of Africa's biggest economies. Industries such as car manufacture, pharmaceuticals, software, electronics, and the oil sector are booming. Yet many residents

▽ **Crowded city**
Lagos's streets are often packed with bumper-to-bumper traffic. The yellow minibuses known as *danfo* are a city institution.

live in poor-quality housing with a lack of basic services such as piped water, healthcare, and education. In 2020, security forces opened fire on protesters against police brutality, while in 2023 currency shortages led to riots, and tensions continue between groups such as the Yoruba, Igbo, and Hausa.

For all its flaws, however, Lagos is a thriving cultural hub. Dishes from across Nigeria such as *eba* (a fried cassava snack) and *egusi* (melon-seed soup) are sold in restaurants and by street vendors and music is everywhere – Afrobeats stars Wizkid and Tiwa Savage were born in the city. Lagos Fashion Week is Africa's biggest fashion event, while Nollywood, Nigeria's film industry, is centred on Lagos. The city's vibrant locations have defined an industry that produces over 2,000 films a year.

Cities of the future

Lagos's historic expansion may be just a taster for what is to come. At current rates, its population could hit 90 million by 2100. And Lagos is not alone. It and fellow megacities Cairo (the largest city in the Arab world) and Kinshasa (the world's largest French-speaking city) are set to be joined by other megacities.

GROWTH OF **A PORT CITY**

This print shows the port of Lagos in 1885. In the first half of the 19th century, Lagos was a Yoruba port that was integral to the trade in enslaved people and palm oil. In 1851, the British navy bombarded the city, ending the slave trade and installing a new Yoruba ruler, Akitoye, who had been ousted as *oba* by his nephew. In 1861, Britain invaded and annexed the city as a British colony. The British seized the remainder of Nigeria in 1886 with Lagos, now the colony's capital, gaining infrastructure such as railways and street lighting.

Dar Es Salaam (Tanzania), Khartoum (Sudan), Nairobi (Kenya), and Luanda (Angola) are all due to pass 10 million inhabitants by 2050, as the urban population grows faster in Africa than on any other continent.

This growth will power economies and reshape global politics. Megacities will face familiar problems such as inequality and challenges with infrastructure and healthcare, as well as new ones, such as climate change. Investment and planning is critical if these cities of the future are to fulfil their potential.

▽ **Landmark bridge**
This cable-stayed bridge stretches for 1.36 km (0.84 miles) and connects the island neighbourhoods of Lekki and Ikoyi.

Sport

Excelling at a range of sports

Africa has a long history of sport. Ancient Egyptians held swimming and athletics contests, while modern North African *fantasia* festivals of horsemanship have roots in ancient Numidia. Many sports were martial, such as the *dambe* boxing of Nigeria's Hausa and Angolan *engolo*, which developed into capoeira (a martial art that combines dance, acrobatics, and music).

Football has also been adopted. The Africa Cup of Nations is the continent's national tournament, pulling in millions of viewers. Successful men's teams include Cameroon, Egypt, Nigeria, Ghana, and Morocco – the first African side to reach the World Cup semi-finals, in 2022. Egypt's Mohamed Salah, Cameroon's Samuel Eto'o, and George Weah (from 2018, Liberia's president) rank among the world's greatest players.

In athletics, East Africans dominate long-distance running, with Eliud Kipchoge of Kenya and Haile Gebrselassie and Kenenisa Bekele of Ethiopia setting multiple world records and winning several Olympic golds each. Other top athletes include triple and long jumper Hugues Fabrice Zango of Burkina Faso, and Kenyan middle-distance runner Faith Kipyegon.

Nigeria, the Democratic Republic of the Congo (DRC), Sudan, Senegal, and Cameroon are key basketball nations. As with football, many of the finest athletes have pursued their career overseas: in the United States' National Basketball Association (NBA), top players such as Hakeem Olajuwon of Nigeria, who played in the 1980s and '90s, and Dikembe Mutombo of the DRC, who played in the 1990s and 2000s, led

△ **Biniam Girmay (Eritrea)**
Eritrean road cyclist Biniam Girnay was African Cyclist of the Year in 2021, 2022, and 2023. At the 2022 *Giro d'Italia*, he triumphed in a Grand Tour stage and the 196-km (122-mile)-long stage 10 after a sprint finish. In 2023, he won a Tour de Suisse stage.

△ **Tobi Amusan (Nigeria)**
Oluwatobiloba Ayomide "Tobi" Amusan is the World, Commonwealth, and African Champion in the 100 metres hurdles. She became the first athlete from Nigeria to win gold at the 2022 World Athletics Championships, setting a new world record of 12.12 seconds in the semi-final, followed by a 12.06 in the final.

△ **Africa Cup of Nations**
Africa's national football tournament, which takes place every two years, is popular on the continent and around the globe. Senegal (pictured) beat Egypt in the 2023 men's event, while South Africa defeated Morocco in the 2022 women's final.

"I am running to **make history**, to show that no human is **limited**."

ELIUD KIPCHOGE, KENYAN MARATHON RUNNER, 2019

the way for current stars such as Cameroonian Joel Embiid of the Philadelphia Sixers. The NBA is also a backer of the Basketball Africa League.

Cricket is popular in some nations that were British colonies, such as South Africa, Zimbabwe, and Namibia. South Africa has won several international tournaments, including the Champions Trophy in 1998. The country hosted the World Cup in 2003 and has its own T20 league. South Africa is also a global force in rugby union, and has triumphed in three World Cups. Namibia, Kenya, and Zimbabwe are increasingly competitive.

Wrestling and boxing are deeply rooted in African cultures, particularly in Senegal and Ghana, respectively. The wrestling style focuses on grappling. In West Africa in particular, competitions are held at festivals with drums and dances. Africans have also fought in Greco-Roman-style wrestling events including the Olympics. In boxing, some of the most successful African fighters on the global stage include Nigeria's Hogan Bassey and Dick Tiger, who were world champions in the 1950s and '60s. In the 1980s and '90s, Azumah Nelson of Ghana won multiple belts. Tennis is less popular, but Africa has produced some notable players, including Tunisian Ons Jabeur, the 2022 runner-up at Wimbledon and the US Open.

Many Africans outcompete the rest of the world at events first introduced by colonial powers. But in some countries, a lack of resources means top athletes move overseas to fulfil their sporting potential.

△ **Decorated runner**
In September 2018, Eliud Kipchoge of Kenya was awarded the gold medal at the 45th Berlin Marathon in Berlin, Germany.

△ **Phiwokuhle Mnguni (South Africa)**
Featherweight Mnguni won bronze at the 2022 Commonwealth Games, becoming the first female South African to win a major boxing medal. South Africa has a strong history of boxing – in 2003 Corrie Sanders became WBO World Champion.

△ **Rwanda vs South Sudan**
Kuany Ngor Kuany is pictured in possession for South Sudan's men's national basketball team during qualifiers for the 2023 World Cup. As a relatively new country and one enduring a cycle of war, South Sudan defied expectations by reaching the World Cup. It played alongside Egypt, Angola, Côte d'Ivoire, and Cabo Verde.

△ **Clive Madande (Zimbabwe)**
Madande is a rising star in Zimbabwean cricket. The wicketkeeper and batter, pictured here in Zimbabwe's capital, Harare, has an impressive record in test and one-day matches. He made his international debut for his country's cricket team in June 2022.

Feminisms

Fighting for women's rights

ALBERTINA SISULU
Centenary
2018

Photograph: Sisulu Family Archives
South Africa
Standard Postage

△ **Stamp of approval**
Born in 1918, South Africa's Albertina Sisulu – "Ma Sisulu" – led thousands of women in a march against apartheid laws in 1956.

The struggle for equality for Africa's women has not been one of upward, linear progression. The considerable authority women lost during colonization had to be rewon after it ended, resulting in feminisms that take different forms.

In many African cultures, women customarily wielded power separately from men through familial structures and cultural and economic organizations. European colonizers imposed Victorian-era values of submissive femininity on the societies they controlled, disregarding the central role of women in producing, processing, and buying and selling food, and ignoring their important positions within their communities.

Finding a way to fight back

In response to this erosion of status, many women in Africa joined the anticolonial struggle. The 1929 Aba Women's War (see p. 219) and the 1947–48 Egba Women's uprising in Nigeria (in which women opposed arbitrary taxes imposed on them by the colonial government) are examples of organized grassroots women's resistance. In Somalia, women used their own genre of poetry, *buraanbur,* to express their concerns and aspirations, while in Tanganyika (modern-day Tanzania) women gathered in dance clubs known as *ngoma* to form communal networks through which they could campaign for their political and social rights. This they sometimes did through performances in song and dance – although these were usually dismissed by colonial officials as little more than noisy entertainments.

Women also played an active role in armed uprisings, including Kenya's Mau Mau uprising of 1952–60 (see pp. 222–23), the Algerian War of Independence of 1954–62 (see pp. 234–35), and the

Second *Chimurenga* in Zimbabwe of 1964–79 (see pp. 252–53). The names of political activists and feminists like Funmilayo Ransome-Kuti (Nigeria), Winnie Mandela (South Africa), Graça Machel (Mozambique), Hawo Tako (Somalia), and Aminatou Haidar (Western Sahara) are synonymous with nationalist movements in their countries.

In more recent times, literature has been an important – and often controversial – means of feminist expression. The protagonist of Egyptian novelist Nawal El Saadawi's *Woman at Point Zero* (1974)

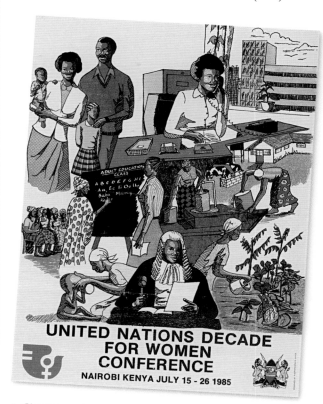

UNITED NATIONS DECADE FOR WOMEN CONFERENCE
NAIROBI KENYA JULY 15 - 26 1985

△ **Charting progress**
Convened for the 10-year anniversary of 1975's International Women's Year, the UN-sponsored "Decade for Women" conference in Kenya drew attention to women's rights in Africa.

"I generally **struggle with labels**, but I acknowledge the importance of **owning the word 'feminism'.**"

MALEBO SEPHODI, SOUTH AFRICAN WRITER

experiences genital mutilation and sexual abuse. Nigerian Flora Nwapa's *Efuru* (1966) depicts an Igbo woman's frustrations with married life. In 1965, Ghana's Ama Ata Aidoo became the first published African female dramatist, and she later went on to serve as her country's Minister for Education. The lives and careers of these women helped to pave the way for post-millennial writers such as Zambia's Namwali Serpell, Zimbabwe's Tsitsi Dangarembga, Côte d'Ivoire's Véronique Tadjo, and Nigeria's Chimamanda Ngozi Adichie (see pp. 302–303).

In the performing arts, the South African singer Miriam Makeba campaigned against apartheid, and for Black civil rights more generally, from the 1960s. She was followed by other outspoken South African singer-activists such as Brenda Fassie and Yvonne Chaka Chaka (see pp. 296–97). The Beninese singer-songwriter Angélique Kidjo is a UNICEF ambassador and a campaigner for the rights of women and girls.

Africa's feminisms

Across the continent, women are working to improve women's lives. In 1982, for example, the Senegalese anti-FGM campaigner Awa Thiam founded the Commission for the Abolition of Sexual Mutilation, while Tanzania's Hope For Girls and Women, set up by Rhobi Samwelly, has been helping girls escape

genital mutilation by providing safe houses and other services since 2017. African women who have been awarded Nobel Prizes include South Africa's Nadine Gordimer (Literature, 1991) and Yemen's Tawakkul Karman along with Liberia's Ellen Johnson Sirleaf (see pp. 290–91) and Leymah Gbowee (Peace, 2011).

African women have adapted feminism to their own contexts. These feminisms take many forms, such as Womanism, which places special focus on the experiences of Black women, and Nego-Feminism, emphasizing negotiation as a way forwards. Africa's feminisms remain irreducibly plural.

△ **Lagos protests**
Protests against Nigeria's notoriously violent Special Anti-Robbery Squad (SARS) took place in 2020. One of SARS' most organized critics was the Feminist Coalition, founded that same year.

ECO **FEMINISM IN AFRICA**

Set up in 1977, the Green Belt Movement (GBM) mobilized women across rural Africa to plant 50 million trees to help prevent desertification. Established in Kenya, it was seen as a threat to male power in a patriarchal society. The movement put its members on the front line of political engagement and protest for decades – none more so than the GBM's visionary founder Wangari Maathai (1940–2011, pictured here). With UN support, her organization expanded across the continent, involving tens of thousands of women in activism. In 2004, Maathai was awarded the Nobel Peace Prize.

Ellen Johnson Sirleaf

Liberian stateswoman and Nobel laureate

The first elected female head of state of an African country, Ellen Johnson Sirleaf served as the 24th president of the Republic of Liberia from 2006–18, becoming an icon of good governance in her country after its long civil war.

Born in the Liberian capital, Monrovia, in 1938, Ellen Johnson Sirleaf was raised by her mother, a teacher, and her father, an attorney, and was educated at the prestigious College of West Africa. Aged 17, she married a young agronomist, James Sirleaf, and the couple moved to the US in 1961. She earned an economics degree from the University of Colorado and a master's in public administration from Harvard University's John F. Kennedy School of Government.

In 1971, Johnson Sirleaf returned to Liberia and was appointed Assistant Minister of Finance a year later. Her public criticism of the government's financial mismanagement attracted national attention and in 1973 she left the Ministry to work for the World Bank in the US. In 1977, she returned to Liberia, becoming Deputy Finance Minister in 1977 and Finance Minister in 1979. The appointment proved short-lived: a coup led by Samuel Doe, a master sergeant, took place, and Johnson Sirleaf was forced to flee the country.

Return to politics

Johnson Sirleaf returned to Monrovia for the general election of 1985, hoping to run for vice president. Instead, she was repeatedly arrested for criticizing Doe's corrupt regime, which had now triggered a period of civil war. During a break in the hostilities in 1997, Sirleaf stood for the presidency, but it was not until the end of the second Liberian Civil War (1999–2003) that she re-entered government. She won the 2005 general election, and in 2006 became the first female president of Liberia, ushering in a period of stability and a time for rebuilding the nation. She established the right to free education for children and passed laws to protect women from domestic violence. After serving a second term from 2011, she retired in 2017; the first peaceful transition of power in her country for 73 years took place in 2018.

△ **Nobel Peace Prize**
In 2011, Johnson Sirleaf was awarded the Nobel Prize for Peace, along with women's rights campaigners Leymah Gbowee of Liberia and Tawakkul Karman of Yemen.

◁ **Campaign for president**
Johnson Sirleaf was energetic in her campaigns for president. She is pictured here running for the first time in 1997, when she earned the epithet "Africa's Iron Lady".

1938 Born in Monrovia

1977 Appointed Deputy Minister of Finance and then Minister of Finance in 1979

1980 Flees Liberia after Samuel Doe seizes power, and works for banks in the US and Kenya

1985 Returns to Liberia and is arrested for criticism of the government; released in 1986 after international pressure

1992 Appointed Director of UN Development Programme's Regional Bureau for Africa

1997 First campaign for president; comes second to eventual winner, Charles Taylor

2005 Wins general election to become president

2011 Jointly awarded the Nobel Peace Prize for work enabling women to participate in the peace-building process

2018 Founds the Ellen Johnson Sirleaf Presidential Center for Women and Development

Cinema

Africa on the big screen

△ **On the move**
Self-financed by director
Djibril Diop Mambéty,
Touki Bouki ("The Journey
of the Hyena") is a
Senegalese road movie.

If early films made by Europeans in and about Africa projected "exotic primitivism", films by Africans have opened up a completely different perspective. They show multiple depictions of Africa from the inside.

Many early "African" films reflected imperialist views. *De Voortrekkers* ("Pioneers", 1915) glorified white colonization in South Africa by the Boers (descendants of Dutch-speaking settlers), while the charismatic presence of Black American actor Paul Robeson in British-Hungarian director Zoltán Korda's *Sanders of the River* (1935) could not save it from promoting white "superiority". Other films, such as *Jim Comes to Jo'burg* (1949), perpetuated this message, as did educational documentaries made by colonial film units.

Independent film-making

After independence, African directors took over the lens, and film became a tool of revolution. In *Sambizanga* (1972), Sarah Maldoror dramatized Angola's anticolonial struggle, while in Senegal, Ousmane Sembène's *Borom Sarret* ("The Wagoner", 1963), and

Black Girl (1966) set the tone for a lifetime of radical film-making. In South Africa, anti-apartheid films like *Mapantsula* (1988) and *Sarafina!* (1993) led the way for post-apartheid films such as Ramadan Suleman's *Zulu Love Letter* (2004), in which two women struggle to come to terms with a legacy of political violence and trauma.

However, independent cinema developed in a piecemeal fashion due to a lack of investment. Funding or support from former colonial powers often came with strings attached: francophone nations could produce more films, but

▷ **Migrant story**
Ousmane Sembène's *Black Girl* follows a Senegalese woman who travels from Dakar to France, where she faces alienation and tragedy.

▷ **Futuristic horror**
Cameroonian director
Jean-Pierre Bekolo describes
his 2005 film *Les Saignantes*
("The Bloodettes") as a "stylized
sci-fi-action-horror hybrid".
The film is a futuristic vision
of female power at play.

> "I believe that **Africans**, in particular, must **reinvent cinema**."

DJIBRIL DIOP MAMBÉTY, SENEGALESE DIRECTOR

productions seen as critical of France were less likely to receive support. Directors such as Safi Faye in Senegal, Gaston Kaboré in Burkina Faso, and Souleymane Cissé in Mali made films distinguished by their meditative concentration on rural life and precolonial knowledge, and were dubbed "return to the source".

There were always many innovators. In Senegal, Djibril Diop Mambéty created a richly surreal world of startling juxtapositions that upended genre expectations. *Touki Bouki* (1973) is fast-paced and youthful, while *Hyenas* (1992) is a revenge tragedy set in the outskirts of Dakar. Guinean Mohamed Camara's *Dakan* ("Destiny", 1997), was the first African film to represent a same-sex love affair.

Contemporary cinema

African film has expanded into genres as diverse as futurism (*Pumzi*, or "Breath", 2009; *District 9*, 2009), LGBTQ+ love (*Rafiki*, 2017; *Inxeba/The Wound*, 2017), romcom (*Tell Me Sweet Something*, 2015), Western (*Five Fingers for Marseilles*, 2017); thriller (*Nairobi Half Life*, 2012), political satire (*The Night of Truth*, 2004) and dramatized documentary (*Otelo Burning*, 2011).

Migration has meant film-makers of African descent are active throughout the diaspora. European-based directors include French-Mauritanian Med Hondo, (*Soleil Ô*, or "Oh, Sun", 1970); Franco-Algerian Mounia Meddour (*Papicha*, or "Rebel Girl", 2019); and British/ Ghanaian John Akomfrah, the UK's representative at the 60th Venice Biennale in 2024. Film-makers born in one part of Africa but living and working in another include Mauritanian-Malian Abderrahmane Sissako, whose *Bamako* (2006) offers a swingeing critique of neoliberal economics and its resulting poverty; and Nigerian-South African Akin Omotoso, whose drama film *Man on Ground* (2011) responds to the phenomenon of township attacks on *makwerekwere*, or non-local "outsiders".

Though women have always been prominent as actors, recognition of their role as film-makers has been slower to arrive. Today, female directors are making their mark across the continent. Wanuri Kahiu's *Rafiki* (or "Friend") was the first Kenyan film to be screened at the Cannes Film Festival, while women are central to Nigeria's "Nollywood", both as actors and directors, and sometimes – like Genevieve Nnaji (*Lionheart*, 2019) – both.

Hampered by lack of distribution, African cinema was for a long time confined to arthouse screenings and film festivals, notably the Panafrican Film and Television Festival of Ouagadougou (FESPACO). In the 1990s, new technology brought about a huge democratizing boom. Nollywood's sensational melodramas and comedies captivate local and diasporic audiences. Today, streaming services make African cinema more accessible than ever before.

▽ **Teen love story**
In *Rafiki*, Wanuri Kahiu offers a tale of lesbian love in a country – Kenya – where same-sex sexual relations are illegal. But this warm drama holds out hope that things may change.

Musical instruments

Music-making across Africa

Africa has a rich variety of Indigenous musical instruments, reflecting the many different musical styles of the continent. Percussion instruments, especially drums, are central to the ceremonies, dances, and songs of many African cultures, and melodic instruments, including various plucked and bowed strings and some wind instruments, are also widespread.

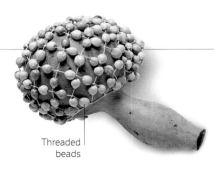

Threaded beads

△ Gourd rattle

Shakers and rattles are found across Africa south of the Sahara. They are often made from hollow gourds containing seeds or loosely wrapped with a network of beads, shells, or nuts.

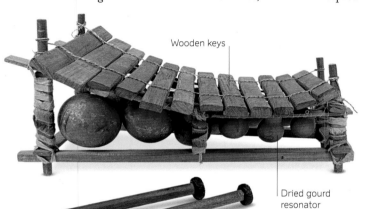

Wooden keys

Dried gourd resonator

△ African xylophone

Various types of xylophone – tuned wooden percussion instruments – are found in Africa, including the *bala* (or *balafon*), seen here, from the Mande region of West Africa and the *marimba* from Southern Africa.

▷ Jembe

The *jembe*, a goblet drum played with bare hands, is said to derive its name from a saying by the Bambara people of West Africa, meaning "everybody gather in peace".

Animal skin

Curved beater

Tensioning strings

Animal skin

Single drumhead

△ Moroccan tar

The *tar* is a variety of tambourine found across North Africa. This 19th-century example from Morocco consists of a decorated wooden frame with metal zills, or jingles, and a green animal skin.

△ Zulu drum

This simple drum in the Zulu style has animal-hide heads stretched over a hollow wooden shell. Drums such as these would accompany Zulu celebrations.

△ Talking drum

Squeezing the strings attached to the drumskins of this West African drum changes the pitch, allowing the player to mimic the cadences of human speech.

▷ Valiha
The *valiha*, considered the national instrument of Madagascar, is a type of tube zither made from bamboo with attached, tensioned strings.

Carved wooden yoke

Bamboo tube

Leather soundboard

△ Begena
The *begena* is a type of wooden lyre used as an accompanying instrument to the spiritual songs of the Amhara people of Ethiopia.

Higher-pitched bell

△ Gankogui bell
Originating from Ghana, Togo, and Benin, the iron double bell, called a *gankogui*, is struck with a wooden beater to produce two different pitches.

MUSICAL **BOW**
Particularly associated with peoples of Southern Africa, the musical bow consists of a single string, usually made of metal, stretched between the two ends of a flexible stick and then struck or plucked. To amplify the sound of the vibrating string, the player's mouth – or, sometimes, a gourd attached to the back of the bow – is used as a resonator.

◁ Kora
Found throughout the Mande diaspora in West Africa, the *kora* is a 21-string calabash (bottle gourd) harp plucked with the index fingers and thumbs.

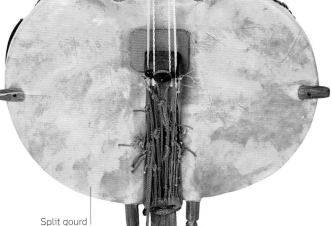

Split gourd body

Carved mouthpiece

Gourd resonator

△ Mbira
The tuned metal keys on a *mbira* are plucked with the thumbs and index fingers to produce sounds of different pitches.

▽ Bondjo
The Congolese *bondjo* is a side-blown trumpet carved from elephant's tusk and wood, originally used in battle but nowadays employed in ceremonies.

Decorated wooden extension

Popular music

The evolution of Indigenous African styles

With its many cultures and musical traditions, Africa has inevitably produced a diverse range of popular music over the course of the 20th and 21st centuries. Regions south of the Sahara in particular developed popular music that fused local styles with elements of Western genres such as jazz, pop, and rock.

Although a predominantly urban phenomenon, African popular music had its roots in the wealth of rural musical traditions, from Yoruba drumming to call and response forms found across the continent, where a soloist sings a phrase, which is then repeated by backing singers. Colonialism in the 19th century brought exposure to Western folk and popular songs, which were gradually assimilated into the Indigenous styles. The process of assimilation accelerated in the 20th century with the advent of jazz and blues (themselves from African roots), which spread to an increasingly urban African audience.

One of the first countries to develop a characteristic popular genre was present-day Ghana, where "palm-wine music" – a fusion of jazz and local styles such as *sikyi*, an Akan genre of dance music – emerged in the pre-World War II period. By the 1950s, this had evolved into the Cuban-inspired highlife, featuring West African rhythms and melodies played on Western guitars and brass instruments, which quickly became popular throughout West Africa.

The 1960s saw the emergence of new hybrid genres, notably in the townships of apartheid-era South Africa. Singers such as Miriam Makeba popularized

△ **Miriam Makeba (1932–2008)**
In a more than 50-year career, South African singer Miriam Makeba became one of the first African musicians to achieve global acclaim, with Xhosa songs such as "Pata Pata" and "Qongqothwane" (the "Click song") inflected with elements of jazz.

△ **Fela Kuti (1938–1997)**
Singer, multi-instrumentalist, bandleader, and political activist Fela Aníkúlápó Kuti is considered to be the originator of the highly influential hybrid Afrobeat genre in the 1960s. As the foremost Nigerian musician of his generation, he used his songs to campaign against Nigerian military rule and dictatorship.

△ **Stella Chiweshe (1946–2023)**
Zimbabwean musician Stella Chiweshe challenged the taboo against female players of the *mbira*, a Shona keyboard instrument. She supported nationalist and women's rights causes and brought Shona culture to a worldwide audience.

> "The **curious beauty** of African music is that it uplifts even as it **tells a sad tale**."
>
> NELSON MANDELA, *LONG WALK TO FREEDOM*

Xhosa songs with jazz inflections, while Zulu music formed the basis for *mbaqanga*, the pop-inspired music of urban Johannesburg. At the same time, a similar process was happening with the creation of *mbalax*, a Senegalese hybrid of local Wolof *sabar* drumming with influences from Latin genres.

Contemporary styles

The collective term "Afropop" refers to many regional varieties of African popular music that are truly Indigenous: African music absorbing Western genres, rather than Western music with an African flavour. As well as the integration of stylistic elements, the various genres of Afropop adopted the instruments of Western pop music, especially guitars, keyboards, and electronics. African instruments still featured strongly in most genres, but these were often amplified, and modern production techniques created a distinctively contemporary sound.

Perhaps paradoxically, these Western-influenced genres often came to symbolize the independence of postcolonial African countries. In Nigeria, for example, Fela Kuti blended Indigenous Yoruba music with highlife and African-American jazz and funk to create Afrobeat, which he used as a vehicle for sociopolitical comment. Less overtly political, but no less influential, was Youssou N'Dour, whose incorporation of multiple styles into Senegalese music stimulated a worldwide interest in African contemporary music.

△ **Youssou N'Dour (1947–)**
Emerging from the *mbalax* dance music of 1970s Senegal, Youssou N'Dour gained an international following with his innovative fusion of Senegalese and other African genres with Islamic chants, jazz, and pop styles.

△ **Salif Keita (1949–)**
After some success as a member of the band Les Ambassadeurs, Salif Keita left his native Mali to pursue a solo career in Paris. Sometimes referred to as the "Golden Voice of Africa", Keita built a global reputation with his eclectic dance-music style, before returning to Mali's capital Bamako in the early 2000s.

△ **Yvonne Chaka Chaka (1965–)**
Born in the township of Soweto, Johannesburg, Yvonne Chaka Chaka became the leading light of South African *mbaqanga* music after her debut in the 1980s. An internationally famous singer, she has also been active in raising global awareness of issues including HIV/AIDS.

"If you don't [handle] **the material**, the work might end up not **having a soul**."

EL ANATSUI, 2011

◁ **Art and artist**
El Anatsui stands in front of his 2004 sculpture *Sasa*, which is 8.4 m (27.6 ft) tall. The artist chose the Ewe word "sasa", meaning patchwork, to refer to the carving up of Africa by European colonial powers.

Bottle-top sculptures

Metal mosaics made by groundbreaking Ghanaian artist

El Anatsui creates wall hangings that, on first glance, may be taken for woven tapestries. In fact, these works — which he makes by creating segments of flattened metal, including bottle caps, that are then stitched together — reconceptualize the function and meaning of cloth, transforming it into an original form of sculpture. Anatsui's aesthetic draws on West African modes while being in dialogue with Western art. His wall hangings ironize Western art history through the transformation of discarded materials into objects of priceless beauty and grandeur. They also reference West African fabric styles, such as Ghanian *kente* and Nigerian *aso-oke*, in which woven strips are sewn together in a process similar to his own.

New forms of expression

El Anatsui's practice chimes with that of other African and African-diaspora artists. By adorning 18th-century figures and interiors in wax-print fabric, British-Nigerian artist Yinka Shonibare similarly uses cloth to question the centrality of a Western perspective on history. With the help of a team of weavers based in Johannesburg, South African artist William Kentridge makes tapestries depicting sociopolitical conditions in his country. Romuald Hazoume, a Yoruba artist from Benin, recycles jerry cans and British painter Chris Ofili uses elephant dung, further exemplifying the infiltration of high art by a trash aesthetic.

Born in Anyako in southern Ghana, El Anatsui trained in sculpture in the central Ghanaian city of Kumasi in the 1960s. Formal art schools had proliferated in Africa during and after colonization. Exposure to a British-influenced school set Anatsui on a search for an Indigenous mode of expression. He began by experimenting with local materials, combining wooden trays used in markets with *adinkra* symbols, breaking and recombining pottery, and carving in wood. From 1975, he has lived in Nsukka, eastern Nigeria, where he works at the University of Nigeria as both artist and teacher.

In Nsukka, El Anatsui stumbled on the material for which he has become famous. The bottles of alcohol from which the discarded caps came had been a medium of colonial exchange. Struck by its historical resonances, he started by beating out the metal and stitching the segments together to form colourful patterns. He works with a team of assistants, laying out bottle caps in blocks of 200 to create a design, photographing them and playing with images on a computer, before painstakingly putting them together.

Displayed and purchased internationally, El Anatsui's hangings have draped the exterior of such buildings as the Alte Nationalgalerie in Berlin, the Royal Academy of Arts in London, and El-Badi Palace (Qasr al-Badī') in Marrakech. In 2023, he created an installation for the Turbine (entrance) Hall at Tate Modern in London.

Combinations of metal caps and seals from bottles

▷ **Shimmering design**
El Anatsui's 2021 artwork, *Wade in the Water*, recalls a song associated with the Underground Railroad. This secret network was established in the 19th century to help enslaved African Americans escape to freedom.

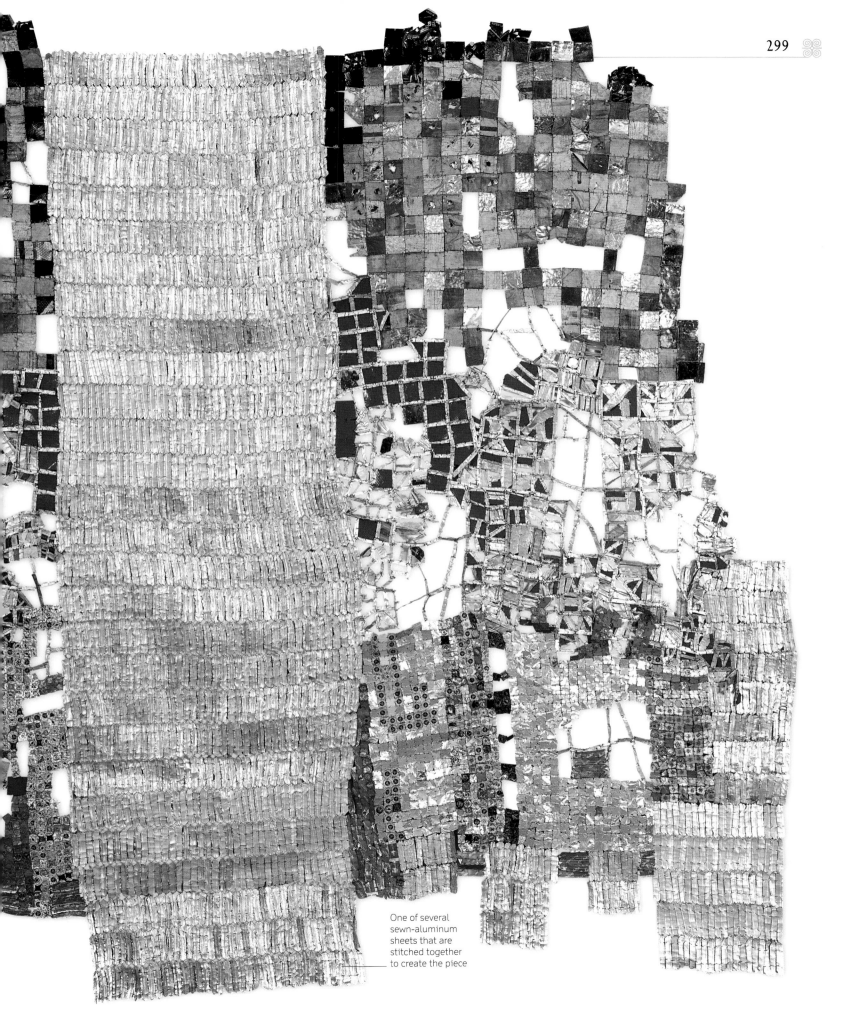

One of several
sewn-aluminum
sheets that are
stitched together
to create the piece

> "In my world, **every human is beautiful.**"
>
> ZANELE MUHOLI, 2020

Art and activism

Identity-affirming photography by Zanele Muholi

Born in Umlazi, a township close to Durban, KwaZulu-Natal, in 1972, Zanele Muholi experienced first-hand the oppression of the South African apartheid regime, intensified by hostility directed at people whose sexuality was considered transgressive. Muholi is non-binary, using the pronouns they/them, and their art focuses on issues of race, gender, and sexuality, observing and honouring the Black LGBTQ+ communities of South Africa.

Muholi's chosen medium is photography, including video and installation, but given their chosen subject matter, they prefer to describe themselves as a "visual activist" rather than a photographer or an artist. This reflects the motivation that runs through their work: to make both the positive and negative aspects of the lives of Black LGBTQ+ people visible. Muholi's first solo exhibition, *Visual Sexuality: Only Half the Picture*, in Johannesburg in 2004 presented images of survivors of hate crimes, their identity and even gender deliberately concealed. The effects of violence directed against South African Black LGBTQ+ people was a subject Muholi returned to in later exhibitions.

As well as highlighting oppressive attitudes towards race, gender, and sexuality, Muholi has devoted much of their work to celebrating especially Black lesbian and trans lives. This they did through portraits, such as those of lesbians in the *Faces and Phases* project which they began in 2006, and the *Brave Beauties* series of portraits of trans women shown in 2014.

Probably the most personal statement they have produced, however, is the series of 365 self-portraits titled *Somnyama Ngonyama* ("Hail the Dark Lioness" in isiZulu, the Zulu language), exhibited in New York in 2015 and in London in 2017, and subsequently published in book form. Photographed in various locations around the world, the arresting images portray Muholi as a series of alter egos, reflecting diverse African cultures, and often with a Zulu name.

In addition to their photographic work, Muholi was a co-founder of a Black lesbian organization, the Forum for the Empowerment of Women, in 2002, and more recently has concentrated on increasing educational opportunities in photography and art for underprivileged young people.

△ **Comb headdress**
In this photograph, entitled *Qiniso, The Sails, Durban* (2019), from the *Somnyama Ngonyama* series, Muholi wears a stylized headdress made of Afro combs, symbolizing pride in Black natural hair. *Qiniso* means "truth" in isiZulu.

▷ **Caught in coils**
Xiniwe at Cassilhaus, North Carolina (2016) captures one of Muholi's alter egos, Xiniwe, with an exaggerated hairstyle and wrapped in snake-like coils, highlighting exoticized representations of African cultures in the West.

Writers

Africa's literary history

African literature stretches back further than that of any other continent. The first writing – Egyptian hieroglyphs – emerged around 3000 BCE. Religious texts were produced from around the 4th century CE in the Christian kingdom of Aksum (modern-day Ethiopia). In areas with an Islamic influence, including North Africa, the Sahel, and East Africa, texts mostly written in Arabic described religion and astronomy. The early Swahili epic poem *Utendi wa Tambuka* (The Story of Tambuka) dramatizes the conflicts between the Arabs, Ottomans, and Byzantines and was first written down in 1728.

Until the 18th century, African history and stories were passed on orally, in the form of proverbs, folklore (featuring animal tricksters such as spiders or tortoises), religious narratives, and love songs. In West Africa, storytellers called *griots* have told the history of a village or family in a mixture of poetry and music for hundreds of years. The tale of the Mandingo (Malinke) hero Sundiata (see pp. 90–91) was told by *griots* for centuries and still shapes our understanding of the Mali Empire.

A wider circulation

When colonizers brought European literary traditions and written languages to Africa, Africans learned these languages and began to write in English and French. First-hand accounts of enslavement such as the *Interesting Narrative of the Life of Olaudah Equiano* were written in English. A formerly enslaved Igbo man, Equiano (c. 1745–97) bought his freedom and settled in London.

△ **Mariama Bâ (1929–81)**
Born into a middle-class Muslim family in Senegal in the 1940s, Bâ took part in the country's feminist movement. She wrote the acclaimed *So Long a Letter* (1979) about a woman's painful experience of a polygamous marriage and the inequalities women face.

△ **Chinua Achebe (1930–2013)**
Nigerian novelist Achebe is known as the "father of African literature". He wrote in English, but used Igbo phrases in novels such as *Things Fall Apart* (1958), which explores the impact of colonial power on an Igbo village. His portrayal of a complex West African society challenged Western ideas of "primitive" Africa.

△ **Nawal El Saadawi (1931–2021)**
A graduate of Cairo University and a qualified doctor, El Saadawi was also a feminist who wrote novels, non-fiction, and short stories. Her focus was on social issues and the impact of religion on women, such as in the *The Hidden Face of Eve* (1977).

"If you **don't like** someone's story, **write your own**."

CHINUA ACHEBE, 1994

By the 20th century, Africans were writing in a range of Western genres. In the Gold Coast (now Ghana), J.E. Casely Hayford (1866–1930) wrote *Ethiopia Unbound* (1911), an influential philosophical novel about colonialism, while *The Girl Who Killed to Save: Nongqause the Liberator* by South African Herbert Isaac Ernest Dhlomo (1903–56), published in 1935, is commonly regarded as the first English-language African play.

Independent voices

This trickle of new, often anticolonial voices became a cascade in the decades that followed. Writers such as Chinua Achebe, Wole Soyinka, and Ngũgĩ wa Thiong'o used African as well as European languages to explore colonialism and identity. Since then, novelists including Tanzanian Abdulrazak Gurnah (1948–) and South Africa's J.M. Coetzee (1940–) have won Nobel prizes and achieved worldwide sales.

In the later 20th century, female writers became more prominent. Zimbabwean Yvonne Vera (1964–2005), Egypt's Nawal El Saadawi, who wrote in Arabic, and Senegal's Mariama Bâ have explored feminism and social issues. In the 21st century, a new generation, including Nigeria's Chimamanda Ngozi Adichie (1977–) and Franco-Senegalese novelist David Diop (1966–) are part of a diaspora of writers driving African literature forward. Authors such as American poet and photographer Teju Cole (1975–) and Jamaica's Marlon James (1970–) show that African writing is as wide-ranging and as vital as ever.

△ **Swahili wordsmith**
Tanzanian poet and author Shaaban bin Robert (1909– 62) wrote poetry, novels, and essays. He promoted the Tanzanian verse style and the Swahili language.

△ **Wole Soyinka (1934–)**
Soyinka's plays often target authority, and he has had to flee his native Nigeria during his career. His work explores Yoruba culture and Western themes and in 1986 he became the first person from Africa south of the Sahara to win the Nobel Prize for Literature.

△ **Ngũgĩ wa Thiong'o (1938–)**
Kenyan novelist, playwright, activist, and academic Ngũgĩ has been a force for change throughout his varied career. Although his first works were in English, he has written primarily in Gikuyu since the 1970s. He has pushed for the rebranding of "English literature" as simply "literature" across Africa.

△ **Chimamanda Ngozi Adichie (1977–)**
Globally successful writer Adichie was born in Nsukka, Nigeria, to Igbo parents. She studied politics and African history in Nigeria and the US. Her novel *Half of a Yellow Sun* (2006) is set during the brutal Nigeria–Biafra War (1967–70) and has won several literary prizes.

The future of Africa

A new momentum

In most of Africa's 54 countries, 70 per cent or more of the population is under the age of 30. In the 21st century, these overwhelmingly youth-dominated societies are looking to harness their economic and cultural potential.

△ **Symbol of solidarity**
The African Union emblem shows palm leaves (representing peace) and interlocking rings (showing solidarity) surrounding a continent without borders.

▽ **Nairobi skyline**
With a population of around 5 million, the Kenyan capital of Nairobi is one of Africa's fastest-growing cities.

In the 20th century, Africa freed itself from colonizing powers as nations across the continent forged their own paths. Now Africa is transforming again. Its population is projected to nearly double over the next few decades, reaching 2.4 billion by 2050, when one in four people around the world will live in Africa. By 2100, the figure is forecast to be one in three.

With a growing population, the demand for goods and services will increase, and Africa has the potential to become a major global player on its own terms. It is rich in resources such as oil, gas, and arable land, and holds around 30 per cent of the world's mineral reserves, including gold, lithium, and cobalt (all used in batteries). Africa's biodiversity provides an opportunity to implement sustainable practices that protect the environment while supporting growth, and the potential of renewable energy such as wind, solar, hydro, and geothermal power is immense.

Turning this potential into long-term prosperity and stability will not be straightforward. Optimism is nothing new: in 1999, Thabo Mbeki, then president of South Africa, spoke of entering "the African century", but economic growth in the 2000s was followed by a dip in the 2010s due to lower commodity prices.

Countries including the Central African Republic, Burundi, and South Sudan regularly rank as the poorest in the world, and conflicts continue to affect several nations. Investment from powers such as China and Russia may have transformed infrastructure in some states, but also points towards the spectre of a new imperialism.

Yet Africa's momentum is becoming unstoppable. The continent is experiencing a digital revolution, with advancements in technology and connectivity transforming various sectors. Mobile communication has played a significant role in leapfrogging traditional

infrastructure, empowering huge numbers of people through access to information, education, healthcare, and financial services.

Nigeria, South Africa, and Egypt all had GDPs of over US$400 million in 2023, and Nigeria is expected to become one of the world's top ten economies in the next 50 years. These African superpowers are attracting more and more commercial opportunities, while other nations including Kenya, Côte d'Ivoire, and the Democratic Republic of the Congo (DRC) are among the fastest-growing economies in the world.

Collaboration and culture

To achieve their potential, African countries must address challenges such as poverty, inequality, and political instability, and ensure that the management of natural resources benefits their citizens and leads to stability and long-term growth.

Intergovernmental organizations such as the African Union (which replaced the Organization of African Unity in 2002) seek to encourage collaboration. The African Union has played a crucial role in promoting peace and its Agenda 2063 seeks to bring about a "prosperous Africa based on inclusive growth and sustainable development" via a roadmap for areas such as industrialization, infrastructure, and lowering trade barriers within the continent. The vision is positive, although – due in part to its consensus-building approach – progress has sometimes been slow.

Africa's future is more than just economic. There is strong interest in preserving Indigenous knowledge, promoting local languages, and reviving arts and crafts. Young and growing populations, as well as changing patterns of migration, will see Africa's cultures evolve and spread through the 21st century.

Popular music, notably West Africa's Afrobeats, has already become a global juggernaut, while African writers and film-makers attract ever-larger international audiences. Cities such as Lagos, Kinshasa, Johannesburg, Cairo, Dakar, and Nairobi burst with creativity, and, as Africa builds a new future, the next big thing could come from anywhere on the continent.

△ **Edo Museum**
This digital visualization shows a planned exhibition space at Edo Museum of West African Art (EMWAA), which will focus on the history of the Kingdom of Benin. It is due to open in 2024 in Benin City, Nigeria.

▷ **Afrobeats**
Nigerian singer Wizkid performs at a tribute to musician Fela Kuti in 2017. In the 1960s, Kuti pioneered Afrobeat and influenced today's Afrobeats style, which also draws on hip-hop and other genres.

"As Africans, we are **proud of our history**, as we are **optimistic** about **our future**."

SOUTH AFRICAN PRESIDENT CYRIL RAMAPHOSA, 2023

Glossary

A

Abbasid Caliphate (750–1258 CE) A Muslim empire that stretched across modern-day Iran, Iraq, Saudi Arabia, and North Africa as far as Tunisia.

Afrikaner (or Boer, from the Dutch for "husbandman," or "farmer") Describes South Africans descended from predominantly Dutch settlers who arrived in 1652.

African Union An organization founded in 2002 to replace the Organization of African Unity (OAU). It promotes solidarity between African states and international cooperation to further economic development in the continent.

Aghlabid dynasty (800–909 CE) An Arab dynasty that ruled modern-day Tunisia, eastern Algeria, and parts of Southern Italy and Sicily in the 9th and early 10th centuries.

Akan An ethnolinguistic grouping of peoples who settled in what is now Ghana, Côte d'Ivoire, and parts of Togo in the 11th–18th centuries.

Aksum (c. 150–1000 CE) A kingdom in East Africa and the Arabian Peninsula.

Almohad Caliphate (1121–1269 CE) An Amazigh (Berber) Muslim empire that stretched across much of North Africa (the Maghreb) and the Iberian Peninsula (al-Andalus).

Almoravid Caliphate (1050s–1147 CE) An Amazigh Muslim empire that encompassed North Africa (the Maghreb) and the Iberian Peninsula (al-Andalus).

Amazigh (pl. Imazighen) A diverse grouping of distinct ethnic groups in North Africa, descendants of pre-Arab inhabitants of the region. Also known as Berber, from the Greek for "[non-Greek speaking] foreigner".

annexation The proclamation of sovereignty by one state over territory outside its domain; often preceded by conquest and military occupation.

anthropoids The group of primates that includes living and fossil monkeys, apes, and humans.

apartheid In South Africa and southwest Africa, the system of institutionalized racial segregation that existed from 1948 to 1994.

Arab Describes Arabic-speaking people who came from the Arabian Peninsula and inhabited much of the Middle East and North Africa.

Asante Empire (1701–1901 CE) A West African state that occupied the area that is now southern Ghana.

Assyria An ancient empire in southwestern Asia that was at its height from about 750 to 612 BCE.

autonomy The right or condition of self-government.

Ayyubid Sultanate (1171–1260 CE) A Muslim empire – founded by Salah al-Din Yusuf ibn Ayyub (commonly known as Saladin) in Egypt – that encompassed much of the Middle East and North Africa.

B

Bamum A Central African kingdom established in the 14th century in what is now northwest Cameroon.

Bantu-speaking people Speakers of any of the approximately 500 Bantu languages spoken in Central and Southern Africa.

Biafra A state that declared its independence from Nigeria in May 1967 and existed until January 1970.

Boer See Afrikaner.

Buganda (c. 14th century–1967, re-established in 1993) A kingdom in Uganda, Central Africa, that was at its most powerful in the 18th and 19th centuries.

Bunyoro (c. 12th century–1967, re-established in 1993) A kingdom in western Uganda that was at its height from the 16th to the 19th centuries.

C

caliph A Muslim civil and religious ruler, regarded as a successor of the Prophet Muhammad.

caliphate An Islamic state, especially one ruled by a single religious and political leader.

Chimurenga A Shona word meaning "uprising" (the Ndebele equivalent is *Umvukela*, meaning "revolutionary struggle"). It refers to the Shona and Ndebele insurrections against the British South Africa Company during the late 1890s – known as the Second Matabele War, or the First *Chimurenga/Umvukela*. In the 1960s and '70s, the Second *Chimurenga/Umvukela,* also known as the Zimbabwe War of Independence, was fought between African nationalist guerrillas and the predominantly white Rhodesian government.

city-state In the ancient world, a city and surrounding land with its own government.

client king A term used in ancient Rome for a ruler in a harmonious but unequal alliance with Rome.

Coptic Christianity One of the oldest churches of Christianity, based in Egypt and said to have been founded by Mark, an apostle and evangelist, in the middle of the 1st century CE.

crown colony A British colony that was administered by a governor appointed by the British monarch on the advice of the UK Government.

Cushite A word used in the Hebrew Bible to refer to Africa and Africans. Cush is identified with the Kingdom of Kush (c. 1070 BCE–c. 550 CE), also known as ancient Sudan.

D

Dahomey Kingdom (c. 1625–1904) A West African power that flourished in the 18th and 19th centuries in southern Benin.

diaspora A population that shares a cultural and regional origin, but currently resides elsewhere. Diasporas come about through immigration and forced movements of people.

Dogon An ancient ethnic group in Mali and Burkina Faso, known for their mask dances and dry stone buildings.

dynasty A line of rulers or leaders from the same family or group, or a period of time when a country or region is ruled by them.

E

emirate A Muslim state ruled by a military commander called an emir.

Ethiopian Empire (1270–1974 CE) A state in the region that is now Ethiopia and Eritrea, founded by the Solomonic dynasty.

F

Fatimid Caliphate (909–1171 CE) A Muslim empire that spanned North Africa to western Saudi Arabia.

forced labour Work that is performed involuntarily – not, as with slavery, because the worker is "owned" (seen as a piece of property), but because of threats such as of violence or death.

French Community An association of states set up in 1958 between France and its remaining African colonies; by the end of 1960, its African members had declared their independence and left, although the association was only officially abolished in 1995.

Fulani Empire (or Sokoto Caliphate) (c. 1800–c. 1900 CE) A West African Muslim theocracy in Cameroon, Burkina Faso, Niger, and Nigeria.

G

Gao A town on the Niger River in Mali that gave rise to a kingdom that, by the end of the 13th century, had become part of the Mali Empire.

Ge'ez An ancient language of Ethiopia that influenced modern Ethiopian languages such as Amharic and that survives as the liturgical language of the Ethiopian Church.

Great Zimbabwe The stone-built capital city of a great medieval kingdom in modern-day Zimbabwe.

H

Hajj The pilgrimage that Muslims are required to make to Mecca – Islam's holiest city – in Saudi Arabia.

Hausa Kingdoms (c. 1000–1815) A loose alliance of trading states in what is now northern Nigeria.

hominid A group consisting of all living and extinct great apes (modern humans, chimpanzees, gorillas, and orang-utans, and all their immediate ancestors).

hominin A group consisting of *Homo sapiens* (modern humans) and extinct ancestors such as *Homo erectus* and *Homo neanderthalensis*.

hut tax Taxation introduced by British colonizers in Africa on a per hut or household basis, payable in money, labour, grain, or stock.

I

Ilé-Ifè (or Ife) A city in southwestern Nigeria, founded by the 4th century BCE and considered to be the oldest city-state of the Yoruba people.

Indentured servitude A contracted period of labour without salary to pay off an indenture or loan.

J

Jolof (or Wolof) Empire
(c. 1200–c. 1600 CE) A West African trading state that dominated inland modern-day Senegal.

K

kandake A title for queens and queen mothers of the Empire of Kush (also known as Nubia) in what is now northern Sudan and southern Egypt.
kabaka The title of the king of Buganda in what is now Uganda.
Kanem-Bornu (c. 800–1893 CE) A trading empire that controlled the area around Lake Chad in West Central Africa.
Khoikhoi Indigenous peoples of Southern Africa, traditionally nomadic herders and hunter-gatherers.
Kongo Kingdom (c. 1390–1862 CE) A western Central African state located in present-day northern Angola, Congo, and the western Democratic Republic of the Congo.

L

Lozi Kingdom (c. 1700s–1890) A state inhabiting the area that is today western Zambia in Central Africa.
Luba Kingdom (1585–1889) A power that arose in what is now the southern Democratic Republic of the Congo.
Lunda Kingdom (c. 1665–c. 1887) A confederation of states in what is now the Democratic Republic of the Congo, northeastern Angola, and northwestern Zambia.

M

madrasa The Arabic word for a place of learning, either religious or secular.
Mahgreb The western part of the Arab world, comprising western and central North Africa, including Mauritania, (disputed) Western Sahara, Morocco, Algeria, Tunisia, and Libya.
Mali Empire (1230–1660 CE) A state in West Africa renowned for the wealth of its rulers, especially Mansa Musa.
Mamluk dynasty (1250–1517 CE) A dynasty that ruled Egypt and Syria, established by formerly enslaved soldiers turned generals.
Mandingo Also known as Mandinka or Malinke, an ethnic group primarily found in southern Mali, the Gambia, and eastern Guinea.
megacity A very large city, typically with a population of over 10 million.

Meroë A city of ancient Kush in present-day Sudan; also the name of the area surrounding the city.
Mfecane The Zulu name (meaning "destruction" or "crushing") for an upheaval among Indigenous peoples in Southern Africa in the first half of the 19th century during the formation of the Zulu Kingdom. Also known by the Sesotho names *Difaqane* or *Lifaqane* (meaning "forced migration").

N

Napata An ancient city of Nubia and Kush, situated in present-day Sudan.
Négritude An anticolonial movement founded in the 1930s by French-speaking African and Caribbean writers living in France.
Neocolonialism A term first used after World War II to describe the use of economic, political, cultural, or other pressures exerted by one state on another, particularly former colonies.
Nri Kingdom (900 CE–present) A state in what is now Nigeria.

O

oba A ruler among various peoples in the Benin region of West Africa.
Organization of African Unity (OAU) A body founded in 1963 to promote self-government, respect for territorial boundaries, and social progress throughout the African continent.
Ottoman Empire (c. 1299–1922) One of the mightiest and longest-lasting dynasties in world history, which controlled much of southeast Europe, North Africa, and western Asia.
Oyo Empire (c. 1300–1896) The largest Yoruba state in West Africa, located in present-day eastern Benin and western Nigeria.

P

palette In ancient Egypt, a decorated stone on which cosmetics were mixed.
Pan-Africanism A worldwide movement that aims to unite and strengthen the relationship between people of African descent.
Phoenicia (c. 2500 BCE–64 BCE) A maritime state that extended along the coastal regions of modern-day Lebanon and parts of Syria and Israel.
protectorate A state or region that is nominally independent, but whose external affairs are controlled by a protector country.

Punic Wars (or Carthaginian Wars) (264–146 BCE) A series of three wars between the Roman Republic and the Carthaginian (Punic) Empire in modern-day Tunisia, as a result of which Rome took control of the western Mediterranean, destroyed Carthage, and enslaved its people.

S

Sahel The semiarid region of West and northern Central Africa extending from Senegal eastwards to Sudan.
San Indigenous hunter-gatherer peoples of Southern Africa, and the oldest surviving cultures of the region.
Semitic Relating to or denoting a family of languages that includes Hebrew, Arabic, Amharic, and Aramaic, as well as certain ancient languages such as Phoenician.
Shia Islam One of two main branches of Islam (the other being the Sunni), which regards Muhammad's cousin and son-in-law Ali ibn Abi Talib and his descendants as the Prophet's rightful successors.
Songhai Empire (1464–1591 CE) A trading state of West Africa, which replaced the Mali Empire as the most important power in the region.
Solomonic dynasty The ruling dynasty of the Ethiopian Empire from the 13th to the 20th centuries.
sphere of influence The claim by one state to have control over a foreign area or territory.
stela (pl. stelae) In the ancient world, an inscribed stone or wooden slab set up for a monumental purpose.
Sufism An Islamic belief and practice in which adherents seek the truth of divine love and knowledge through direct personal experience of God.
sultanate A state or country that is ruled by a sultan, or Muslim sovereign.
Sunni Islam The largest of the two major branches of Islam (the other being the Shia), which recognizes the first four caliphs as the Prophet Muhammad's legitimate successors.
Swahili Bantu-speaking people of Zanzibar and the adjacent coast of Africa; also the language spoken.

T

Tellem The name (meaning "those who were before us") used by the Dogon for the people who inhabited their region in Mali before them.

theocracy A system of government by religious leaders.
Tifinagh The script used to write Amazigh languages.
tributary state In premodern times, the subordinate relationship of one state to another, involving the sending of regular tokens of submission, or tributes, such as gold, goods such as cattle or crops, or enslaved people.
Tukulor Empire (c. 1850–1893) A Muslim theocracy in West Africa founded by cleric Al-Hajj Umar Tal.

U

Umayyad Caliphate (661–750 CE) The second Muslim caliphate established after the death of the Prophet Muhammad, which, at its peak, controlled the Middle East, parts of India, much of North Africa, and Spain.

V

vassal state A country that has limited independence and only has the rights and privileges that a more powerful country has given to it.
Vodun A West African religion practised by peoples in Benin, Togo, Ghana, and Nigeria; elements of it are found in the Haitian religion of Vodou, brought there by enslaved Africans.

W

Wagadou Empire (or ancient Ghana) (600–1000 CE) A trading empire in parts of what is now Mauritania and Mali.

X

Xhosa An group of related peoples in Southern Africa who speak Xhosa, a Bantu language.

Y

Yoruba A West African ethnic group who inhabit parts of Nigeria, Benin, and Togo, a region known as Yorubaland.

Z

Zagwe Kingdom (c. 900–c 1200 CE) A dominant state in the northern parts of Ethiopia and Eritrea that was ruled by the Zagwe dynasty, whose best-known emperor, Lalibela, is said to have built the magnificent rock-hewn churches named after him.
Zulu Kingdom (1816–1887) A monarchy in Southern Africa founded by Shaka kaSenzangakhona (known as Shaka Zulu).

Index

Acknowledgments

DK would like to thank the following for their help with this book:
Professor Gérard Chouin at William & Mary University, Virginia, US, and Professor Mark Gillings at Bournemouth University, UK, for assistance with the Oyo-Ile walls map (p.112); James Anthony Gardner, Tony Humphries, Keith Shiri, and Dr. Hengameh Ziai for additional consultancy; Sophie Adam, Diana Loxley, and Bonnie Macleod for editorial assistance; Jessica Tapolcai for design assistance; Sarah Smithies for picture research advice; Steve Crozier, Butterfly Creative Services Ltd. for image retouching; Manpreet Kaur for picture logging; Mrinmoy Mazumdar, Raman Panwar, and Vishal Bhatia (Creative Technical Support team); Diana Vowles for proofreading; and Helen Peters for indexing.

Friedrichs (tr); Ian Nellist (crb). **95 Getty Images:** AFP / Michele Cattani (tl). **UN/DPI Photo:** Tiecoura N'daou (br). **96-97 Getty Images:** Xavier ROSSI / Gamma-Rapho. **98 Bridgeman Images:** G. Dagli Orti / © NPL - DeA Picture Library (crb). **The Metropolitan Museum of Art:** Theodore M. Davis Collection, Bequest of Theodore M. Davis, 1915 (cl). **99 Bridgeman Images:** Freer Sackler Gallery / Freer Gallery of Art, Smithsonian Institution. **100 akg-images:** Album / Oronoz (cra). **Alamy Stock Photo:** Luis Dafos (bc); The Picture Art Collection (cla). **101 Alamy Stock Photo:** Album. **103 akg-images:** Erich Lessing (br). **Alamy Stock Photo:** VPC Travel Photo (cr). **104 Bibliotheque de l'Institut de France:** Ms 2414 f.151 A verso (crb). **Courtesy of the New Orleans Museum of Art:** Acc.No.97.138 (bl). **105 Bridgeman Images:** Pictures from History (tl). **The Metropolitan Museum of Art:** Gift of John and Evelyn Kossak, The Kronos Collections, in honor of Martin Lerner, 1983 (r). **106 Alamy Stock Photo:** Horst Friedrichs (cla). **Reuters:** Florin Iorganda (crb). **107 Bridgeman Images:** Heini Schneebeli. **108 Alamy Stock Photo:** Chronicle (t). **Getty Images:** Universal Images Group / Werner Forman (bl). **109 akg-images:** Andr Held (br). **Alamy Stock Photo:** Album (tr). **110 Alamy Stock Photo:** Omoniyi Ayedun Olubunmi (cl). Bridgeman Images: Dirk Bakker (br). **111 akg-images:** Andrea Jemolo (r). **Alamy Stock Photo:** CMA / BOT (tl). **112 © The Trustees of the British Museum. All rights reserved:** (bl). **113 Alamy Stock Photo:** Penta Springs Limited / Artokoloro (br). **The Charles Deering McCormick Library of Special Collections and University Archives:** Justine Cordwell Papers, Northwestern University Archives (tl). **114 The National Archives:** (bl). **Photo Scala, Florence:** Christie's Images, London (cra). **115 Alamy Stock Photo:** Historic Images (br); World History Archive (tc). **Wikipedia:** Peoples of All Nations by Northcote W. Thomas, The Amalgamated Press Ltd, London, 1922 (cra). **116 akg-images:** Andr Held (c); Andrea Jemolo (b). **Bridgeman Images:** Dirk Bakker (cl, tr, cr). **© The Trustees of the British Museum. All rights reserved:** (cr/Pendant). **117 akg-images:** Andr Held (t); Werner Forman Archive / British Museum, London (br). **Bridgeman Images:** Dirk Bakker (cr, bl); Andrea Jemolo (cl). **118 Alamy Stock Photo:** History and Art Collection (cl). **The Metropolitan Museum of Art:** Mariana and Ray Herrmann Gift, 2015 (bc). **119 Alamy Stock Photo:** The Picture Art Collection (br); Tim Wege (t). **120 Alamy Stock Photo:** Thomas Cockrem. **121 Alamy Stock Photo:** John Elk III (bl). **122-123 Getty Images:** Moment / Jon Bratt. **124 Getty Images:** Pictures from History / Universal Images Group (cla, br). **125 Alamy Stock Photo:** Album (br). **126 Alamy Stock Photo:** Dorling Kindersley ltd (cra). **Bridgeman Images:** Photo Josse (bc). **127 Alamy Stock Photo:** Old Books Images (t). **Getty Images:** Eric Lafforgue / Art in All of Us / Corbis (br). **128 Alamy Stock Photo:** Florilegius (cla). **Getty Images:** Universal Images Group / Werner Forman (bc). **129 akg-images:** Pictures From History. **130 Alamy Stock Photo:** MET / BOT (crb). **The Metropolitan Museum of Art:** Gift of Mr. and Mrs. Klaus G. Perls, 1991 (clb). **131 The Metropolitan Museum of Art:** The Michael C. Rockefeller Memorial Collection, Bequest of Nelson A. Rockefeller, 1979. **132 The Metropolitan Museum of Art:** The Michael C. Rockefeller Memorial Collection, Gift of Nelson A. Rockefeller, 1965. **133 The Metropolitan Museum of Art:** The Michael C. Rockefeller Memorial Collection, Gift of Nelson A. Rockefeller, 1972 (crb). **134 Alamy Stock Photo:** imageBROKER.com GmbH & Co. KG / Stefan Auth (crb). **Bridgeman Images:** Zev Radovan (cb). **Getty Images:** DDP / Oliver Lang (clb). **135 Alamy Stock Photo:** Chronicle (cb). **Getty Images:** Popperfoto (crb). **The Metropolitan Museum of Art:** Mr. and Mrs. Klaus G. Perls, 1991 (clb). **136 Alamy Stock Photo:** Christopher Scott. **137 Alamy Stock Photo:** Fine Art Images / Heritage Images (bl). **© The Trustees of the British Museum. All rights reserved:** (tr). **138 Alamy Stock Photo:** Gallo Images / Denny Allen (tc). **140 Alamy Stock Photo:** INTERFOTO / History (bl); robertharding / Ian Griffiths (br). **141 Bridgeman Images:** Heini Schneebeli (t). LOT-ART: (br). **142 Getty Images:** Werner Forman / Universal Images Group (bl). **Photo Scala, Florence:** Image copyright The Metropolitan Museum of Art / Art Resource (c). **143 The Metropolitan Museum of Art:** Rogers Fund, 1988 (crb); The Michael C. Rockefeller Memorial Collection, Gift of Nelson A. Rockefeller, 1969 (c). **144-145 Brooklyn Museum:** Gift of Marcia and John Friede (b). **145 Mary (Polly) Nooter Roberts:** (tl). **146 Alamy Stock Photo:** John Warburton-Lee Photography / Nigel Pavitt (t). **© The Trustees of the British Museum. All rights reserved:** (br). **147 Alamy Stock Photo:** The Picture Art Collection (br). **Getty Images:** Universal Images Group / Pictures from History (tc). **148 Getty Images:** Dea Picture Library / De Agostini. **149 Alamy Stock Photo:** CPA Media Pte Ltd / Pictures From History (ca); World History Archive (br). **150 Alamy Stock Photo:** Aninka Bongers-Sutherland (crb); Tribaleye Images / Tribal Textiles / Jamie Marshall (cb). **The Metropolitan Museum of Art:** Purchase, Mrs. Howard J.

Barnet Gift, 2012 (clb). **151 Alamy Stock Photo:** Thomas Cockrem (clb); Nick Greaves; Agfa Awards Winner (cb). **Getty Images:** Sepia Times / Universal Images Group (crb). **152 Alamy Stock Photo:** Eric Lafforgue (bl). **Dorling Kindersley:** Dave King / Pitt Rivers Museum, University of Oxford (ca). **152-153 Alamy Stock Photo:** Art World (b). **153 Dorling Kindersley:** Dave King / Pitt Rivers Museum, University of Oxford (t). **154-155 Alamy Stock Photo:** Tariq Zaidi / ZUMA Wire. **156-157 Courtesy of the New Orleans Museum of Art:** Francoise Billion Richardson Fund, 90-306 (c). **156 Alamy Stock Photo:** Interfoto / Fine Arts (bc). **Photo Scala, Florence:** The Metropolitan Museum of Art / Art Resource (l). **157 Alamy Stock Photo:** Jon Arnold Images Ltd / Gavin Hellier (cra). **158-159 Bridgeman Images:** North Carolina Museum of Art. **160 The Metropolitan Museum of Art:** Gift of Mr. and Mrs. Klaus G. Perls, 1991 (bl). **161 akg-images:** Heritage Images / Fine Art Images (crb). Alamy Stock Photo: Pictorial Press Ltd (tr). **Getty Images:** DEA / G. DAGLI ORTI / De Agostini (cra). **163 Alamy Stock Photo:** GRANGER - Historical Picture Archive (t). Library of Congress, Washington, D.C.: LC-USZ62-34160 (b). **164-165 Alamy Stock Photo:** VTR. **166 The Metropolitan Museum of Art:** Louis V. Bell and Rogers Funds (bl). **167 Alamy Stock Photo:** Pictorial Press Ltd (tr). Rijksmuseum Amsterdam: (b/x3). **168 Alamy Stock Photo:** ART Collection (bl); Chronicle (t). **169 Alamy Stock Photo:** Album (br); Florilegius (tc). **170 Alamy Stock Photo:** World History Archive (ca). University of Southern California: (bl). **171 The Metropolitan Museum of Art:** Purchase, The Fred and Rita Richman Foundation Gift and Rogers Fund, 2000. **172 Alamy Stock Photo:** history_docu_photo. **173 Alamy Stock Photo:** Old Images (clb); World History Archive (cra). **174 Alamy Stock Photo:** North Wind Picture Archives (cr); Ariadne Van Zandbergen (bl). **175 Mary Evans Picture Library:** (t). **176 Alamy Stock Photo:** Oscar Espinosa (t); Boaz Rottem (bl). **177 Bridgeman Images:** Heini Schneebeli (bl). **Getty Images:** Popperfoto / Paul Popper (tr). **178 Alamy Stock Photo:** Historic Images (cla). Fowler Museum at UCLA: (b). **179 Bridgeman Images:** Look and Learn. **180 National Portrait Gallery, London. 181 Getty Images:** Archive Photos / Fotosearch (cb); Hulton Archive / Heritage Images (cra). **182 Alamy Stock Photo:** Science History Images (cla). **The Metropolitan Museum of Art:** Gift of Ernst Anspach, 1999 (c). **183 Alamy Stock Photo:** Penta Springs Limited / Artokoloro (c). **Dreamstime.com:** Fabian Plock (tr). **184-185 The Metropolitan Museum of Art:** Purchase, Lila Acheson Wallace, Drs. Daniel and Marian Malcolm, Laura G. and James J. Ross, Jeffrey B. Soref, The Robert T. Wall Family, Dr. and Mrs. Sidney G. Clyman, and Steven Kossak Gifts, 2008. **185 The Metropolitan Museum of Art:** Purchase, Lila Acheson Wallace, Drs. Daniel and Marian Malcolm, Laura G. and James J. Ross, Jeffrey B. Soref, The Robert T. Wall Family, Dr. and Mrs. Sidney G. Clyman, and Steven Kossak Gifts, 2008 (tr). **186 Alamy Stock Photo:** CPA Media Pte Ltd / Pictures From History (cla); UtCon Collection (br). **© The Trustees of the British Museum. All rights reserved:** (bl). **187 Alamy Stock Photo:** WBC ART (r). **189 Alamy Stock Photo:** CPA Media Pte Ltd / Pictures From History (tl). **190-191 Bridgeman Images:** British Library Board. All Rights Reserved (t). **190 Alamy Stock Photo:** INTERFOTO / Fine Arts (br). **191 Dorling Kindersley:** Wallace Collection, London / Geoff Dann (cr). **192 Alamy Stock Photo:** Album (cla); Holden History (cb). **193 The Metropolitan Museum of Art:** The Michael C. Rockefeller Memorial Collection, Purchase, Nelson A. Rockefeller Gift, 1967. **194 Alamy Stock Photo:** Chronicle (crb); Jorge Fernandez (t). **195 Bridgeman Images:** Archives Charmet / Bernatz, Johann Martin (1802-1878) (after) / German (1802-1878). **196-197 Photo Scala, Florence:** Muse de l'Arme, Paris. Dist. RMN-Grand Palais (b). **196 Getty Images:** De Agostini (cla). **197 Alamy Stock Photo:** Historic Images (t). **198 Alamy Stock Photo:** Penta Springs Limited (bl); Stock Imagery (tr). **Photo Scala, Florence:** The Metropolitan Museum of Art / Art Resource (cra, c, cl, br). **199 akg-images:** François Gunet (tr). **Bridgeman Images:** Brooklyn Museum / Gift of Marcia and John Friede (br). **The Metropolitan Museum of Art:** Purchase, Mrs. Howard J. Barnet Gift, 2015 (bc); The Michael C. Rockefeller Memorial Collection, Purchase, Nelson A. Rockefeller Gift, 1967 (l); The Michael C. Rockefeller Memorial Collection, Bequest of Nelson A. Rockefeller, 1979 (tc); The Michael C. Rockefeller Memorial Collection, Gift of Nelson A. Rockefeller, 1972 (c). Photo Scala, Florence: The Metropolitan Museum of Art / Art Resource (cr). **200 Alamy Stock Photo:** The History Collection (cra). **Getty Images:** Photo12 / Universal Images Group (bl). **201 Alamy Stock Photo:** World History Archive (bc). **Getty Images:** DeAgostini (t). **202-203 Library of Congress, Washington, D.C.:** Njoya, Sultan Of Bamoun, 1876?-1933, Cartographer. Bamum. [Cameroon: producer not identified, Between to 1919, 1912]. **204 Alamy Stock Photo:** Universal Images Group North America LLC / PHAS / UIG. **205 Alamy Stock Photo:** Colaimages (cra); Scherl / Sddeutsche Zeitung Photo (br). **206 Getty Images:** Gamma-Rapho / Jean-Noel De Soye (bl). **207 Alamy Stock Photo:** Historica Graphica Collection / Heritage Images (tr, b). **208 Alamy Stock Photo:** GL Archive. **209 Alamy Stock Photo:** CBW (crb); Pictorial Press (tr). **© The Trustees of the British Museum. All rights reserved:** (ca). **210 Alamy Stock Photo:** Chronicle (cla). **210-211 Alamy Stock Photo:** Granger - Historical Picture Archive (b). **211 Alamy Stock Photo:** Svintage Archive (tc). **212 Alamy Stock Photo:** Svintage Archive (bl). **Brooklyn Museum:** Arts of Africa / Purchased with funds given by Mr. and Mrs. Alastair B. Martin, Mrs. Donald M. Oenslager, Mr. and Mrs. Robert E. Blum, and the Mrs. Florence A. Blum Fund (cra). **213 Alamy Stock Photo:** Photo12 / Archives Snark (tr). **The New York Public Library:** (bc). **214 Alamy Stock Photo:** IanDagnall Computing (bl); Science History Images (t). **215 Alamy Stock Photo:** Chronicle. **216 Alamy Stock Photo:** Zuri Swimmer (cla). **Getty Images:** Universal Images Group (br). **217 Alamy Stock Photo:** Alto Vintage Images (tr); Ariadne Van Zandbergen (tc). **218 Alamy Stock Photo:** Historic Images (cra); Vinard Collection (bl). **219 © The Trustees of the British Museum. All rights reserved. 220 Alamy Stock Photo:** Classic Collection 3. **221 © The Trustees of the British Museum. All rights reserved:** (crb). **Dreamstime.com:** Dolphfyn (ca). **222 Alamy Stock Photo:** The Print Collector / Heritage Images (crb). **Getty Images:** Bert Hardy / Picture Post / Hulton Archive / Stringer (t). **223 Alamy Stock Photo:** Art Collection 2 (bl); Prisma Archivo (tr). **224-225 Photo Scala, Florence:** The Metropolitan Museum of Art / Art Resource. **226 Getty Images / iStock:** E+ / PictureLake (bl). **227 Alamy Stock Photo:** Everett Collection Historical (cra); World History Archive (tr). **Getty Images:** Hulton Archive / Keystone / Stringer (crb). **228 Alamy Stock Photo:** Alto Vintage Images (br); Peregrine (cra). **229 Alamy Stock Photo:** Agefotostock / Historical Views (t). **Getty Images:** James O Jenkins / Bolton & Quinn / AFP (br). **230 Alamy Stock Photo:** NBP / piemags. **231 Alamy Stock Photo:** Associated Press (bl); D and S Photography Archives (tr). **Getty Images:** Universal Images Group Editorial / Photo 12 (tc). **232 Alamy Stock Photo:** History and Art Collection (crb); Pictorial Press Ltd (clb). **Getty Images:** Bettmann (cb). **233 Getty Images:** AFP / STF (clb); Lipnitzki / Roger Viollet (cb); Bettmann (crb). **Photo Scala, Florence:** RMN-Grand Palais / Dist. / Diouf, Ibrahima (20th cent.) (tr). **234 Alamy Stock Photo:** Dragan Ilic (cla); Photo12 / Ann Ronan Picture Library (bl). **235 TopFoto:** Heritage-Images. **236 Alamy Stock Photo:** Charles O. Cecil (cr). **237 Alamy Stock Photo:** The Print Collector / Heritage Images (tr). **Getty Images:** Bettmann (b). **238 Getty Images:** AFP / STR / Stringer. **239 Alamy Stock Photo:** Photo12 / Ann Ronan Picture Library (ca). **Getty Images:** Rolls Press / Popperfoto (crb). **240 akg-images:** African Pictures (PTY) Ltd (bl). **Getty Images:** Bettmann (t). **241 Getty Images:** Bettmann (br). **Shutterstock.com:** Mirt Alexander (tr). **242 Getty Images:** Bettmann. **243 Alamy Stock Photo:** Historic Collection (crb); Sura Nualpradid (c). **244-245 Josef and Anni Albers Foundation:** Courtesy of Xaritufoto and Le Korsa.. **246 Alamy Stock Photo:** Grant Rooney (br). **Getty Images:** AFP / Trevor Samson (ca). **247 Getty Images:** Hulton Archive. **248 Getty Images:** Archive Photos / Ben Martin (cla); Archive Photos / David Hume Kennerly (bl). **249 Getty Images:** Corbis Historical / Michael Nicholson (b). **250 Getty Images:** CILO / Gamma-Rapho. **251 Alamy Stock Photo:** Keystone Press (clb). **Getty Images:** AFP / Alexander Joe / Staff (cra). **252 Alamy Stock Photo:** Peter Jordan (t). **Getty Images:** AFP / Alexander Joe / Staff (crb). **253 Alamy Stock Photo:** Brian Harris (br). **254 Getty Images:** Sygma / Alain Nogues (cla); Sygma Premium / William Campbell (bl). **255 Alamy Stock Photo:** Mike Abrahams (b). **Photo Scala, Florence:** Photo Smithsonian American Art Museum / Art Resource (tr). **256-257 Photo Scala, Florence:** The Art Institute of Chicago / Art Resource, NY. **258 Alamy Stock Photo:** Pictorial Press Ltd (br). **Getty Images:** Keystone-France / Gamma-Keystone (cl). **259 Alamy Stock Photo:** Borislav Marinic (br). **Getty Images:** Michel Huet / Gamma-Rapho (tr). **260 Alamy Stock Photo:** GFC Collection (t). **261 Alamy Stock Photo:** Associated Press / Uncredited (bc); Marion Kaplan (tr). **262 Getty Images:** - / AFP. **263 Alamy Stock Photo:** Contraband Collection (tl). **Getty Images:** Pierre Guillaud / AFP (br). **264 Alamy Stock Photo:** Mike Goldwater (cb); Trinity Mirror / Mirrorpix (clb). **Getty Images:** Marco Di Lauro / Stringer (crb). **265 Alamy Stock Photo:** Associated Press / Samir Bol (crb). **Getty Images:** Corbis / VCG / David Turnley (cb); Sygma / Patrick Robert - Corbis (clb). **266 Getty Images:** Patrick Durand / Sygma (ca). **266-267 Getty Images:** Paris Match Archive / Gysembergh Benoit (c). **267 Getty Images:** AFP / Pascal Guyot / Staff (br). **268 Getty Images:** AFP / STF / Staff (bc). **Reuters:** Juda Ngwenya (cla). **269 Alamy Stock Photo:** Associated Press / Denis Farrell (t). **Getty Images:** AFP / Keith Schamotta / Staff (br). **270 Getty Images:** Thomas Imo / Photothek. **271 Getty Images:** Eli

Weinberg / Apic / Hulton Archive (tr); The Chronicle Collection / Allan Tannenbaum (crb). **272 Photo Scala, Florence:** The Metropolitan Museum of Art / Art Resource. **274 Courtesy of SMAC Gallery/Southern Guild:** (bl). **275 Alamy Stock Photo:** AfriPics.com (tr). **Getty Images:** AFP / Issouf Sanogo (cr); AFP / Pius Utomi Ekpei (crb). **276-277 Jennifer Okpoko:** (tc). **276 Getty Images:** Gallo Images Editorial (bl); Hulton Archive / Heritage Images (cr). **Jennifer Okpoko:** (tl). **277 Getty Images:** AFP / Gulshan Khan (b). **Jennifer Okpoko:** (tr). **278 Alamy Stock Photo:** LMA / AW (crb); Universal Images Group North America LLC / DeAgostini / A. Dagli Orti (cra). **Photo Scala, Florence:** Princeton University Art Museum, / Art Resource NY (tc, bl); Princeton University Art Museum / Art Resource NY (crb/Cap). **278-279 Dreamstime.com:** Fabrizio Cianella (t). **279 Alamy Stock Photo:** CPA Media Pte Ltd. / Pictures From History (cr); John Warburton-Lee Photography / Nigel Pavitt (tr); Penta Springs Limited / Artokoloro (crb). **Brooklyn Museum:** Gift of Thomas Alexander (cb). **Photo Scala, Florence:** The Metropolitan Museum of Art / Art Resource (bl). **280 Alamy Stock Photo:** Nature Picture Library / Christophe Courteau (crb); Omoniyi Ayedun Olubunmi (clb). **© UNESCO:** DCP, 2011 (cb). **281 Alamy Stock Photo:** Africa Media Online / Rogan Ward (crb); Eric Lafforgue (clb). Reuters: Tiksa Negeri (cb). **282 Science Photo Library:** Thierry Berrod, Mona Lisa Production (bl). **283 Alamy Stock Photo:** Martin Harvey (t). **Getty Images:** Junior Kannah / AFP (br). **284 Getty Images:** Anadolu Agency (bl). **285 Alamy Stock Photo:** Antiqua Print Gallery (tc). **Shutterstock.com:** Dr Craig (b). **286 Getty Images:** AFP / Glyn Kirk (cb); Velo / Tim de Waele (clb); AFP (crb). **287 Alamy Stock Photo:** Associated Press / Markus Schreiber (cra). **Getty Images:** Anadolu Agency (cb); Robert Cianflone (clb); Gallo Images (crb). **288 Alamy Stock Photo:** Peregrine (cla). Collection IAV-Atria: Copyright unknown (br). **289 Getty Images:** Micheline Pelletier / Corbis (bc). Reuters: Temilade Adelaja (t). **290 Getty Images:** Micheline Pelletier / Corbis. **291 Alamy Stock Photo:** NTB / Cornelius Poppe / Scanpix Norway / POOL (cra). **Getty Images:** AFP / Issouf Sanogo / Staff (clb). **292 Alamy Stock Photo:** Photo 12 / Cinegrit (t). Posteritati: (br). **293 Alamy Stock Photo:** Lifestyle pictures (br); Photo 12 / A7A collection (tc). **294 Alamy Stock Photo:** Chrisstockphoto (cla); Yuri Kevhiev (tr); Zoonar / Aliaksei Hintau (br). **Dreamstime.com:** Dario Lo Presti (cb). **The Metropolitan Museum of Art:** The Crosby Brown Collection of Musical Instruments (bl). **295 Alamy Stock Photo:** Chrisstockphoto (bl); Fortune Fish (c); Eric Lafforgue (cra). **Getty Images:** Universal History Archive / Universal Images Group (cr). **Photo Scala, Florence:** The Metropolitan Museum of Art / Art Resource (br). **296 Getty Images:** PoPsie Randolph / Michael Ochs Archives / Donaldson Collection (clb); David Corio / Redferns (cb); Frans Schellekens / Redferns (crb). **297 Alamy Stock Photo:** Mariano Garcia (cb). **Getty Images:** Suhaimi Abdullah (clb); Michael Loccisano / Staff (crb). **298-299 © El Anatsui. Courtesy of El Anatsui Studio:** Photo courtesy Brandywine Workshop and Archives.. **298 Alamy Stock Photo:** Independent / Tom Pilston (tc). **300 Yancey Richardson Gallery:** Courtesy of the Artist and Yancey Richardson, New York. **301 Yancey Richardson Gallery:** Courtesy of the Artist and Yancey Richardson, New York. **302 africamediaonline. com:** (clb). **Getty Images:** David Degner (crb). **Shutterstock.com:** The LIFE Picture Collection / Carlo Bavagnoli (cb). **303 Getty Images:** Awakening / Simone Padovani (cb); Gamma-Rapho / Frederic Reglain (clb); LightRocket / SOPA Images (crb). **304 Getty Images:** Photodisc / Buena Vista Images (b). **305 Alamy Stock Photo:** Associated Press / Sunday Alamba (crb). **Edo Museum of West African Art:** (t).

All other images © Dorling Kindersley

BRINGING HISTORY TO LIFE

FOREWORD BY
DAVID OLUSOGA

AFRICA

THE DEFINITIVE VISUAL
HISTORY OF A CONTINENT

IMPERIAL

CHINA

THE DEFINITIVE
VISUAL HISTORY

ANCIENT

EGYPT

THE DEFINITIVE
VISUAL HISTORY

ANCIENT

ROME

THE DEFINITIVE
VISUAL HISTORY

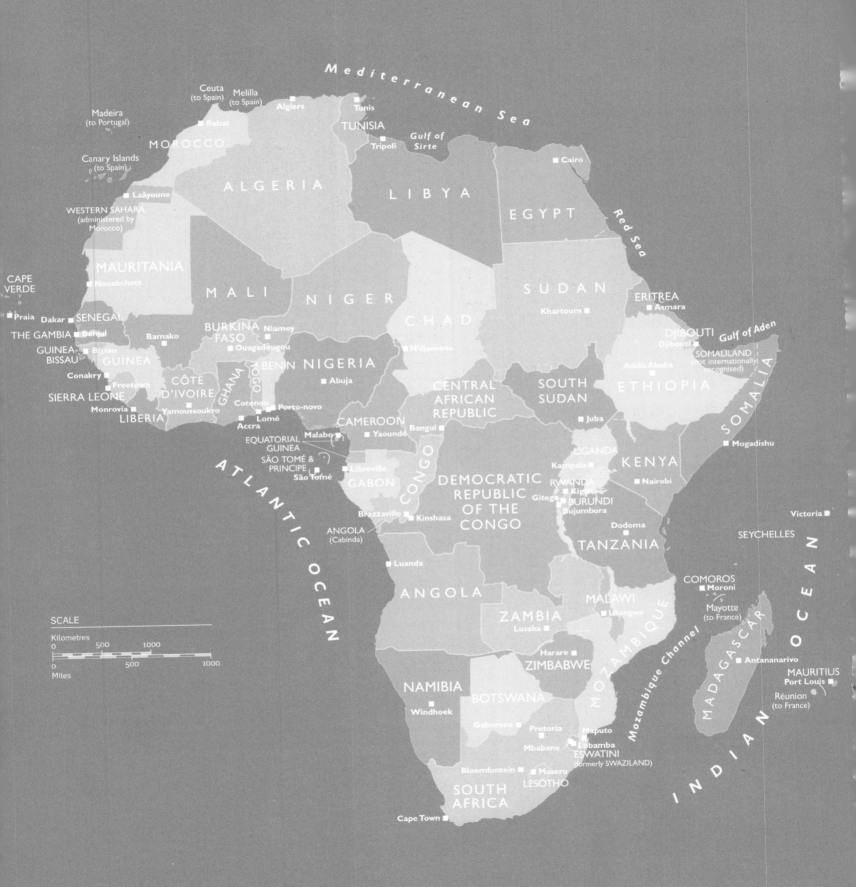

Mediterranean Sea

Ceuta
(to Spain)
Melilla
(to Spain)
Algiers
Tunis
Madeira
(to Portugal)
Rabat
TUNISIA
Gulf of
Sirte
Tripoli
MOROCCO

Canary Islands
(to Spain)

ALGERIA
LIBYA
EGYPT
Cairo
Red Sea

Laâyoune
WESTERN SAHARA
(administered by
Morocco)

MAURITANIA
MALI
NIGER
SUDAN
ERITREA
Asmara
Khartoum

CAPE
VERDE
Nouakchott
CHAD
DJIBOUTI
Gulf of Aden
Djibouti

Praia
Dakar
BURKINA
FASO
Niamey
N'djamèna
Addis Ababa
SOMALILAND
(not internationally
recognised)

THE GAMBIA
SENEGAL
Bamako
Banjul
Ouagadougou
NIGERIA
SOUTH
SUDAN
ETHIOPIA

GUINEA-
BISSAU
Bissau
GUINEA
BENIN
Abuja
CENTRAL
AFRICAN
REPUBLIC
SOMALIA

Conakry
Freetown
CÔTE
D'IVOIRE
TOGO
GHANA
Cotonou
Porto-novo
Juba
Mogadishu

SIERRA LEONE
Monrovia
Yamoussoukro
Lomé
Accra
CAMEROON
Bangui
UGANDA
KENYA

LIBERIA
EQUATORIAL
GUINEA
Malabo
Yaoundé
Kampala
Nairobi

SÃO TOMÉ &
PRÍNCIPE
Libreville
CONGO
DEMOCRATIC
REPUBLIC
OF THE
CONGO
RWANDA
Kigali
BURUNDI
Bujumbura
Gitega

São Tomé
GABON
Victoria

ATLANTIC OCEAN
Brazzaville
Kinshasa
TANZANIA
Dodoma
SEYCHELLES

ANGOLA
(Cabinda)

Luanda
COMOROS
Moroni

ANGOLA
MALAWI
Mayotte
(to France)

SCALE
ZAMBIA
Lilongwe
MADAGASCAR
Antananarivo

Kilometres
0   500   1000
Lusaka
MAURITIUS
Port Louis

Miles
0   500   1000
Harare
ZIMBABWE
Réunion
(to France)

NAMIBIA
BOTSWANA
MOZAMBIQUE
Mozambique Channel

Windhoek
Gaborone
Pretoria
Maputo
Lobamba

Mbabane
ESWATINI
(formerly SWAZILAND)

Bloemfontein
Maseru
LESOTHO

SOUTH
AFRICA
Cape Town

INDIAN OCEAN